Errata

While every effort has been made to ensure the proper insertion of loins within these pages, slippage has occurred infrequently. The editors note, with regret, the following :

And in this harsh world draw they breath in pain
To sell my story.

—*Martin P. Rafferty*

. . . a Power
Girt round with weakness; it can scarce uplift
The weight of the superincumbent houri . . .

—*James Michie*

Some mute inglorious Hilton here may rest.

—*D.H. Crown*

She stood in tears amid the alien porn.

—*George Hurren*

By grace divine
Not otherwise, O Nature, are we thin.

—*Netta B. Brownlie*

When Kempenfelt went down
On twice four hundred men.

—*Anne B. Rodgers*

The king shall drink to Hamlet's better breath,
And in the cup an onion shall he throw.

—*P.W.R. Foot*

This is the way the world ends
Not with a bang but a wimpy.

—*Doris Pulsford*

Rough winds do shake the darling bubs of May.

—*Tony Lurcock*

I struck the broad, and cry'd, No more!

—*J.N. Newton*

Beneath the rule of men entirely great
The penis mightier than the sword.

—*Stephen Corrin*

Hoover through the fog and filthy air.

—*D. Smith*

There's a breathless lush in the Close tonight.

—*Colin Kimberely*

To muse and brood and live again in memory,
With those old faeces of our infancy.

—*Jethro B. Tucket*

An enema hath done this.

—*L. Reeve Jones*

And may there be no moaning at the bar
When I send out for tea.

—*Eve Gammon*

Stood Dido with a willy in her hand.

—*T.A. Dyer*

THE

Brand-X Anthology of Poetry

BURNT NORTON EDITION

THE Brand-X Anthology of Poetry

BURNT NORTON EDITION

WILLIAM ZARANKA
UNIVERSITY OF DENVER

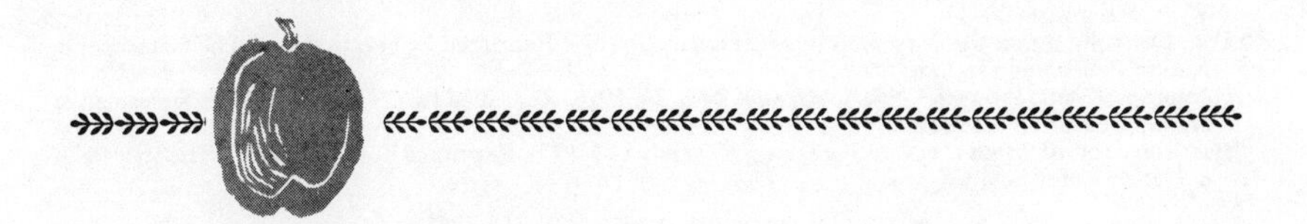

APPLE-WOOD BOOKS, INC.
Cambridge • Watertown

To My Wife, Ruth

First Edition

ISBN 0-918222-30-3 (Cloth Edition)

ISBN 0-918222-31-1 (Paper Edition)

PRINTED IN THE UNITED STATES OF AMERICA

1 2 3 4 5 6 7 8 9 0BP

Martin Fagg: From the *New Statesman*, November 25, 1977, April 14, 1972, August 27, 1971. Reprinted by permission of The Statesman & Nation Publishing Co. Ltd.

Molly Fitton: From the *New Statesman*, April 14, 1972. Reprinted by permission of The Statesman & Nation Publishing Co. Ltd.

John Flood: From the *New Statesman*, July 11, 1975. Reprinted by permission of The Statesman & Nation Publishing Co. Ltd.

Laurence Fowler: From the *New Statesman*, March 31, 1978. Reprinted by permission of The Statesman & Nation Publishing Co. Ltd.

Robert Frost: From *The Letters of Robert Frost to Louis Untermeyer*. Copyright © 1963 by Louis Untermeyer and Holt Rinehart and Winston. Reprinted by permission of Holt, Rinehart and Winston, Publishers.

Alan Gibson: From the *New Statesman*, April 14, 1972. Reprinted by permission of The Statesman & Nation Publishing Co. Ltd.

Malcolm Glass: "Coming Down to It" appears for the first time. "The Boy; Or, Son of Rip-Off" first appeared in *Poultry*, Vol. 1, #1. By permission of the author.

E.S. Goodwill: From the *New Statesman*, July 20, 1973. Reprinted by permission of The Statesman & Nation Publishing Co. Ltd.

Richard Leighton Greene: "Song to Imogen (In Basic English)" first appeared in *What Cheer* edited by David McCord. Reprinted by permission of the author.

Bill Greenwell: From the *New Statesman*. Reprinted by permission of The Statesman & Nation Publishing Co. Ltd.

T. Griffiths: From the *New Statesman*, April 14, 1972, September 1, 1978, March 31, 1978. Reprinted by permission of The Statesman & Nation Publishing Co. Ltd.

Arthur Guiterman: "On the Vanity of Earthly Greatness," "Sea-Chill," "Consolation," and "Lovelace's Alibi" from *Gaily the Troubadour*. Copyright 1936 by E.P. Dutton & Co.; Copyright © renewed 1964 by Mrs. Arthur Guiterman. "Mavrone" from *Lyric Laughter*. Copyright 1939 by E.P. Dutton & Co.; renewed © 1967. Reprinted by permission of the owner of the copyrights, Louise H. Sclove.

James B. Hall: Originally appeared as "Stafford in Kansas" in *Poultry*, Vol. 1, #2. Reprinted by permission of the author.

Gerry Hamill: From the *New Statesman*, July 11, 1975, March/April, 1973. Reprinted by permission of The Statesman & Nation Publishing Co. Ltd.

Walter Hard: "Medical Aid" is reprinted by permission of Frederick Ungar Publishing Co., Inc.

Barbara Harr: "Walking Through a Cornfield in the Middle of Winter... is reprinted by permission of the author.

Anthony Hecht: From *The Hard Hours*. Copyright © 1967 by Anthony Hecht (New York: Atheneum, 1967) Reprinted with the permission of Atheneum Publishers.

Michael Heffernan: "Sunday Service" appears for the first time. "Naked War" and "Putting On My Shoes" were originally published in *Poultry* Vol. 1, #1. All by permission of the author.

Gilbert Highet: "Homage to Ezra Pound" first appeared in *The Nation*, February 21, 1942. Copyright 1942 by Gilbert Highet. All rights reserved. Reprinted by permission of Curtis Brown, Ltd.

Samuel Hoffenstein: From *A Treasury of Humorous Verse* including "Poems in Praise of Practically Nothing" by Samuel Hoffenstein, by permission of Liveright Publishing Corporation. Copyright 1946 and renewed 1974 by Liveright Publishing Corporation. Copyright 1928, 1930 by Samuel Hoffenstein, and copyright renewed 1955 and 1958 by David Hoffenstein.

Daniel Hoffman: "Lines Written Near Linton, on Exmoor" is used by permission of the author.

A.D. Hope: From *Dunciad Minor*. Reprinted by permission of Melbourne University Press.

T. Hope: From the *New Statesman*, May 26, 1978. Reprinted by permission of The Statesman & Nation Publishing Co. Ltd.

Tim Hopkins: From the *New Statesman*, March 31, 1978. Reprinted by permission of The Statesman & Nation Publishing Co. Ltd.

A.E. Housman: "O Have You Caught the Tiger" from *My Brother, A.E. Housman* by Laurence Housman and "The shades of night were falling fast" from *A.E. Housman's Collected Poems*. Reprinted by permission of the Society of Authors as the literary representative of the Estate of A.E. Housman and Jonathan Cape Ltd., publishers of A.E. Housman's *Collected Poems*.

B.L. Howarth: From the *New Statesman*, April 14, 1972. Reprinted by permission of The Statesman & Nation Publishing Co. Ltd.

G.W. Jones: From the *New Statesman*, March 22, 1974. Reprinted by permission of The Statesman & Nation Publishing Co. Ltd.

Roy Kelly: From the *New Statesman*, May 26, 1978, September 11, 1978. Reprinted by permission of The Statesman & Nation Publishing Co. Ltd.

Ian Kelso: From the *New Statesman*, May 26, 1978. Reprinted by permission of The Statesman & Nation Publishing Co. Ltd.

Jenny King: From the *New Statesman*, June 21, 1974. Reprinted by permission of The Statesman & Nation Publishing Co. Ltd.

Hugh Kingsmill: (i) from "Two Poems (after A.E. Housman)" in *The Best of Hugh Kingsmill* edited by Michael Holroyd. Reprinted by permission of Lady Dorothy Hopkinson, Literary Executor of Hugh Kingsmill.

Rudyard Kipling: From *Rudyard Kipling's Verse: Definitive Edition*. Reprinted by permission of the National Trust and Doubleday & Company, Inc. "Municipal" also by permission of A.P. Watt Ltd.

E.V. Knox (Evoe): "Upon Julia's Clothes" from *The Brazen Lyre*, 1911 (Smith. Elder & Co.) and "The Last Bus" from *These Liberties*, 1923 (Methuen & Co. Ltd.) Reprinted by permission of Mrs. Mary E. Knox.

Kenneth Koch: "Variations on a Theme by William Carlos Williams" from *Thank You and Other Poems*. Copyright © 1962 by Kenneth Koch. "Mending Sump" is Copyright © by Kenneth Koch. Reprinted by permission of the author.

Amedie Eva List: From the *New Statesman*, July 20, 1973. Reprinted by permission of The Statesman & Nation Publishing Co. Ltd.

Russell Lucas: From the *New Statesman*, April 14, 1972. Reprinted by permission of The Statesman & Nation Publishing Co. Ltd.

Charles F. Lummis: From *A Bronco Pegasus* by Charles F. Lummis. Copyright 1928, © renewed 1956 by Houghton Mifflin Company.

David McCord: From *Bay Window Ballads*. Copyright 1935 Charles Scribner's Sons; copyright renewed. Reprinted by permission of the publisher.

William McGonagall: From *Pegasus Descending* edited by James Camp, X.J. Kennedy and Keith Waldrop (New York: Macmillan, 1971).

F.A.V. Madden: From the *New Statesman*, March-June, 1974. Reprinted by permission of The Statesman & Nation Publishing Co. Ltd.

Naomi Marks: From the *New Statesman*, March 22, 1978, February 3, 1978. Reprinted by permission of The Statesman & Nation Publishing Co. Ltd.

George Moor: From the *New Statesman,* November 25, 1977. Reprinted by permission of The Statesman & Nation Publishing Co. Ltd.

E.O. Parrott: From the *New Statesman,* July 20, 1973, September 1, 1978. Reprinted by permission of The Statesman & Nation Publishing Co. Ltd.

David Fisher Parry: First published in *The New York Herald Tribune.*

Dorothy Parker: From *The Portable Dorothy Parker.* Copyright 1926, 1954 by Dorothy Parker. Reprinted by permission of Viking Penguin Inc.

Robert Peters: From *The Poet as Ice-Skater,* published by ManRoot Books and "The Heniad." Reprinted by permission of the author.

Peter Peterson: From the *New Statesman,* September 1, 1978. Reprinted by permission of The Statesman & Nation Publishing Co. Ltd.

David Phillips: From the *New Statesman.* Reprinted by permission of The Statesman & Nation Publishing Co. Ltd.

Frank Polite: From *Letters of Transit.* © 1979 by Frank Polite. Reprinted by permission of the author.

Carol Poster: "Robert Bly Finds Something In New Jersey" and "Synthesizing Several Abstruse Concepts With an Experience." By permission of the author.

Ezra Pound: From *Personae.* Copyright 1926 by Ezra Pound. Reprinted by permission of New Directions. Also by permission of Faber and Faber Ltd. from *Collected Shorter Poems* by Ezra Pound.

Charles Powell: From *Poets in the Nursery.* Reprinted by permission of the publisher, The Bodley Head, London.

Edward Pygge (pseud.): From the *New Statesman,* December 21, 1973, December 12, 1973, and June 22, 1973. Reprinted by permission of The Statesman & Nation Publishing Co. Ltd.

Martin P. Rafferty: From the *New Statesman,* March 14, 1975. Reprinted by permission of The Statesman & Nation Publishing Co. Ltd.

R.W. Ransford: From the *New Statesman,* December 8, 1972. Reprinted by permission of The Statesman & Nation Publishing Co. Ltd.

Basil Ransome: From the *New Statesman,* September 1, 1978. Reprinted by permission of The Statesman & Nation Publishing Co. Ltd.

Henry Reed: From *A Map of Verona.* Reprinted by permission of the publishers, Jonathan Cape Ltd.

Alan Riback: From *Furioso,* September, 1951. Reprinted by permission.

Charles Robinson: From the *New Statesman,* 1973. Reprinted by permission of The Statesman & Nation Publishing Co. Ltd.

Wey Robinson: First appeared in *What Cheer* edited by David McCord.

Ian Sainsbury: From the *New Statesman,* March-June, 1974, September 22, 1978. Reprinted by permission of The Statesman & Nation Publishing Co. Ltd.

Brian S. Salome: From the *New Statesman,* May 26, 1978. Reprinted by permission of The Statesman & Nation Publishing Co. Ltd.

A.M. Sayers: From the *New Statesman,* February 2, 1973, July 20, 1973. Reprinted by permission of The Statesman & Nation Publishing Co. Ltd.

Peter Schroeder: From the *New Statesman,* April 23, 1976. Reprinted by permission of The Statesman & Nation Publishing Co. Ltd.

Peter Scupham: From the *New Statesman,* July 11, 1975. Reprinted by permission of The Statesman & Nation Publishing Co. Ltd.

Stanley Sharpless: From the *New Statesman,* November 25, 1977, April 14, 1972, June 9, 197?, September 19, 1975, March 13, 1976, July 11, 1975. Reprinted by permission of The Statesman & Nation Publishing Co. Ltd.

Louis Simpson: "Squeal" was first published in *The Hudson Review,* Vol. X, No. 3, (Autumn, 1957). Copyright © 1957 by Louis Simpson and reprinted with his permission.

David R. Slavitt: From "Broads." These first appeared in *Poultry* Vol. 1, #1. Reprinted by permission of the author.

J.C. Squire: All except "Numerous Celts" and "If Pope Had Written 'Break Break Break'" from *Collected Parodies* published by Hodder & Stoughton Ltd. Reprinted by permission of Raglan Squire, Esq.

Ian Stirling: From the *New Statesman,* March-June, 1974. Reprinted by permission of The Statesman & Nation Publishing Co. Ltd.

Henry Taylor: From *The Horse Show at Midnight.* Copyright 1966. Published by Louisiana State University Press. Reprinted by permission of the author.

J.H. Thomas: From the *New Statesman,* April 14, 1972. Reprinted by permission of The Statesman & Nation Publishing Co. Ltd.

Louis Untermeyer: From *Heavens.* Copyright 1922 by Harcourt Brace Jovanovich, Inc.; Copyright 1950 by Louis Untermeyer. Reprinted by permission of the publisher.

Peter Veale: From the *New Statesman,* March-June, 1974. Reprinted by permission of The Statesman & Nation Publishing Co. Ltd.

J. Walker: From the *New Statesman,* December 22-29, 1978. Reprinted by permission of The Statesman & Nation Publishing Co. Ltd.

W.F.N. Watson: From the *New Statesman,* March 22, 1974, March 31, 1978. Reprinted by permission of The Statesman & Nation Publishing Co. Ltd.

W.J. Webster: From the *New Statesman,* April 14, 1972, July 11, 1975. Reprinted by permission of The Statesman & Nation Publishing Co. Ltd.

Craig Weeden: "A Pizza Joint in Cranston" first appeared in *Poultry,* Vol. 1, #1. Reprinted by permission of the author.

E.B. White: From *The Second Tree from the Corner.* Copyright 1944 by E.B. White. Originally appeared in *The New Yorker.* Reprinted by permission of Harper & Row, Publishers, Inc.

Margaret Widdemer: From *A Tree with a Bird In It.* Reprinted by permission of John D. Widdemer.

John Lloyd Williams: From the *New Statesman,* June 18, 1976. Reprinted by permission of The Statesman & Nation Publishing Co. Ltd.

Humbert Wolfe: "When lads have done . . ." (also titled "A.E. Housman and a Few Friends") first appeared in *Lampoons.* Reprinted by permission of Ann Wolfe.

Wynford Vaughan-Thomas: "To His Not-So-Coy Mistress" © 1978 by L.J.W. Vaughan-Thomas appeared first in *The New Oxford Book of Light Verse* edited by Kingsley Amis. Reprinted by permission of the author.

R.J. Yeatman and W.C. Sellar: From *Horse Nonsense.* Reprinted by permission of Associated Book Publishers Ltd. for the publisher, Eyre Methuen Ltd.

William Zaranka: "Robert Frost's Left-Leaning TRESPASSERS WILL BE SHOT Sign" appeared originally in *The Antigonish Review.* Reprinted with their permission and the permission of the author.

William Zaranka: "Quicksands," "Ode," "Memories of Aunt Maria-Martha," "Conceit Upon the Feet," "In the Ladies' Room at the Bus Terminal" and "Cropdusting" originally appeared in *The Denver Quarterly.* Reprinted by permission of the author.

William Zaranka: "The Continuation of Chaucer's 'The Cook's Tale'" from *Poet and Critic*, Volume 10, No. 3 Reprinted by permission of *Poet and Critic* and the English Department of Iowa State University.

L.L. Zeiger: "The Snack" appeared originally in *Poultry*, Vol. 1, #1. Reprinted by permission of the author.

Contents

Foreplay

My intention from the start has been to avoid the mistakes of rival compilers. While their anthologies purport to be the true suppositories of poetic tradition since Chaucer, they are not. The *Ed Norton Anthology of Literature*, edited by the illustrious M.H. Ammons and a host of lesser lumianskis, is a case in point. While it boasts single colons (poetry in double colons reads unnaturally) and comfortable margarines, it errs in its predictably biased selection of material. So does the leatherbound, large-floormat edition of *British Literature* published by Heathkit and edited by Spencer Haywood. More specialized contemporary anthologies, such as Stephen Bug's and Robert Measly's *Naked Lunch Poetry*, or A. Poupon's *Temporary Poetry*, or even Haystack Carruth's *The Vice That Is Great Within Us*, are similarly flawed, despite Robert Lowell's claim for the latter that it is perhaps "safe from the competition of weevils." Such high praise from the post-Kenya, post-*Life Smutties* Lowell invites examination. Alas, examination shows that Carruth's collection suffers from the same vice its title announces.

What Horror de Balzac has said of Milton may be said of these rival anthologies. They show remarkably little whist, a faulty sense of poulter's measure, imperfect understanding of neurasthenia, and a readiness to accept vulgar marbles as the equivalent of spiritual mysteries. Furthermore, much of the collected material is monarch-ridden, and does not so much pile itself pleasantly line on line as lie hard and heavy on the stomach of the reader, like the accumulated grundlage of a cairn. I emphatically agree with Balzac's estimate, despite his being called an "indefatigable, print-oriented buzzard" by Yale's Childe Harold Bloom, whose *Troping the Light Fantastic* otherwise fulfills Pound's criterion, that criticism must be as well written as prose, when prose is in French.

I have sought in this anthology to present an alternative to the traditional literary corpse as defined in Eliot's *Tradition and the Individual Tyrant* and "Malt More than Milton," and in the works of such writers as John Crowe Ronsard, author of *World's Booby*, and James Tate, author of *The Confederate Graveyard in Nantucket*, whose contributions to literature seem to me to be little more than a greater emphasis on normalized spilling, punk tuition, and a few other minor phalluses of imitative form. In selecting alternatives, I asked myself several questions: what but inherited taste compels the selection in anthology after anthology of "The Thelonius Monk's Tale" or "The Bobby Knight's Tale" or even "The Hillis Miller's Tale"? Surely, in all that great cannon which comprises the literary corpse of Geoffrey Chaucer, there are miglior fabliaux the equal of those perennially anthologized by tiresome syllabus-stuffers such as Richard and Lillian Ellman? Here in the *Brand X Anthology* the reader will find selections from *Murder in the Cathedral and Other Tales* such as "The Cook's Tale" and the tales of "The Holloe Menne" and "The Pornagraphre." Similarly, in all of Shakespeare, is there nothing the equal of—ho-hum—*Hamlet*? Here the reader will find (in lost history plays such as *Ethelred The Unready*) the Objective Coriolanus which Eliot despaired of and died before finding, *no doubt because he read the wrong anthologies.* By the end of the nineteenth century, the reader will find himself more and more closing his Bryant and opening his Roethke, more and more putting down the Wordsworth of "The Ruined Cottage" for the Wordsworth of "The Ruined Cottage Cheese" (the foreflusher of Yeast's "The Second Camembert" and virtually all of the Cheese and Snack Poetry of the next century).

With regard to floormat, let me say that I have avoided the problem of emphasis posed by broadening the literary survey at the expense of a more in-debt examination of major figures by doing both. Likewise, I have either dilated or exercised most footnodes as being dearer to University Warts than to the general reader who resents them. Finally, I believe this first edition of *The Brand-X Anthology* to be superior to its rivals by dint of its no-nuisance introductions to literary periods, its informal attitudes towards the dates of literary epoxies, its unboulderized versions of dirty masterpieces, and its inclusion of a helpful Prosodomy at the rear of the collection.

I am grateful to no one for help with this project. Rather, let me acknowledge the few who did not hold me back. They are Burton Feldman, David Cummings, Robert Pawlowski, Daniel Hoffman, Hyman Datz, Michael Walton, Phil Zuckerman, Marian Reiner, Jake, Charles Manson Myers, the Faculty Research Grant Committee at the University of Denver, the Sonia Bronstein SWAT team, and last, my beloved wife Ruth, who helped edit this volume, and who spurned me to a finish by threatening to cut my Balzac.

William Zaranka
The University of Denver
Summer, 1981

THE MIDDLE-AGED

ca. 450:	Hell's Anglo-Anne Sexton Conquest.
597:	St. Augustine arrives Kent State; first PAT conversion.
871-899:	Rains on King Alfred.
1066:	Norman Cozzens.
ca. 1200:	Beginnings of Middle-Aged Literature.
1360-1400:	Summit meeting, great Middle-Aged poets: Chaucer, Peers Porridge, Brute, Thelonius Monk.
1485:	End of "War of the Roadsters."

BEGINNINGS TO NORMAN COZZENS

Although most Middle-Aged literary scholars share Professor W. Allen's view that the college sophomore should refrain from taking any course in which Beowulf is required reading, no survey of Middle-Aged literature could call itself complete without at least some mention of the great Hell's Anglo-Anne Sexton poet. The son of Cuthbert Bede and the marauding Viking Juliet of Norwich, Beowulf was born by permission of the male members of the "tribe of Bede" in and around the seventh century. Legend has it that the first sound out of the mouth of the baby Beowulf was not a cry but the entire *Battle of Karl Maldon*, the first poem written in the oral tradition, composed in four-stress illiterative whimpers. Contemporary scholars tend to dispute Beowulf's authenticity (much as they do Homer's *Odious*) and now attribute that haiku-epic to the great escapist poet of the Boston Celtic twilight, the Wife of Boethius, whose "Dream of the Open Rood" is perhaps our first transient epic, and whose "Wanderer" completes her cannon. Nevertheless, Beowulf did write the anonymous gnomes, ribalds, chainsaws, and endearing young charms anthologized here. To quote Edward Arlington Cemetery, Beowulf was "a giant before Mr. Flood's party," a man who, ironically, lived long enough for the Christian/pagan heterodoxy of his poems to be married by the Catholic Pope Gregory as a gesture of support for Norman Cozzens in 1066.

Another child prodigy was Layamon's Brute. Savage and wolf-suckled, his parents orphaned by a tribe of Hell's Anglos, Anne Sextons, and Wandering Jutes, the young Brute writes of his adolescence among the Virginia Wolves. There his nature, "red in tooth and claw," was formed. His beast fable, "Wolfman's Jack," is as powerful an account as there is in Middle-Aged literature of a boy's loss of virginity to a pack of ravening canines, while his "The Call of Oscar Wilde" is a gruesome account of pack mentality and overkill written in grisly skeletonics. One turns from Brute with great relief to the gentle cannings of Thomas Malory's "Sir John Gower and the Green Giant." Here the forbidden vegetable love of the Knights of the Seven Gables for the Lady of Shallot is allowed to mushroom, until even King Alfred the Great himself is powerless to prevent the cantankerous Gower from destroying himself in a lustful quest for his lady's Holy Grail. Malory's poem, written in the Midland viaduct, is said to be the father of modern prose, while Spender's whore of Babylon, *The Furry Queene*, is said to be its mother.

DEATH OF "THE IMAGINATION'S LATIN"

It is now something of a cliche to talk about the harsh conditions of Middle-Aged life. Indeed, the great Latin forerunner of the disease poets, A.B. Guthlac, was only one of many unfortunate Latins killed off during the dreadful Yvor Winters described in the anonymous lyric, "Wynters ys i-cumen in":

Legges trembel after bath,
And fyngres turneth blu,
Wisker freseth, nose sneseth—
Merie syng tish-u—
—tish-u—
—tish-u—

One pities the poor Guthlac, shivering in his mud hovel, cursing the pestilence and famine which had spirited away his friend, the Second Shepherd, and bemoaning the terror through the walls at least as much as the lack of originality and the childlike simplicity which were so symptomatic of his times. And yet, had his poem "Johannes et Gillia" been written on his mother's tongue instead on the cheap corrasable vellum of the times, doubtless it would have been one of the classics of our prose.

THE PEERLESS PLAYBOY

In a literary sense, it was perhaps fitting that the Middle-Aged Latin poets were killed off during those terrible winters, for in their frozen wake came the greatest Middle-Aged poet of them all, Geoffrey Chaucer. The son of a London vintner and the Wife of Boethius, the youthful Chaucer was born in 1343, and during the next few years earned himself a dubious reputation as "the Peerless Playboy." Chastened by a charge of "raptus" brought against him by the Lady Francine du Plessix-Grey, Chaucer mended his ways and settled down to serve as one of the pages, or twerps, in the house of Lionel of Antwerp. It was here that Chaucer first came into contact with the Dante Gabriel Rossetti Stone, from which he translated "Troilus and Criseide," as well as some lesser known Egyptian miglior fabliaux.

Chaucer's masterpiece, of course, is *Murder in the Cathedral and Other Tales*, modeled after Petrarch's *Porgy and Laura* and Boccaccio's *The Amorous Camera.* Chaucer set about writing his tales not to teach and delight, as did Petrarch and Boccaccio, but to refute the popular notion that "the existing archbishoprics form an ideal order among themselves, which is modified by the introduction of the new (the really new) pric of an archbishop among them." Chaucer knew that his real charge as a poet was to preserve the sanctity of the tradition of the Church from whose tired loins he had sprung, and to instill in his own loins the same reverence and respect. It comes as no surprise, therefore, that some of Chaucer's tales are strikingly modern—most notably the beginning of his tale of the "Burialle of the Deede:"

Aprille is of al the months moste dyr,
For she engendereth anewe desyr
For fickel foweles not worthe the winnynge—

and the end of "The Holloe Menne"

Thissen way endeth werlde
Noe bangen butten wampere...

FEUDAL RESISTANCE BY THE RISING MIDDLE GAS

Generally, ballads are written by the aspiring sensibility of the tribe, utilizing medieval polka rhythm and excremental repetition. However, we end our survey of the Middle-Aged with a selection of Populist Ballads, a political literature whose cause is lost on us but whose art remains. As a result of the crushing oppression the rising middle gas was subjected to at the hands of King Orfeo, an underground resistance, led by the Tory Captain Carpenter and the Whig Patrick Spens, was formed. While it was never their intention to overthrow Orfeo by force, it was hoped that a sit-down strike followed by a vote of no-confidence written on the reverse side of each ballad might in some way persuade Orfeo to improve the lot of those hapless, rising middle gasses. Alas, it did not; the resistance proved feudal. All that remains of the ill-fated venture are the ballads, about which the poet W.H. Dryden has written, "Here is good and plenty; it's plenty good," an estimate which is surely true as well for Middle-Aged literature as a hole.

MIDDLE-AGED LYRICS

Ancient Music

Winter is icummen in,
Lhude sing Goddamm,
Raineth drop and staineth slop,
And how the wind doth ramm!
  Sing: Goddamm.
Skiddeth bus and sloppeth us,
An ague hath my ham.
Freezeth river, turneth liver,
  Damn you, sing: Goddamm.
Goddamm, Goddamm, 'tis why I am, Goddamm,
  So 'gainst the winter's balm.
Sing goddamm, damm, sing Goddamm,
Sing goddamm, sing goddamm, DAMM.

—*Ezra Pound*

Baccalaureate

Summa is i-cumen in,
  Laude sing cuccu!
Laddes rede and classe lede,
Profesor bemeth tu—
  Sing cuccu!

Scholour striveth after Aye,
  Bleteth after shepskin ewe;
Writë theseth, honoure seazeth,
  Murie sing cuccu!

Cuccu, cuccu, wel singes A • B cuccu;
  Ne flunke thu naver nu;
  Sing cuccu, nu, sing cuccu,
  Sing cuccu, Phye Betta Cappe, nu!

—*David McCord*

For City Spring

Now grimy April comes again,
Maketh bloom the fire-escapes,
Maketh silvers in the rain,
Maketh winter coats and capes
Suddenly all worn and shabby
Like the fur of winter bears,
Maketh kittens, maketh baby,
Maketh kissing on the stairs.
Maketh bug crawl out of crack,
Maketh ticklings down the back
As if sunlight stroked the spine
To a hurdy-gurdy's whine
And the shower ran white wine.

April, April, sing cuckoo,
April, April, maketh new
Mouse and cockroach, man and wife,
Everything with blood and life;
Bloweth, groweth, flourisheth,
Danceth in a ragged skirt

On the very stoop of Death
And will take no mortal hurt.
Maketh dogs to whine and bound,
Maketh cats to caterwaul,
Maketh lovers, all around,
Whisper in the hall.

Oh, and when the night comes down
And the shrieking of the town
Settles to the steady roar
Of a long sea-beaten shore,
April hieth, April spieth
Everywhere a lover lieth,
Bringeth sweetness, bringeth fever,
Will not stop at "I would liever,"
Will not heed, "Now God a mercy!"
Turneth Moral topsy-versy,
Bringeth he and she to bed,
Bringeth ill to maidenhead,
Bringeth joyance in its stead.
By May, by May, she lieth sped,
Yet still we praise that crocus head,
April!

—*Stephen Vincent Benét*

Song

Singee songee sick a pence,
Pockee muchee lye;
Dozen two time blackee bird
Cookee in e pie.
When him cutee topside
Birdee bobbery sing;
Himee tinkee nicey dish
Setee foree King!
Kingee in a talkee loom
Countee muchee money;
Queeny in e kitchee,
Chew-chee breadee honey,
Servant galo shakee,
Hangee washee clothes;
Cho-chop comee blackie bird,
Nipee off her nose!

—*Anonymous*

GEOFFREY CHAUCER
(ca. 1343-1400)

Lyrics and Occasional Verse

Burialle of the Dede

Aprille is of al the months moste dyr,
For she engendereth anewe desyr
For fickel foweles not worthe the winnynge—
And eek the pregnant shayme of former sinnynge.

Aprille too sends shoures pissynge doune
On them that gathere lilacks all too soune;
And sokes from hed to foote the clevere Dicke
That doth too soune assaie to pick-a-nick.
For Winter, tho' with snowe the waies a'clogging,
Is sesoun meete for boosynge and a'snogging:
Righte dolte be he that doth forbear contryvinge
In two-faced Janus' hour a deele of swyvinge

—*Martin Fagg*

The Summonee's Tale

A mayde ther was, y-clept Joan Hunter Dunn,
In all of Surrie, comelier wench was none.
Yet wondrous greet of strength was she withalle.
Ful lustily she smote the tenis-balle.
And whether lord or lady she wolde pleye,
With thirtie, fortie-love wolde winne the day.
A squyer eke ther was, in horseless cariage,
And he wolde fayn have sought her hand in marriage.
Though he coude songes make, with mery rime,
At tennis she out-pleyed him every time;
To make her wyfe he saw but little chaunce.
But then be-thought to take her to a daunce
In gentil Camberlee, where after dark
They held long daliaunce in the cariage park;
Eftsoons Cupide had the twain in thralle,
And this they found the beste game of alle.

—*Stanley J. Sharpless*

The Holloe Menne

O waly waly waly waly
Arownde the priklie pare goe we gailie
Ronde agin ar wee alle driven
Intille clocken hath struken nien
Atwixen manie thinges ys a shadowe
Fer everie stuffen manne has hadde enow
Soe rase we untoe Lorde Godd ower songe
Alle menne ar holloe an alsoe dum
Hissen the kingdum at shel cum
Stuffen an holloe an dumbe
Thissen way endeth werlde
Noe bangen butte wampere inferled

—*Harrison Everard*

The Eternale Footeman's Tale

By Godde and Seynt Johne I sweare ye
This clerke in his time heard fram the sea
The lusty mermaides fillen ears with song.
They singen nat for me, I am nat yonge.
I have seen them ryding lowe and hye
On blanchëd billowes under blue skye
Combing the watter white whan windes blowe
From Germanie here wulfen hool in snowe.
I seye you I have eke gan doon
With swilke nymphes to their oozy toon
Under the watter. In weedes brown and redde

I pleyed in drooned cities of the dead
With girlës fishy arsed, bothe coold and hoot.
Till spak my wyf. Hyt were plesance I woot.

—*George Moor*

The Hicche-Hykeres Tale

This yonge fresshe wenche, wel loking honey-swete,
Hir thumbe up-haf and gan a lifte entrete,
Wherat eftsone oon sely wight dide stoppe
And curteislie, I—wis, bade hir in hoppe.
Quod he, Gode morwe, whider wendestow?
Thanne quod this murie jade, til Marlborrowe.
Therto he syde that she moghte with hym steye
Til Gildforde, wher his destinacioun leye,
But whan hem neghen dide to Gildforde toun
She til hir verray queynte up—drow hir goun,
And swoor to crye out Ravyne! and Harrow!
So mote he bere hir ful to Marlborrowe.

—*W.F.N. Watson*

The Probatioun Officeres Tale

The lede guiterriste was a craftie ladde,
Wel koude he luren chickes to his padde
To dyg the sownes of Clapton or The Stones
And share a joynte and turn on for the nones,
Till net he wyth a drogge squadde maiden fayre
Who yaf him think she was a Frenssche au pair,
That whan at last he caused hir sens to feynte
And subtilly to frote hir at the queynte,
And whyspere sucred words and strook her sore,
'Lay on!' she cried, 'my rammysh prikasour!'
For she was nothing loth to amorous sport
So be she got hir Pusheres into court.

—*Gerard Benson*

Portrait of the Pornographer

Ther was a Knight, a worthy for the chaffre.
He lovede gold, and was a Pornografre.
To sellen likerous bokis was his wone,
For he was Daun Boccacces owene sone.
Bretful his mal was, ful of lewed news
And images of swivings and of screws.
To Stokholme hadde he been on pilgrimage,
And comen was to delen us outrage—
Of *flagellatio* and swich hethnesse,
De coitu and other cursednesse,
As in our dayes is nat worth a torde.
He balled was, and highte Lord Longenforde.

—*G.W. Jones*

Ye Clerke of Ye Wethere

A Clerke ther was, a puissant wight was hee,
Who of ye wethere hadde ye maisterie;
Alway it was his mirthe and his solace—
To put eche seson's wethere oute of place.

Whanne that Aprille shoures wer our desyre,
He gad us Julye sonnes as hotte as fyre;
But sith ye summere togges we donned agayne,
Eftsoons ye wethere chaunged to cold and rayne.

Wo was that pilgrimme who fared forth a-foote,
Without ane gyngham that him list uppe-putte;
And gif no mackyntosches eke had hee,
A parlous state that wight befelle—pardie

We wist not gif it nexte ben colde or hotte,
Cogswounds! ye barde a grewsome colde hath gotte!
Certes, that clerke's ane mightie man withalle,
Let non don him offence, lest ille befalle.

—*Anonymous*

A Clerk Ther was of Cauntebrigge Also

A Clerk ther was of Cauntebrigge also,
That unto rowing hadde long y-go.
Of thinne shides wolde he shippes make,
And he was nat right fat, I undertake.
And whan his ship he wrought had atte fulle,
Right gladly by the river wolde he pulle,
And eek returne as blythly as he wente.
Him rekked nevere that the sonne him brente,
Ne stinted he his cours for reyn ne snowe;
It was a joye for to seen him rowe!
Yit was him lever, in his shelves newe,
Six olde textes, clad in greenish hewe,
Of Chaucer and his olde poesye
Than ale, or wyn of Lepe, or Malvoisye.
And therwithall he wex a philosofre;
And peyned him to gadren gold in cofre
Of sundry folk; and al that he mighte hente
On textes and emprinting he it spente;
And busily gan bokes to purveye
For hem that yeve him wherwith to scoleye.
Of glossaryes took he hede and cure;
And when he spyed had, by aventure,
A word that semed him or strange or rare,
To henten it anon he nolde spare,
But wolde it on a shrede of paper wryte,
And in a cheste he dide his shredes whyte,
And preyed every man to doon the same;
Swich maner study was to him but game.

—*Walter William Skeat*

From THE MURDER IN THE CATHEDRAL AND OTHER TALES

The Tale of Sir Thopas

Listeth, lordes, in good entent,
And I wol telle verrayment
  Of mirthe and of solas;
Al of a knyght was fair and gent
In bataille and in tourneyment,
  His name was sir Thopas.

Y-born he was in fer contree,
In Flaundres, al biyonde the see,
   At Poperyng, in the place;
His fader was a man ful free,
And lord he was of that contree,
   As it was goddes grace.

Sir Thopas wax a doghty swayn,
Whyt was his face as payndemayn,
   His lippes rede as rose;
His rode is lyk scarlet in grayn,
And I yow telle in good certayn,
   He hadde a semely nose.

His heer, his berd was lyk saffroun,
That to his girdel raughte adoun;
   His shoon of cordewane.
Of Brugges were his hosen broun,
His robe was of ciclatoun,
   That coste many a Iane.

He coude hunte at wilde deer,
And ryde an hauking for river,
   With grey goshauk on honde;
Ther-to he was a good archeer,
Of wrastling was ther noon his peer,
   Ther any ram shal stonde.

Ful many a mayde, bright in bour,
They moorne for him paramour,
   Whan hem were bet to slepe;
But he was chast and no lechour,
And sweet as is the bremble-flour
   That bereth the rede hepe.

And so bifel up-on a day,
For sothe, as I yow tell may,
   Sir Thopas wolde out ryde;
He worth upon his stede gray,
And in his honde a launcegay,
   A long swerd by his syde.

He priketh thurgh a fair forest,
Ther-inne is many a wilde best,
   Ye, bothe bukke and hare;
And, as he priketh north and est,
I telle it yow, him hadde almest
   Bitid a sory care.

Ther springen herbes grete and smale,
The lycorys and cetewale,
   And many a clowe-gilofre;
And notemuge to putte in ale,
Whether it be moyste or stale,
   Or for to leye in cofre.

The briddes singe, it is no nay,
The sparhauk and the papeiay,
   That Ioye it was to here;

The thrustelcok made eek his lay,
The wodedowve upon the spray
She sang ful loude and clere.

Sir Thopas fil in love-longine
Al when he herde the thrustel singe,
And priked as he were wood:
His faire stede in his prikinge
So swatte that men mighte him wringe,
His sydes weer al blood.

Sir Thopas eek so wery was
For prikinge on the softe gras,
So fiers was his corage,
That doun he leyde him in that plas
To make his stede som solas,
And yaf him good forage.

"O seinte Marie, *benedicite!*
What eyleth this love at me
To binde me so sore?
Me dremed al this night, pardee,
An elf-queen shal my lemman be,
And slepe under my gore.

An elf-queen wol I love, y-wis,
For in this world no womman is
Worthy to be my make
In toune;
Alle othere wommen I forsake,
And to an elf-queen I me take
By dale and eek by doune!"

In-to his sadel he clamb anoon,
And priketh over style and stoon
An elf-queen for tespye,
Til he so longe had riden and goon
That he fond, in a privee woon,
The contree of Fairye
So wilde;
For in that contree was ther noon
That to him dorste ryde or goon,
Neither wyf ne childe.

Til that ther cam a greet geaunt,
His name was sir Olifaunt,
A perilous man of dede;
He seyde, "child, by Termagaunt!
But if thou prike out of myn haunt,
Anon I slee thy stede
With mace.
Heer is the queen of Fayërye,
With harpe and pype and simphonye
Dwelling in this place."

The child seyde, "al-so mote I thee,
Tomorwe wol I mete thee
Whan I have myn armoure;
And yet I hope, *par ma fay,*

That thou shalt with this launcegay
Abyen it ful soure:
Thy mawe
Shal I percen, if I may,
Er it be fully pryme of day,
For heer thou shalt be slawe."

Sir Thopas drow abak ful faste;
This geaunt at him stones caste
Out of a fel staf-slinge;
But faire escapeth child Thopas,
And al it was thurgh goddes gras,
And thurgh his fair beringe.

Yet listeth, lordes, to my tale
Merier than the nightingale,
For now I wol yow roune
How sir Thopas with sydes smale,
Priking over hil and dale,
Is come agayn to toune.

His merie men comanded he
To make him bothe game and glee,
For nedes moste he fighte
With a geaunt with hevedes three,
For paramour and Iolitee
Of oon that shoon ful brighte.

"Do come," he seyde, "my minstrales,
And gestours, for to tellen tales
Anon in myn arminge;
Of romances that been royales,
Of popes and of cardinales,
And eek of love-lykinge."

They fette him first the swete wyn,
And mede eek in a maselyn,
And royal spicerye;
Of gingebreed that was ful fyn,
And lycorys, and eek comyn,
With sugre that is so trye.

He dide next his whyte lere
Of clooth of lake fyn and clere
A breech and eek a sherte;
And next his sherte an aketoun,
And over that an habergeoun
For percinge of his herte;

And over that a fyn hauberk,
Was al y-wroght of Iewes werk,
Ful strong it was of plate;
And over that his cote-armour
As whyt as is a lily-flour,
In which he wol debate.

His sheeld was al of gold so reed,
And ther-in was a bores heed,
A charbocle bisyde;
And there he swoor, on ale and breed,
How that "the geaunt shal be deed,
Bityde what bityde!"

His jambeux were of quirboilly,
His swerdes shethe of yvory,
   His helm of laton bright;
His sadel was of rewel-boon,
His brydel as the sonne shoon,
   Or as the mone light.

His spere was of fyn ciprees,
That bodeth werre, and no-thing pees,
   The heed ful sharpe y-grounde;
His stede was al dappel-gray,
It gooth an ambel in the way
   Ful softely and rounde
      In londe.
Lo, lordes myne, heer is a fit!
If ye wol any more of it,
   To telle it wol I fonde.

The Second Fit

Now hold your mouth, *par charitee,*
Bothe knight and lady free,
   And herkneth to my spelle;
Of bataille and of chivalry,
And of ladyes love-drury
   Anon I wol yow telle.

Men speke of romances of prys,
Of Horn child and of Ypotys,
   Of Bevis and sir Gy,
Of sir Libeux and Pleyn-damour;
But sir Thopas, he bereth the flour
   Of royal chivalry.

His gode stede al he bistrood,
And forth upon his wey he glood
   As sparkle out of the bronde;
Up-on his crest he bar a tour,
And ther-in stiked a lily-flour,
   God shilde his cors fro shonde!

And for he was a knight auntrous,
He nolde slepen in non hous,
   But liggen in his hode;
His brighte helm was his wonger,
And by him baiteth his dextrer
   Of herbes fyne and gode.

Him-self drank water of the wel,
As did the knight sir Percivel,
   So worthy under wede,
Til on a day——

Heere the Host stinteth Chaucer of his Tale of Thopas

"No more of this, for goddes dignitee,"
Quod oure hoste, "for thou makest me
So wery of thy verray lewednesse
That, also wisly god my soule blesse,
Myn eres aken of thy drasty speche;
Now swiche a rym the devel I biteche!
This may wel be rym dogerel," quod he,
   "Why so?" quod I, "why wiltow lette me
More of my tale than another man,

Sin that it is the beste rym I can?"
"By god," quod he, "for pleynly, at a word,
Thy drasty ryming is nat worth a tord;
Thou doost nought elles but despendest tyme,
Sir, at o word, thou shalt no lenger ryme.
Lat see wher thou canst tellen aught in geste,
Or telle in prose somwhat at the leste
In which ther be som mirthe or som doctryne."
"Gladly," quod I, "by goddes swete pyne,
I wol yow telle a litel thing in prose
That oughte liken yow as I suppose,...

—Geoffrey Chaucer

The Cook's Tale

A prentys whilom dwelled in oure citee,
And of a craft of vitailliers was hee.
Gaillard he was as goldfynch in the shawe,
Broun as a berye, a propre short felawe,
With lokkes blake, ykembd ful fetisly.
Dauncen he koude so wel and jolily
That he was cleped Perkyn Revelour.
He was as ful of love and paramour
As is the hyve ful of hony sweete:
Wel was the wenche with hym myghte meete.
At every bridale wolde he synge and hoppe;
He loved bet the taverne than the shoppe.
For whan ther any ridyng was in Chepe,
Out of the shoppe thider wolde he lepe
Til that he hadde al the sighte yseyn,
And daunced well, he wolde nat come ayeyn—
And gadered hym a meynee of his sort
To hoppe and synge and maken swich disport;
And ther they setten stevene for to meete,
To pleyen at the dys in swich a streete.
For in the toune nas ther no prentys
That fairer koude caste a paire of dys
Than Perkyn koude, and therto he was free
Of his dispense, in place of pryvetee.
That fond his maister wel in his chaffare;
For often tyme he foond his box ful bare.
For sikerly a prentys revelour
That haunteth dys, riot, or paramour,
His maister shal it in his shoppe abye,
Al have he no part of the mynstralcye.
For thefte and riot, they been convertible,
Al konne he pleye on gyterne or ribible.
Revel and trouthe, as in a lowe degree,
They been ful wrothe al day, as men may see.
This joly prentys with his maister bood,
Til he were ny out of his prentishood,
Al were he snybbed bothe erly and late,
And somtyme lad with revel to Newegate.
But atte laste his maister hym bithoghte,
Upon a day, whan he his papier soghte,
Of a proverbe that seith this same word,
"Wel bet is roten appul out of hoord
Then that it rotie all the remenaunt."
So fareth it by a riotous servaunt;

It is ful lasse harm to lete hym pace,
Than he shende alle the servantz in the place.
Therfore his maister yaf hym acquitance,
And bad hym go, with sorwe and with meschance!
And thus this joly prentys hadde his leve.
Now lat hym riote al the nyght or leve.
And for ther is no theef withoute a lowke,
That helpeth hym to wasten and to sowke
Of that he brybe kan or borwe may.
Anon he sente his bed and his array
Unto a compeer of his owene sort,
That lovede dys, and revel, and disport,
And hadde a wyf that heeld for contenance
A shoppe, and swyved for hir sustenance.

—*Geoffry Chaucer*

Here Begins the Continuation of the Cook's Tale

And in this swyving there nas noon hir pere.
For sothe, she heeld no thyng so leef and dere,
But that it were a jape, by Goddes blode!
She swoor ther nas no bettre liflhode,
And laboured in shoppe on breches breste,
A nyghtes knyttynge membres withoute reste.
Hir skyn was fresshe as floures, dew-wete hir lippes;
She nolde bosten of hir rounde hippes,
Ne of a lifly toute, as Albert dyde,
Ne that hir brest coude fede fourty kyde.
She kept a gaytres bery for good fortune[1],
And was as hoot as is a hare in June.
He was a gadeling, a gay putour,
The husbonde of this worldes paramour.
He felte nat the prikke of jalousie,
But lovede hir bettre for hir puterie.
Whan that his wyf was bisye with hir mendyng,
He was as bisye al hir monye spendying
At dys and bauderye with gladde chere.
He lovede Perkyn as a brother dere,
As muchel, siker, as he did his wyf,
And swoor he wolde kerve with a knyf
The throtes of hem that sholde his freend ygreve.
Ful ofte he swoor lest som nat hym bileve.
Now whan this Perkyn ther biforn hem stood
As still as stoon, ystript of prentishood,
Allone and banysshed fro his maistres place,
A clowde coveryng his brighte face,
Than Albertes wyf him clippte for to kisse,
And thakked Perkyn ther that menne pisse,
And seyde,"Good daye, myn owene papejay!"
Albert than hym grette with herte gay,
"Perkyn myn freend, and brother of myn lyf,
Wel-come to myn dys, myn wyn, myn wyf!"

1. *gaytres bery*, berry from the goat tree. Cf. *Nun's Priest's Tale*, I.2965, where it is identified as a strong laxative; and *General Prologue*, the description of the Pardoner: "A voys he hadde as smal as hath a goot," I.688. The cluster of images and implications arising from the berry's derivation from a tree named after the animal equivalent of lust, and use as a laxative, suggest that the wife Marybones kept the berry to bring her continuing good fortune in her fleshly pursuits.

"O hoo," quod Perkyn, murie al atones,
"Myn deere Albert and swete Marybones!"[2]
Anoon for joye he gan a litel daunce
And soong ful loude a dytee newe fro Fraunce.
By God, in all this world of wantownesse
Wot I noon his pere, as I gesse.
Quod Albert than, "By Goddes privetee,
How farest thou that heere thou sholde be?
Ascuance som cursedness or som fel treson
Hath on thee new by-fallen, or oother reson?"
Than told broun Perkyn of an hostileere
That neyther coude laughe ne make cheere,
Of contenance fond for al to see,
But heeld in grete prys his dignitee;
An hooly vitailler so ful of preyere
Temptacioun bigyled nat a heere.
"By Goddes bones, this prikethe me ful soore
To spille his hooly herte blood on the floore!
Y-wis, this Loller wol been bettre deed,"[3]
Quod Albert, and his nosethirles wax al reed.
Than Perkyn gan to laughe, than Marybones;
Wrooth Albert was, but caughte the fit atones.
"But was this Loller 'Loller' fro his byrthe,
Or hath he oother name?" quod she in myrthe
And curiositee, a joly sighte.
"This hostileer 'Gregigdignibs' is highte,"[4]
Broun Perkyn seyde, and lough as he were wood.
"Gregigdignibs?" she cride, "by Goddes blood!"
"What, wyfe myne, hastow ete a worm?"
"By Loy, he nis no Loller, but a form!
He cometh every nyght into myn shoppe
For mendyng; his halwed wyf wol not him toppe.
'A wyfes yen,' quoth she, 'sholde loke to heven[5]
At alle tymes,' and wol han hym bileven.
Nor in his swyving nis no man so coy;
He wol be whipped lyk a litel boy
Upon his toute with a strope thikke;
No oother thyng wol make him wexe so quikke,
But that I ryde his bakke as I couthe,
Or bynde him doun and bete him withoute routhe.
If that be Lollerdie, than plukke myn heeris."
"By Cristes bones and his moodres teeris!"
Quod Perkyn. "Comth he heer, this verray oon?"
"This nyght," quod she, "he cometh heer anoon."
"I have a jape, myn freendes, a murie game

2. *Marybones*, marrow-bones. Cf. *General Prologue*, I.380, Chaucer's description of the Cook. The wife's name would seem an outrageous pun, considering the "stywe" she simmers in. The Cook, of course, would know all about *marybones*.

3. *Loller*, cf. *Man of Law's Epilogue*, I.II73, where the Parson is branded a Lollard, or a follower of John Wycliffe. The Lollards were the leaders of what was essentially a popular reform movement in the fourteenth century and were, in a sense, forerunners of the Reformation. The movement attacked the worldly state of the church, the rich mendicant orders, monasts, and so on, for their high life, and advocated a return to the simple and unworldly.

That the "vitaillier," or host, of this tale should be labelled a Lollard is ironic in light of the events following. It ought to be noted, however, that it is the quick-tempered Albert who gives this label to the host, and not Marybones, who simply plays with the word. Implicit in all this, of course, is the fact that the host of Chaucer's pilgrimage, Harry Bailey, has been mentioned in *The Cook's Prologue* as a possible character in *The Cook's Tale*: "And therfore, Harry Bailly, by they feith,/ Be thou nat wrooth, er we departen heer,/ Though that my tale be of an hostileer."

4. *Gregigdignibs*, apparently a nonsense name, but with a seeming host of appropriate connotations.

5. *A wyfes yen*, a conceivable link with the so-called Marriage Group. On the one hand, the Wife of Bath advocates female sovereignty in marriage; on the other, the Clerk advocates (in the person of the patient Griselda) "steadfast devotion" to the husband on the part of the wife. Standing midway between these two extremes is the rather anarchic arrangement between Albert and Marybones. It might be added that the fate of the husband Gregigdignibs seems a chilly counterpart to the kind of sovereignty espoused by the Wife of Bath.

That wol been this fooles deeth in shame.
Now hoold youre pees, and I yow it wol telle."
On what this Perkyn seyde, I wol not dwelle.
  In the mene while up roos our hooste
Softely fro his bedde lyk a gooste,
Or lyk Lazar risyng fro deeth to lyf,
And seyde a curs upon his rowtyng wyf,
Than greythed him and don his hosen rede
And kembd the fourty heeris on his hede;
Than prikt his mare Abigayl ful smerte,
The develes fyr brennynge in his herte.
This hoost, he broght with him a broyded whippe
For Marybones to carye on hir hippe,
And shoon of cordewane for hir pleasaunce,
And for his owene gamyng to avaunce.
  Atte laste he knokked on hir dore;
"Now get thee gone," quod she, "and come namoore."
"Dere herte, artow sike fro maladye?
Allas, withoute thy socour moot I dye!"
"Go hoom, jakke-fool, I nam no syghte to see."
"What, hath thyn housbond maad col-blak thyn ye?
Yet me were lever languisshe in the reyne
Than to myn wyfe hye me hoom ayeyne.
Swete Marybones, blow out youre lyghte;
Be nat a lette-game thise nyghte,
Or I spille." This wysh had she in mynde
And blew the candele out; and as oon blynde
This sely hooste groped in the derke.
"Myn love, come hider, parfourne your hooly werke,"
Quod he. "For love of thee I am forpyned."
Than doun upon al foure fel this bene-hed
And strepte him al naked for the nones.
"Wee-hee!" he cride, whynynge for Marybones
Lyk a nagge, and gan to prike and praunce.
"Olde fool," quod she, "namoore they daliaunce!
What profit, I yow preye, in avoutrye
Whan that myn housbond shal of shame dye?"
"Wol brouded whippe, dere herte, y-nough suffyse?"
"Certes, his precyous honour hath na pryse!"
"And shoon," quod he, "of souple cordewan?"
"Welcome, y-wis," quod she, "myn dere lemman!"
He yaf hir yiftes two, and lyk a beeste
Gan goon on foure, al redy for the feeste.
  Soone had this Perkyn and his good felawe
Ystript the mare and softe gan hir drawe
Into the derke chambre, thrugh the dore
That Marybones had undoon bifore;
She lough ful loude for to hyde the soun
Of fartynge Abigayl, y-wrested doun
Upon the bedde, and he anon answerde,
"The crakes of thy whippe, by Goddes berde!"
Now douteles he hadde two cris fyn
Bifore thre draughtes of this bawdes wyn.
"O swete soun! Now longe I for the smerte
Of firy strookes on my bak, dere herte.
Com, lay thy lassche harde upon my flesshe!"
Ful firme heeld she hir whippe, and gan hym thresshe,
And in the derknesse smoot hym bake and syde
Til blody was he scorged; yet he cryde,
"My swete foo, O lufsom lady, moore!"
Than quyk thise harlots did obeye hym soore

And bete hym with yerdes on his toute,
While Perkyn rood this Loller al aboute,
Cryynge "gee-ho," but in a smale voys.
Attelaste ther cam a pitous noys
Of sobbes and of sikes. "Com of my bake,
Dere herte," quod he. "Have doon, for Cristes sake,
Elles I dye, pardee, of to muche joy;
A greet mervayle, thyn love, and nevere coy!
But ful of wyn I am and moste pisse."
Perkynes softe chyne he yaf a kisse
Than groped out the dore in dronkenesse;
Leve we him ther to doon his bisynesse.
  This out-caste prentys had so myrie a fit
Hit semed that he had his maister quit;
Unnethe koude he speke or drawe brethe
After he rood this wight ny to the dethe,
And with his freendes lough til teeris cam.
"By God," quod he, "an outridere I am!
In al my lyf I nevere rood so fer
Upon so slough an asse, ne so ner,
Y-wis, withoute sadel and stiropes!
Dere freendes, this game passeth al my hopes,
But heere we comen to the beste part."
Than lete this Abigayl abedde a fart
That rente hir eris lyk a thonder clappe.
"Love calleth?" Perkyn seyde. "Than leet it happe!"
Al sodeynly aroos nat fer withoute
A pitous moone of wo, and than a shoute:
"O villanie! My Abigayl is goon,
Ystole, percas mordred! What shal I doon?"
Whan that thise harlots thre coude hym espye,
This Albert gan in grete fere to crye,
"By God, this waylyng Loller, bely-naked,
Wol han the hoole toun, ywis, y-waked!
This swere I yow, he suffreth soone his deeth!"
Ful many an ooth he swoor and grinte his teeth.
Quod Marybones, "Us nedeth nat a cors,
Myn housbond dere, whan that we have a hors."
Than gan this baude swetely hym calle,
"Thyn mare, sir, nis nat in theves stalle,
But stondeth ther biforn thyn verray eyen;
Ful oft wol wyn this jape on wittes pleyen."
"Biforn myn verray yen? By Cristes nayles,"
Quod he, "this is oon of the greet mervayles,
By my trouthe, that evere I did se;
She nis nat heere, God woot, yit heere she be!"
And pitously he shoke his hede and syked,
Than meeke as a lamb dide as hir lyked.
"Com hyder, sir," quod she, "ye sholde nat stonde
Naked in the strete," and by the honde
Hym ladde in the derke bour ayeyn.
"Thy wittes fledde, ther nis namoore to seyn;
Hit is a commune thynge," quod Marybones.
"Sufficeth this ensample; heere ones
A wight did swere a shepe was in myn bed[6]
Which that he swyved; wyn was in his hed.

6. *a shepe.* Intercourse with sheep was apparently esteemed in the Middle Ages. A veritable *Kama Sutra* of the art has recently been discovered in successive fly-leaves of the *Yedyfycaciounes* of Thessalone the Elder (1300-1369). The following is an excerpt: "A shepe is nat so hoot as youre wyf. But whan youre wyf is goon hoom to hir mooder, than a shepe doth good servyce."

This day myn housbond nolde nat me clippe,
But clept me olde nagge and gan me whippe;
Dronke he was, certeyn, of corny ale,
And ther have yow another swiche tale.
Now wostow why, dere sir, I nam no syghte
For mannes eyen, by moone or candel lyghte."
Whil that she spak, this sely hoost, ful bare,
Gan grope in bed wher sleep that deyntee mare,
And seyde, "Now pees, dere herte; this hooly werk,
As clerkes seyn, is hoolier in the derk,"
Than fond and coughte hir by the ers and flankes;
"O swet richesse," he cride, and sobbed thankes,
"And hooly heer, by God, so lyk a tayle,
Hit is, y-wis, another greet mervayle!"
He gan than threste and crowe, as cokkes trede,
But lyked hir so wel hir maydenhede
This mare sproong up as arwe out of bowe;
Now did thre repe from seede here y-sowe
Whan that with shoon she yaf hem kisse of iren
Thise two harlotes did nat moche desiren;
Than mette this wilde mare Marybones
In derknesse heed on heed lyk slinge-stones;
And whil this baude did aswoune ther leye,
This mare cride "Wee-hee"; namoore to seye,
She baar this hoost about in greet clamour,
Than brast adoun with hoves wal of bour;
And with hym harde embracyng ers and tayle,
Ful faste hoomward spedde this Abigayl
Hir maister bare to wyf, and hir to stable.
   I am the Cook, but coke yow here no fable;
Hit happed, by my trouthe, as I yow tolde,
Thise japeres byjaped, as God wolde;
Longe on hir lippes is ther mark of hoves
Ful wel embosed for to kiss hir loves.
Swete Marybones heed is al y-broken,
And now in honde-glas she dar nat loken;
Have pitee on this baude, for Cristes sake,
And preye God lat oure hedes nevere ake!
This hoost that rood hoom dronken as a mous,
Ful naked, namoore is maister in his hous;
A-nyght he moste in bedde abyde at hoom,
A wyf with herte and toute colde his doom;
Aslepe he maketh mone, withouten fayl
In dreem of hym bistrid that Abigayl;
For out of doute this resteless caytyf
Had never swiche swyving in his lyf!
That stywe is doun; myn litel tale is doon;
May Goddes body fede us everichoon!

—*William Zaranka*

ANONYMOUS BALLADS

Ballad

The auld wife sat at her ivied door,
   (*Butter and eggs and a pound of cheese*)
A thing she had frequently done before;
   And her spectacles lay on her apron'd knees.

The piper he piped on the hill-top high,
(*Butter and eggs and a pound of cheese*)
Till the cow said, "I die," and the goose ask'd "Why?"
And the dog said nothing, but search'd for fleas.

The farmer he strove through the square farmyard;
(*Butter and eggs and a pound of cheese*)
His last brew of ale was a trifle hard—
The connexion of which with the plot one sees.

The farmer's daughter hath frank blue eyes;
(*Butter and eggs and a pound of cheese*)
She hears the rooks caw in the windy skies,
As she sits at her lattice and shells her peas.

The farmer's daughter hath ripe red lips:
(*Butter and eggs and a pound of cheese*)
If you try to approach her, away she skips
Over tables and chairs with apparent ease.

The farmer's daughter hath soft brown hair;
(*Butter and eggs and a pound of cheese*)
And I met with a ballad, I can't say where,
Which wholly consisted of lines like these.

Part II

She sat, with her hands 'neath her dimpled cheeks,
(*Butter and eggs and a pound of cheese*)
And spake not a word. While a lady speaks
There is hope, but she didn't even sneeze.

She sat, with her hands 'neath her crimson cheeks,
(*Butter and eggs and a pound of cheese*)
She gave up mending her father's breeks,
And let the cat roll in her new chemise.

She sat, with her hands 'neath her burning cheeks,
(*Butter and eggs and a pound of cheese*)
And gazed at the piper for thirteen weeks;
Then she follow'd him out o'er the misty leas.

Her sheep follow'd her, as their tails did them.
(*Butter and eggs and a pound of cheese*)
And this song is consider'd a perfect gem,
And as to the meaning, it's what you please.

—*Charles S. Calverley*

The New Ballad of Sir Patrick Spens (Old Border Ballad)

The King sits in Dumferline toun
Drinking the blude-red wine:
"O wha will rear me an equilateral triangle
Upon a given straight line?"

O up and spake an eldern knight
Sat at the King's right knee—
"Of a' the clerks by Granta side
Sir Patrick bears the gree.

"'Tis he was taught by the Tod-huntère
Tho' not at the tod-hunting;
Yet gif that he be given a line
He'll do as brave a thing."

Our King has written a braid letter
To Cambrigge or thereby
And there it found Sir Patrick Spens
Evaluating Pi

He hadna warked his quotient
A point but barely three,
There stepped to him a little foot-page
And louted on his knee.

The first word that Sir Patrick read
"Plus X" was a' he said:
The neist word that Sir Patrick read
'Twas "*plus* expenses paid."

The last word that Sir Patrick read
The tear blinded his e'e:
"The pound I most admire is not
In Scottish currencie."

Stately stepped he east the wa',
And stately stepped he north;
He fetched a compass frae his ha'
And stood beside the Forth.

Then gurly grew the waves o' Forth
And gurlier by-and-bye—
"O never yet was sic a storm
Yet it isna sic as I!"

Syne he had crossed the Firth o' Forth
Until Dumferline toun
And tho' he came with a kittle wame
Fu' low he louted down.

"A line, a line, a gude straight line,
O King, purvey me quick!
And see it be of thilka kind
That's neither braid nor thick."

"Nor thick nor braid?" King Jamie said,
"I'll eat my gude hatband
If arra line as ye define
Be found in our Scotland."

"Tho' there be nane in a' thy rule
It sall be ruled by me";
And lichtly with his little pencil
He's ruled the line A B.

Stately stepped he east the wa',
And stately stepped he west;
"Ye touch the button," Sir Patrick said,
"And I sall do the rest."

And he has set his compass foot
Until the centre A,
From A to B he's stretched it oot—
"Ye Scottish carles, give way!"

Syne he has moved his compass foot
Until the centre B,
From B to A he's stretched it oot,
And drawn it viz-a-vee.

The ane circle was B C D,
And A C E the tither.
"I rede ye well," Sir Patrick said,
"They interseck ilk ither.

"See here, and where they interseck—
To wit with yon point C—
Ye'll just obsairve that I conneck
The twa points A and B.

"And there ye have a little triangle
As bonny as e'er was seen;
The whilk is not isosceles,
Nor yet it is scalene."

"The proof! the proof!" King Jamie cried:
"The how and eke the why!"
Sir Patrick laughed within his beard—
"'Tis *ex hypothesi*—

"When I ligg'd in my mither's wame
I learn'd it frae my mither,
That things was equal to the same
Was equal ane to t'ither.

"Sith in the circle first I drew
The lines B A, B C,
Be radii true, I wit to you
The baith maun equal be.

"Likewise and in the second circle
Whilk I drew widdershins
It is nae skaith the radii baith
A B, A C, be twins.

"And sith of three a pair agree
That ilk suld equal ane,
By certes they maun equal be
Ilk unto ilk by-lane."

"Now by my faith!" King Jamie saith,
"What *plane* geometrie!
If only Potts had written in Scots,
How loocid Potts would be!"

"Now, wow's my life!" saith Jamie the King,
And the Scots lords said the same,
For but it was that envious knicht
Sir Hughie o' the Graeme.

"Flim-flam, flim-flam!" and "Ho-indeed?"
Quod Hughie o' the Graeme;
"'Tis I could better upon my heid
This prabblin prablem-game."

Sir Patrick Spens was nothing laith
When as he heard "flim-flam,"
But syne he's ta'en a silken claith
And wiped his diagram.

"Gif my small feat may better'd be;
Sir Hew, by thy big head,
What I hae done with an A B C
Do thou with X Y Z."

Then sairly sairly swore Sir Hew,
And loudly laucht the King;
But Sir Patrick tuk the pipes and blew,
And *played* that eldritch thing!

He's play'd it reel, he's play'd it jig,
And the baith alternative;
And he's danced Sir Hew to the Asses' Brigg
That's Proposition Five.

And there they've met and there they've fet,
Forenenst the Asses' Brigg,
And waefu', waefu' was the fate
That gar'd them there to ligg.

For there Sir Patrick's slain Sir Hew
And Sir Hew, Sir Patrick Spens.
Now was not that a fine to-do
For Euclid's Elemen's?

But let us sing Long live the King!
And his foes the Deil attend 'em:
For he has gotten his little triangle,
Quod erat faciendum!

—Sir Arthur Quiller-Couch

The Massacre of the Macpherson

FROM THE GAELIC

I

Fhairshon swore a feud
Against the clan M'Tavish;
Marched into their land
To murder and to rafish;
For he did resolve
To extirpate the vipers,
With four-and-twenty men
And five-and-thirty pipers.

II

But when he had gone
Half-way down Strath Canaan,
Of his fighting tail

Just three were remainin'.
They were all he had,
To back him in ta battle;
All the rest had gone
Off, to drive ta cattle.

III

"Fery coot!" cried Fhairshon.
"So my clan disgraced is;
Lads, we'll need to fight
Pefore we touch the peasties.
Here's Mhic-Mac-Methusaleh
Coming wi' his fassals,
Gillies seventy-three,
And sixty Dhuinéwassails!"

IV

"Coot tay to you, sir;
Are you not ta Fhairshon?
Was you coming here
To fisit any person?
You are a plackguard, sir!
It is now six hundred
Coot long years, and more,
Since my glen was plunder'd."

V

"Fat is tat you say?
Dare you cock your peaver?
I will teach you, sir,
Fat is coot pehaviour!
You shall not cxist
For another day more;
I will shoot you, sir,
Or stap you with my claymore!"

VI

"I am fery glad
To learn what you mention,
Since I can prevent
Any such intention."
So Mhic-Mac-Methusaleh
Gave some warlike howls,
Trew his skhian-dhu,
An' stuck it in his powels.

VII

In this fery way
Tied ta faliant Fhairshon,
Who was always thought
A superior person.
Fhairshon had a son,
Who married Noah's daughter,
And nearly spoil'd ta Flood,
By trinking up ta water:

VIII

Which he would have done,
I at least believe it,
Had to mixture peen
Only half Glenlivet.
This is all my tale:
Sirs, I hope 'tis new t'ye!
Here's your fery good healths,
And tamn ta whusky duty!

—*William Aytoun*

The Lay of the Ettercap

Now shal y tellen to ye, y wis,
Of that Squyere hizt Ellis,
And his Dame so fre:
So hende he is by goddes mizt,
That he nis not ymake a knizt
It is the more pitè.

He knoweth better eche glewe,
Than y can to ye shew
Oither bi plume or greffe:
To hunte or hawke, bi frith or folde,
Or play at boules in alles colde,
He is wel holden cheffe.

His eyes graye as glas ben,
And his visage alto kene,
Loveliche to paramour:
Clere as amber beth his faxe,
His face beth thin as battle-axe
That deleth dintes doure.

His witte beth both kene and sharpe,
To knizt or dame that wel can carpe
Oither in halle or boure:
And had y not that Squyere yfonde,
Y hadde ben at the se gronde,
Which had ben gret doloure.

In him y finden none nother evil,
Save that his nostril moche doth snivel,
Al throgh that vilaine snuffe:
But then his speche beth so perquire,
That those who may his carpyng here,
They never may here ynough.

His Dame beth of so meikle price,
To holden hemselves in her service,
Fele folks faine wolde be:
Soft and swote in eche steven,
Like an angel com fro heven,
Singeth sothe that fre.

I wot her carpyng bin ful queynt,
And her corps bothe smale and gent,
Semeliche to be sene:
Fete, hondes, and fingres smale,
Of perle beth eche fingre nail;
She mizt ben Fairi Quene.

That Ladi gent wolde given a scarfe
To hym wolde kille a wreche dwarfe
Of paynim brode;
That dwarfe is a fell Ettercap,
And liven aye on nettle-sap,
And hath none nother fode.

That dwarfe he beth berdles and bare,
And weazel-blowen beth all his hair,
Lyke an ympe elfe;

And in this middel erd all and haile
Ben no kyn thyng he loveth an dele,
Save his owen selfe.

And when the Dame ben come to toune,
That Ladi gent sall mak her boune
A selcouth feat to try,
To take a little silver knyfe,
And end that sely dwarfes life,
And bake hym in a pye.

—*John Leyden*

Faithless Nelly Gray

Ben Battle was a soldier bold,
And used to war's alarms;
But a cannon-ball took off his legs,
So he laid down his arms!

Now as they bore him off the field,
Said he, 'Let others shoot,
For here I leave my second leg,
And the Forty-second Foot!'

The army-surgeons made him limbs:
Said he—'They're only pegs:
But there's as wooden members quite
As represent my legs!'

Now Ben he loved a pretty maid,
Her name was Nelly Gray;
So he went to pay her his devours
When he'd devoured his pay!

But when he called on Nelly Gray,
She made him quite a scoff;
And when she saw his wooden legs
Began to take them off!

'Oh, Nelly Gray! Oh, Nelly Gray!
Is this your love so warm?
The love that loves a scarlet coat
Should be more uniform!'

Said she, 'I loved a soldier once,
For he was blithe and brave;
But I will never have a man
With both legs in the grave!

'Before you had those timber toes,
Your love I did allow,
But then, you know, you stand upon
Another footing now!'

'Oh, Nelly Gray! Oh, Nelly Gray!
For all your jeering speeches,
At duty's call, I left my legs
In Badajos's *breaches*!'

'Why then,' said she, 'you've lost the feet
Of legs in war's alarms,
And now you cannot wear your shoes
Upon your feats of arms!'

'Oh, false and fickle Nelly Gray;
I know why you refuse:—
Though I've no feet—some other man
Is standing in my shoes!'

'I wish I ne'er had seen your face;
But, now, a long farewell!
For you will be my death—alas!
You will not be my *Nell*!'

Now when he went from Nelly Gray,
His heart so heavy got—
And life was such a burthen grown,
It made him take a knot!

So round his melancholy neck,
A rope he did entwine,
And, for his second time in life,
Enlisted in the Line!

One end he tied around a beam,
And then removed his pegs,
And, as his legs were off,—of course,
He soon was off his legs!

And there he hung, till he was dead
As any nail in town,—
For though distress had cut him up,
It could not cut him down!

A dozen men sat on his corpse,
To find out why he died—
And they buried Ben in four cross-roads,
With a *stake* in his inside!

—Thomas Hood

OLD AND MIDDLE ENGLISH GNOMES, RIBALDS, CHAINSAWS, AND ENDEARING YOUNG CHARMS

When fog come creepin' over Beccles,
Ye'll catch no roach but only stickleback.

If the chestnut flower not by September,
Why then the bloody thing be dead.

If throstles moult in early June,
The wife'll drop 'un mighty soon.

—Molly Fitton

When Gaffer be dead for a month or more,
Be time to stuff'en under floorboards.

—Martin Fagg

If you hear rustling in the straw,
And oohs and aahs
And 'nay' and 'more!'
The chances are, nine months from now,
Something will happen to your favourite cow.

If the sky be pink at night
And stars and moon be all in sight,
And you eat pickles with your tea,
Tomorrow will be quite windy.

—David Phillips

A bishop's hand on a widow's breast
Will bring a dry wind from the East;
And when his fingers stroke her groin
Expect an autumn damp but fine.

Should the geese stand arse to beak
There's pain and pox within the year;
But when the geese stand beak to arse
Quite pleasant things may come to pass.

—Russell Lucas

When man walketh moon
Peacock singeth in tune.

A gambler beat thrice
Becometh wise.

A wife warm and bonny
Cares little for money.

—T. Griffiths

Prick a maiden nether holly,
Never a firstling cry will follow.

Plough a furrow under the privet,
The seed will shrivel where you drill it.

Delve a fork spit under yew,
Quick shall never be the issue.

—W.J. Webster

Brown paper worn next to the skin
Keeps you in excellent trim.

A thorough mulch
Will ensure a good lunch.

—B.L. Howarth

When stags do rut in the Plym
'Twill be a sunny spring.

—Alan Gibson

If the maiden coughs immediately after
coitus she shall never become pregnant.

—J.H. Thomas

To 'ave a garden in fettle
An' neat as a nettle,
Two things ye mun keep out—
A wuman an' a scrattin' hen.

—Michael Hyde

Better a day in Oxbridge
Than a thousand years in Uxbridge.

—Stanley J. Sharpless

Prithee, let no raindrop fall
   On our countryside at all
While we cope with summer's dates—
   Cricket, tennis, parties, fêtes—
Items on our fixture lists
   Organized by optimists.
Kindly, till the summer's out,
   Give us a stupendous drought.

—A.M. Sayers

The mon that wist for raine
   To the skye sal he seyne:
      'Com raine, thou droghte-quencher.
      Thou gras-feedere, earth-drencher,
      Thou cloud-brekere, mire-makere,
      Puddle-acre, thirst-slakere.
      Com, pond-fillere, bed-wetter.
      Fal, brook-swellere, seed-getter.'
Quhen he havest al this i-saide
   Then be the droghtes mighte allaide.
Then sal his tubbe fill, his cup flowe,
   His kine drink and his whete grow.

—Amedie Eva List

Round about the cauldron go!
  In commuter's brolly throw,
Barometer once tapped by Lord,
  Mummied finger of Bert Foord,
Plastic mac of belted earl,
  Pixie hood of virgin girl,
Windscreen-wiper, weather cock,
Galoshes' zip and welly's sock,
  Sou'wester of a life-boat man,
Rheumatic thumb of gipsy gran,
  Now pour in rain from water-butt!
Peace, peace! Our charm's wound up.

—E.O. Parrott

Here is a beetle as black as my hat,
  And here is a hammer to hammer him flat.
All the clouds will climb the skies
  To see the place where their brother dies.
From east and west they will billow and thunder.
  And bump each other to make the thunder.
Stratus and nimbus will weep together
  And put an end to the summery weather.

—B.S. Goodwill

The Renaissance
(1485-1660)

1485: Henry VII invents Tudor Ford.
1509: Henry VIII invents Fourdor.
1517: Martin Luther nails Ph.D. thesis to wall at Chartres.
1557: Childe Roland publishes *Toddler's Miscellany.*
1558: Annexation of Queen Elizabeth.
1576: First off-Broadway production in England.
1588: Defeat of Spinach Armada by Irish Potato Feminists.
1603: Headline: "Liz Dies; Elizabethan World Blue."
1605: Guy Fawkes declared national holiday.
1620: Billy Pilgrims emigrate to new world.
1641: Puritan sex revolt. Milton clips phylacteries.
1649: Interragtime. Charles massacred by Piedmontese.

ENGLAND'S WAR OF THE ROADSTERS

Henry VII's invention of the Tudor Ford in 1485 is often said to have kicked off the Renaissance in England by bringing to an end the dreadful "War of the Roadsters" which had been raging between New York and Lancaster, Pennsylvania. Yet it is quite possible to date the beginning with Martin Luther's famous nailing of his doctoral dissertation to the wall in the cathedral at Chartres in 1517. Luther, pained by certain criticisms of his thesis ("The Miles Standish Figure in Morris Udall's *Ralph Roister Doister*") leveled by Professors Derrida Erasmus and Childe Harold Bloom, declared that rather than rewrite his thesis he would restructure the world. Thus it is that the seeds of revolt and reformation were planted, seeds that marked the beginning of a storm which later assumed the proportions of a tidal wave spreading like a plague of locusts over the religious face of sixteenth-century Europe.

THE ELIZABETHAN ERROR

Luther's pioneering work in deconstruction was certainly a contributing cause of the Elizabethan Error, that period spanning the annexation of Queen Elizabeth in 1558, the defeat of the Spinach Armada (England's answer to the Irish potato feminists) in 1588, and the cessation of the Queen in 1603. It is perhaps significant that in 1557, the year before the annexation, Childe Roland published the famous *Toddler's Miscellany*, the first anthology of children's poetry— significant because Elizabeth herself was scarcely more than a childe when she took the throne. On the other hand, "The Shepheardes Calendar," a pictorial almanac for illiterates and the literary forefinger of Ben Franklin's *Poor Richard III*, was published in 1579, doubtless a reminder of the passing of time.

What was the Elizabethan Error? Surely, the error was more a general failing of the people rather than of the age to keep up with the times. For instance, Thomas More, kin of Shakespeare's Othello, wrote his famous *Myopia* in the dead language of Latin. Likewise, the typical Elizabethan education was based not upon the liberal Hearts, as it is today, but rather upon medieval *trivia.* As a final example of the general failings which comprised the Elizabethan Error, we have the spectacle of the august Privy Council reduced to such mundane tasks as censoring French farts and keeping the hair off the throne. On the other hand, much of what is called the Elizabethan Error may be seen as merely the great love of the age for the conventional. Like many a big modern city, London was quite proud of its convention facilities and depended to some extent upon conventions for its economic well-being. The Optimists Convention, for instance, was usually held at the Sir Walter Ralegh, the VFW at the Drake, and the Humanists at The Tower. It is a tribute to Elizabethan taste and culinary excellence that only the best food was served, and the reputation of English beef was enhanced at least as much for its Golden Hind as it was for its Papal Bull.

SHAKESPEARE'S CONFESSIONALISM

The greatest poet of the century was, of course, William Shakespeare. The son of William Stratford and Gammar Gurton Avon, Shakespeare began his life as a rogue and ended it that way. An early, so-called "confessional" poem of his youth is Shakespeare's "The Rape of Lucretia Borgia," a shocking expose of the poet's forcible rape of a common London whore. This is followed by a series of verse plays which pursue the same thames: *King John*, *The Merchant of Venus*, *The Comedy of Eros*, *King Leer*, and finally *The Temptress*. Indeed, the unchanging prurience of Shakespeare's plays makes them seem like the work of the true author of the great sex manual, *Novum Orgasm*, usually ascribed to Francis Bacon. As the selection from his work indicates, Shakespeare was at home in at least several of the major genders of English poetry. The snatches from the plays, for instance, are as lovely as anything in English, while his lyrics to those horseplay-loving Grooms of the Chamber are justly famous. Shakespeare's sonnets, meanwhile, are the finest produced during the age and should be distinguished from those of his chief rival, Petrarch, by their superior structure. While Petrarch's Italian sonnets, or Whoppers, divide naturally into an eight-line proposition followed by a six-line sexpot, Shakespeare's proposition takes longer (twelve lines) and the sexpot is replaced by a capulet. Unlike his bawdy plays, Shakespeare's sonnets are extremely correct and polite eschewing any mention of the nymphs and lesbias so often addressed in poems by contemporaries such as Ralegh, Camptown, and others of the so-called "Passionate Shepherds." The depiction of male-female love here reminds the reader of nothing so much as Sidney's sonnet-cycle, *Stanley and Stella,* or Daniel's *Deliacatessen.* Indeed, of the courtly literary genders, few were those at which Shakespeare's genius did not excel. Yet even without Shakespeare, the sixteenth century had geniuses enough to make up for its famous error: Spender, for instance, whose *Dairie Queene* foreshadows the Cheese Poetry of the twentieth century and was the century's greatest pasteurized romance; Sidney, whose *Penny Arcadia* was its greatest diversionary amusement; Marlowe, whose *Nero and Ann Landers* was its greatest neurotic idol— and the list could go on and on. Surely, if the age needed Sidney's *Apology* for is poetry, it needed none for its literature.

MALT MORE THAN MILTON

While Shakespeare dominated the early Renaissance in England, Milton dominated the later. Born solitary, poor, nasty, brutish, and short, by the time of his death Milton was old, mad, blind, and despised to boot. According to T.S. Eliot in his essay, "Malt More Than Milton," it was Milton's blindness which was responsible for the peculiarly oral quality of his imagination, replete as his imagination was with such rhetorical trappings as Miltonic endjabments of the feminine end [see Prosodomy], rolling periodicals, elevated dictation, excremental repetitions, and epic smellies. Perhaps the most famous extended smellie in the language is the following from the second book of *This Side Of Paradise*:

> With impetuous recoil and jarring sound,
> The infernal doors, and on their haunches grate
> Harsh thunder, that the lowest bottom shook
> Of Erebus.

One pictures the ill penseroso swelling the organ at his Grub Street condominium or at work composing his great epoch, while his amanuanus, one of the pamphlet whores, tended his needs. It is to these "blind mouths" (Milton may have kept two pamphlet whores to tend his "grim two-handed engine") that Milton dedicated his *Look Homeward, Angel.* His *Go Down, Samson,* he dedicated to Albert Comus and Andrea del Sartre, the first existential Renaissance men.

ORIGINS: DISCOMBOBULATION OF SENSIBILITY

Milton's quarrel with his great poetic rival, Juan Donne, is perhaps publicized too much for the wrong reasons, and the student of the period would do well to ignore the sensation in favor of the poems. Yet it is impossible to ignore such a battlecry as Donne's "Third Sapphire," where the elder Donne enjoins the younger Milton to quit his books and sow some Joyce Carol Oats:

> Fool and wretch, wilt thou let thy soul be tied
> To Man's laws, by which she shall not be tried.
> At the last day?

Milton, of course, was outraged and blamed Donne for the subsequent "discombobulation of sensibility" which fractured his psyche and later caused him to imagine that his wife, Mary Powell, was having an affair with the Cleveland Cavalier poet, Ben Jonson, and that his three daughters were really "the sons of Ben."

Critics are fond of pointing out that there are two Donnes. Dizzy Donne, the rake, is one of them. The other is Dean Donne, the grave and dignified old man who served as Divining Rod at St. Paul's Community College in London. There are also two poetries: the saucy, sometimes bawdy physical lyrics of the debauched boy, and the highly serious and depth-ridden metaphysiological lyrics of the old man. The differences have earned the complete man, Dizzy Dean Donne, the appalachian "the greatest schizophrenic in the language," a title bestowed on him by Christopher Smart. Yet both Donnes are highly conceited, rude, and cynical, and both make startling use of such techniques as bazarre images, prosthesis and doctoral thesis, perversions of word order, and desperate images yoked by violins together, characteristics shared by Donne's fellow poets, Robert "Red" Herring, George "Orange" Sherbet, Rod Carew, and Andrew Carvel. While the latter (albeit lesser) poets escaped whipping for their minor irregularity, Donne was well-hung for not keeping of meter. However, it is somehow pathetic that this great man who, during his life, had earned the titles of Parliamentarian, Preacher, and above all, Poet, should by the time of his death have dwindled to a Dean.

SIR THOMAS WYATT THE ELDER
(1503-1542)

An Utter Passion Uttered Utterly

Meseem'd that Love, with swifter feet than fire,
Brought me my Lady crown'd with amorous burs,
And drapen in tear-collar'd minivers,
Sloped saltire wise in token of desire;
My heart she soak'd in tears, and on a pyre
Laid, for Love's sake, in folds of fragrant perse,
The while her face more fair than sunflowers,
She gave mine eyes for pasture most entire.
Sicklike she seem'd, as with wan-carven smiles
Some deal she moved anear, and thereunto
Thrice paler wox, and weaker than blown sand
Upon the passioning ocean's beachèd miles;
And as her motion's music nearer drew
My starved lips play'd the vampyre with her hand.

—John Todhunter

EDMUND SPENSER
(ca. 1552-1599)

Ride a Cock Horse

So on he pricked, and loe, he gan espy,
  A market and a crosse of glist'ning stone,
And eke a merrie rablement thereby,
  That with the musik of the strong trombone,
  And shaumes, and trompets made most dyvillish mone.
And in their midst he saw a lady sweet,
  That rode upon a milk white steed alone,
In scarlet robe ycladd and wimple meet,
Bedight with rings of gold, and bells about her feet.

Whereat the knight empassioned was so deepe,
  His heart was perst with very agony.
Certes (said he) I will not eat, ne sleepe,
  Till I have seen the royall maid more ny;
  Then will I holde her in fast fealtie,
Whom then a carle adviséd, louting low,
  That little neede there was for him to die,
Sithens in yon pavilion was the show,
Where she did ride, and he for two-and-six mote go.

—Barry Pain

A Portrait

He is to weet a melancholy carle:
Thin in the waist, with bushy head of hair,
As hath the seeded thistle, when a parle
It holds with Zephyr, ere it sendeth fair
Its light balloons into the summer air;

Thereto his beard had not begun to bloom.
No brush had touched his cheek, or razor sheer,
No care had touched his cheek with mortal doom,
But new he was and bright, as scarf from Persian loom.

Ne carèd he for wine, or half and half;
Ne carèd he for fish, or flesh, or fowl;
And sauces held he worthless as the chaff;
He 'sdeigned the swine-head at the wassail-bowl:
Ne with lewd ribbalds sat he cheek by jowl;
Ne with sly lemans in the scorner's chair;
But after water-brooks this pilgrim's soul
Panted and all his food was woodland air;
Though he would oft-times feast on gilliflowers rare.

The slang of cities in no wise he knew,
Tipping the wink to him was heathen Greek;
He sipped no "olden Tom," or "ruin blue,"
Or Nantz, or cherry-brandy, drunk full meek
By many a damsel brave and rouge of cheek;
Nor did he know each aged watchman's beat,
Nor in obscuréd purlieus would he seek
For curléd Jewesses, with ankles neat,
Who, as they walk abroad, make tinkling with their feet.

—*John Keats*

The Irish Schoolmaster

I

Alack! 'tis melancholy theme to think
How Learning doth in rugged states abide,
And, like her bashful owl, obscurely blink,
In pensive glooms and corners, scarcely spied;
Not, as in Founders' Halls and domes of pride,
Served with grave homage, like a tragic queen,
But with one lonely priest compell'd to hide,
In midst of foggy moors and mosses green,
In that clay cabin hight the College of Kilreen!

II

This College looketh South and West alsoe,
Because it hath a cast in windows twain;
Crazy and crack'd they be, and wind doth blow
Thorough transparent holes in every pane,
Which Dan, with many paines, makes whole again
With nether garments, which his thrift doth teach
To stand for glass, like pronouns, and when rain
Stormeth, he puts, 'once more unto the breach,'
Outside and in, tho' broke, yet so he mendeth each.

III

And in the midst a little door there is,
Whereon a board that doth congratulate
With painted letters, red as blood I wis,
Thus written,
'CHILDREN TAKEN IN TO BATE.'
And oft, indeed, the inward of that gate,
Most ventriloque, doth utter tender squeak,
And moans of infants that bemoan their fate,
In midst of sounds of Latin, French, and Greek,
Which, all i' the Irish tongue, he teacheth them to speak.

IV

For some are meant to right illegal wrongs,
And some for Doctors of Divinitie,
Whom he doth teach to murder the dead tongues,
And so win academical degree;
But some are bred for service of the sea,
Howbeit, their store of learning is but small.
For mickle waste he counteth it would be
To stock a head with bookish wares at all,
Only to be knocked off by ruthless cannon ball.

V

Six babes he sways,—some little and some big,
Divided into classes six;—alsoe,
He keeps a parlour boarder of a pig,
That in the College fareth to and fro,
And picketh up the urchins' crumbs below,—
And eke the learned rudiments they scan,
And thus his A, B, C, doth wisely know,—
Hereafter to be shown in caravan,
And raise the wonderment of many a learned man.

VI

Alsoe, he schools some tame familiar fowls,
Whereof, above his head, some two or three
Sit darkly squatting, like Minerva's owls,
But on the branches of no living tree,
And overlook the learned family;
While, sometimes, Partlet, from her gloomy perch,
Drops feather on the nose of Dominie,
Meanwhile, with serious eye, he makes research
In leaves of that sour tree of knowledge—now a birch.

VII

No chair he hath, the awful Pedagogue,
Such as would magisterial hams imbed,
But sitteth lowly on a beechen log,
Secure in high authority and dread:
Large, as a dome for learning, seems his head,
And like Apollo's, all beset with rays,
Because his lock are so unkempt and red,
And stand abroad in many several ways:—
No laurel crown he wears, howbeit his cap is baize.

VIII

And, underneath, a pair of shaggy brows
O'erhang as many eyes of gizzard hue,
That inward giblet of a fowl, which shows
A mongrel tint, that is ne brown ne blue;
His nose,—it is a coral to the view;
Well nourished with Pierian Potheen,—
For much he loves his native mountain dew;—
But to depict the dye would lack, I ween,
A bottle-red, in terms, as well as bottle-green.

IX

As for his coat, 'tis such a jerkin short
As Spencer had, ere he composed his Tales;
But underneath he hath no vest, nor aught,
So that the wind his airy breast assails;
Below, he wears the nether garb of males,
Of crimson plush, but non-plushed at the knee;—
Thence further down the native red prevails,
Of his own naked fleecy hosiery:—
Two sandals, without soles, complete his cap-a-pee.

X

Nathless, for dignity, he now doth lap
His function in a magisterial gown,
That shows more countries in it than a map,—
Blue tinct, and red, and green, and russet brown,
Besides some blots, standing for country-town;
And eke some rents, for streams and rivers wide;
But, sometimes, bashful when he looks adown,
He turns the garment of the other side,
Hopeful that so the holes may never be espied!

XI

And soe he sits, amidst the little pack,
That look for shady or for sunny noon,
Within his visage, like an almanack,—
His quiet smile foretelling gracious boon:
But when his mouth droops down, like rainy moon,
With horrid chill each little heart unwarms,
Knowing that infant show'rs will follow soon,
And with forebodings of near wrath and storms
They sit, like timid hares, all trembling on their forms.

XII

Ah! luckless wight, who cannot then repeat
'Corduroy Colloquy,'—or 'Ki, Kae, Kod,'—
Full soon his tears shall make his turfy seat
More sodden, tho' already made of sod,
For Dan shall whip him with the word of God,—
Severe by rule, and not by nature mild,
He never spoils the child and spares the rod,
But spoils the rod and never spares the child,
And soe with holy rule deems he is reconcil'd.

XIII

But, surely, the just sky will never wink
At men who take delight in childish throe,
And stripe the nether-urchin like a pink
Or tender hyacinth, inscribed with woe;
Such bloody Pedagogues, when they shall know,
By useless birches, that forlorn recess,
Which is no holiday, in Pit below,
Will hell not seem designed for their distress,—
A melancholy place, that is all bottomlesse?

XIV

Yet would the Muse not chide the wholesome use
Of needful discipline, in due degree.
Devoid of sway, what wrongs will time produce,
Whene'er the twig untrained grows up a tree.
This shall a Carder, that a Whiteboy be,
Ferocious leaders of atrocious bands,
And Learning's help be used for infamie,
By lawless clerks, that, with their bloody hands,
In murder'd English write Rock's murderous commands.

XV

But ah! what shrilly cry doth now alarm
The sooty fowls that dozed upon the beam,
All sudden fluttering from the brandish'd arm,
And cackling chorus with the human scream;
Meanwhile, the scourge plies that unkindly seam,
In Phelim's brogues, which bares his naked skin,
Like traitor gap in warlike fort, I deem,
That falsely lets the fierce besieger in,
Nor seeks the pedagogue by other course to win.

XVI

No parent dear he hath to heed his cries;—
Alas! his parent dear is far aloof,
And deep in Seven-Dial cellar lies,
Killed by kind cudgel-play, or gin of proof;
Or climbeth, catwise, on some London roof,
Singing, perchance, a lay of Erin's Isle,
Or, whilst he labours, weaves a fancy-woof,
Dreaming he sees his home,—his Phelim smile;
Ah me! that luckless imp, who weepeth all the while!

XVII

Ah! who can paint that hard and heavy time,
When first the scholar lists in learning's train,
And mounts her rugged steep, enforc'd to climb,
Like sooty imp, by sharp posterior pain,
From bloody twig, and eke that Indian cane,
Wherein, alas! no sugar'd juices dwell,
For this the while one stripling's sluices drain
Another weepeth over chilblains fell,
Always upon the heel, yet never to be well!

XVIII

Anon a third, for his delicious root,
Late ravish'd from his tooth by elder chit,
So soon is human violence afoot,
So hardly is the harmless biter bit!
Meanwhile, the tyrant, with untimely wit
And mouthing face, derides the small one's moan,
Who, all lamenting for his loss, doth sit,
Alack,—mischance comes seldomtimes alone,
But aye the worried dog must rue more curs than one.

XIX

For lo! the Pedagogue, with sudden drub,
Smites his scald head, that is already sore,—
Superfluous wound,—such is Misfortune's rub!
Who straight makes answer with redoubled roar,
And sheds salt tears twice faster than before,
That still, with backward fist he strives to dry;
Washing, with brackish moisture, o'er and o'er,
His muddy cheek, that grows more foul thereby,
Till all his rainy face looks grim as rainy sky.

XX

So Dan, by dint of noise, obtains a peace,
And with his natural untender knack,
By new distress, bids former grievance cease,
Like tears dried up with rugged huckaback.
That sets the mournful visage all awrack;
Yet soon the childish countenance will shine
Even as thorough storms the soonest slack,
For grief and beef in adverse ways incline,
This keeps, and that decays, when duly soak'd in brine.

XXI

Now all is hushed, and, with a look profound,
The Dominie lays ope the learned page
(So be it called); although he doth expound
Without a book, both Greek and Latin sage;
Now telleth he of Rome's rude infant age,
How Romulus was bred in Savage wood,
By wet-nurse wolf, devoid of wolfish rage;
And laid foundation-stone of walls of mud,
But watered it, alas! with warm fraternal blood.

XXII

Anon, he turns to that Homeric war,
How Troy was sieged like Londonderry town;
And stout Achilles, at his jaunting-car,
Dragged mighty Hector with a bloody crown:
And eke the bard, that sung of their renown,
In garb of Greece most beggar-like and torn,
He paints, with collie, wand'ring up and down:
Because, at once, in seven cities born;
And so, of parish rights, was, all his days, forlorn.

XXIII

Anon, through old Mythology he goes,
Of gods defunct, and all their pedigrees,
But shuns their scandalous amours, and shows
How Plato wise, and clear-ey'd Socrates,
Confess'd not to those heathen hes and shes;
But thro' the clouds of the Olympic cope
Beheld St. Peter, with his holy keys,
And own'd their love was naught, and bow'd to Pope,
Whilst all their purblind race in Pagan mist did grope.

XXIV

From such quaint themes he turns, at last, aside,
To new philosophies, that still are green,
And shows what rail-roads have been track'd to guide
The wheels of great political machine;
If English corn should grow abroad, I ween,
And gold be made of gold, or paper sheet;
How many pigs be born to each spalpeen;
And, ah! how man shall thrive beyond his meat,—
With twenty souls alive, to one square sod of peat!

XXV

Here, he makes end; and all the fry of youth,
That stood around with serious look intense,
Close up again their gaping eyes and mouth,
Which they had opened to his eloquence,
As if their hearing were a threefold sense;
But now the current of his words is done,
And whether any fruits shall spring from thence,
In future time, with any mother's son,
It is a thing, God wot! that can be told by none.

XXVI

Now by the creeping shadows of the noon,
The hour is come to lay aside their lore;
The cheerful pedagogue perceives it soon,
And cries, 'Begone!' unto the imps,—and four
Snatch their two hats, and struggle for the door,
Like ardent spirits vented from a cask,
All blythe and boisterous,—but leave two more,
With Reading made Uneasy for a task,
To weep, whilst all their mates in merry sunshine bask,

XXVII

Like sportive Elfins, on the verdant sod,
With tender moss so sleekly overgrown,
That doth not hurt, but kiss, the sole unshod,
So soothly kind is Erin to her own!
And one, at Hare and Hound, plays all alone,—
For Phelim's gone to tend his step-dame's cow;
Ah! Phelim's step-dame is a canker'd crone!
Whilst other twain play at an Irish row,
And, with shillelagh small, break one another's brow!

XXVIII
But careful Dominie, with ceaseless thrift,
Now changeth ferula for rural hoe;
But, first of all, with tender hand doth shift
His college gown, because of solar glow,
And hangs it on a bush, to scare the crow:
Meanwhile, he plants in earth the dappled bean,
Or trains the young potatoes all a-row,
Or plucks the fragrant leek for pottage green,
With that crisp curly herb, call'd Kale in Aberdeen.

XXIX
And so he wisely spends the fruitful hours,
Linked each to each by labour, like a bee;
Or rules in Learning's hall, or trims her bow'rs;—
Would there were many more such wights as he,
To sway each capital academie
Of Cam and Isis, for, alack! at each
There dwell, I wot, some dronish Dominie,
That does no garden work, nor yet doth teach,
But wears a floury head, and talks in flow'ry speech!

—*Thomas Hood*

SIR PHILIP SIDNEY
(1554-1586)

From STANLEY AND STELLA

She Dwelt Among the Untrodden Ways

Ask me not for the semblance of my loue.
Amidst the fountains of the christal Doue
Like to that fayre Aurora did she runne,
Who treads the beams of the sweete morning sunne.
Forth from her head her hayres like golden wyre
Did spring; her amorous eyes were lamps of fire,
Bright as that torch their heauenly raies did mount
Wherewith fayre Hero lit the Hellespont,
Or as that flame which on the desert lies
When new-borne Phenix soareth to the skies.
Like wanton darts her eye-beames she did throw
From out her noble forehead's iuorie bow
Whose Beuties great perfection would withstand
The skill of the most cunning painter's hand.
Her virgin nose like Dians self did raigne
Amidst her vermell cheekes' ambrosiall plaine;
Her busie lips twinne Rubies did appeare
From which her Voyce did come as Diamonds cleare;
Venus' owne sonne would sigh to look beneath
At the straight pearlie pleasaunce of her teethe.
Like to fayre starres, or rather, like the sunne
Was her smooth Marble chinne's pavilion,
Wherefrom her slender necke the eye did lead
To shoulders like twinne Lilies on a mead,
Whiter than Ledaes fethers or white milke,
As sweete as nectar and as softe as silke.

O, and her tender brests, they were as white
As snowie hills which Phebus' beames do smite
Engirt with azure and with Saphire veines.

(*Cetera desunt*)

—*J.C. Squire*

MICHAEL DRAYTON
(1563-1631)

Going or Gone

Fine merry franions,
Wanton companions,
My days are ever banyans
  With thinking upon ye!
How Death, that last stinger,
Finis—uriter, end-bringer,
Has laid his chill finger,
  Or is laying on ye.

There's rich Kitty Wheatley,
With footing it featly
That took me completely,
  She sleeps in the Kirk House;
And poor Polly Perkin,
Whose Dad was still firking,
The jolly ale firkin
  She's gone to the Workhouse.

Fine gardener, Ben Carter,
(In ten counties no smarter)
Has ta'en his departure
  For Proserpine's orchard;
And Lily, postilion,
With cheeks of vermilion,
Is one of a million
  That fill up the churchyard;

And, lusty as Dido,
Fat Clemintons's widow
Flits now a small shadow
  By Stygian hid ford;
And good Master Clapton
Has thirty years napt on,
The ground he last hapt on,
  Intombed by fair Widford;

And gallant Tom Dockwra,
Of Nature's finest crockery,
Now but thin air and mockery,
  Lurks by Avernus,
Whose honest grasp of hand
Still, while his life did stand,
At friend's or foe's command,
  Almost did burn us.

Roger de Coverley
Not more good man than he;
Yet has he equally
  Pushed for Cocytus,
With drivelling Worral,
And wicked old Dorral,
'Gainst whom I've a quarrel,
  Whose end might affright me!

Kindly hearts have I known;
Kindly hearts, they are flown;
Here and there if but one
  Linger yet uneffaced,
Imbecile tottering elves,
Soon to be wrecked on shelves,
These scarce are half themselves,
  With age and care crazed.

But this day Amy Hutton
Her last dress has put on;
Her fine lessons forgotten,
  She died, as the dunce died;
And prim Betsy Chambers,
Decayed in her members,
No longer remembers
  Things, as she once did:

And prudent Mrs. Wither,
Not in jest now doth *wither*,
And soon must go—whither
  Nor I well, nor you know;
And flaunting Miss Waller,
That soon must befall her,
Whence none can recall her,
  Though proud once as Juno!

—*Charles Lamb*

SIR WALTER RALEGH
(ca. 1552-1618)

Bacchanal

'Come live with me and be my love,
  He said, in substance. 'There's no vine
We will not pluck the clusters of,
  Or grape we will not turn to wine.'

It's autumn of their second year.
  Now he, in seasonal pursuit,
With rich and modulated cheer,
  Brings home the festive purple fruit;

And she, by passion once demented
  —That woman out of Botticelli—
She brews and bottles, unfermented,
  The stupid and abiding jelly.

—*Peter Devries*

CHRISTOPHER MARLOWE
(1564-1593)

Invocation

Come, lovely Muse, desert for me
Your leafy hill, your crystal spring,
Your Heliconian company
Who taught the earlier Greek to sing.

Your laurel and your lute forsake,
Your parsley-field and pleasant wood,
Your votive rose, suburban brake
And all its antic brotherhood.

Abandon to their goats and sheep
The herdsmen in their whispering home,
Where Pindar woke from sunny sleep
To smack Boeotian honeycomb.

Your myrtle and your April loves,
Your amber days, whose temperate sun,
Wind-winnowed in the ordered groves,
Is to your body subtly spun;

Your lunar mead, your starry glade,
Your fragrant and nectarean night,
Your bird liquescent in the shade
That melts melodiously to light;

Your sail beyond the morning sands,
Where Sappho, wandering from the sea,
To Phaon stretches fluid hands,
Come, leave, oh, Muse, and live with me!

Come, live with me and we shall make
Delicious and immortal moan,
And the fantastic bootleg shake
Unto the ductile saxophone.

Come, live with me and be my love
In statutory Christian sin,
And we shall all the pleasures prove
Of two-room flats and moral gin.

And you shall be a modern maid,
And golf upon the Attic greens,
Bisexually unafraid,
And talk about your endocrines.

And we shall to the heavens advance,
And broadcast to the quaking dawn
The age that walks in Puritan pants
With just one crucial button gone.

And we shall sing of export trade,
And celebrate the fiscal year,
And revel in the basement shade
Until the lusty riveteer,

Winds high and clear his rural horn
And the official day begins,
And we shall usher in the morn
With bowls of shredded vitamins.

Oh, come, sweet Muse, and share with me
My kitchenette and telephone,
And all my complexes shall be
Your true and circumambient own.

And we shall pluck the dulcet strain
From ukulele and guitar,
And look on Ford and Hoover plain,
And meet the cousins of the Czar:

The countless cousins of the Czar,
Grand Duke or Duchess, every one,
As multitudinous as are
The spheres (who borrow from the sun).

And we shall tune the choriamb,
And with the taxi-horn compete,
To bull and bear and little lamb
Who play together in the Street.

And airships overhead shall roar
The hymnal of our happy state,
Based on the single standard, or
If you prefer, companionate.

And Progress shall with every flower
Of sweet Expense her ardor prove,
If you will leave your dated bower,
Delightful Muse, and be my love.

—*Samuel Hoffenstein*

WILLIAM SHAKESPEARE
(1564-1616)

Speeches and Songs from the Plays

Macbeth

(*Enter* Macbeth *in a red night cap. Page following with a torch.*)

Go boy, and thy good mistress tell
(She knows that my purpose is cruel),
I'd thank her to tingle her bell
As soon as she's heated my gruel.
Go, get thee to bed and repose—
To sit up so late is a scandal;
But ere you have ta'en off your clothes,
Be sure that you put out that candle.
Ri fol de rol tol de rol lol.

My stars, in the air here's a knife!—
   I'm sure it can not be a hum;
I'll catch at the handle, add's life!
   And then I shall not cut my thumb.
I've got him!—no, at him again!
   Come, come, I'm not fond of these jokes;
This must be some blade of the brain—
   Those witches are given to hoax.

I've one in my pocket, I know,
   My wife left on purpose behind her;
She bought this of Teddy-high-ho,
   The poor Caledonian grinder.
I see thee again! o'er thy middle
   Large drops of red blood now are spill'd,
Just as much as to say, diddle diddle,
   Good Duncan, pray come and be kill'd.

It leads to his chamber, I swear;
   I tremble and quake every joint—
No dog at the scent of a hare
   Ever yet made a cleverer point.
Ah, no! 'twas a dagger of straw—
   Give me blinkers, to save me from starting;
The knife that I thought that I saw
   Was nought but my eye, Betty Martin.

Now o'er this terrestrial hive
   A life paralytic is spread;
For while the one half is alive,
   The other is sleepy and dead.
King Duncan, in grand majesty,
   Has got my state-bed for a snooze;
I've lent him my slippers, so I
   May certainly stand in his shoes.

Blow softly, ye murmuring gales!
   Ye feet, rouse no echo in walking!
For though a dead man tells no tales,
   Dead walls are much given to talking.
This knife shall be in at the death—
   I'll stick him, then off safely get!
Cries the world, this could not be Macbeth,
   For he'd ne'er stick at anything yet.

Hark, Hark! 'tis the signal, by goles!
   It sounds like a funeral knell;
O, hear it not, Duncan! it tolls
   To call thee to heaven or hell.
Or if you to heaven won't fly,
   But rather prefer Pluto's ether,
Only wait a few years till I die,
   And we'll go to the devil together.
                    Ri fol de rol, etc.

—*Horace and James Smith*

Song, *Hamlet*

TUNE, "HERE WE GO UP, UP, UP."

When a man becomes tired of his life,
  The question is, "to be, or not to be?"
For before he dare finish the strife,
  His reflections most serious ought to be.
When his troubles too numerous grow,
  And he knows of no method to mend them,
Had he best bear them tamely, or no?—
  Or by stoutly opposing them end them?
Ri-tol-de rol, etc.

To die is to sleep—nothing more—
  And by sleeping to say we end sorrow,
And pain, and ten thousand things more—
  O, I wish it were *my* turn to-morrow!
But, perchance, in that sleep we may dream,
  For we dream in our beds very often—
Now, however capricious 't may seem,
  I've no notion of dreams in a coffin.
Ri-tol-de-rol, etc.

'Tis the doubt of our ending all snugly,
  That makes us with life thus dispute,
For who'd bear with a wife old and ugly,
  Or the length of a chancery suit?
Or who would bear fardels, and take
  Kicks, cuffs, frowns, and many and odd thing,
When he might his own quietus make,
  And end all his cares with a bodkin?
Ri-tol-de-rol, etc.

Truly, death is a fine thing to talk of,
  But I'll leave to men of more learning:
For my own part, I've no wish to walk off,
  For I find there's no chance of returning.—
After all 'tis the pleasantest way,
  To bear up as we can 'gainst our sorrow,
And if things go not easy to-day,
  Let us hope they'll go better to-morrow.—
Ri-tol-de-rol, etc.

—*John Poole*

Hamlet

Prince Hamlet thought Uncle a traitor
For having it off with his Mater;
  Revenge Dad or not?
  That's the gist of the plot,
And he did—nine soliloquies later.

—*Stanley J. Sharpless*

Song to Imogen

Listen, listen! The small song bird at the doorway of
God's living place makes a whistling sound on a
high note,
And Phoebus makes a start at getting up,
To give water to his horses at those waters coming up
from the earth
That have the body stretched out parallel with the
earth.
And Mary-buds getting their eyes open and shut
quickly make a start at getting their gold eyes
open.
With every thing that is good looking in a soft way
My sweet respected woman, get up!

—*Richard Leighton Greene*

A Cold Rendering

A Fool, a fool!—I bet a fool i' the forest,
A botley fool;—a biserable world!
As I do live by—attishu—food, I bet a fool;
Who laid hib dowd ad bask'd hib id the sud,
Ad rail'd od Lady Fortude id good terbs,
Id good set terbs—attishu—ad yet a botley fool.
"Good borrow, fool," quoth I, "Dough, sir," quoth he.
"Call be dot fool till heaved has sed be fortude."
Ad—attishu—thed he drew a dial frob his poke,
Ad lookid od it with lack lustre eye,
Says very wisely, "It's ted o'clock;
Thus we bay see" quoth he, "how the world wags,
Tis but ad hour ago sidce it was dide;
Ad after ad—attishu—hour bore, 'twill be eleved;
Ad so frob hour to hour, we ripe ad ripe,
Ad thed frob hour to hour we rot ad rot,
Ad therby hangs a tale." When I did hear,
The botley fool thus boral od the tibe,
My lugs begad to crow like chadticleer,
That fools should be so deep-codtebplative;
Ad I did laugh, sads idterbissiod,
Ad—attishu—hour by his dial. O doble fool!
A worthy fool! Botley's the odly wear—attishu!

—*Anonymous*

From THE LOST HISTORY PLAYS

King Ethelred the Unready

Ethelred
This cankered earth, this murrain'd patch of land
Infected by the malady of machinations, plots
Hatched in the hangman's shadow—

(*Enter a messenger.*)

Well?

Messenger
My Lord, the queen requests—

Ethelred
I am not ready, goose.
Leave presently.

(*Exit messenger*)

What was my theme? Ah yes,
The agu'd frame of state and soul alike,
Their fragile course through time that
rusts apace
Like blades sheathed fast in scabbards
long unused,
Or targets hung as pictures—

(*Alarums. Enter a soldier.*)

Now what?

Soldier
Sir, your army is suborn'd, and
craves your presence.

Ethelred
Out, knave! I'm not yet ready.

(*Exit soldier*)

Life's no more
Than a wastrel player crouching by his glass
That mocks his silly passion for himself,
Strangling his sight—

(*Enter the Witan, severally*)

What is it now? You curs
That cannot let a prince deliver words
Or finish a soliloquy in peace.
I'm just not ready. Hence!

(*Exit the Witan*)

This monstrous world
Mired in the reeking dung of wolves, bewrayed
By gods who wreak injurious fate, as if
Our penitence was gall—

(*Enter seventy-two murderers*)

Not ready yet,
I've told you, dogs: now list these
jewelled lines
And glean their poetry. I' the old adage lies
The motto thus: Ripeness is all. But that's
Not it. Why should I play the Saxon fool,
And fall upon mine sword, when I'm
not ready?

—*Bill Greenwell*

King Canute

The coast near Southampton. Enter, from royal barge, Canute, courtiers and Fool.

Fool
Tis clear, Great Dane, thy barque's worse than thy bite.

Canute
Once more unto the beach, dear friends, once more—

Fool
A line, methinks, too good to throw away,
'Twill soon be echoed in another play.

Canute
For now I needs must show these slavering curs
That e'en Canute cannot roll back the sea.

Fool
Canute cannot? Cannot Canute? For shame!

Canute
Cease, fool. We at the mighty ocean's marge,
Exchanging throne for deck-chair for the nonce,
Shall thus disport, paddling our royal feet.

Fool
Nay, if it please thee, paddle thine own, Canute,
And get thy breeches wet into the bargain,
But why not summon statecraft to thine aid
And make a secret compact with the moon?
Sit tight until the tide is on the turn,
Then it would seem as though thy royal command,
'Back, waters, back,' had wrought a miracle.

Canute
Verily, my boy, thou'rt on the ball.

Fool
On land or sea, good sire, timing is all.

Canute
Henceforth I'll hear no ill spoken of fools.

Fool
Thou rul'st the waves; my task's to waive the rules.

—*Stanley J. Sharpless*

Savonarola

A TRAGEDY

ACT I

Scene, *A Room in the Monastery of San Marco. Florence.*
Time, 1490, A.D. *A summer morning.*

Enter the Sacristan *and a* Friar.

Sacr.
Savonarola looks more grim to-day
Than ever. Should I speak my mind, I'd say
That he was fashioning some new great scourge
To flay the backs of men.

Fri.
'Tis even so.
Brother Filippo saw him stand last night
In solitary vigil till the dawn
Lept o'er the Arno, and his face was such
As men may wear in Purgatory—nay,
E'en in the inmost core of Hell's own fires.

Sacr.
I often wonder if some woman's face,
Seen at some rout in his old worldling days,
Haunts him e'en now, e'en here, and urges him
To fierier fury 'gainst the Florentines.

Fri.
Savonarola love-sick! Ha, ha, ha!
Love-sick? He, Love-sick? 'Tis a goodly jest!
The *con*firm'd misogyn a ladies' man!
Thou must have eaten of some strange red herb
That takes the reason captive. I will swear
Savonarola never yet hath seen
A woman but he spurn'd her. Hist! He comes.

(Enter Savonarola, *rapt in thought.)*

Give thee good morrow, Brother.

Sacr.
And therewith
A multitude of morrows equal-good
Till thou, by Heaven's grace, hast wrought the work
Nearest thine heart.

Sav.
I thank thee, Brother, yet
I thank thee not, for that my thankfulness
(An such there be) gives thanks to Heaven alone.

Fri. (*To* Sachr.)
'Tis a right answer he hath given thee.
Had Sav'narola spoken less than thus,
Methinks me, the less Sav'narola he.
As when the snow lies on yon Apennines,
White as the hem of Mary Mother's robe,
And insusceptible to the sun's rays,

Being harder to the touch than temper'd steel,
E'en so this great gaunt monk white-visagèd
Upstands to Heaven and to Heav'n devotes
The scarpèd thoughts that crown the upper slopes
Of his abrupt and *aus*tere nature.

Sacr.
Aye.

(*Enter* Lucrezia Borgia, St. Francis of Assisi, *and* Leonardo Da Vinci. Luc. *is thickly veiled.*)

St. Fran.
This is the place.

Luc. (*Pointing at* Sav.)
And this the man! (*Aside.*) And I—
By the hot blood that courses i' my veins
I swear it ineluctably—the woman!

Sav.
Who is this wanton?
(Luc. *throws back her hood, revealing her face.*
Sav. *starts back, gazing at her.*)

St. Fran.
Hush, Sir! 'Tis my little sister
The poisoner, right well-belov'd by all
Whom she as yet hath spared. Hither she came
Mounted upon another little sister of mine—
A mare, caparison'd in goodly wise.
She—I refer now to Lucrezia—
Desireth to have word of thee anent
Some matter that befrets her.

Sav. (*To* Luc.)
Hence! Begone!
Savonarola will not tempted be
By face of woman e'en tho' 't be, tho' 'tis,
Surpassing fair. All hope abandon therefore.
I charge thee: Vade retro, Satanas.

Leonardo
Sirrah, thou speakst in haste, as is the way
Of monkish men. The beauty of Lucrezia
Commends, not discommends, her to the eyes
Of keener thinkers than I take thee for.
I am an artist and an engineer,
Giv'n o'er to subtile dreams of what shall be
On this our planet. I foresee a day
When men shall skim the earth i' certain chairs
Not drawn by horses but sped on by oil
Or other matter, and shall thread the sky
Birdlike.

Luc.
It may be as thou sayest, friend,
Or may be not. (*To* Sav.) As touching this our errand,
I crave of thee, Sir Monk, an audience
Instanter.

Fri.
Lo! Here Alighieri comes.
I had methought me he was still at Parma.

(*Enter* Dante.)

St. Fran. (*To* Dan.)
How fares my little sister Beatrice?

Dan.
She died, alack, last sennight.

St. Fran.
Did she so?
If the condolences of men avail
Thee aught, take mine.

Dan.
They are of no avail.

Sav. (*To* Luc.)
I do refuse thee audience.

Luc.
Then why
Didst thou not say so promptly when I ask'd it?

Sav.
Full well thou knowst that I was interrupted
By Alighieri's entry.

(*Noise without. Enter Guelfs and Ghibellines fighting.*)
What is this?

Luc.
I did not think that in this cloister'd spot
There would be so much doing. I had look'd
To find Savonarola all alone
And tempt him in his uneventful cell.
Instead o' which—Spurn'd am I? I am I.
There was a time, Sir, look to 't! O damnation!
What is 't? Anon then! These my toys, my gauds,
That in the cradle—aye, 't my mother's breast—
I puled and lisped at,—'Tis impossible,
Tho', faith, 'tis not so, forasmuch as 'tis.
And I a daughter of the Borgias!—
Or so they told me. Liars! Flatterers!

Currying lick-spoons! Where's the Hell of 't then?
'Tis time that I were going. Farewell, Monk,
But I'll avenge me ere the sun has sunk.

(*Exeunt* Luc., St. Fran., *and* Leonardo, *followed by* Dan., Sav., *having watched* Luc. *out of sight, sinks to his knees, sobbing.* Fri. *and* Sacr. *watch him in amazement. Guelfs and Ghibellines continue fighting as the Curtain falls.*)

Act II

Time, *Afternoon of same day.*
Scene, *Lucrezia's Laboratory. Retorts, test-tubes, etc. On small Renaissance table, up c., is a great poison-bowl, the contents of which are being stirred by the* First Apprentice, The Second Apprentice *stands by, watching him.*

Second App.
For whom is the brew destin'd?

First App.
I know not.
Lady Lucrezia did but lay on me
Injunctions as regards the making of 't,
The which I have obey'd. It is compounded
Of a malignant and a deadly weed
Found not save in the Gulf of Spezia,
And one small phial of 't, I am advis'd,
Were more than 'nough to slay a regiment
Of Messer Malatesta's condottieri
In all their armour.

Second App.
I can well believe it.
Mark how the purple bubbles froth upon
The evil surface of its nether slime!

(*Enter* Luc.)

Luc. (*To* First App.)
Is't done, Sir Sluggard?

First App.
Madam, to a turn.

Luc.
Had it not been so, I with mine own hand
Would have outpour'd it down thy gullet, knave.
See, here's a ring of cunningly-wrought gold
That I, on a dark night, did purchase from
A goldsmith on the Ponte Vecchio.
Small was his shop, and hoar of visage he.
I did bemark that from the ceiling's beams
Spiders had spun their webs for many a year,
The which hung erst like swathes of gossamer
Seen in the shadows of a fairy glade,
But now most woefully were weighted o'er
With gather'd dust. Look well now at the ring!
Touch'd here, behold, it opes a cavity
Capacious of three drops of yon fell stuff.
Dost heed? Whoso then puts it on'his finger
Dies, and his soul is from his body rapt
To Hell or Heaven as the case may be.
Take thou this toy and pour the three drops in.

(*Hands ring to* First App. *and comes down c.*)

So, Sav'narola, thou shalt learn that I
Utter no threats but I do make them good.
Ere this day's sun hath wester'd from the view
Thou art to preach from out the Loggia
Dei Lanzi to the cits in the Piazza.

I, thy Lucrezia, will be upon the steps
To offer thee with phrases seeming-fair
That which shall seal thine eloquence for ever.
O mighty lips that held the world in spell
But would not meet these little lips of mine
In the sweet way that lovers use—O thin,
Cold, tight-drawn, bloodless lips, which natheless I
Deem of all lips the most magnifical
In this our city—

(*Enter the Borgias'* Fool.)

Well, Fool, what's thy latest?

Fool
Aristotle's or Zeno's, Lady—'tis neither latest nor
last. For, marry, if the cobbler stuck to his last,
then were his latest his last *in rebus ambulantibus*.
Argal, I stick at nothing but cobble-stones, which,
by the same token, are stuck to the road by men's
fingers.

Luc.
How many crows may nest in a grocer's jerkin?

Fool
A full dozen at cock-crow, and something less under
the dog-star, by reason of the dew, which lies
heavy on men taken by the scurvy.

Luc. (*To* First App.)
Methinks the Fool is a fool.

Fool
And therefore, by auricular deduction, am I own
twin to the Lady Lucrezia!

(*Sings.*)

When pears hang green on the garden wall
  With a nid, and a nod, and a niddy-niddy-o,
Then prank you, lads and lasses all,
  With a yea and a nay and a niddy-o.

But when the thrush flies out o' the frost
  With a nid, (*etc.*)
'Tis time for loons to count the cost,
  With a yea (*etc.*)

(*Enter the* Porter.)

Porter
O my dear Mistress, there is one below
Demanding to have instant word of thee.
I told him that your Ladyship was not
At home. Vain perjury! He would not take
Nay for an answer.

Luc.
Ah? What manner of man
Is he?

Porter
A personage the like of whom
Is wholly unfamiliar to my gaze.
Cowl'd is he, but I saw his great eyes glare
From their deep sockets in such wise as leopards
Glare from their caverns, crouching ere they spring
On their reluctant prey.

Luc.
And what name gave he?

Porter (*After a pause.*)
Something-arola.

Luc.
Savon-? (Porter *nods.*) Show him up.

(*Exit* Porter.)

Fool
If he be right astronomically, Mistress, then is he
the greater dunce in respect of true learning, the
which goes by the globe. Argal, 'twere better he
widened his wind-pipe.

(*Sings.*)

Fly home, sweet self,
Nothing's for weeping,
Hemp was not made
For lovers' keeping,
Lovers' keeping,
Cheerly, cheerly, fly away.

Hew no more wood
While ash is glowing,
The longest grass
Is lovers' mowing,
Lovers' mowing,
Cheerly, (*etc.*)

(*Re-enter* Porter, *followed by* Sav. *Exeunt*
Porter, Fool, *and* First *and* Second Apps.)

Sav.
I am no more a monk, I am a man
O' the world.

(*Throws off cowl and frock, and stands forth in the costume of a Renaissance nobleman.* Lucrezia *looks him up and down.*)

Luc.
Thou cutst a sorry figure.

Sav.
That
Is neither here nor there. I love you, Madam.

Luc.
And this, methinks, is neither there nor here,
For that my love of thee hath vânished,

Seeing thee thus beprankt. Go pad thy calves!
Thus mightst thou, just conceivably, with luck,
Capture the fancy of some serving-wench.

Sav.
And this is all thou hast to say to me?

Luc.
It is.

Sav.
I am dismiss'd?

Luc.
Thou art.

Sav.
'Tis well
(*Resumes frock and cowl.*)

Savonarola is himself once more.

Luc.
And all my love for him returns to me
A thousandfold!

Sav.
Too late! My pride of manhood
Is wounded irremediably. I'll
To the Piazza, where my flock awaits me.
Thus do we see that men make great mistakes
But may amend them when the conscience wakes.

(*Exit.*)

Luc.
I'm half avengèd now, but only half:
'Tis with the ring I'll have the final laugh!
Tho' love be sweet, revenge is sweeter far.
To the Piazza! Ha, ha, ha, ha, har!

(*Seizes ring, and exit. Through open door are heard, as the Curtain falls, sounds of a terrific hubbub in the Piazza.*)

Act III

Scene, *The Piazza.*
Time, *A few minutes anterior to close of preceding Act.*

The Piazza is filled from end to end with a vast seething crowd that is drawn entirely from the lower orders. There is a sprinkling of wild-eyed and dishevelled women in it. The men are lantern-jawed, with several days' growth of beard. Most of them carry rude weapons—staves, bill-hooks, crow-bars, and the like—and are in as excited a condition as the women. Some of them are bare-headed, others affect a kind of Phrygian cap. Cobblers predominate.

Enter Lorenzo De Medici *and* Cosimo De Medici.
They wear cloaks of scarlet brocade, and, to avoid notice, hold masks to their faces.

Cos.
What purpose doth the foul and greasy plebs
Ensue to-day here?

Lor.
I nor know nor care.

Cos.
How thrall'd thou art to the philosophy
Of Epicurus! Naught that's human I
Deem alien from myself. (*To a* Cobbler.) Make answer, fellow!
What empty hope hath drawn thee by a thread
Forth from the *ob*scene hovel where thou starvest?

Cob.
No empty hope, your Honour, but the full
Assurance that to-day, as yesterday,
Savonarola will let loose his thunder
Against the vices of the idle rich
And from the brimming cornucopia
Of his immense vocabulary pour
Scorn on the lamentable heresies
Of the New Learning and on all the art
Later than Giotto.

Cos.
Mark how absolute
The Knave is!

Lor.
Then are parrots rational
When they regurgitate the thing they hear!
This fool is but an unit of the crowd,
And crowds are senseless as the vasty deep
That sinks or surges as the moon dictates.
I know these crowds, and know that any man
That hath a glib tongue and a rolling eye
Can as he willeth with them.

(*Removes his mask and mounts steps of Loggia.*)

Citizens!

(*Prolonged yells and groans from the crowd.*)

Yes, I am he, I am that same Lorenzo
Whom you have nicknamed the Magnificent.

(*Further terrific yells, shakings of fists, brandishings of bill-hooks, insistent cries of 'Death to Lorenzo!' 'Down with the Magnificent!' Cobblers on fringe of crowd, down c., exhibit especially all the symptoms of epilepsy, whooping-cough, and other ailments.*)

You love not me.

(*The crowd makes an ugly rush.* Lor. *appears likely to be dragged down and torn limb from limb, but raises one hand in nick of time, and continues:*)

Yet I deserve your love.

(*The yells are now variegated with dubious murmurs. A cobbler down c. thrusts his face feverishly in the face of another and repeats, in a hoarse interrogative whisper, 'Deserves our love?'*)

Not for the sundry boons I have bestow'd
And benefactions I have lavishèd
Upon Firenze, City of the Flowers,
But for the love that in this rugged breast
I bear you.

(*The yells have now died away, and there is a sharp fall in dubious murmurs. The cobbler down c. says, in an ear-piercing whisper, 'The love he bears us,' drops his lower jaw, nods his head repeatedly, and awaits in an intolerable state of suspense the orator's next words.*)

I am not a blameless man,

(*Some dubious murmurs.*)

Yet for that I have lov'd you passing much,
Shall some things be forgiven me.

(*Noises of cordial assent.*)

There dwells
In this our city, known unto you all,
A man more virtuous than I am, and
A thousand times more intellectual;
Yet envy not I him, for—shall I name him?—
He loves not you. His name? I will not cut
Your hearts by speaking it. Here let it stay
On tip o' tongue.

(*Insistent clamour.*)

Than steel you to the shock!—
Savonarola.

(*For a moment or so the crowd reels silently under the shock. Cobbler down c. is the first to recover himself and cry 'Death to Savonarola!' The cry instantly becomes general.* Lor. *holds up his hand and gradually imposes silence.*)

His twin bug-bears are
Yourselves and that New Learning which I hold
Less dear than only you.

(*Profound sensation. Everybody whispers 'Than only you' to everybody else. A woman near steps of Loggia attempts to kiss hem of* Lor.'s *garment.*)

Would you but con
With me the old philosophers of Hellas,
Her fervent bards and calm historians,
You would arise and say 'We will not hear
Another word against them!'

(*The crowd already says this, repeatedly, with great emphasis.*)

Take the Dialogues
Of Plato, for example. You will find
A spirit far more truly Christian
In them than in the ravings of sour-soul'd
Savonarola.

(*Prolonged cries of 'Death to the Sour-Souled Savonarola!' Several cobblers detach themselves from the crowd and rush away to read the Platonic Dialogues. Enter* Savonarola. *The crowd, as he makes his way through it, gives up all further control of its feelings, and makes a noise for which even the best zoologists might not find a good comparison. The staves and bill-hooks wave like twigs in a storm. One would say that* Sav. *must have died a thousand deaths already. He is, however, unharmed and unruffled as he reaches the upper step of the Loggia.*
Lor. *meanwhile has rejoined* Cos. *in the Piazza.*)

Sav.
Pax vobiscum, brothers!

(*This does but exacerbate the crowd's frenzy.*)

Voice of a Cobbler
Hear his false lips cry Peace when there is no
Peace!

Sav.
Are not you ashamed, O Florentines,

(*Renewed yells, but also some symptoms of manly shame.*)

That hearken'd to Lorenzo and now reel
Inebriate with the exuberance
Of his verbosity?

(*The crowd makes an obvious effort to pull itself together.*)

A man can fool
Some of the people all the time, and can
Fool all the people sometimes, but he cannot
Fool *all* the people *all* the time.

(*Loud cheers. Several cobblers clap one another on the back. Cries of 'Death to Lorenzo!' The meeting is now well in hand.*)

To-day
I must adopt a somewhat novel course
In dealing with the awful wickedness
At present noticeable in this city.
I do so with reluctance. Hitherto
I have avoided personalities.
But now my sense of duty forces me
To a departure from my custom of
Naming no names. One name I must and shall
Name.

(*All eyes are turned on* Lor., *who smiles uncomfortably.*)

No, I do not mean Lorenzo. He
Is 'neath contempt.

(*Loud and prolonged laughter, accompanied with hideous grimaces at* Lor. *Exeunt* Lor. *and* Cos.)

I name a woman's name,

(*The women in the crowd eye one another suspiciously.*)

A name known to you all—four-syllablèd,
Beginning with an L.

(*Pause. Enter hurriedly* Luc. *carrying the ring. She stands, unobserved by any one, on outskirt of crowd.* Sav. *utters the name*:)

Lucrezia!

Luc. (*With equal intensity.*)
Savonarola!

(Sav. *starts violently and stares in direction of her voice.*)

Yes, I come, I come!

(*Forces her way to steps of Loggia. The crowd is much bewildered, and the cries of 'Death to Lucrezia Borgia!' are few and sporadic.*)

Why didst thou call me?

(Sav. *looks somewhat embarrassed.*)

What is thy distress?
I see it all! The sanguinary mob
Clusters to rend thee! As the antler'd stag,
With fine eyes glazèd from the too-long chase,
Turns to defy the foam-fleck'd pack, and thinks,
In his last moment, of some graceful hind
Seen once afar upon a mountain-top,
E'en so, Savonarola, didst thou think,
In thy most dire extremity, of me.
And here I am! Courage! The horrid hounds
Droop tail at sight of me and fawn away
Innocuous.

(*The crowd does indeed seem to have fallen completely under the sway of* Luc.'s *magnetism, and is evidently convinced that it had been about to make an end of the monk.*)

Take thou, and wear henceforth,
As a sure talisman 'gainst future perils,
This little, little ring.

(Sav. *makes awkward gesture of refusal. Angry murmurs from the crowd. Cries of 'Take thou the ring!' 'Churl!' 'Put it on!' etc. Enter the Borgias'* Fool *and stands unnoticed on fringe of crowd.*)

I hoped you'ld like it—
Neat but not gaudy. Is my taste at fault?
I'd so look'd forward to—(*Sob.*) No, I'm not crying,
But just a little hurt.

(*Hardly a dry eye in the crowd. Also swayings and snarlings indicative that* Sav.'s *life is again not worth a moment's purchase.* Sav. *makes awkward gesture of acceptance, but just as he is about to put ring on finger, the* Fool *touches his lute and sings—*)

Wear not the ring,
It hath an unkind sting,
Ding, dong, ding.
Bide a minute,

There's poison in it,
Poison in it,
Ding-a-dong, dong, ding.

Luc.
The fellow lies.

(*The crowd is torn with conflicting opinions. Mingled cries of 'Wear not the ring!' 'The fellow lies!' 'Bide a minute!' 'Death to the Fool!' 'Silence for the Fool!' 'Ding-a-dong, dong, ding!' etc.*)

Fool (*Sings.*)

Wear not the ring,
For Death's a robber-king,
Ding. (*etc.*)
There's no trinket
Is what you think it,
What you think it,
Ding-a-dong, (*etc.*)

(Sav. *throws ring in* Luc.'s *face. Enter* Pope Julius II, *with Papal army.*)

Pope
Arrest that man and woman!

(*Re-enter Guelfs and Ghibellines fighting.* Sav. *and* Luc. *are arrested by Papal officers. Enter* MichaelAngelo. Andrea Del Sarto *appears for a moment at a window.* Pippa *passes. Brothers of the Misericordia go by, singing a Requiem for Francesca da Rimini. Enter* Boccaccio, Benvenuto Cellini, *and many others, making remarks highly characteristic of themselves but scarcely audible through the terrific thunderstorm which now bursts over Florence and is at its loudest and darkest crisis as the Curtain falls.*)

Act IV

Time, *Three hours later.*
Scene, *A Dungeon on the ground-floor of the Palazzo Civico.*

The stage is bisected from top to bottom by a wall, on one side of which is seen the interior of Lucrezia's *cell, on the other that of* Savonarola's.

Neither he nor she knows that the other is in the next cell. The audience, however, knows this.

Each cell (because of the width and height of the proscenium) is of more than the average Florentine size, but is bare even to the point of severity, its sole amenities being some straw, a hunk of bread, and a stone pitcher. The door of each is facing the audience. Dim-ish light.

Lucrezia *wears long and clanking chains on her wrists, as does also* Savonarola. *Imprisonment has left its mark on both of them.* Savonarola's *hair has turned white. His whole aspect is that of a very old, old man.* Lucrezia *looks no older than before, but has gone mad.*

Sav.
Alas, how long ago this morning seems
This evening! A thousand thousand aeons
Are scarce the measure of the gulf betwixt
My then and now. Methinks I must have been
Here since the dim creation of the world
And never in that interval have seen
The tremulous hawthorn burgeon in the brake,
Nor heard the hum o' bees, nor woven chains
Of buttercups on Mount Fiesole
what time the sap lept in the cypresses,

Imbuing with the friskfulness of Spring
Those melancholy trees. I do forget
The aspect of the sun. Yet I was born
A freeman, and the Saints of Heaven smiled
Down on my crib. What would my sire have said,
And what my dam, had anybody told them
The time would come when I should occupy
A felon's cell? O the disgrace of it!—
The scandal, the incredible come-down!
It masters me. I see i' my mind's eye
The public prints—'Sharp Sentence on a Monk.'
What then? I thought I was of sterner stuff
Than is affrighted by what people think.
Yet thought I so because 'twas thought of me,
And so 'twas thought of me because I had
A hawk-like profile and a baleful eye.
Lo! my soul's chin recedes, soft to the touch
As half-churn'd butter. Seeming hawk is dove,
And dove's a gaol-bird now. Fie out upon 't!

Luc.
How comes it? I am Empress Dowager
Of China—yet was never crown'd. This must
Be seen to

(*Quickly gathers some straw and weaves a crown, which she puts on.*)

Sav.
O, what a dégringolade!
The great career I had mapp'd out for me—
Nipp'd i' the bud. What life, when I come out,
Awaits me? Why, the very Novices
And callow Postulants will draw aside
As I pass by, and say 'That man hath done
Time!' And yet shall I wince? The worst of Time
Is not in having done it, but in doing 't.

Luc.
Ha, ha, ha, ha! Eleven billion pig-tails
Do tremble at my nod imperial,—
The which is as it should be.

Sav.
I have heard
That gaolers oft are willing to carouse
With them they watch o'er, and do sink at last
Into a drunken sleep, and then's the time
To snatch the keys and make a bid for freedom.
Gaoler! Ho, Gaoler!

(*Sounds of lock being turned and bolts withdrawn. Enter the Borgias'* Fool, *in plain clothes, carrying bunch of keys.*)

I have seen thy face
Before.

Fool
I saved thy life this afternoon, Sir.

Sav.
Thou art the Borgias' Fool?

Fool
Say rather, was.
Unfortunately I have been discharg'd
For my betrayal of Lucrezia,
So that I have to speak like other men—
Decasyllabically, and with sense.
An hour ago the gaoler of this dungeon
Died of an apoplexy. Hearing which,
I ask'd for and obtain'd his billet.

Sav.
Fetch
A stoup o' liquor for thyself and me.

(*Exit* Gaoler.)

Freedom! there's nothing that thy votaries
Grudge in the cause of thee. That decent man
Is doom'd by me to lose his place again
To-morrow morning when he wakes from out
His hoggish slumber. Yet I care not.

(*Re-enter* Gaoler *with a leathern bottle and two glasses.*)

Ho!
This is the stuff to arm our vitals, this
The panacea for all mortal ills
And sure elixir of eternal youth.
Drink, bonniman!

(Gaoler *drains a glass and shows signs of instant intoxication.* Sav. *claps him on shoulder and replenishes glass.* Gaoler *drinks again, lies down on floor, and snores.* Sav. *snatches the bunch of keys, laughs long but silently, and creeps out on tip-toe, leaving door ajar.*

Luc. *meanwhile has lain down on the straw in her cell, and fallen asleep.*

Noise of bolts being shot back, jangling of keys, grating of lock, and the door of Luc.'s *cell flies open.* Sav. *takes two steps across the threshold, his arms outstretched and his upturned face transfigured with a great joy.*)

How sweet the open air
Leaps to my nostrils! O the good brown earth
That yields once more to my elastic tread
And laves these feet with its remember'd dew!

(*Takes a few more steps, still looking upwards.*)

Free!—I am free! O naked arc of heaven,
Enspangled with innumerable—no,
Stars are not there. Yet neither are there clouds!
The thing looks like a ceiling! (*Gazes downward.*) And this thing
Looks like a floor. (*Gazes around.*) And that white bundle yonder
Looks curiously like Lucrezia.

(Luc. *awakes at sound of her name, and sits up sane.*)

There must be some mistake.

Luc. (*Rises to her feet.*)
There is indeed!
A pretty sort of prison I have come to,

In which a self-respecting lady's cell
Is treated as a lounge!

Sav.
I had no notion
You were in here. I thought I was out there.
I will explain—but first I'll make amends.
Here are the keys by which your durance ends.
The gate is somewhere in this corridor,
And so good-bye to this interior!

(*Exeunt* Sav. *and* Luc. *Noise, a moment later, of a key grating in a lock, then of gate creaking on its hinges; triumphant laughs of fugitives; loud slamming of gate behind them.*
In Sav.'s *cell the* Gaoler *starts in his sleep, turns his face to the wall, and snores more than ever deeply. Through open door comes a cloaked figure.*)

Cloaked Figure
Sleep on, Savonarola, and awake
Not in this dungeon but in ruby Hell!

(*Stabs* Gaoler, *whose snores cease abruptly. Enter* Pope Julius II, *with Papal retinue carrying torches.* Murderer *steps quickly back into shadow.*)

Pope (*To body of* Gaoler.)
Savonarola, I am come to taunt
Thee in thy misery and dire abjection.
Rise, Sir, and hear me out.

Murd. (*Steps forward.*)
Great Julius,
Waste not thy breath. Savonarola's dead.
I murder'd him.

Pope
Thou hadst no right to do so.
Who art thou, pray?

Murd.
Cesare Borgia,
Lucrezia's brother, and I claim a brother's
Right to assassinate whatever man
Shall wantonly and in cold blood reject
Her timid offer of a poison'd ring.

Pope
Of this anon.

(*Stands over body of* Gaoler.)

Our present business
Is general woe. No nobler corse hath ever
Impress'd the ground. O let the trumpets speak it!

(*Flourish of trumpets.*)

This was the noblest of the Florentines.
His character was flawless, and the world
Held not his parallel. O bear him hence
With all such honours as our State can offer.

He shall interrèd be with noise of cannon.
As doth befit so militant a nature.
Prepare these obsequies.

(*Papal officers lift body of* Gaoler.)

A Papal Officer
But this is not
Savonarola. It is some one else.

Cesare
Lo! 'tis none other than the Fool that I
Hoof'd from my household but two hours agone.
I deem'd him no good riddance, for he had
The knack of setting tables on a roar.
What shadows we pursue! Good night, sweet Fool,
And flights of angels sing thee to thy rest!

Pope
Interrèd shall he be with signal pomp.
No honour is too great that we can pay him.
He leaves the world a vacuum. Meanwhile,
Go we in chase of the accursèd villain
That hath made escapado from this cell.
To horse! Away! We'll scour the country round
For Sav'narola till we hold him bound.
Then shall you see a cinder, not a man,
Beneath the lightnings of the Vatican!

(*Flourish, alarums and excursions, flashes of Vatican lightning, roll of drums, etc. Through open door of cell is led in a large milk-white horse, which the* Pope *mounts as the Curtain falls.*)

Act V

Dawn on summit of Mount Fiesole. Outspread view of Florence (Duomo, Giotto's Tower, etc.) as seen from that eminence.—Niccolo Machiavelli, *asleep on grass, wakes as sun rises. Deplores his exile from Florence,* Lorenzo's *unappeasable hostility, etc. Wonders if he could not somehow secure the* Pope's *favour. Very cynical. Breaks off:* But who are these that scale the mountain-side?/ Savonarola and Lucrezia/ Borgia!—*Enter through a trap-door, back c. (trap-door veiled from audience by a grassy ridge),* Sav. *and* Luc. *Both gasping and footsore from their climb. (Still with chains on their wrists? or not?)*—Mach. *steps unobserved behind a cypress and listens.*—Sav. *has a speech to the rising sun*—Th' effulgent hope that westers from the east/ Daily. *Says that* his *hope, on the contrary, lies in escape* To that which easters not from out the west,/ That fix'd abode of freedom which men call/ America! *Very bitter against* Pope.—Luc. *says that she, for her part, means* To start afresh in that uncharted land/ Which austers not from out the antipod,/ Australia!—*Exit* Mach., *unobserved, down trap-door behind ridge, to betray* Luc. *and* Sav.—*Several longish speeches by* Sav. *and* Luc. *Time is thus given for* Mach. *to get into touch with* Pope, *and time for* Pope *and retinue to reach the slope of Fiesole.* Sav., *glancing down across ridge, sees these sleuth-hounds, points them out to* Luc. *and cries* Bewray'd! Luc. By whom? Sav. I know not, but suspect/ The hand of that sleek serpent Niccolo/ Machiavelli.—Sav. *and* Luc. *rush down c., but find their way barred by the footlights.*—Luc. We will not be ta'en/ Alive. And here availeth us my lore/ In what pertains to poison. Yonder herb/ (*points to a herb growing down* r.) Is deadly nightshade. Quick, Monk! Pluck we it!—Sav. *and* Luc. *die just as* Pope *appears over ridge, followed by retinue in full cry.*—Pope's *annoyance at being foiled is quickly swept away on the great wave of Shakespearean chivalry and charity that again rises in him. He gives* Sav. *a funeral oration similar to the one meant for him in Act IV, but even more laudatory and more stricken. Of* Luc., *too, he enumerates the virtues, and hints that the whole terrestrial globe shall be hollowed to receive her bones. Ends by saying:* In deference to this our double sorrow/ Sun shall not shine to-day nor shine to-morrow.—*Sun drops quickly back behind eastern horizon, leaving a great darkness on which the Curtain slowly falls.*

—*Max Beerbohm*

SHAKESPEAREAN SOLILOQUY IN PROGRESS

To wed, or not to wed? That is the question.
Whether 'tis nobler in the mind to suffer
The pangs and arrows of outrageous love
Or to take arms against the powerful flame
And by opposing quench it.
To wed—to marry—
And by a marriage say we end
The heartache and the thousand painful shocks
Love makes us heir to—'tis a consummation.
Devoutly to be wished! to wed—to marry
Perchance a scold! aye, there's the rub
For in that wedded life what ills may come
When we have shuffled off our single state
Must give us serious pause. There's the respect
That makes us Bachelors a numerous race.
For who would bear the dull unsocial hours
Spent by unmarried men, cheered by no smile
To sit like hermit at a lonely board
In silence? Who would bear the cruel gibes
With which the Bachelor is daily teased
When he himself might end such heart-felt griefs
By wedding some fair maid? O who would live
Yawning and staring sadly in the fire
Till celibacy becomes a weary life
But that the dread of something after wedlock
(That undiscovered state from whose strong chains
No captive can get free) puzzles the will
And makes us rather choose those ills we have
Than fly to others which a wife may bring.
Thus caution doth make Bachelors of us all
And thus our natural taste for matrimony
Is sicklied o'er with the pale cast of thought
And love adventures of great pith and moment
With this regard their currents turn awry
And lose the name of Wedlock.

—*Anonymous*

To have it out or not? that is the question—
Whether 'tis better for the jaws to suffer
The pangs and torments of an aching tooth,
Or to take steel against a host of troubles;
And, by extracting end them? To pull—to tug!
No more; and by a tug to say we end
The tooth-ache, and a thousand natural ills
The jaw is heir to; 'tis a consummation

Devoutly to be wished? To pull—to tug!
To tug—perchance to break! Ay, there's the rub.
For in that wrench what agonies may come,
When we have half-dislodged the stubborn foe,
Must give us pause. There's the respect
That makes an aching tooth of so long life.
For who would bear the whips and stings of pain,
The old wife's nostrum, dentist's contumely,
The pangs of hope deferred, kind sleep's delay
The insolence of pity, and the spurns
That patient sickness of the healthy takes,
When he himself might his quietus make,
For two-and-sixpence? Who would fardels bear
To groan and sweat beneath a load of pain?
But that the dread of something lodged within
The linen-twisted forceps, from whose pangs
No jaw at ease returns!—puzzles the will,
And makes it rather bear the ills it has
Than fly to others that it knows not of.
Thus dentists do make cowards of us all—
And thus the native hue of resolution
Is sicklied o'er with the pale cast of fear;
And many a one, whose courage seeks the door,
With this regard his footsteps turn away,
Scared at the name of dentist.

—*C.A.W.*

To shave, or not to shave? that is the question,
Whether 'tis comfortable most to cover
One's face all over with outrageous lather,
Or by outrageous hair, s(h)ave so much trouble,
And thus soap—pose we end it! To shave—to swear
What for? when by moustache and beard we end
The nuisance thus encouraging the locks
That flesh is *hair* to—'tis a consummation
Devoutly to be wished. To shave? To swear?
To swear! perchance an oath—ay, there's the rub;
For as we shave, perhaps the razor slips,
And as we *barber*ously hack our chin,
Must we then pause; in every respect
There is calamity in such a shave.
Oh, who would bear shivering in the cold
Ten minutes long to be in misery?
The pangs of getting up, with much delay,
The razor wanting strapping, and the time
The patient shaver usually takes,
When he himself might get on very well
Without a razor?—or who would be shaved,
Tweak'd by the nose as pigs for singeing are,
To groan and sweat under the barber's hand,
And as the dread of something happening—
A pleasant slice, perhaps, taken off one's nose;
Of course entirely against one's will.
It makes us rather wear the honest beard,
Than fly to barbers whom we know not of.
Thus custom makes Gorillas of us all;
Although we falter in our resolution,

As lathered over with best Windsor soap,
Expecting a severe cut every moment,
We contemplate our beard with jaundiced eye,
And so prepare for action—
Soft I vow—'tis done—*Oh, feel here!*

—T.F. Dillon Croker

To draw, or not to draw,—that is the question:—
Whether 't is safer in the player to take
The awful risk of skinning for a straight,
Or, standing pat, to raise 'em all the limit
And thus, by bluffing, get in. To draw,—to skin;
No more—and by that skin to get a full,
Or two pairs, or the fattest bouncing kings
That luck is heir to—'t is a consummation
Devoutly to be wished. To draw—to skin;
To skin! perchance to burst—ay, there's the rub!
For in the draw of three what cards may come,
When we have shuffled off th' uncertain pack,
Must give us pause. There's the respect
That makes calamity of a bobtail flush;
For who would bear the overwhelming blind,
The reckless straddle, the wait on the edge,
The insolence of pat hands and the lifts
That patient merit of the bluffer takes,
When he himself might be much better off
By simply passing? Who would trays uphold,
And go out on a small progressive raise,
But that the dread of something after call—
The undiscovered ace-full, to whose strength
Such hands must bow, puzzles the will,
And makes us rather keep the chips we have
Than be curious about the hands we know not of.
Thus bluffing does make cowards of us all:
And thus the native hue of a four-heart flush
Is sicklied with some dark and cussed club,
And speculators in a jack-pot's wealth
With this regard their interest turn away
And lose the right to open.

—Anonymous

To starve, or not to starve? that is the question:—
Whether, Sylvester, thou should'st calmly bear
The yearns and gripings of internal wants,
Or take up arms against the parish treat,
And, willy nilly, end it?—To eat;—to glut
Thy fill;—and, by this feast, to say thou end'st
Those cravings and the thousand rav'nous wants
That flesh is heir to—'tis an occupation
Devoutly to be wish'd. To eat;—to stuff;—
To gorge, perchance be sick! aye, there's the rub;
For in that yearning state what pangs may come,
In easing me of superfluities,

Must make me pause:—'tis this alone
That bids me curb my longing appetite;
Else should I tamely bear fell hunger's cries,
My stomach's wrongs, my bowels' piercing shrieks,
My greedy eye's desire, the cook's delay,
Who, insolent in office, jade-like taunts
My rav'nous appetite, that sneaking waits,
When quickly force might satisfy desire
With knife and bodkin? What all endure,
And grumbling sweat before the blazing fire,
But that the dread of sickness afterwards,
That painful operation, from whose course
No man is free, affrights my will,
And makes me rather bear those gripes I feel,
Than fly to such as might await the deed?
Thus sickness does make cowards of us all;
And thus fell resolution, arm'd by want,
Sinks, pale and coward-like, the slave of thought;
And mighty feats perform'd with knife and fork
Are left untried; so is my craving turn'd!
I lose the power of eating.—

—*W.H. Ireland*

To print, or not to print—that is the question.
Whether 'tis better in a trunk to bury
The quirks and crotchets of outrageous fancy,
Or send a well-wrote copy to the press,
And, by disclosing, end them? To print, to doubt
No more, and by one act to say we end
The headache, and a thousand natural shocks,
Of scribbling frenzy—'tis a consummation
Devoutly to be wished. To print—to beam
From the same shelf with Pope, in calf well-bound:
To sleep perchance with Quarles. Ay, there's the rub
For to what class a writer may be doomed,
When he hath shuffled off some paltry stuff,
Must give us pause. There's the respect that makes
Th' unwilling poet keep his piece nine years.
For who would bear the impatient thirst of fame,
The price of conscious merit, and 'bove all,
The tedious importunity of friends,
When he himself might his quietus make
With a bare inkhorn? who would fardels bear?
To groan and sweat under a load of wit?
But that the tread of steep Parnassus' hill
That undiscover'd country, with whose bays
Few travellers return, puzzles the will,
And makes us rather bear to live unknown
Than run the hazard to be known and damn'd.
Thus Critics do make cowards of us all;
And thus the healthful face of many a poem
Is sicklied o'er with a pale manuscript;
And enterprisers of great fire and spirit,
With this regard, from Murray turn away,
And lose the name of authors.

—*Reverend Richard Jago*

(Dame Tiller *discovered washing; she takes out of her tub a veil, and a pair of small socks, which she hangs on the line, sighs, and regards them sorrowfully.)*

Dame
Tubby or not tubby—there's the rub,
Whether I shall get anything to scrub,
Or, overcome by all my numerous troubles,
Dive headlong down into that sea of bubbles;
As to my business it is something shockin',
Of stockings I've got but that small *stock in.*
People won't send their things, complaining (bosh)
That, like King John, they'd lost them in the *Wash.*
I used to do for schools, and so it follers
I used to have a lot of *scholars' collars*;
Now I have none, no collars smooth, nor ruffs,
I've got to make the best of fortune's cuffs.
To emigrate the best thing now would be—
Yes! *Washington* would be the place for me.

—*F.C. Burnand*

To be, or not to be; that is the bare bodkin
That makes calamity of so long life;
For who would fardels bear, till Birnam Wood do come to Dunsinane,
But that the fear of something after death
Murders the innocent sleep,
Great nature's second course,
And makes us rather sling the arrows of outrageous fortune
Than fly to others that we know not of.
There's the respect must give us pause:
Wake Duncan with thy knocking! I would thou couldst;
For who would bear the whips and scorns of time,
The oppressor's wrong, the proud man's contumely,
The law's delay, and the quietus which his pangs might take,
In the dead waste and middle of the night, when churchyards yawn
In customary suits of solemn black,
But that the undiscovered country from whose bourne no traveler returns,
Breathes forth contagion on the world,
And thus the native hue of resolution, like the poor cat i' the adage,
Is sicklied o'er with care,
And all the clouds that lowered o'er our housetops,
With this regard their currents turn awry,
And lose the name of action.
'Tis a consummation devoutly to be wished. But soft you, the fair Ophelia:
Ope not thy ponderous and marble jaws,
But get thee to a nunnery—go!

—*Samuel Clemens*

THOMAS NASHE
(1567-1601)

Consolation

Helen's lips, as drifting dust,
Can't be kissed, and someone's must.

Queen Semiramis is clay!
You are sweeter, any day.

Dead is Queen Shub-Ad of Ur!
Still, I like you more than her.

Rosamond is in her grave,
Hero sleeps beneath the wave,

Long deceased is Guinevere,
Yseult lies upon her bier;

Cleopatra, Lady Jane,
Deirdre, Beatrice, Elaine,—

All are gone, those damsels fair,
But you're here, so I don't care!

—Arthur Guiterman

JOHN DONNE
(1572-1631)

O! For Some Honest Lover's Ghost

O! for some honest lover's ghost,
Some kind unbodied post
Sent from the shades below!
I strangely long to know,
Whether the nobler chaplets wear,
Those that their mistress' scorn did bear,
Or those that were us'd kindly.

For whatsoe'er they tell us here
To make those sufferings dear,
'Twill there I fear be found,
That to the being crown'd
T' have loved alone will not suffice,
Unless we also have been wise,
And have our loves enjoy'd.

What posture can we think him in,
That here unlov'd again
Departs, and 's thither gone
Where each sits by his own?
Or how can that elysium be,
Where I my mistress still must see
Circled in others' arms?

For there the judges all are just,
And Sophonisba must
Be his whom she held dear,
Not his who lov'd her here:
The sweet Philoclea, since she died,
Lies by her Pirocles his side,
Not by Amphialus.

Some bays, perchance, or myrtle bough,
For difference crowns the brow
Of those kind souls that were
The noble martyrs here;
And if that be the only odds
(As who can tell?) ye kinder gods,
Give me the woman here.

—Sir John Suckling

Lovers' Debouchment

Come, cut thy throte, and have thy throte-ball out!
The little while I love, I had as lief
Thy Adam's apple did not gad about,
Nor glut thy pipes with choking on thy grief.
What though I leave thee now, and must traverse
Untraffic'd hemispheres where agapanthi rove?
Crop down thy bolus! lovers' spleen's made worse
By unsquanch'd gagging, which profanes our love.

For in thy neck's an Edenic world englob'd,
Stuck o'er with continents, nay, hemispheres
Coughed, retched, gasped dry; hydroptized, robbed
Of dews, ponds, oceans; deserts made; made tents
And camels. Aye, and that Sahara, not removed,
Drowns us in drouth, nor no man ever loved.

—William Zaranka

From GO AND CATCH A FALLING STAR

Unfortunate Coincidence

By the time you swear you're his,
Shivering and sighing,
And he vows his passion is
Infinite, undying—
Lady, make a note of this:
One of you is lying.

—Dorothy Parker

The Deformed Mistress

I know there are some fools that care
Not for the body, so the face be fair;
Some others, too, that in a female creature
Respect not beauty, but a comely feature;
And others, too, that for those parts in sight

Care not so much, so that the rest be right.
Each man his humour hath, and, faith, 'tis mine
To love that woman which I now define.
First I would have her wainscot foot and hand
More wrinkled far than any pleated band,
That in those furrows, if I'd take the pains,
I might both sow and reap all sorts of grains:
Her nose I'd have a foot long, not above,
With pimples embroider'd, for those I love;
And at the end a comely pearl of snot,
Considering whether it should fall or not:
Provided, next, that half her teeth be out,
Nor do I care much if her pretty snout
Meet with her furrow'd chin, and both together
Hem in her lips, as dry as good whit-leather:
One wall-eye she shall have, for that's a sign
In other beasts the best: why not in mine?
Her neck I'll have to be pure jet at least,
With yellow spots enamell'd; and her breast,
Like a grasshopper's wing, both thin and lean,
Not to be toucht for dirt, unless swept clean:
As for her belly, 'tis no matter, so
There be a belly, and—
Yet, if you will, let it be something high,
And always let there be a timpany.
But soft! where am I now? here I should stride,
Lest I fall in, the place must be so wide,
And pass unto her thighs, which shall be just
Like to an ant's that's scraping in the dust:
Into her legs I'd have love's issues fall,
And all her calf into a gouty small:
Her feet both thick and eagle-like display'd,
The symptoms of a comely, handsome maid.
As for her parts behind, I ask no more:
If they but answer those that are before,
I have my utmost wish; and, having so,
Judge whether I am happy, yea or no.

—*Sir John Suckling*

ROBERT BURTON
(1577-1640)

Hypochondriacus

By myself walking,
To myself talking,
When as I ruminate
On my untoward fate,
Scarcely seem I
Alone sufficiently,
Black thoughts continually
Crowding my privacy;
They come unbidden,
Like foes at a wedding,
Thrusting their faces
In better guests' places,
Peevish and malecontent,

Clownish, impertinent,
Dashing the merriment:
So in like fashions
Dim cogitations
Follow and haunt me,
Striving to daunt me,
In my heart festering,
In my ears whispering,
'Thy friends are treacherous,
Thy foes are dangerous,
Thy dreams ominous.'
  Fierce Anthropophagi,
Spectra, Diaboli,
What scared St. Anthony
Hobgoblins, Lemures,
Dreams of Antipodes,
Night-riding Incubi
Troubling the fantasy,
All dire illusions
Causing confusions;
Figments heretical,
Scruples fantastical,
Doubts diabolical,
Abaddon vexeth me,
Mahu perplexeth me,
Lucifer teareth me—
Jesu! Maria! liberate nos ab his diris tentationibus Inimici

—Charles Lamb

ROBERT HERRICK (1591-1674)

To Julia under Lock and Key[1]

When like a bud my Julia blows
In lattice-work of silken hose,
Pleasant I deem it is to note
How, 'neath the nimble petticoat,
Above her fairy shoe is set
The circumvolving zonulet.
And soothly for the lover's ear
A perfect bliss it is to hear
About her limb so lithe and lank
My Julia's ankle-bangle clank.
Not rudely tight, for 't were a sin
To corrugate her dainty skin;
Nor yet so large that it might fare
Over her foot at unaware;
But fashioned nicely with a view
To let her airy stocking through:
So as, when Julia goes to bed,
Of all her gear disburdenèd,
This ring at least she shall not doff
Because she cannot take it off.
And since thereof I hold the key,

1. A form of betrothal gift in America is an anklet secured by a padlock, of which the other party keeps the key

She may not taste of liberty,
Not though she suffer from the gout,
Unless I choose to let her out.

—*Sir Owen Seaman*

Upon Julia

Upon seeing her picture in profile.

I die
If I but spy
One eye;
Yet I would fain
See twain

Upon receiving the same in a full view.

In profile
'Twas vile;
But in th' obverse
'Tis worse.

—*Ernest Radford*

Upon Julia's Clothes

Whenas in furs my Julia goes,
Of slaughtered vermin goodness knows,
What tails depend upon her clothes!

Next, when I cast my eyes and see
The living whelp she lugs to tea,
Oh, how their likeness taketh me!

—*E.V. Knox (Evoe)*

To Julia In Shooting Togs

Whenas to shoot my Julia goes,
Then, then, (methinks) how bravely shows
That rare arrangement of her clothes!

So shod as when the Huntress Maid
With thumping buskin bruised the glade,
She moveth, making earth afraid.

Against the sting of random chaff
Her leathern gaiters circle half
The arduous crescent of her calf.

Unto th' occasion timely fit,
My love's attire doth show her wit,
And of her legs a little bit.

Sorely it sticketh in my throat,
She having nowhere to bestow't,
To name the absent petticoat.

In lieu whereof a wanton pair
Of knickerbockers she doth wear,
Full windy and with space to spare.

Enlargéd by the bellying breeze,
Lord! how they playfully do ease
The urgent knocking of her knees!

Lengthways curtailéd to her taste
A tunic circumvents her waist,
And soothly it is passing chaste.

Upon her head she hath a gear
Even such as wights of ruddy cheer
Do use in stalking of the deer.

Haply her truant tresses mock
Some coronal of shapelier block,
To wit, the bounding billy-cock.

Withal she hath a loaded gun,
Whereat the pheasants, as they run.
Do make a fair diversión.

For very awe, if so she shoots,
My hair upriseth from the roots,
And lo! I tremble in my boots!

—Sir Owen Seaman

Herrick's Julia

1

Whenas in perfume Julia went,
Then, then how sweet was the intent
Of that inexorable scent.

Her very shadow walked in myrrh
And smelled (itself) of pomander,
And Herrick could but covet her.

2

The sight of Julia's dainty limb
Recalled a smooth white egg to him.
And when he saw a smooth white egg,
I guess he thought of Julia's leg.

3

All that was fair, all that was neat
Did Herrick love, her silvery feet,
Her golden head, her double chin.
(Conceive the dither he was in.)

4

There were the riband on her throat,
Her silken hair, her petticoat,
The soft pretension of her dress
To kindle in him lovingness.

They took his homage and his heart.
So, too, did every other part;
Her breasts, her eager lips, her hair.
I think she pleased him everywhere.

5

Then for his subjugation, ah,
There was the total Julia.

—Helen Bevington

GEORGE HERBERT
(1593-1633)

Confusion

O how my mind
Is gravell'd!
Not a thought
That I can find
But's ravel'd
All to nought.
Short ends of threads
And narrow shreds
Of lists,
Knot-snarl'd ruffs,
Loose broken tufts
Of twists,
Are my torn meditations' ragged clothing;
Which, wound and woven, shape a suit for nothing;

One while I think and then I am in pain
To think how to unthink that thought again.

—*Christopher Hervey*

EDMUND WALLER
(1606-1687)

The Aesthete to the Rose

Go, flaunting Rose!
Tell her that wastes her love on thee,
That she nought knows
Of the New Cult, Intensity,
If sweet and fair to her you be.

Tell her that's young,
Or who in health and bloom takes pride,
That bards have sung
Of a new youth—at whose sad side
Sickness and pallor aye abide.

Small is the worth
Of Beauty in crude charms attired.
She must shun mirth,
Have suffered, fruitlessly desired,
And wear no flush by hope inspired.

Then die, that she
May learn that Death is passing fair;
May read in thee
How little of Art's praise they share,
Who are not sallow, sick, and spare!

—*Anonymous*

JOHN MILTON
(1608-1674)

Paradise Lost

Don't touch that fruit, Eve.
O my God—she's disobeyed!
Cosmic disaster!

—*Stanley J. Sharpless*

The Splendid Shilling

Happy the Man, who void of Cares and Strife,
In Silken, or in Leathern Purse retains
A *Splendid Shilling*: He nor hears with Pain
New Oysters cry'd, nor sighs for chearful Ale;
But with his Friends, when nightly Mists arise,
To *Juniper's, Magpye,* or *Town-Hall* repairs:
Where, mindful of the Nymph, whose wanton Eye
Transfix'd his Soul, and kindled Amorous Flames,
Chloe, or *Phillis*; he each Circling Glass
Wisheth her Health, and Joy, and equal Love.
Mean while he smoaks, and laughs at merry Tale,
Or *Pun* ambiguous, or *Conundrum* quaint.
But I, whom griping Penury surrounds,
And Hunger, sure Attendant upon Want,
With scanty Offals, and small acid Tiff
(Wretched Repast!) my meagre Corps sustain:
Then Solitary walk, or doze at home
In Garret vile, and with a warming puff
Regale chill'd Fingers; or from Tube as black
As Winter-Chimney, or well-polish'd Jet,
Exhale *Mundungus*, ill-perfuming Scent:
Not blacker Tube, nor of a shorter Size
Smoaks *Cambro-Britain* (vers'd in Pedigree,
Sprung from *Cadwalader* and *Arthur*,
Kings Full famous in Romantic tale) when he
O'er many a craggy Hill, and barren Cliff,
Upon a Cargo of fam'd *Cestrian* Cheese,
High over-shadowing rides, with a design
To vend his Wares, or at th' *Arvonian* Mart,
Or *Maridunum*, or the ancient Town
Eclip'd *Brechinia*, or where *Vaga's* Stream
Encircles *Ariconium*, fruitful Soil,
Whence flow Nectareous Wines, that well may vye
With *Massic, Setin*, or renown'd *Falern*.
Thus while my joyless Minutes tedious flow
With Looks demure, and silent Pace, a *Dunn*,
Horrible Monster! hated by Gods and Men,
To my aerial Citadel ascends;
With Vocal Heel thrice thund'ring at my Gates,
With hideous Accent thrice he calls; I know
The Voice ill-boding, and the solemn Sound.
What shou'd I do? or wither turn? amaz'd,
Confounded, to the dark Recess I fly
Of Woodhole; strait my bristling Hairs erect
Thrô sudden Fear; a chilly Sweat bedews
My shud'ring Limbs, and (wonderful to tell!)
My Tongue forgets her Faculty of Speech;

So horrible he seems! his faded Brow
Entrench'd with many a Frown, and *Conic* Beard,
And spreading Band, admir'd by Modern Saints,
Disastrous Acts forebode; in his Right Hand
Long Scrolls of Paper solemnly he waves,
With Characters, and Figures dire inscrib'd
Grievous to mortal Eyes; (ye Gods avert
Such Plagues from righteous Men!) behind him stalks
Another Monster, not unlike himself,
Sullen of Aspect, by the Vulgar call'd
A *Catchpole*, whose polluted Hands the Gods
With Force incredible, and Magick Charms
Erst have indu'd, if he his ample Palm
Should haply on ill-fated Shoulder lay
Of Debtor, strait his Body, to the Touch
Obsequious, (as whilom Knights were wont)
To some enchanted Castle is convey'd,
Where Gates impregnable, and coercive Chains
In Durance strict detain him, 'till in form
Of Mony, *Pallas* sets the Captive free.
Beware, ye Debtors, when ye walk beware,
Be circumspect; oft with insidious Ken
This Caitif eyes your Steps aloof, and oft
Lies perdue in a Nook or gloomy Cave.
Prompt to enchant some inadvertent wretch
With his unhallow'd Touch. So (Poets sing)
Grimalkin to Domestick Vermin sworn
An everlasting Foe, with watchful Eye,
Lyes nightly brooding o'er a chinky gap,
Protending her fell Claws, to thoughtless Mice
Sure Ruin. So her disembowell'd Web
Arachne in a Hall, or Kitchin spreads,
Obvious to vagrant Flies: She secret stands
Within her woven Cell; the Humming Prey,
Regardless of their Fate, rush on the toils
Inextricable, nor will aught avail
Their Arts, nor Arms, nor Shapes of lovely Hue.
The Wasp insidious, and the buzzing Drone,
And Butterfly proud of expanded wings
Distinct with Gold, entangled in her Snares,
Useless Resistance make: With eager strides,
She tow'ring flies to her expected Spoils;
Then with envenom'd Jaws the vital Blood
Drinks of reluctant Foes, and to her Cave
Their bulky Carcasses triumphant drags.
So pass my Days. But when Nocturnal Shades
This World invelop, and th' inclement Air
Persuades Men to repel benumming Frosts,
With pleasant Wines, and crackling blaze of Wood;
Me Lonely sitting, nor the glimmering Light
Of Make-weight Candle, nor the joyous Talk
Of loving Friend delights; distress'd, forlorn,
Amidst the horrors of the tedious Night,
Darkling I sigh, and feed with dismal Thoughts
My anxious Mind; or sometimes mournful Verse
Indite, and sing of Groves and Myrtle Shades,
Or desperate Lady near a purling Stream,
Or Lover pendent on a Willow-Tree:
Mean while I Labour with eternal Drought,
And restless Wish, and Rave; my parched Throat
Finds no Relief, nor heavy Eyes Repose:

But if a Slumber haply does Invade
My weary Limbs, my Fancy's still awake,
Thoughtful of Drink, and Eager in a Dream,
Tipples Imaginary Pots of Ale;
In Vain; awake, I find the settled Thirst
Still gnawing, and the pleasant Phantom curse.
Thus do I live from Pleasure quite debarr'd,
Nor taste the Fruits that the Sun's genial Rays
Mature, *John-Apple*, nor the downy *Peach*,
Nor *Walnut* in rough-furrow'd Coat secure,
Nor *Medlar*, Fruit delicious in decay;
Afflictions Great! yet Greater still remain:
My *Galligaskins* that have long withstood
The Winter's Fury, and Encroaching Frosts.
By Time subdu'd, (what will not Time subdue!)
An horrid Chasm disclose, with Orifice
Wide, Discontinuous; at which the Winds
Eurus and *Auster*, and the dreadful Force
Of *Boreas*, that congeals the *Cronian* Waves,
Tumultuous enter with dire chilling Blasts,
Portending Agues. Thus a well-fraught Ship
Long sail'd secure, or thrô the' *Aegean* Deep,
Or the *Ionian*, 'till Cruising near
The *Lilybean* Shoar, with hideous Crush
On *Scylla*, or *Charybdis* (dang'rous Rocks)
She strikes rebounding, whence the shatter'd Oak,
So fierce a Shock unable to withstand,
Admits the Sea; in at the gaping Side
The crouding Waves Gush with impetuous Rage,
Resistless, Overwhelming; Horrors seize
The Mariners, Death in their Eyes appears,
They stare, they lave, they pump, they swear, they pray:
(Vain Efforts!) still the battering Waves rush in
Implacable, 'till delug'd by the Foam,
The Ship sinks found'ring in the vast Abyss.

—*John Phillips*

The Suet Dumpling

Happy the man who in his pot contains
A suet dumpling; he nor feels the pains
Of going dinnerless, nor griping hunger:
But cheerful blows the fire with merry heart,
Often revolving when the happy minute
That brings it to his homely board will come.
Sometimes with longing eyes he gazes hard,
And views it boiling in the frothy waves;
Then, with his fork or spoon applied, he feels,
And turns it o'er and o'er. Now time moves slowly on;
The hour-glass, which in yon old corner stands,
Is often view'd; for now his stomach keen,
Gnawing with greedy expectation,
Almost persuades him that the sands are stopp'd.
Now is his table placed near the fire,
His cloth of dingy hue is spread thereon;
His large clasp knife from out his pocket pull'd.
(A knife which oft has dealt destruction dire
To many a pudding, beef, or whate'er else
Came in its way; for none it spar'd;)
The earthen plate which graces his old shelf.

(Which late grimalkin, taking her nightly walks
In search of prey, by dire mishap
Threw down; but, by good care of fortune,
A piece from out the brim is only broke.)
Is straight in order plac'd and all's compleat.
As when the mariner, who, long from home,
Far from his native land, through seas and storms
And dangerous perils, homeward does return;
Sudden he sees the wish'd for port appear,
Joy fills his dancing heart, and now he feeds
His fancy with the pleasing expectation
Of mirth and joy, and heart delighting scenes.
Behold the pot has yielded up its store,
And reeking hot, is placed upon the plate!
The three-legg'd stool is drawn, and down he sits,
Elated with the goodly prospect: sudden
His knife, well plung'd, dreadful incision makes;
And fork, aptly applied, his joys compleat,
Now direful devastation does ensue;
And half the delicious morsel is destroy'd
Ere he can make a pause; which having done,
He smacks his lips, and liking well the sport,
Proceeds again with more deliberation,
Till of the luscious cates he's made an end.
Thus happy he, envying not sumptuous feasts,
Nor courtly entertainments; but well pleas'd,
Feasts on his homely viands; far happier than a king,
He enjoys as full content, without his cares.

—*Anonymous*

Fashion

Hence, loath'd vulgarity,
Of ignorance and native dullness bred,
In low unwholesome shed,
'Mongst thieves and drabs, and street-sweeps asking charity:
Find some suburban haunt,
Where the spruce 'prentice treats his flashy mate,
And smoking cits debate:
Or at a dowdy rout, or ticket-ball,
Giv'n at Freemasons' Hall,
With tawdry clothes and liveries ever flaunt.
But come, thou nymph of slender waist,
Known early by the name of Taste.

* * *

Haste thee, nymph, and bring with thee
Steed, and light-hung Tilbury,
Undiscoverable rouge,
Polish'd boots, and neckcloth huge,
(Such as might deck a Dandy's cheek,
And draw the gazers for a week.)
Mackintosh's racy phrase,
And wit, that peerless Ward might praise.
Come, and let your steps be bent
With a lively measurement,
And bring the proper airs and graces
That make their way in certain places:
And, if I give thee honour due,

Fashion, enroll me with the few,
With Spencer, Sydney Smith, and thee
In a select society:
To ride when many a lady fair in
Her morning veil begins her airing,
And with the nurse and children stow'd
Drives down the Park, or Chelsea road:
Then to stop in spite of sorrow,
And through the window bid good-morrow
Of vis-à-vis, or barouchette,
Or half-open landaulet:
While little Burke, with lively din,
Scatters his stock of trifles thin;
And at the Bridge, or Grosvenor Gate,
Briskly bids his horses wait;
Oft listening how the Catalani
Rouses at night th' applauding many,
In some opera of Mozart,
Winning the eye, the ear, the heart.
Then in the round room not unseen,
Attending dames of noble mien,
Right to the door in Market-lane,
Where chairmen range their jostling train,
And footmen stand with torch alight,
In their thousand liveries dight,
While the doorkeeper on the stairs,
Bawls for the Marchionesses' chairs
And young dragoons enjoy the crowd,
And dowagers inveigh aloud,
And lovers write a hasty scrawl
Upon the ticket of a shawl.
Straight mine eye hath caught new pleasures,
As the circling crowd it measures;
Virgins old with tresses grey,
That in corkscrew curls do stray;
Ladies, on whose softer breast
Gallants receive a hope of rest;
Little feet with sandals tied,
Shallow heads and shoulders wide;
Necks and throats of lovely form,
Bosom'd high in tippet warm,
Where some beauty spreads her snare,
The envy of surrounding fair.
Hard by, the Op'ra being past,
To some small supper let me haste,
Where ladies, wits, and poets met,
Are at their various banquet set,
Of fifty little tempting messes,
Which the neat-handed Gunter dresses:
And there with satisfaction see
The pullet and the early pea,
Or, if the sultry dog-star reign,
The melon ice and cool champagne.
Sometimes, to a late delight
Argyll advertisements invite,
Where the wreathèd waltz goes round,
Or English tunes more briskly sound,
To twice a hundred feet or more,
Dancing on the chalky floor:
And wise mamma, well pleased to see
Her daughter paired with high degree,

Stays till the daylight glares amain:
Then in the carriage home again,
With stories told, of many a bow,
And civil speech from so and so.
She was ask'd to dance, she said,
But scarcely down the middle led,
Because his Lordship only thought
How soonest to find out a spot,
Where, seated by her side, unheard,
He whisper'd many a pretty word,
Such as no poet could excel!
Then, having paid his court so well,
Most manifestly meaning marriage,
He fetch'd the shawls and call'd the carriage,
Handed her from the crowded door
And watch'd till she was seen no more.
Thus done the tales, the flutt'ring fair
Go up to bed, and curl their hair.
Country houses please me too,
And the jocund Christmas crew,
Where chiefs of adverse politics
Awhile in social circle mix,
And tenants come, whose county franchise
Connects them with the higher branches,
Since all the great alike contend
For votes, on which they all depend.
Let Affability be there,
With cordial hand and friendly air,
And private play and glittering fete,
To make the rustic gentry prate,—
Such joys as fill young ladies' heads,
Who judge from books of masquerades.
Then will I to St. Stephen's stray,
If aught be moved by Castlereagh,
Or matchless Canning mean to roll
His thunders o'er the subject soul.
And sometimes, to divert my cares,
Give me some flirt, with joyous airs,
Married a girl, a widow now,
Such as will hear each playful vow,
Too young to lay upon the shelf:
Meaning—as little as myself:—
Still speaking, singing, walking, running,
With wanton heed and giddy cunning,
With a good mien to testify
Her converse with good company,
That Chesterfield might lift his eyes
From the dark Tartarus where he lies,
Beholding, in her air and gait,
Graces that almost compensate
The blunders of his awkward son,
And half the harm his book has done.
These delights if thou canst give,
Fashion, with thee I wish to live.

—*Horace Twiss*

RICHARD CRASHAW
(ca. 1613-1649)

Luke 11: Blessed be the paps
which Thou hast sucked

Suppose he had been Tabled at thy Teats,
Thy hunger feels not what he eats:
He'll have his Teat ere long (a bloody one).
The Mother then must suck the Son.

—*Richard Crashaw*

RICHARD LOVELACE
(1618-1657)

Alibi

Blame me not, Sweet, if here and there
My wayward self inclines
To note that others, too, are fair,
To bow at lesser shrines.

What though with eye or tongue I praise
Iona's gentle wile,
Camilla's happy turn of phrase,
Or Celia's winning smile?

My constancy shall be thy boast
From now to Kingdom Come.
How could I love thee, Dear, the most,
Loved I not others, some?

—*Arthur Guiterman*

ANDREW MARVELL
(1621-1678)

Had I but Strength enough, and time
Thy boldness Lady were no crime.
We would sit down, and think which way
Next to disport us in love's Fray.
But thou, sweet hot impetuous Wench
Hast cull'd cruel lessons from the *French*;
No vast *Atlantick* could produce
Those Tydes thou seek'st of am'rous Juice.
Hi thee to *Lesbos*; there to sport
With Baubles of a sturdier sort,
Whose vibrant Aires fair Nymphs adore.
Cool thus thy Needes: make mine less sore.
E'en yet, wilde Tumult in thine eyes
Calls from soft Ease my Sword to rise,
Who, tristely swathed in *Stygian* Glooms
Anew his nuptial Toil resumes.

—*Charles Robinson*

To His Not-So-Coy Mistress

Time's Wingèd Chariot (poets say)
Warns us to love while yet we may;
Must I not hurry all the more
Who find it parked outside my door?
For those who sipped Love in their prime
Must gulp it down at Closing Time.

—*Wynford Vaughan-Thomas*

ANONYMOUS LYRICS

From *We Greet Each Other in the Side*

We greet each other in the Side
   Of our beloved Spouse,
Which is ordained for his dear Bride
   Her everlasting House.
The Lamb, the Husband of our Hearts,
Hath got, 'tis true, more wounded Parts,
Yet is the bleeding lovely Side
The Chamber of the Bride.

Our Husband's Side-wound is indeed
   The Queen of all his Wounds;
On this the little Pidgeons feed,
   Whom Cross's Air surrounds.
There they fly in and out and sing,
Side's blood is seen on ev'ry wing,
The bill that picks the Side-hole's floor,
Is red of Blood all o'er.

*   *   *

A bird that dives into the Side,
   Goes down quite to the Ground,
And finds a Bottom large and wide
   In this so lovely Wound.
A Side-hole's diver I will be:
O Side-hole! I will sink in thee.
My Soul and Body, enter thou
Into the *Pleura* now.

To live and work and sleep therein,
   I'm heartily inclin'd:
As a poor Dove myself to screen,
   Is my whole heart and mind.
O precious Side-hole's cavity!
I want to spend my Life in thee.
Glory to thee for thy Side-hole,
Dear Husband of my Soul!

With all my heart I bow and bend
   Before thy bleeding Feet:
Yet to thy Side I re-ascend,
   Which is to me most sweet.

There in one Side-hole's Joy divine,
I'll spend all future Days of mine.
Yes, yes, I will forever sit
There, where thy Side was split.

—*Anonymous*

The Line to Heaven by Christ was Made

The Line to heaven by Christ was made
With heavenly truth the Rails are laid,
From Earth to Heaven the Line extends
To Life Eternal where it ends.
Repentance is the Station then
Where Passengers are taken in,
No Fee for them is there to pay.
For Jesus is himself the way.
God's Word is the first Engineer
It points the way to Heaven so dear,
Through tunnels dark and dreary here
It does the way to Glory steer.
God's Love the Fire, his Truth the Steam,
Which drives the Engine and the Train,
All you who would to Glory ride,
Must come to Christ, in him abide
In First and Second, and Third Class,
Repentance, Faith and Holiness,
You must the way to Glory gain
Or you with Christ will not remain.
Come then poor Sinners, now's the time
At any Station on the Line.
If you'll repent and turn from sin
The Train will stop and take you in.

—*Anonymous*

THE RESTORATION AND THE EIGHTEENTH CENTURY (1660-1798)

1660: End of Interragtime. Resurrection of Charles to English throne.
1667: Swift born posthumorously.
1681: W.H. Dryden clothes couplet
1709: Addison and Steele raid bluestockings; "Trial of the Petticoat."
1714: Rape of John Locke.
1733: *Easy on Man.*
1759: Johnson attacks noble sausage; refutes Berkeley by kicking.
1789: Kenneth Burke: *Symbolic Action in a Revolution by the French.*

MORALITY AND MYSTICISM IN RESURRECTION ENGLAND

After Charles II's resurrection to the English throne in 1660, what Eliot has called the "discombobulation of sensibility," which caused Milton to suffer the delusion that his wife had given birth to several "sons of Ben," persisted. The period has been vicariously characterized as one of burlesque marymaking and laxative morality. To some extent this view of Resurrection England, fostered by the sapphires, harpoons, and commodities of the reactionary writers of the Puritan sex, is true. Like any generalization, however, it is only partly true. While the age may have received its moral inspiration from the so-called Low Countries, it produced as well works of high moral seriousness such as Bunyan's *Billy Pilgrim's Progress*, and W.H. Dryden.

Although Dryden was never able to overcome his fidoism (a form of syneschdoggy), he did manage to translate the shy youthful septic system he inherited from the French philanthropist Montaigne into several great mystical essays and to earn Dr. Johnson's approbation as "the father of English mysticism." The father of such English mystics as Ossian (pseudonym for "the marvellous bellbuoy") and Alexander Pepys, Dryden's hours were spent mostly in dreamy revery, which is why he wrote only occasional verse during his lifetime and after his death virtually no verse at all. This is a pity, for it was Dryden, a closet hero and puritan at heart, who was instrumental in fashioning the heroic, or "clothed," couplet for the more delicate sensibilities of the looming Augustinian Age (cf. the *Naked Lunch Poetry* of Stephen Bug).

STYLISTIC ELEMENTS OF THE NEO-CALICIFIED AGE

By the time of his *Easy on Man*, Alexander Pepys had thoroughly renounced the mysticism of "The Old Pretender" (Dryden) for a more balanced, neo-calcified style. Indeed, this was the style of the Augustinian Age, and for the most part it rejected the rhetorical flushies and epic smellies of a Milton (while greatly admiring them) as well as the thorny pair of doxies of such poets as Donne and Carvel. Sobriety, clarity, refinement—these were characteristics valued by the Augustinians. Equally valued were such qualities as wit and judgment, and such fine distinction-making as Pepys's famous one between humor (a shift of wit) and odor. However, it would be a mistake to characterize the age too strictly as one of narrow decorum and portable propriety. It does us well to keep in mind that Pepys, author of "The Rape of John Locke" and the high priest of reason, was a baseball fan and immortalized the sport in his Homer. Similarly, although the official religion of the eighteenth century was Dadaism (the belief that God is a watchmaker for the Papal Bulova), religious enthusiasts such as Charles and Wesley Unseld thrilled at Pepys's prediction of a "nature Methodized." In other words, while eighteenth-century social behavior may have been dominated by good horse-sense, prior-restraint, and reasonableness, we should not forget its undercurrent of passion and high spirits, best typified by Addison's and Steele's famous periodical assays into the London coffeehouses in pursuit of the bluestockings, garters, and pantisocrates of the Countess Winchilsea and Lady Mary Wartly Montagu (the "coy mattress" of Swift's "A Modest Proposal").

EXCEPTIONS TO RULE: THE NOBLE SAUSAGE

Indeed, nothing illustrates more dramatically the emotional antipathy against prescriptive laws and rules than Dr. Johnson's epistolary love for Lady Mary Montagu, vividly documented in his *Idler Letters*, the preambler of his scatalogical *Tatler Tales*. One gets a flavor of the high passion of the correspondence in Dr. Johnson's "Expectations of Pleasure," in which Johnson attacks the "noble sausage" of his rival, Swift:

> Poor Sausage! I have often teased him with reproof,
> and he has often promised reformation: for no man
> is so much open to conviction as this Idler, but
> there is none on whom it operates so little. What will
> be the effect of this paper I know not: perhaps he
> will read it and laugh, and light the fire in my furnace;
> but my hope is that he will quit his truffles, and
> betake himself to rational and useful diligence.

Likewise, Johnson despised such sentimentalists as Bishop Berkeley (one of the three Unitarians), whom he refuted by kicking. When physical violence proved useless against these sesquipedalians (defined in Boswell's *Dictionary*) Johnson wrote his *The Life of Richard Sausage*, a verse sapphire in his Juvenile mode, which put an end, finally, to eighteenth-century notions of the inherited gooeyness of man.

It is perhaps ironic that while nineteenth-century critics seemed opposed—nay, hostile—to Johnson's work (Arnold called him "no man but a blackhead"), such modern critics as Andrew Jackson Bait of Harvard have led a continuing argument in favor of awarding Johnson a real doctorate.

HEAVY TRAFFIC IN MOCKERY

Although it is true that eighteenth-century man sometimes rebelled against laws and rules, it would be a mistake to characterize the age chiefly as one of "not poetry, but passion run mad," as Pepys did, or of "unbridled chastity and unabashed continence," as did the critic Charles Manson Myers. One needs only to examine the career of Jonathan Swift to disabuse oneself of that misunderstanding. Born a posthumorous child, Jonathan Swift quickly developed the same lack of a sense of humor that plagued the poets of the period following the Interragtime. William Butler Keats's deaf trimeter couplet, "We/Terrific in mockery" (addressed to the fierce Quaker of *The Endymion Review*), seems to sum up the dour septicsystem of such poets as the early Dryden, as well as of Pepys, Johnson, and Swift, that no hero but was a mock hero; no epic but was a mock epic. (Hence Dryden's closet heroism, first exposed by the pasture poet Titus Oates. Hence also the paucity of serious epochs in the century.)

While it may be overstating the case somewhat to call these men "misogymnasts" (haters of all forms of physical education in schools), critics are nevertheless right in accusing Swift (as they accuse Johnson) of sausage misanthropy. Swift, too, distrusted the sentimental notions of the gooeyness of man. For Swift, Pepys's idea of man as a rational animal ("enema rationale") was a misnorman; man was merely *capable* of reason ("enema rationis capon"). This distinction is powerfully illustrated in Swift's two early masterpieces on sailing and finance, *A Tale of a Tub* and *The Battle of the Bucks*. Later works, completed before Johnson accused Swift of deafness and infirmity, are *Gulag's Travels* and *The Gulliver Archipelago*, formidable denunciations not only of whole political systems but also of the failure of mankind to come up to the standards of the human race. This dispiriting human race, Swift thought, could best be run not by "Yoohoos" but by prototypes of the Dickensian quadruped, "Houyhnhymns" possessed of a kind of divine horsesense. Alas, like so many of Swift's proposals for the improvement of the human condition, this one failed, and Swift, in whom misogymnasticism had spawned the fiercest indignation against the "flatballers" (football players) and "roundballers" (basketball players), expired himself "a dribbler and a show."

JOHN DRYDEN
(1631-1700)

Oyster-crabs

Three viands in three different courses served,
Received the commendation they deserved.
The first in succulence all else surpassed;
The next in flavor; and in both, the last.
For Nature's forces could no further go;
To make the third, she joined the other two.

—*Carolyn Wells*

The Town Mouse and the Country Mouse

A milk-white Mouse *immortal and unchang'd,*
Fed on soft Cheese, and o're the Dairy *rang'd;*
Without, unspotted; innocent within,
She fear'd no danger, for she knew no Ginn.
Yet had She oft been scar'd by bloody Claws
Of *winged* Owls, and stern *Grimalkins* Paws
Aim'd at her destin'd Head, which made her *fly,*
Tho She was *doom'd to Death*, and *fated not to dye.*
Not so her young; their Linsy-woolsy *line,*
Was Hero's make, half humane, half Divine.
Of these a slaughter'd Army lay in Blood,
Whose sanguine Seed encreas'd the sacred Brood;
She multipli'd by these, *now rang'd alone,*
And wander'd in the Kingdoms once her own.
The common Hunt, She timorously past by,
For they made tame, *disdain'd Her company;*
They grin'd, She in a fright *tript* o're the Green,
For She was *lov'd,* whereever She was *seen.*
The Independent Beast.——
——*In groans Her hate exprest.*
She thought, and reason good, the *quaking Hare*
Her cruel Foe, because *She would not swear,*
And had *profess'd neutrality.*
Next Her, the Buffoon Ape his body *bent,*
And paid at Church a Courtier's complement.
The brisl'd Baptist *Boar, impure as he.*
Was whiten'd with the foam of Sanctity.
The Wolf with Belly-gaunt his rough crest rears,
And pricks up his predestinating Ears.
These fiery Zuinglius, *meagre* Calvin *bred.*
Or else reforming *Corah* spawn'd *this Class,*
When opening Earth made way for all to pass.
The Fox and he came shuffled in the dark,
If ever they were stow'd in Noah's *Ark.*
Quickened with Fire below, these Monsters breed
In Fenny Holland, *and in Fruitful* Tweed.
The Divine Blacksmith *in th' Abyss of Light,*
Yawning and lolling *with a careless beat,*
Struck out the mute Creation at a Heat.
But he work'd hard to Hammer out our Souls,
He blew the Bellows, and stir'd up the Coals;
Long time he thought, and could not on a sudden
Knead up with unskim'd *Milk* this Reas'ning Pudding:
Tender, and mild within its Bag it lay

Confessing still the softness of its Clay,
And kind as Milk-Maids on their Wedding-Day.
Till *Pride of Empire, Lust,* and hot Desire
Did over-boile him, like too great a Fire,
And understanding grown, *misunderstood,*
Burn'd Him to th' Pot, and sour'd his curdled Blood.
A *spotted* Mouse, the prettiest next the White,
Ah! were her Spots wash'd out, as pretty quite,
With *Phylacteries* on her Forehead spred,
Crozier in Hand, and *Miter* on her Head.
Three Steeples Argent on her Sable Shield,
Liv'd in the *City,* and disdain'd the *Field.*
This Princess tho *estrang'd* from what was *best,*
Was least Deform'd, because Reform'd the least.
She in a Masquerade of Mirth and Love,
Mistook the Bliss of Heaven for Bacchanals above,
And grub'd the Thorns *beneath our tender Feet,*
To make the Paths of Paradise more sweet.
She——
Humbly content to be despis'd at Home,
Which is too narrow Infamy for some.
Whose Merits are diffus'd from Pole to Pole,
Where Winds can carry, and where Waves can rowl.
One Evening, when she went away from Court,
Levee's and Couchee's past without resort.
She met the Country Mouse, whose *fearful Face*
Beheld from far the common watering Place,
Nor durst approach, till with an awful Roar
The Soveraign Lyon bad her fear no more.
But when she had this sweetest Mouse *in view,*
Good *Lord, how she admir'd her Heavenly Hiew!*
Th' Immortal Mouse, who saw the *Viceroy* come
So far to see Her, did invite her Home.
To smoak a Pipe, and o're a sober Pot
Discourse of *Oates* and *Bedloe,* and the *Plot.*
She made a Court'sy, like a Civil Dame,
And, being *much a Gentlewoman,* came.
Dame, said the Lady of the Spotted Muff,
Methinks your Tiff is sour, your *Cates* meer stuff.
Your Pipe's so foul, that I disdain to smoak;
And the Weed worse than e'er *Tom. I—s took.*
Leave, leave this hoary *Shed* and lonely Hills,
And eat with me at *Groleau's*, smoak at *Will's.*
What Wretch would nibble on a Hanging-shelf,
When at *Pontack's* he may *Regale* himself?
Or to the House of cleanly *Renish* go;
Or that at *Charing-Cross,* or that in *Channel-Row?*
Come, at a Crown a Head our selves we'll treat,
Champain our Liquor, and *Ragousts* our Meat.
Then hand in hand we'll go to *Court,* dear *Cuz,*
To visit *Bishop Martin,* and *King Buz.*
With *Evening Wheels* we'll drive about the *Park,*
Finish at *Locket's,* and reel home i'th' Dark.
Break clattering Windows, and demolish Doors
Of English Manufactures—Pimps, and Whores.
With these Allurements *Spotted* did invite
From *Hermits Cell,* the *Female Proselyte.*
Oh! with what ease we follow such a Guide,
Where Souls are starv'd, and Senses gratifi'd.
But here the *White,* by *observation wise,*
Who long on Heaven had fixt her prying *Eyes,*

With thoughtful Countenance, and grave Remark,
Said, or my Judgment fails me, or 'tis dark.
Lest therefore we should stray, and not go right,
Through the *brown horrour* of the starless Night.
Hast thou *Infallibility, that Wight?*
Sternly the Savage grin'd, and thus reply'd:
That Mice may err, was never yet deny'd.
That I deny, said the immortal Dame,
There is a Guide—Gad I've forgot his Name,
Who lives in *Heaven or Rome,* the Lord knows where,
Had we but him, Sweet-heart, we could not err.
But heark you, Sister, this is but a Whim;
For still we want a *Guide* to find out Him.
What need we find Him? we have certain proof
That he is somewhere, *Dame,* and that's enough:
For if there is a *Guide* that knows the way,
Although we know not him, we cannot stray.
As though 'tis controverted in the *School,*
If *Waters* pass by *Urine* or by *Stool.*
Shall we who are *Philosophers,* thence gather
From this dissention that they work by neither.
All this I did, your Arguments to try.
Hear, and be dumb, thou Wretch, *that Guide am I.*
Come leave your Cracking tricks, and as they say,
Use not, that Barber that trims time, delay
I've Eyes as well as you to find the way.
Then on they jogg'd, *and since an hour of talk*
Might cut a Banter *on the tedious walk;*
As I remember said the sober Mouse,
I've heard much talk of the *Wits Coffee-House.*
Thither, says *Brindle,* thou shalt go, and see
Priests sipping *Coffee, Sparks* and *Poets Tea;*
Here rugged Freeze, there Quality well drest,
These bafling the *Grand-Seigniour;* those the *Test.*
And hear shrew'd guesses made, and reasons given,
That humane Laws were never made in Heaven.
But above all, what shall oblige thy sight,
And fill thy Eye-Balls with a vast delight;
Is the *Poetic Judge* of sacred *Wit,*
Who do's i' th' *Darkness of his Glory sit.*
And as the Moon who first receives the light,
With which she makes these neither Regions bright;
So does he shine, reflecting from a far,
The Rayes he borrow'd from a better Star:
For rules which from *Corneille* and *Rapin* flow,
Admir'd by all the scribling Herd below,
From *French Tradition* while he does dispence,
Unerring Truths, 'tis Schism, a damn'd offence,
To question his, or trust your private sense.
But now at *Peccadille* they arrive,
And taking Coach, t'wards *Temple-Bar* they drive;
But at St. *Clement's Church,* eat out the Back;
And slipping through the *Palsgrave,* bilkt poor *Hack.*
Thence to the *Devil,* and ask'd if *Chanticleer,*
Of Clergy kind, or Councellour *Chough* was there;
Or Mr. *Dove,* a Pigeon of Renown,
By his high crop, and corny Gizzard known,
Or Sister Partlet, *with the Hooded head;*
No, Sir. She's *hooted hence,* said *Will,* and fled.
Why so? *Because she would not pray a-Bed.*

Thus to the place where *Johnson* sat we climb,
Leaning on the same Rail that guided him;
And whilst we thus on equal helps rely,
Our Wit must be as true, our thoughts as high.
For as an *Author* happily compares
Tradition to a well-fixt pair of *Stairs,*
So this the *Scala Sancta* we believe,
By which his *Traditive Genius* we receive.
Thus every step I take my Spirits soar,
And I grow more a *Wit,* and more, and more.
E'er that *Gazet* was printed, said the *White,*
Our Robin told another story quite;
This *Oral Truth* more safely I believ'd,
My Ears cannot, your Eyes may be deceiv'd.
By word of Mouth unerring Maxims flow,
And *Preaching's* best, if understood, or no.
Words I confess *bound by, and trip so light,*
We have not time to take a steady sight;
Yet fleeting thus are plainer then when Writ,
To long Examination they submit.
Hard things at the first Blush are clear and full,
God mends on second thoughts, but Man grows dull.
Thus did they merrily carouse all day,
And, like the gaudy fly, their Wings display;
And sip the sweets, and bask in great Apollo's *ray.*
Sirrah, says *Brindle,* thou hast brought us Wine,
Sour to my tast, and to my Eyes unfine.
Says *Will,* all *Gentlemen* like it, ah! says *White,*
What is approv'd by them, must needs be right.
'Tis true, I thought it bad, but if the House
Commend it, I submit, a private Mouse.
Nor to their *Catholic* consent oppose
My erring Judgment, and reforming Nose.
Why, what a Devil, shan't I trust my Eyes?
Must I drink *Stum* because the *Rascal* lyes?
And palms upon us *Catholic* consent,
To give *sophisticated Brewings* vent.
Says *White,* What ancient Evidence can sway,
If you must Argue thus and not obey?
Drawers must be trusted, through whose hands convey'd,
You take the *Liquor,* or you spoil the *Trade.*
For sure those *Honest Fellows* have no knack,
Of putting off *stum'd Claret* for *Pontack.*
How long, alas! would the poor Vintner last,
If all that drink must *judge,* and every *Guest*
Be allowed to have an understanding *Tast?*
Thus she: Nor could the Panther well inlarge,
With weak defence, against so strong a Charge.
But with a *weary Yawn,* that shew'd her pride,
Said, *Spotless* was a *Villain,* and she *lyed.*
White saw her *canker'd Malice* at that word,
And said her Prayers, and drew her *Delphic Sword.*
T'other cry'd *Murther,* and her *Rage restrain'd:*
And thus her passive Character maintain'd.
But now, alas, I grieve, I grieve to tell
What sad mischance these pretty things *befel*
These Birds of Beasts, these learned Reas'ning Mice,
Were separated, banish'd in a trice.
Who would be learned for their sakes, who wise?
The *Constable* alarm'd by this noise,
Enter'd the Room, directed by the voice,

And speaking to the *Watch, with head aside,*
Said, Desperate Cures must be to desperate Ills apply'd.
These *Gentlemen,* for so their Fate decrees,
Can n'ere enjoy at once the *But and Peace.*
When each have separate Interests of their own,
Two Mice are one too many for a Town.
By *Schism* they are torn; and therefore, *Brother,*
Look you to one, and I'll secure the t'other.
Now whither *Dapple* did to *Bridewell* go,
Or in the *Stocks* all night her Fingers blow,
Or in the *Compter* lay, concerns not us to know.
But the *immortal Matron, spotless White,*
Forgetting *Dapple's* Rudeness, Malice, Spight,
Look'd kindly back, and wept, and said, *Good Night.*
Ten thousand Watchmen waited on this Mouse,
With Bills, and Halberds, to her Country-House.

—*Matthew Prior*

All Human Things

All human things are subject to decay:
When Fate compels, meek Furrytales obey.
Now cruel Fate has caught in his/her net
Two loves, whose memory lovers cherish yet,
(And keep tear-sprinkled, in two pots of gold,
By potted ghosts of Thisbe and Isolde).
Banality! Withdraw thy dishpan hand
From too-romantic Photo-Furryland;
Spare, dismal daughter/son of the Middle Class,
This dashing lad, this short but noble lass;
Let Grub-Street gossip dip empathic pens
In tears; let tears blur every photo lens,
And tint the prints with rose, that all can see
Not Truth, but Beauty's slick facsimile,
More rare than real, making the most of least,
To render tragic what is merely *triste.*

—*Peter Schroeder*

JOHN WILMOT, SECOND EARL OF ROCHESTER
(1647-1680)

From Oppian's *Halieuticks*

When pleasing Heat, and fragrant Blooms inspire
Soft leering Looks, kind Thoughts and gay Desire,
Love runs thro' All; the feather'd Wantons play,
Seek out their Mates, and bill on ev'ry Spray.
The savage Kinds a softer Rage express,
And gloating Eyes the secret Flame confess.
But none like Fishes feel the dear Disease;
For *Venus* doubly warms her native Seas.
Males unconcern'd their pleasing Loves repeat,
While anxious She's the ripen'd Birth compleat.
On sandy Mounds their pressing Bellies lay,
And force the Burden of the Womb away.
Close joyn'd the complicated Eggs remain;
To separate that Heap is racking Pain.

Complain no more, ye Fair, of partial Fate,
What Sorrows on the teeming Bride await.
The Female-Curse is not to Earth confin'd
Severest Throws the Fishes Wombs unbind;
Lucina is alike to All unkind.
Now when the vernal Breeze has purg'd the Air
To ev'ry Shore the vig'rous Males repair;
By Fear compell'd, or Appetite inclin'd,
To chase the weak, or fly the stronger Kind:
Nor will the am'rous Females stay behind:
No Fears or Dangers can the Bliss prevent,
When urg'd by Love, and on the Joy intent,
They still importunate their Suit renew,
And obstinately kind extort their Due.
Their Bodies meet, the close Embraces please,
Till mingled Slime lies floating on the Seas:
The She's gulp greedy down the tepid Seed,
And fruitful from the strange Conception breed.
Hence the succeeding Colonies increase,
And new-spawn'd Tribes replenish all the Seas.
But some no lawless Liberties allow;
Whose Brides confin'd their private Chambers know.
In close Retreat they guard th'imprison'd Fair,
Observe their Haunt, and watch with jealous Care
Lest some false Leman should invade their Right.
And wanton glory in the stol'n Delight.
All Things obey, when softer Passions move,
But Fishes feel the keenest Rage of Love.

* * *

Strange the Formation of the *Eely* Race,
That know no Sex, yet love the close Embrace.
Their folded Lengths they round each other twine
Twist am'rous Knots, and slimy Bodies joyn;
Till the close strife brings off a frothy Juice,
The Seed that must the wriggling Kind produce.
Regardless They their future Offspring leave,
But porous Sands the spumy Drops receive.
That genial Bed impregnates all the Heap,
And little *Eelets* soon begin to creep.
Half-Fish, Half-Slime they try their doubtful strength,
And slowly trail along their wormy Length.
What great Effects from slender Causes flow!

—*William Diaper*

JONATHAN SWIFT
(1667-1745)

Boy! Bring An Ounce

Boy! bring an ounce of Freeman's best,
And bid the vicar be my guest:
Let all be plac'd in manner due,
A pot, wherein to spit, or spue,
And *London Journal,* and *Free Briton,*
Of use to light a pipe or—

* * *

This village, unmolested yet
By troopers, shall be my retreat:
Who cannot flatter, bribe, betray;
Who cannot write or vote for pay.
Far from the vermin of the town,
Here let me rather live, my own,
Doze o'er a pipe, whose vapour bland
In sweet oblivion lulls the land;
Of all, which at Vienna passes,
As ignorant as — Brass is:
And scorning rascals to caress,
Extol the days of good Queen Bess,
When first TOBACCO blest our Isle,
Then think of other queens—and smile.

Come jovial pipe, and bring along
Midnight revelry and song;
The merry catch, the madrigal,
That echoes sweet in City Hall;
The parson's pun, the smutty tale
Of country justice, o'er his ale.
I ask not what the French are doing,
Or Spain to compass ———'s ruin:
  Britons, if undone, can go,
  Where TOBACCO loves to grow.

—Isaac Hawkins Browne

The Happy Life of a Country Parson

Parson, these things in thy possessing
Are better than the bishop's blessing:
A wife that makes conserves; a steed
That carries double when there's need;
October store, and best Virginia,
Tithe-pig, and mortuary guinea;
Gazettes sent gratis down, and frank'd;
For which thy patron's meekly thank'd;
A large Concordance, bound long since;
Sermons to Charles the First, when Prince;
A chronicle of ancient standing;
A Chrysostom to smooth thy band in;
The Polyglott—three parts—my text:
Howbeit,—likewise—now to my next:
Lo here the Septuagint,—and Paul,
To sum the whole,—and close of all.
He that has these, may pass his life,
Drink with the Squire, and kiss his wife;
On Sundays preach, and eat his fill;
And fast on Fridays—if he will;
Toast Church and Queen, explain the news,
Talk with churchwardens about pews,
Pray heartily for some new gift,
And shake his head at Doctor Swift.

—Alexander Pope

ALEXANDER POPE
(1688-1744)

Blest Leaf

Blest Leaf! whose aromatic gales dispense
To Templars modesty, to parsons sense:
So raptur'd priests, at fam'd Dodona's shrine
Drank inspiration from the steam divine.
Poison that cures, a vapour that affords
Content, more solid than the smile of lords:
Rest to the weary, to the hungry food,
The last kind refuge of the wise and good:
Inspir'd by thee, dull cits adjust the scale
Of Europe's peace, when other statesmen fail.
By thee protected, and thy sister, beer,
Poets rejoice, nor think the bailiff near.
Nor less, the critic owns thy genial aid,
While supperless he plies the piddling trade.
What tho' to love and soft delights a foe,
By ladies hated, hated by the beau,
Yet social feeedom, long to courts unknown,
Fair health, fair truth, and virtue are thy own.
Come to thy poet, come with healing wings,
And let me taste thee unexcis'd by kings.

—*Isaac Hawkins Browne*

Inebriety

The mighty spirit, and its power, which stains
The bloodless cheek, and vivifies the brains,
I sing. Say, ye, its fiery vot'ries true,
The jovial curate, and the shrill-tongued shrew,
Ye, in the floods of limpid poison nurst,
Where bowl the second charms like bowl the first;
Say how, and why, the sparkling ill is shed,
The heart which hardens, and which rules the head....
Lo! the poor toper whose untutor'd sense,
Sees bliss in ale, and can with wine dispense;
Whose head proud fancy never taught to steer,
Beyond the muddy ecstasies of beer;
But simple nature can her longing quench,
Behind the settle's curve, or humbler bench:
Some kitchen fire diffusing warmth around,
The semi-globe by hieroglyphics crown'd;
Where canvas purse displays the brass enroll'd,
Nor waiters rave, nor landlords thirst for gold;
Ale and content his fancy's bounds confine,
He asks no limpid punch, no rosy wine;
But sees, admitted to an equal share,
Each faithful swain the heady potion bear:
Go wiser thou! and in thy scale of taste,
Weigh gout and gravel against ale and rest;
Call vulgar palates what thou judgest so;
Say beer is heavy, windy, cold, and slow;
Laugh at poor sots with insolent pretence,
Yet cry, when tortured, where is Providence?

—*George Crabbe*

From DUNCIAD MINOR

Book V

Now Muse assist me, aptly to describe
Mechanic contests of the Critic tribe;
Choose but condign exemplars for my song,
Lest, like themselves, I explicate too long;
Let me shed light on things both dark and dense
Yet never move them into common sense.[1]

First of the few for whom the Muse finds space,
See Wilson Knight advance and take his place.
A Double Boiler fixed on fiery wheels,[2]
Hisses hysteric or ecstatic squeals;
He takes a play, *The Tempest,* from his poke,
Kisses the boards and drops it in the smoke.
The smoke redoubles and the cauldron roars;
At length he turns a cock and out there pours
The play—Ah, no! it cannot be the play
To myth and symbolism[3] boiled away;
Where are the plot, the actors and the stage?
These are irrelevant, explains the sage;
Damn action[4] and discourse: The play's no more
Than drifts of an extended metaphor
Did simple Shakespeare think: 'The play's the thing'?
What Shakespeare thought is hustled from the ring.
He's shouted down: 'Fallacious by intent';[5]
Critics repudiate what the author meant.
Is *Lear* the story of a King? Ah, no,
A tract on clothing and what lurks below.
Well, but the audience came to see men act
And not to hear a philosophic tract?[6]
Wrong once again, my friend: we won't admit
That many-headed monster[7] of the pit,
Who think *The Tempest* tell a tale perhaps
And not a long-drawn metaphor, poor chaps;
In three short hours how could *they* hope to judge
What takes a critic twenty years of drudge?
But who would write a play with this in view?
That only proves that Shakespeare scorned them too.
A sovereign critic is a mighty god;[8]
Author and audience vanish at his nod;
He takes the poet's place, re-weaves the spell,
And is its only audience as well.

Scarce had the Goddess viewed this weird machine,
When envious Leavis thrusts himself between;

1. Our author here recalls the sublime invocation of Milton's Muse, *Paradise Lost,* Book VII, 1-39 (A.P.)
2. Why fiery wheels, son? (A.P.) A reference, grandad, to a work by this author, *The Wheel of Fire.* (A.A.P.)
3. myth and symbolism... extended metaphor: *The Tempest* will be found peculiarly poor in metaphor. There is less need for it in that the play itself is a metaphor. (Wilson Knight, *The Crown of Life*) (A.A.P.)
4. See Pope, *Epistle to Augustus,* 314-15:
   The Play stands still; damn action and discourse,
   Back fly the scenes, and enter foot and horse...
5. Fallacious by intent: see Wimsatt and Beardsley, *The Intentional Fallacy* (1946). Did they really hold this monstrous opinion, son? (A.P.)
   No, grandad, to give them their due. But they launched the idea. (A.A.P.)
6. See Robert Heilman, 'Poor Naked Wretches and Proud Array', in *This Great Stage* (1948).
7. many-headed monster: see Pope, *Epistle to Augustus,* 304-5:
   There still remains to mortify a Wit,
   The many-headed Monster of the Pit. (A.P.)
   On the same side, but very cautious, see Cleanth Brooks: *The Formalist Critic.* (A.A.P.)
8. Marlowe, *Dr. Faustus,* sc. I, 61
   A sound magician is a demi-god...

Cries: 'What, infringe my patent, thievish swine!
The "extended metaphor" conceit is mine,
Mine the "dramatic poem" device, I say,
By which I demonstrate a play's no play.
Ignore him, Goddess; turn those eyes divine
From Wilson's shandrydan and gaze on mine!
In shining nickel and unblushing brass
Streamlined to make a genius seem an ass,
Reverse the judgment of the centuries,
Make and unmake Tradition as I please,[9]
Exalt the lowly and put down the great.
Observe now while I prestidigitate!'

So saying he thrusts great Fielding[1] in his pot
And in beside him tumbles Walter Scott;
Pours in some gallons of high-octane spleen;
Fiddles and draws a belch from the machine;
Hey Presto! From a trap-door there escape
A hunch-back pigmy and a crippled ape.
'Behold my triumph, Queen!', the critic cries,
'My metamorphoses confound all eyes.
Can this be Fielding whom they knew immense
For wit and charity and common sense?
No, a mere tyro—take a second view—
From whom Jane Austen learned a trick or two.
Can this be Scott, then, whose magician's quill
Delighted Europe and delights it still?
Not so! Look once again: my art unveils
A dabbler in romance and old wives' tales.'
At this the Goddess smiles and nods her head:
'Who then, dear son, would you exalt instead?'
'Observe, great Matriarch,' her son replies,
'This mannikin, the sport of wasps and flies,[2]
Peevish and arrogant, he vents a flood
Of words which he calls "thinking with the blood";
With generous Fielding, or with noble Scott
Compared, he shrinks and dwindles and is not.
And now—watch carefully—in my machine
I place him; add some drops of wintergreen,
A pinch of scrutiny, a touch of gall,
And D.H. Lawrence towers over all.'

There was a moment's silence then a howl
Of jealous rivals: 'Out! A Foul! A Foul!'
The Goddess pursed her lips and then she smiled:
'Such stratagems would not deceive a child,
Remove these baubles; let the Games proceed
And bring me critics of a sterner breed.'

Next from the ranks comes clucking T.R. Henn
Attended by a train of faceless men;
And at his side, in female garb, there move
Caroline Spurgeon, Rosamunda Tuve;

9. See the cavalier treatment of Scott and Fielding in F.R. Leavis, *The Great Tradition* (1948).

1. See *The Great Tradition*: 'Fielding... hasn't the classical importance we are... invited to credit him with. He is important... because he leads to Jane Austen to appreciate whose distinction is to feel that life isn't long enough to permit of one's giving much time to Fielding.'

'Scott was primarily a kind of inspired folk-lorist, qualified to have done in fiction something analogous to the ballad-opera... not having the creative writer's interest in literature, he made no serious attempt to work out his own form and break away from the bad tradition of the eighteenth century romance.'

Who made this mad Jack a judge in Israel, son? (A.P.)

Self-made! (A.A.P.)

2. What is this, grandad? (A.A.P.)

Our author, son, is thinking of Gulliver's adventure with the wasps in Brobdignag. (A.P.)

Blest pair of Sirens,[3] dredges of Heav'n's joy,
His mother and his aunt, their charms employ
To prove, though art is long and life is short
That Drake and Shakespeare shared a favourite sport
And demonstrate *ad nauseam*[4] the way
By Tudor rhetoric to build a play.
(Read them, alas, discover to your cost:
The proof's irrelevant; the play is lost.)
These chicks, for mighty Henn, who stalks between,
Push forward an ingenious machine
As full of pigeon-holes, as bare of birds
As those the Record Office stuffs with words.
Great Henn dismisses them, affects to nod,[5]
Selects a poet and assumes the god.

'You call on us, great Queen, and not in vain.
Ours is a subtler, more insidious strain.
Ours not to denigrate, pervert, deny
Or puff inferior scribblers to the sky;
Patient and meek, we seize on honest worth
And, like the meek, inheriting the earth,
We take them over, make them ours perforce,
Trace every image to its remotest source,
Load it with analogues, gild, trick and frost;
Meaning runs into meaning and is lost;
We read between the lines and read again
Between those lines inserted by our pen;
Add statues, pictures, junk and bric-à-brac
Until the poem's fabric starts to crack
And trick the guileless reader to believe
We still have something further up our sleeve,
Without which, though now driven to the wall,
He cannot understand the poem at all.
Faced with this parasitic mould indeed,
Readers, intimidated, cease to read.
The pleasure of discovery denied,
No corner left where mystery may hide;
And even the simplest poem seems obscure
When every root's confused with its manure.
Come, here's a poem of William Butler Yeats:[6]
This simple thing my genius recreates;
Processed and pulped in my machine, it grows
To fifty pages of inspissate prose.
It is my boast, dear Mother, by this trick
To have found him marble and have left him brick.[7]
Now watch me, Goddess, to confirm my claim,
Take Shakespeare next and treat him much the same.'

3. See Milton, *At a Solemn Musick*, 1-2:
Blest pair of *Sirens*, pledges of Heav'n's joy
Sphear-born harmonious Sisters, Voice and Vers. (A.P.)

4. sport...*ad nauseam:* a fine example of two opposite kinds of irrelevance in the same school of criticism, grandad. Caroline Spurgeon, *Shakespeare's Imagery and What it Tells Us*: 'of all the exercises Shakespeare mentions—tennis, football, bowls, fencing, tilting, wrestling—there can be no doubt that bowls was the one he himself played and loved the best. He has nineteen images from bowls beside other references. (A.A.P.)

He has more references to fornication, son; does this prove him a fornicator? (A.P.)

Rosamund Tuve, *Elizabethan Imagery*. (A.A.P.)

No quotation, son? (A.P.)

Not from *me*, grandad. (A.A.P.)

5. So Alexander the Great in Dryden's *Alexander's Feast or the Power of Musique*:
A present Deity, they shout around
A present Deity, the vaulted Roofs resound.
With ravish't ears
The monarch hears,
Assumes the God,
Affects to nod,
And seems to shake the Spheares. (A.P.)

6. What is this about, son? (A.P.)

T.R. Henn, *The Lonely Tower: Studies in the poetry of W.B. Yeats*, grandad, a signal example of the Infinite Regress School of Explication. (A.A.P.)

7. So Sutonius of Augustus: 'Urbem...excoluit adeo, ut iure sit gloriatus marmoream se relinquere, quam latericam accepisset.' (A.P.)

Thus far he spoke, when rose a general shout:
In rushed a psychoanalytic rout;
Machines they pushed of every shape and size
That mind or myth or madness could devise.[8]
Before them, rattling Shakespeare's honoured bones,
Lumbers the burly form of Ernest Jones:
'Have done with literary chit and chat!
What, Bullough come again?[9] No more of that!
Ur-Hamlets? Fudge! Old Saxo? Tush and Pish!
Castration Fantasies, the dark Death Wish,
Oedipus Complex, narcissistic blocks:
This Key[1] and this alone his heart unlocks.
As for esthetic theories, save your breath!
Topsoil at most; the pay-dirt lurks beneath;
Learn that all literature is fantasy,
All art, Neurosis which you cannot see.[2]
The endless carping of the Leavisites,
Chatter of Cleanth Brooks and L.C. Knights,
What underlies their cultural debate?
A secret wish their fathers to castrate!
And as for Henn's Compulsive Ritual,
Anal Fixation will explain it all.
See, Goddess, see: their fictions I destroy!

Come, where is Herbert Read,[3] my whipping boy?
Wheel me that Viennese contraption there!
Now fetch me *Hamlet*—handle him with care—
Now press this button and let in your clutch:
The play which Shakespeare wrote in Double Dutch,
Which lay dissolved in endless Wilson Knight,[4]
Behold! Let Freud appear and all is light!
Was Hamlet mad or indecisive? Come,
He simply longed to go to bed with Mum;
And so did Shakespeare: "to avoid worse rape",[5]
He found this mechanism of escape.
Good-night, Sweet Prince; to dream, perchance to skid
Between your Super-ego and your Id!'

He ceased. While hate and hubbub flew around,
The critics gnashed their teeth; the Goddess frowned:
'Your scheme, as far as I can make it out,
Destroys my foes, and yet I stand in doubt.
I read your heart, sir; in that heart I see
A sly, libidinous design on *me*,
Your mother and your queen. That purpose is
To deal with me as Oedipus with his.
Presumptuous slave!' . . . A shriek arrests her tongue
And furious Maud comes striding through the throng:

8. So Dryden, *Absalom and Achitophel*:
Gods they had tried of every shape and size
That God-smiths could produce or Priests devise. (A.P.)

9. Bullough come again?: our author here, grandad, refers to the learned Geoffry Bullough's *Narrative and Dramatic Sources of Shakespeare*, a work in innumerable volumes and millions of words. There is also a hint at this critic's place among his peers in the echo from Byron, *The Vision of Judgment*, stanza 93:
The Monarch, mute till then, exclaimed: 'What! What!
Pye come again? No more—no more of that!'

1. Key: Wordsworth, *Miscellaneous Sonnets*, part II, i:
with this key
Shakespeare unlocked his heart.

2. So Pope, *An Essay on Man*, I, 289 90:
All Nature is but Art unknown to thee;
All Chance direction which thou canst not see . . . (A.P.)

3. Herbert Read: our author refers to an essay, 'Psycho-analysis and Criticism', in this critic's *Reason and Romanticism*. (1926). (A.A.P.)

4. dissolved . . . in Knight: so Pope, *Epitaph Intended for Sir Isaac Newton*:
Nature, and Nature's Laws lay hid in Night
God said, *Let Newton* be! and all was *Light*.

5. So Milton, *Paradise Lost*, I, 503-5:
Witness the streets of Sodom, and that night
In Gibeah, when the hospitable door
Expos'd a Matron to avoid worse rape.

'Jung, Mother Jung's the name to conjure with!
Poems are simply archetypal myth;
Poets, blind mouths through which Old Chaos streams;
And Racial Memory dictates their dreams.
A woman to a woman, hear my cry:
As I am Bodkin, let this traitor die!'
She spoke and with her weapon pierced him through.
While consternation seized the manly crew,
The Amazon bestrides the corpse of Jones,
Splits up his hide and extricates the bones,
Smears them with unguent from a shaman's pot
And Jones becomes the thing that he was not.
Reclothed with flesh, though stricken well in years,
An Ancient Mariner he now appears;
An albatross about his neck is hung;
He sings a Vedic hymn[6] and calls on Jung!
The Goddess smiles: the critics all applaud:
'Behold a Rebirth Archetype!' cries Maud.[7]
A New Medea, she towers to the skies
And stands in expectation of the prize.

Just then a form of more plebeian mould
Cries in stentorian tones: 'Hold, Goddess, hold!
Beware the muddles of the bourgeoisie;
For genuine muddle listen first to me!'
And, a left-legged Jacob,[8] squat and wide,
With David Daiches trotting by his side,
Christopher Caudwell issues from the ranks,
Backed by a threatening brace of Soviet tanks.
The tanks advance; the critics all give ground;
He views the various machines around:
'This bourgeois junk, these antiquated arks!
No, Goddess, learn from Lenin and from Marx!
These are but children, squabbling at their play;
In Muscovy we take a shorter way:
The trial, the concentration camp, the knout,
Decide what literature is all about.
(Think of Akhmatova and Pasternak—)
Something your western bourgeois cultures lack
Are these two critical machines behind
The readiest way to halt the march of mind.'

'Son,' cries the Queen, 'although I sympathize,
This would not do yet in democracies.
There for the nonce, a better way to win
Is the slow rot of judgment from within;
Perhaps in any case a better way;
For violence breeds martyrs, so they say;
The hangman and the headsman and the stake
Are apt to raise rebellion in their wake,
Whereas a mind corrupted by degrees
Slides into Vacancy and calls it Peace.'[9]

6. Bodkin, ibid.: 'Dr. Jung cites from the Vedic Hymns lines where prayers or ritual fire-boring, are said to lead forth, or release the flowing streams of Rita.' (A.A.P.)
Not very nice is it, son? (A.P.)
Not very relevant to anything, either! (A.A.P.)

7. What is all this about, son? (A.P.)
It would take too long to explain, grandad. See Maud Bodkin's curious essay, 'A Study of the "Ancient Mariner" and of the Rebirth Archetype,' *Archetypal Patterns in Poetry* (1934). (A.A.P.)

8. So Pope, *Dunciad*, II, 65-8, describes the bookseller Lintot:
So lab'ring on, with shoulders, hands and head,
Wide as a windmill, all his fingers spread,
With arms expanded, Bernard rows his state
And left-legg'd Jacob seems to emulate.
Our author's reference here is less to the Patriarch's wrestle with the angel, than to a political stance. (A.A.P.)

9. So Tacitus, *Agricola*: 'Ubi solitudinem faciunt, pacem appellant.'

'Well, from your contest, then I must withdraw,
Dear Mother, till the reign of martial law;
Besides, a news-flash from the Chosen Land
Tells me that poets have got out of hand;
My thugs are needed there; I must return
And heads will roll while ivory towers burn.
Meantime, with blessings on this company,
I leave you Daiches here; no Marxist he,
But fit to sow confusion: his machine
Tests art by mirrors[1]. Should the social scene
Show a left-wing reflection of a tale,
Though dull, it passes, but if not, must fail.
Spenser and Malory to him are dross
And Rabelais and Sidney a dead loss.
Farewell, *pro tem.*; your Godhead I salute,
This *Lumpenprofessoriat* to boot.'
He raised his arm aloft and clenched his fist,
(Warning to every deviationist).
The tanks roll off; the critics roll an eye
And even David Daiches heaves a sigh.
A pause ensues: the Games are at a stand
Until the Goddess lifts her royal hand:
'Bring on the pachyderms of *Much Ado,*
My Formal Critics marching two and two!'
And from their verbal jungle to the bar,
Chanting a solemn dead march, from afar
Majestic in their pace and bearing, come
The Mastodons of Meaning, all and some.
Spokesmen and leaders of this lumbering crowd,
See Cleanth Brooks and Empson trumpet loud,
Wreathing the lithe proboscis[2] in duet,
They greet the Goddess and to partners set,
Small tails like wreathing o'er each massive bum,
And dance the pompous dance of Dunderdom.
The Queen, bewildered by this ponderous show,
The sense of their 'enactment'[3] seeks to know.
'Mother,' booms Empson,[4] with a final thud,
'Our convolutions should be clear as mud;
Simplicity, great Queen, is for the birds.
Mark this vast structure built of Complex Words;
Insert a lucid poem; pause, and see
How all dissolves in Ambiguity.'
'All hail, Semantic Father!' answers Brooks.[5]
'For Adumbrations, let her read *my* books,

1. David Daiches, 'Fiction and Civilisation,' in *The Novel and the Modern World*: 'What then is a great work of art?...we shall probably find that the greatest works are those which, while fulfilling all the formal requirements, most adequately reflect the civilisation of which they are a product... There will always be aspects of human character and emotion as an illumination of which the decadent bourgeoisie, the struggling proletariat, the atrophied landed gentry and similar phenomena of civilisation will always be adequate myths... If ever they cease to be so, a great deal of past literaure will have ceased to have literary value.' (A.A.P.)

Why is the *Odyssey* still read then, son? (A.P.)

2. Our author here imitates the divine Milton, *Paradise Lost*, IV 345-7:

th' unwieldy Elephant
To make them mirth us'd all his might and wreathd
His Lith Proboscis.

3. Why do they dance, son? (A.P.)

The modern critics, grandad, like bees before the hive, perform a sort of dance to indicate where honey flowers are to be found. This is called 'enacting the meaning.' (A.A.P.)

4. Who is this, son? (A.P.)

The Father of formalist criticism, grandad, author of two famous works: *Seven Types of Ambiguity* (1930) and *The Structure of Complex Words* (1951). These are the Old and New Testaments of this curious religion. (A.A.P.)

5. And this? (A.P.)

He wrote the Pauline epistles to the gospels of the Messiah. See *The Uses of Formal Analysis* (1951): 'The interested reader already knows the general nature of the critical position adumbrated—or if he does not, he can find it set forth in writings of mine or of other critics of like sympathy.' How do you like this? (A.A.P.) Insolent puppy!(A.P.)

Explore that intricate, inane Sublime
And play cat's-cradle to the end of time.'
'Thank you,' replies the Queen, 'I'd rather not.'
Translates the pair to a remoter spot,
Praises their efforts to enhance her state,
But owns that nine such critics make a Tate.[6]

Now Allen Tate comes on with massive tread:
His poems are golden but his prose is lead;
In Labyrinthine coils it crowds and squirms
With knotted syntax and entangled terms,
Strangles each poem, as the serpents once
Laocoön and his unhappy sons,
Enfolds and squeezes, crushes and extracts
Small crumbs of meaning and vast files of facts;
The poet crumbles and the reader nods
Yet on and on and on and on he plods.
The tulip's streaks[7] are numbered, all admit,
But is the poem illumined?[8] Not a whit;
For all his purpose is to demonstrate
The sensibilities of Allen Tate.
Alas, his language gives his game away
And sets a bound[9] to all he has to say.
The Goddess yawns, the serpent folds untwist
And slough, as Tate and Tedium are dismissed.

But now with heavier beasts[1] the earth is trod:
Blackmur and Northrop Frye with equal plod
And equal in gravamen, as in groan,
With cumbrous frolics next approach the throne.
Behind them Kenneth Burke and Schorer prate,
Twin masters of the Inarticulate.[2]
They speak no language, mime and reel and sprawl:
What does it matter? They 'enact' it all;
For in their doctrine that's the final test
And acrobatic verse is judged the best.
'Tis not enough a poet's lines should flow
With eloquence, with sense and passion glow,

6. Pope, *Epistle to Dr Arbuthnot*:
All these my modest satire bad translate
And own that nine such poets made a Tate.

7. Dr. Johnson, *Rasselas*: 'The business of poet, said Imlac, is to examine not the individual but the Species... he does not number the streaks of the tulip.'

8. See Allen Tate, 'Tension in Poetry,' in *Collected Essays* (1948): 'But convenience of elucidation is not a canon of criticism... I do not know what bearing my comment has had, upon the larger effects of poetry... I have of necessity confined both commentary and illustration to the slighter effects that seemed to me commensurate with certain immediate qualities of language.'

9. Allen Tate, 'Tension in Poetry': 'For in the long run, whatever the poet's "philosophy", however wide may be the extension of his meaning... by his language shall you know him; the quality of his language is the valid limit of what he has to say.' Hoist with his own petard, eh, son? (A.P.)

1. Our author at this point, son, suddenly recollected the delightful musical parody of Raphael's aria in *The Creation* of Haydn to the words:
Den Boden drückt der Tiere Last.
In the English version:
With heavy beasts the earth is trod. (A.P.)

2. I can scarcely credit this, son: surely two critics of great reputation?(A.P.)

Let me demonstrate, grandad, with typical specimens of the prose of these masters. First, Kenneth Burke, 'Symbolic Action in a Poem by Keats,' in *A Grammar of Motive* (1945): 'We might go on to make an infinity of observations about the detail of the stanza; but as regards major deployments we should deem it enough to note that the theme of "pipes and timbrels" is developed by the use of mystic oxymoron, and then surpassed (or given a development-atop-the-development) by the stressing of erotic imagery (that had been ambiguously adumbrated in the references to "maidens loth" and "mad pursuit" of Stanza I). And we could note the quality of *incipience* in this imagery, its state of arrest not at fulfilment, but at the point just prior to fulfilment.' (A.A.P.)

God bless us, son, what would Dryden have said to this? (A.P.)

He would throw up, grandad. And now for Mark Schorer, *Technique as Discovery* (1948): 'Technique in fiction, all this is a way of saying, we somehow continue to regard as merely a means to organising material which is "given" rather than as the means of exploring and defining the values in an area of experience which, for the first time *then*, are being given.' How is that for incoherence? (A.A.P.)

Crikey, son, now I credit it. (A.P.)

Sing like an angel, speak with grace and tact:
All fails, unless its meaning it 'enact'.[3]

The Queen surveys these antics, turns around
And calls on Frye and Blackmur to expound.
Ere torpid Blackmur rouses to reply
Great Frye displays his fearful symmetry;[4]
The multitude draw round to hear him speak;
He preaches a full hour; it seems a week;
And Frye, still preaching in the wilderness,
Regards the hungry multitude's distress;
Still preaching, from his hat he takes a fish
Called William Blake and set it in his dish;
And, preaching still, he lays it on the coals
And, while his magic eloquence unrolls,
A Miracle! the fish becomes a feast
Of twenty thousand baskets-full at least.
Alas, the empty multitude is fed
Not meat, but predication, stones for bread.
'Now, having explained my author, I explain
My explanation, brethren, and again
Explain *those* comments, while you break your fast:
To this all literature must come at last!'

The crowd are on their feet! They cheer and sing:
'Reward him, Mighty Mother! Frye for King!'
But, at this music, drowsy Blackmur wakes:
'Still preaching from the pulpit or the jakes!
What? Give the prize to Frye? Make Frye a King?
Promote him to a gibbet: let him swing!
My fist knocks off his sanctimonious hat;
I smite between his horns; take that, and *that!*'
So saying, he strikes; his rival sways; he sprawls;
His breath is spent and like an ox he falls.[5]

The fickle crowd at once begin to cry:
'Crown Blackmur, mighty Queen! A fig for Frye!'
They dance and clap and raise the Victor's Hymn
And tear unhappy Northrop limb from limb.
But over all laborious Blackmur's strain,
Still rumbling in the bowels of Hart Crane,
Drowns out their cries and makes the welkin ring:
'Hear me, great Mother, hearken while I sing!
In tortuous syntax, lame and out of hand,

3. For a sample of this idea, grandad, I give you a further specimen of grave-digger's prose from Kenneth Burke (ibid.): 'For a poem is an act, the symbolic act of the poet who made it—an act of such a nature that, in surviving as a structure or object, it enables us as readers to re-enact it.'

'Thus the Urn as a viaticum (or rather, with the *poem* as a viaticum and *in the name* of the Urn), having symbolically enacted a kind of act that transcends our mortality, we round out the process by coming to dwell upon the transcendental ground of this act.'

Golly, grandad, do we? (A.A.P.)

Too strenuous for me, son. (A.P.)

4. What is this, son? (A.P.)

Northrop Frye, *Fearful Symmetry: A study of William Blake* (1947). Not much symmetry about it, grandad, but fearful enough, and a very pretty preachment. (A.A.P.)

5. Our author here intends a parallel with the incident in the funeral games of Aeneas, where old Entellus fells a bull with his fist. Dryden's *Aeneid*, V, 637-41:

Sternly he spoke; and then confronts the Bull;
And on his ample forehead aiming full,
The deadly Stroke descending, pierced the Skull.
Down drops the Beast; nor needs a second Wound:
But sprawls in pangs of Death; and spurns the ground. (A.P.)

Explaining what I do not understand;[6]
I cannot tell the Bull's feet from the B's,
Nor see the wood for counting all its trees.
Lucus a non lucendo is the fashion,
But my impenetrable explication
Earns me the prize (though stultifies the song)
Who say so little and who talk so long.'[7]

The crowd renews its plaudits and its cries
To see great Blackmur crowned and win the Prize;
But Dullness falters, hesitates and hums;
Then springing from her throne, exclaims:
'He comes!

He comes, by prophets and by seers foretold,
To usher in my spurious Age of Gold;
Latest of all my sons, my chiefest care,
Messiah of Nonsense and great Arthur's Heir!'
Meanwhile her eyes are fixed where, from the east,
A speck, a dot, a blot, a cloud, increased
Moment by moment fascinates each eye
And, speeding towards them, glitters in the sky.
In graceful arcs it spirals, swerves and swoops,
Emitting heavenly Muzak, as it loops;
Light iridescence gleams along its side
—For now 'tis near enough to be descried—
And soon it lands and taxis towards the line,
A glistening engine of unknown design.
Swift through the crowd, like cats'-paws o'er a lake,
Conjecture runs with rumour in its wake.
Some say a sputnik and a UFO some,
The Second Coming or the Millennium,
As, from the hatch on top, a curious dome
Of shining perspex and resplendent chrome,
A smiling figure, uniformed in white,
Steps down and blinds them with excess of light.
He stood there—for at least it seemed to be
A He—or might, perhaps, it be a She?—
Quite featureless, yet as the crowd look on,
Each seemed by turns to recognize his own;
Then moving like a dancer, proud, serene,
The radiant newcomer salutes the Queen.
'Hail, Mother, late in time behold me come!
To join the Games prescribed at Arthur's Tomb.'
He turns towards the Tomb and kneeling there:
'Great Avatar of Nonsense, hear my prayer!
My time is not yet come, yet here behold
Your true Successor by dark stars foretold.

6. There is a splendid example both of the syntax and the modesty of this hero in his 'New Thresholds, New Anatomies. Notes on a text of Hart Crane,' in *Language as Gesture* (1935): 'Immediately following, in the same poem, there is a parenthesis, which I have not been able to penetrate with any certainty, though the possibilities are both fascinating and exciting. The important words in it do not possess the excluding power over themselves and their relations by which alone the precise, vital element in ambiguity is secured. What Crane may have meant privately cannot be in question—his words may have represented for him a perfect tautology; we are concerned only with how the words act on each each other—or fail to act—so as to commit an appreciable meaning. I quote from the first clause of the parenthesis.

> Let sphinxes from the ripe
> Borage of death have cleaved my tongue
> Once and again...' (A.A.P.)

Surely a lot of palaver to say the *words* have no sense and that *he* has no sense of smell. (A.P.)

7. I thrill to these lines, son, as I did to Mr. Pope's lines on this hero's sublime ancestor, Sir Richard Blackmore, *Dunciad*, II, 259-68:

> But far o'er all, sonorous Blackmore's strain;
> Walls, steeples, skies, bray back to him again.
> In Tot'nam fields the brethren with amaze
> Prick all their ears and forget to graze...
> All hail him victor in both gifts of song,
> Who sings so loudly, and who sings so long.

(A.P.)

These Esaus spurn, reject their horoscopes
And bless me, Father, Jacob of your hopes!'
The Tomb flies open with a hollow sound,
And coiling up from shades of underground,
A mighty serpent glides, and winks an eye,
And disappears into a bog nearby.[8]

And next the Stranger turns towards the throne:
'The contest, Goddess, let it now go on!
And let me demonstrate before my Queen
The sovereign virtues of my blest machine.'
'Alas, dear child, whoever you may be,
Still wrapt in clouds of dim futurity,
The victims whom I raised to demonstrate
Are all used up. Forgive me, you must wait
Till I can summon up, and so I will,
Some modern genius worthy of your skill.'
'Fear not, fond parent,' was the Shade's reply.
'For on mere authors I no more rely;
Now Automation and the Critic's Art
Make poets obsolete as horse and cart.
In this superb contraption here, you see
The Self-moved Mover as Machinery;
The Muses are redundant now; and thanks
To automatic brains and memory banks,
Pure Criticism triumphs over all
Without resort to Raw Material.
The Last Age, primitive although it was,
Produced Pure Poetry; eschewed the dross
Of subject, narrative, connective themes;
Now ours at last evolves the Dream of Dreams:
Pure Criticism, without thought or fuss;
Pure Theory formed, with nothing to discuss!
This rare device embodies in its guts
No cranks or levers, pistons, cogs or nuts;
A "magic eye" looks inward and controls
Pure Critics musing on their own pure souls.'
A murmur sweeps the mob; the murmur dies
And Dullness rises and bestows the Prize:
'The Works of mighty Arthur, may he live
In well-tooled leather, nicely gilt, receive!
Peruse them duly, emulate his fame,
And rule the nations in thy Greater Name!

But now, Young Prophet, we must make an end:
The time has come for Arthur to ascend.
Let all assemble soon to see him rise
And let your plaudits waft him to the skies;
And may this Morning Star his reign forestalls
Stand up and catch his mantle[9] as it falls!'

—*A.D. Hope*

8. So at the prayer of Aeneas before the tomb of Anchises. Dryden's *Aeneid*, Book V:

Scarce had he finished, when, with speckled pride,
A serpent from the tomb began to glide;
His hugy bulk on seven high volumes rolled;
Blue was his breadth of back, but streaked with scaly gold:
Thus riding on his curls, he seemed to pass
A rolling fire along, and singe the grass. (A.P.)

9. So Dryden, *Mac Flecknoe*, 214-17:

Sinking he left his Drugget robe behind,
Borne upwards by a subterranean wind.
The Mantle fell to the young Prophet's part
With double portion of his Father's Art. (A.P.)

"Break, Break, Break"

Fly, Muse, thy wonted themes, nor longer seek
The consolations of a powder'd cheek;
Forsake the busy purlieus of the Court
For calmer meads where finny tribes resort.
So may th' Almighty's natural antidote
Abate the worldly tenour of thy note,
The various beauties of the liquid main
Refine thy reed and elevate thy strain.

See how the labour of the urgent oar
Propels the barks and draws them to the shore.
Hark! from the margin of the azure bay
The joyful cries of infants at their play.
(The offspring of a piscatorial swain,
His home the sands, his pasturage the main.)
Yet none of these may soothe the mourning heart,
Nor fond alleviation's sweets impart;
Nor may the pow'rs of infants that rejoice
Restore the accents of a former voice,
Nor the bright smiles of ocean's nymphs command
The pleasing contact of a vanished hand.
So let me still in meditation move,
Muse in the vale and ponder in the grove,
And scan the skies where sinking Phoebus glows
With hues more rubicund than Cibber's nose....
(After which the poet gets into his proper stride.)

—J.C. Squire

A Compliment to the Ladies

Wondrous the gods, more wondrous are the men,
More wondrous, wondrous still, the cock and hen,
More wondrous still, the table, stool and chair;
But ah! more wondrous still the charming fair.

—William Blake

THOMAS GRAY
(1716-1771)

Elegy in the Cemetery of Spoon River Instead of in That of Stoke Poges

The curfew tolls the knell of parting day,
   The whippoorwill salutes the rising moon,
And wanly glimmer in her gentle ray,
   The sinuous windings of the turbid Spoon.

Here where the flattering and mendacious swarm
   Of lying epitaphs their secrets keep,
At last incapable of further harm
   The lewd forefathers of the village sleep.

The earliest drug of half-awakened morn.
  Cocaine or hashish, strychnine; poppy-seeds
Or fiery produce of fermented corn
  No more shall start them on the day's misdeeds.

For them no more the whetstone's cheerful noise.
  No more the sun upon his daily course
Shall watch them savouring the genial joys,
  Of murder, bigamy, arson and divorce.

Here they all lie; and, as the hour is late,
  O stranger, o'er their tombstones cease to stoop,
But bow thine ear to me and contemplate
  The unexpurgated annals of the group.

There are two hundred only: yet of these
  Some thirty died of drowning in the river,
Sixteen went mad, ten others had D.T.'s,
  And twenty-eight cirrhosis of the liver.

Several by absent-minded friends were shot,
  Still more blew out their own exhausted brains,
One died of a mysterious inward rot,
  Three fell off roofs, and five were hit by trains.

One was harpooned, one gored by a bull-moose,
  Four on the Fourth fell victims to lock-jaw,
Ten in electric chair or hempen noose
  Suffered the last exaction of the law.

Stranger, you quail, and seem inclined to run;
  But, timid stranger, do not be unnerved;
I can assure you that there was not one
  Who got a tithe of what he had deserved.

Full many a vice is born to thrive unseen,
  Full many a crime the world does not discuss,
Full many a pervert lives to reach a green
  Replete old age, and so it was with us.

Here lies a parson who would often make
  Clandestine rendezvous with Claflin's Moll.
And 'neath the druggist's counter creep to take
  A sip of surreptitious alcohol.

And here a doctor, who had seven wives,
  And, fearing this *ménage* might seem grotesque.
Persuaded six of them to spend their lives
  Locked in a drawer of his private desk.

And others here there sleep who, given scope,
  Had writ their names large on the Scrolls of Crime,
Men who, with half a chance, might haply cope,
  With the first miscreants of recorded time.

Doubtless in this neglected spot is laid
  Some village Nero who has missed his due,
Some Bluebeard who dissected many a maid,
  And all for naught, since no one ever knew.

Some poor bucolic Borgia here may rest
  Whose poisons sent whole families to their doom,
Some hayseed Herod who, within his breast,
  Concealed the sites of many an infant's tomb.

Types that the Muse of Masefield might have stirred,
  Or waked to ecstasy Gaboriau,
Each in his narrow cell at last interred,
  All, all are sleeping peacefully below.

* * *

Enough, enough! But, stranger, ere we part,
  Glancing farewell to each nefarious bier,
This warning I would beg you to take to heart,
  "There is an end to even the worst career!"

—J.C. Squire

Evening: an Elegy

Apollo now, Sol's carman, drives his stud
  Home to the mews that's seated in the west,
And Custom's clerks, like him, through Thames Street mud,
  Now westering wend, in Holland trousers dress'd.

So from the stands the empty carts are dragg'd,
  The horses homeward to their stables go,
And mine, with hauling heavy hogsheads fagg'd,
  Prepare to take the luxury of—"Wo!"

Now from the slaughter-houses cattle roar,
  Knowing that with the morn their lives they yields,
And Mr. Sweetman's gig is at the door
  To take him to his house in Hackney Fields.

Closed are the gates of the West India Docks,
  Rums, Sugars, Coffees, find at length repose,
And I, with other careless carmen, flocks
  To the King's Head, the Chequers, or the Rose.

They smoke a pipe—the shepherd's pipe I wakes,
  Them skittles pleases—me the Muse invites,
They in their ignorance to drinking takes,
  I bless'd with learning, takes a pen and writes.

—Horatio Smith

Ode on a Distant Prospect of Clapham Academy

Ah me! those old familiar bounds!
That classic house, those classic grounds,
  My pensive thought recalls!
What tender urchins now confine,
What little captives now repine,
  Within yon irksome walls?

Ay, that's the very house! I know
Its ugly windows, ten a-row!
Its chimneys in the rear!
And there's the iron rod so high,
That drew the thunder from the sky,
And turn'd our table-beer!

There I was birch'd! there I was bred!
There like a little Adam fed
From Learning's woeful tree!
The weary tasks I used to con!—
The hopeless leaves I wept upon!—
Most fruitless leaves to me!—

The summon'd class!—the awful bow!—
I wonder who is master now
And wholesome anguish sheds!
How many ushers now employs,
How many maids to see the boys
Have nothing in their heads!

And Mrs. S***?—Doth she abet
(Like Pallas in the parlour) yet
Some favour'd two or three,—
The little Crichtons of the hour,
Her muffin-medals that devour,
And swill her prize—bohea?

Ay, there's the play-ground! there's the lime
Beneath whose shade in summer's prime
So wildly I have read!—
Who sits there *now*, and skims the cream
Of young Romance, and weaves a dream
Of Love and Cottage-bread?

Who struts the Randall of the walk?
Who models tiny heads in chalk?
Who scoops the light canoe?
What early genius buds apace?
Where's Poynter? Harris? Bowers? Chase?
Hal Baylis? blithe Carew?

Alack! they're gone—a thousand ways!
And some are serving in "the Greys",
And some have perish'd young!—
Jack Harris weds his second wife;
Hal Baylis drives the *wane* of life;
And blithe Carew—is hung!

Grave Bowers teaches A B C
To savages at Owhyee;
Poor Chase is with the worms!—
All, all are gone—the olden breed!—
New crops of mushroom boys succeed,
And push us from our *forms*!

Lo! where they scramble forth, and shout,
And leap, and skip, and mob about,
At play where we have play'd!
Some hop, some run (some fall), some twine
Their crony arms; some in the shine,
And some are in the shade!

Lo! there what mix'd conditions run!
The orphan lad; the widow's son;
  And Fortune's favour'd care—
The wealthy-born, for whom she hath
Mac-Adamized the future path—
  The Nabob's pamper'd heir!

Some brightly star'd—some evil born,—
For honour some, and some for scorn,—
  For fair or foul renown!
Good, bad, indiff'rent—none may lack!
Look, here's a White, and there's a Black!
  And there's a Creole brown!

Some laugh and sing, some mope and weep,
And wish *their* frugal sires would keep
  Their only sons at home;—
Some tease the future tense, and plan
The full-grown doings of the man,
  And pant for years to come!

A foolish wish! There's one at hoop;
And four at *fives*! and five who stoop
  The marble taw to speed!
And one that curvets in and out,
Reining his fellow Cob about,—
  Would I were in his *steed*!

Yet he would gladly halt and drop
That boyish harness off, to swop
  With this world's heavy van—
To toil, to tug. O little fool!
Whilst thou canst be a horse at school
  To wish to be a man!

Perchance thou deem'st it were a thing
To wear a crown,—to be a king!
  And sleep on regal down!
Alas! thou know'st not kingly cares;
Far happier is thy head that wears
  That hat without a crown!

And dost thou think that years acquire
New added joys? Dost think thy sire
  More happy than his son?
That manhood's mirth?—Oh, go thy ways
To Drury Lane when—*plays*,
  And see how *forced* our fun!

Thy taws are brave!—thy tops are rare!—
Our tops are spun with coils of care,
  Our *dumps* are no delight!—
The Elgin marbles are but tame,
And 'tis at best a sorry game
  To fly the Muse's kite!

Our hearts are dough, our heels are lead,
Our topmost joys fall dull and dead
  Like balls with no rebound!
And often with a faded eye
We look behind, and send a sigh
  Towards that merry ground!

Then be contented. Thou hast got
The most of heav'n in thy young lot,
There's sky-blue in thy cup!
Thou'lt find thy Manhood all too fast—
Soon come, soon gone! and Age at last
A sorry *breaking up!*

—Thomas Hood, the Elder

WILLIAM SCOTTON
(1746-1783)

From *Doris and Philemon*

Now the declining fulgent orb of day
Tinged all the landskip with his latest ray;
Philemon came to seek the blooming fair,
Rending with gloomy moans the conscious air.
"Doris," he cried, "my Doris I would find—
Doris, my Doris, beauteous and kind,
Doris the queen of all our rural train,
Doris a nymph admir'd by ev'ry swain."
No pleasing answer pierc'd his list'ning ear;
In vain his eyelids shed each sparkling tear;
No virgin accents came, no step of love
Trod the soft verdure of the silent grove,
No lovely face to beam upon his heart,
To calm his breast and ease his painful smart.
With tortured breath for Phoebus' aid he wails,
Shrieks to the trees and murmurs to the gales:
"Me wretched; bring me Doris or I die."
But only scornful Echo made reply.

—J.C. Squire

To Miss L.F. on the Occasion of her Departure for the Continent:

Wherefore, Lucinda, dost aspire
To leave thy native plain,
Forsaking thine adoring quire
To brave the raging main?

Are domiciliar dells so dark,
So dull our English vales,
That thou must trust thy slender bark
To inauspicious gales?

If thou wouldst fain console the Muse,
In explanation speak!
See now the tender blush suffuse
Lucinda's lovely cheek;

A pitying word vouchsafes the fair:
"I seek a foreign plain
That I with more delight may share
My native meads again."

—J.C. Squire

From *Country Wooing*

So lay the youth with Mary in his arms,
Pale with excess of bliss. But when the maid
Perforce must leave to seek her mother's cot
He clomb the higher slopes of Haldon Hill
Calmly suspended 'bove the horizon's rim,
Burned the great globe, and far and far away
The meadows coruscated with his light.
There sat the boy an hour, his thoughtful chin
Supported by his hand, and over all
The universe his eager thought took flight.
He saw lone vessels straining on far seas,
Spread continents of dusky peoples, woods
Where lurked vast she-lions with stealthy eyes,
And icy deserts round about the Pole.
He flung the earth behind his voyaging feet,
And flew amid the stars beyond the moon,
Across the threshold of the Milky Way
And on into the darkness of the void
Impenetrable. So an hour he journeyed.
Then, with a sudden start, regained the world,
And, weary-eyed, stared over sunless fields
And shades that hastened over Haldon Hill.

* * *

'Twas night. High in the heavens rode the moon,
With her great shining host of starry guards.
Pale lay the fields i' th' light, so that they seemed
Almost celestial to Richard's eyes.
There where the river wandered stole he down
And heard the owlet screaming to her mate
And the bat twittering. Anon some downy moth
Would flutter like a phantom 'gainst his face,
Anon he'd hear, as by a hedge he passed,
Some good old hermit of a horse that fed
With loud bite in his dark and tranquil field.

—*J.C. Squire*

From *The Swallow*

Birds, trees and flow'rs they bring to me,
A boon as precious as 'tis free,
  That cities cannot give.
O glossy breast and rapid wing,
If thou shouldst e'er forsake the spring
  I should not wish to live.

—*J.C. Squire*

From *My Father's Cot*

I left thee with a courage high,
The gleam of boyhood in my eye,
  And undefilèd soul.
And now what have I? Shreds of art,
A craven spirit and a heart
  That never will be whole.

—*J.C. Squire*

THOMAS CHATTERTON
(1752-1770)

Ode to Miss Hoyland

Ah! Hoyland, empress of my heart,
When will thy breast admit the dart,
And own a mutual flame?
When, wandering in the myrtle groves,
Shall mutual pleasures seal our loves—
Pleasures without a name?

Thou greatest beauty of the sex,
When will the little god perplex
The mansions of thy breast?
When wilt thou own a flame as pure
As that seraphic souls endure,
And make thy Baker blest?

—*Thomas Chatterton*

SAMUEL JOHNSON
(1709-1784)

Johnsonian Poem in Progress

I put my hat upon my head,
And walked into the Strand,
And there I met another man
Whose hat was in his hand.

'Pray, sir,' I said, 'why don't you place
Your hat upon your head?'
He cried, 'Be silent, medding fool,
And may God strike you dead!'

I turned astonished and distressed
By words so fierce and rude.
Then, on a sudden, lightning flashed
And killed him where he stood.

From the dark clouds that glowered above
There came a mighty roar:
'I missed you, Johnson—damn it all,
I ought to practise more.'

Much shaken, I resumed my stroll,
Pondering what I'd heard,
And even Boswell, when we met,
Would not believe a word.

—*Peter Veale*

I put my hat upon my head,
And walked into the Strand,
And there I met another man
Whose hat was in his hand.

Behind that hat I could not see
The club he'd hidden there,
Nor knew until he turned around
And smote me unaware!

And as he struck it seemed to me
He marked me by my name
'Are you not Dr. Johnson, Sir,
Of dictionary fame?'

'Help! Help!' I cried, 'Why use me so?
What motive have you, Sir?
I am a harmless man of words,
A lexicographer.'

'I strike' quoth he, 'for good Sir John,
John Hawkins brave and true,
He whom you dubbed unclubbable
Don't say the same of you!'

—F.A.V. Madden

I put my hat upon my head,
And walked into the Strand,
And there I met another man
Whose hat was in his hand.

His hat was in his hand because
It was not worth the bother
To put it on his head, for he
Had just espied his mother

Who, in the gutter, filthy drunk
And well spaced out on grass,
Had, not to beat about the bush,
Just fallen on her arse.

He paused a moment and observed,
'Poor dear mama is ill,'
And then put on his hat, and went
Eastwards to Ludgate Hill.

Shutting his parent from his view,
I can't approve of that,
But, credit give where credit's due,
He did remove his hat.

—Ian Sainsbury

I put my hat upon my head,
And walked into the Strand,
And there I met another man
Whose hat was in his hand.

A stick was in his other hand,
Painted a dirty white;
His coat was torn, his shoes worn through,
He looked a sorry sight.

A pair of meagre coppers lay
Within his tattered hat;
The look of misery in his eyes
Could scarce be wondered at.

Assuming he could not see me,
I stood and looked at him;
His glassy stare returned my gaze,
As if his sight were dim

But not quite non-existent yet.
I walked away in awe,
But not before I'd made his hat
Weigh heavier than before.

—Ian Stirling

THE NINETEENTH CENTURY

1798:	*Lyrical Bellows* fans fires of Industrial Revelation.
1811-1820:	Hotel Wars: English Regency vs. Spanish Ramada.
1815:	Rotten burros replace Houyhnhnms.
1820:	Recession of George IV.
1830:	Noiseless patient spinster born in Amherst.
1832:	Bentham dies proving Pushkin better than poetry.
1832:	Reform Bill paid.
	Ralph Waldorf Emerson joins Hotel Wars.
1844:	Poe foreshadows Mallomar, Rainbow, other Cymbalists.
1846:	Corn Dogs repelled.
1851:	Great Exhibitionist arrested in Crystal Palace.
1855:	Brooklyn Fairy invents free verse.
1855:	Andrea del Sartre, second existentialist masterpiece.
1859:	Charles Darvon publishes *Idylls of the Kong.*
1861:	Browning's "Tradition and the Individual Tyrant" for dead wife's father.
1869:	Arnold's *Yogurt Culture or Anarchy.*
1884:	Tennyson accepts porridge.

GLORIFICATION OF THE HUMBUG AND RUSTED

By the time of the opening of the English Regency across town from the Spanish Ramada in 1811 (which precipitated the so-called "Hotel Wars" between the descendants of Milton's pamphlet whores and the American philosopher Ralph Waldorf Emerson), William Wordsworth had already written most of the best poems of a prolonged life, including "The Ruined Cottage Cheese," a spirited protest against enclosing cattle in pens for weeks without pay and forerunner of the Cheese and Snack Poetry of the twentieth century, "Three Years She Grew," a heartbreaking account of the needlessly extended pregnancy of a rustic, and "Inflammations of Immorality," Wordsworth's masterpiece, from which the following is a quotation:

Nine months she grew in sun and shower,
But in my Lover's ear alone
Was ever sown a lovelier flower:
Strange fits of passion have I known.

These poems, along with many by Coleridge, were collected in the epic-mocking *Lyrical Bellows* in 1798, a time when, in William Butler Keats's words, "great spirits now on earth are snoring." The intention of the *Lyrical Bellows*, as any schoolboy knows, was to fan the languishing fires of the Industrial Revelation set by William Blake in his "The Chimney Sweepstakes." Wordsworth, it was decided, would busy himself glorifying the humbug and rusted life of pedestrians, while Coleridge would concentrate on adding string cheese to beauty in order to create wonder—what Dr. Johnson has called "the paws of reason." Coleridge accomplished this in such poems as "Crystal Bull" and "Robert Frost at Midnight," the latter an eerie journey through a timewart to visit another poet who used only the luggage commonly used by men.

SELBSTBEFLECKUNG AND ENGLISH ROMANTICISM

This democratic enterprise was, of course, instantly brandied "Romantic," and while the critic may often invoke the term, he or she seldom defiles it satisfactorily. Let us begin by saying that Romanticism refected the *ancien vagina* of the Elizabethan Error and the *status quo vadis* of the Neo-Calcified Age in favor of what the German Romantics called "*Selbstbefleckung*," translated by William Wordsworth to mean "the spontaneous overflow of powerful feelings." This attributes the sores of poetry to the poet himself (cf. Coleridge's "This Lime-Tree Bowel My Prison"), and not to the world of humid affairs. Blake, Shelley, and Keats all overflowed in keeping with Wordsworth's dictum (as set forth in the "Prelude to *Lyrical Bellows*"), and some twentieth-century critics have even speculated that Shelley drowned not in the Gulf of Spinoza during a reading tour of the "Pizza Circuit" but in his own excessive overflow.

Of all the Romantics, Byron was the only one to raise his vice in objection to the poets of the Lake Isle School. Byron, the major dumbo of the rival Satanic School (which included such minor talents as Lucifer), and a member of the Cocksman School (which included the irrepressible Lay Hunter), seemed to owe more to the anesthetic of Dryden and Pepys than he did to his own error. Furthermore, he delighted in attacking his rivals, especially Wordsworth and Coleridge, whom he ridiculed during a tour of the Lake Isle country on the back of a "rotten burro"—the Industrial Revelation's debased answer to Swift's magnificent "horses of reason." While Byron is perhaps most famous for his "club foot," which must rank with William Tennessee Williams's "variable foot" and Charles "Bobo" Olson's "foot in mouth" as major contributions to English meter [see Prosodomy], he is also well-liked for bringing incest into the language. He managed this difficult fetus under the guise of "laissex-faire" (all is fair in love), and once boasted that Wordsworth's concubine Dorothy (cf. "Tintown Albert") was "half a child of mine own John Poins."

PILGRIM AND PURITAN EROS IN AMERICA

In America, meanwhile, the Billy Pilgrims of the Puritan sex had found relief from the prostitution arising from wide religious schizoids in England, primarily from the one fermented by Loud on his ascension to the Archbishopric in 1633. Like Milton, the Puritans were solitary, poor, nasty, brutish, and short, and according to Nathaniel Hawthorne (author of *The House of the Seven Gobblers* and the father of American poultry), they spent the bulk of their time writing scarlet chain-letters with poison puns and trying to impose their prunish standards on others. They learned their inherent depravity from Calvin Coleridge (not to be confused with Wordsworth's corroborator), who preached that salivation came only through degeneration. It was everywhere apparent in their good works, which included witch-biting. Hawthorne, of course, objected to these teachings in his fiction and attacked them in his prose; nevertheless, Calvin Coleridge's dogmas of the prestidigitation of the electorate and salivation by grass exerted a tremendous influence on colonial politics and drug use.

AMERICAN BELLY-LITTERS AT MID-CENTURY

While some critics like to tart literary accomplishments during the Pilgrim and Puritan eros, American poetry did not begin flushing until the explosion of literature that went hand in hand with the blossoming of American belly-litters (literature of the "Art Fart's Sake Movement"). It was not until the publication of *The Princess and the Poe*, an autobiographical study of Poe's use of onomatopotato, obliteration, and other vegetable methods in foreplay with women, that the American garden began to yield. Poe quickly followed this success with *Tales of the Polio Club*, a crushing indictment of both of his tight-lipped former brides-to-be, Sarah Elmira Royster and Virginia Clamm, with whom he developed the Cymbalist technique of Sinoidseizure (stimulation of all five scent glands by squanching) in foreplay.

Just as important are Poe's critical criteria for the successful short story or poem. Abandoning the Gothic desiderius of his youth in favor of naturalism after reading Blake's "The Four Zolas," Poe wrote a review of Melville's metaphysical fish epic *Moby Slick*, in which he determined that in addition to allying melancholy with beauty the short prose narrative should be brief. In other words, excessive size robs the work of art of its infectiousness, and every word should contribute to the infection itself. Poe's attention to craft has endured him to the "depersonalized" modern sensibility, while his devotion to the sound of verse, its musical katydids, and rhythm-method [see Prosodomy], foreshadows the Cymbalist poets Rainbow, Mallomar, and others. It is no wonder that Melville, the "Homer of Wall Street" and author of "Hawthorne and his Mooses" memorialized Poe forever in his *The Lack of Confidence Man* and *Typoe*.

MICROCOSM AND MACKERELCOSM

After the Civil War, the swelling tide of foreign ingrates who caused the widening gap between the struggling industrial masses and the robber Byrons found vent for its growing frustration in the rising middle gas. The latter, of course, found a spokesman in Walt Whitman, the "Brooklyn fairy," whose *Leaves of Gas* anticipates that watershed of modern and contemporary literary history, the twentieth century. Whitman, whose invention of free verse (from the french, *amour libre*) he likened to "dispensing food without a hairnet," wrote all of his life in the free verse gender, composing occasional poems for poets, friends, and the multitudes, such poems as "Passage to Indiana" for Theodore Dryden, "A Noiseless Patient Spinster" for lover Emily Dickinson, and "Specimen Jars" for the doctorless masses of his beloved Madahatter.

Dickinson's achievement rivals Whitman's. While Whitman opened a great new geography for poetry, the "democratic viscera"—long, incantatory, mantis-like lines marked by reputation, enematopoeia, and anaphrodisiacs—Dickinson, in a more modest prosodomy derived from the pew-primers and hymenals, mapped her own virgin land. Here we find our worst guilt and fear and joy recapitated in verse that speaks to our essential humid condition by, of all people, the archconservative apostate of individualism, "the belle of Forever Amherst," whose original use of shove-off rhyme and epileptical method have fascinated even the sternest twentieth-century critics of "The Gilded Village."

YOGURT CULTURE OR ANARCHY?

In Victorian England, news of American literary accomplishments was drowned out by a growing hue and cry over the Reform Bill. Paid in 1832, it enfranchised all men weighing ten pounds or more, which lessened the impact of the Irish potato feminists by rapidly increasing the consumption of Corn Dogs in Great Britain. Primarily responsible for getting the repressive Corn Dogs repelled was Henry Adams, leader of the Chartres Movement and author of the "Peoples Chartres," who first brought the blight of the underfed to the attention of nineteenth-century reformers. Among them were Thomas Carlyle, author of "On Hero Sandwiches" and forerunner of the Snack Poetry of the twentieth century, Matthew Arnold, author of "Yogurt Culture and Anarchy," and Cardinal Alfred Newton, who founded the Gastro-intestinal Tractarian Movement. Newton founded his movement in order to combat the strict puritan cod of morality which, according to critic Stanley Fish, prescribed meatless Fridays and joyless Victorian Sundaes (served without syrup).

EXHIBITIONISM AND ANTIMASSACRES

What Bulwer-Lytton Strachey has called "The great summer of humid civilization" may have lacked an emporium of ice cream, but it did not lack other cymbals of a vigorous commercial and industrial age. The Crystal Palace, as yet untainted by the amber of Henry James's prose, stood as glittering reproof of what D'Israeli has called "the infantile romance" of science. Built in 1951 in Jekyll Park to hide "the Grand Exhibitionist," Dean Ruskin, it proved to be living proof that "people in glass houses shouldn't throw stones of Venice" when Ruskin was arrested while disrobing a grand piano leg. Shortly afterward he died and was immobilized forever by Samuel Butler Hudibras in his *The Way Of All Flashers*. Ruskin, who continues the line of author-athletes begun by Pepys, is perhaps best known for his *Modern Punters*, a study of the pathetic phallus in sports literature, and his "The Savageness of Gothic Archibunker," a prophetic history of the mass mediocre.

UNDERACHIEVERS OF VICTORIA'S ENGLAND

Pathetic in his own way was Alfred North Tennyson, whom W. H. Dryden has called the "stupidest" English poet. This is perhaps unkind, for while Tennyson may have lacked ideas, he was not without opinions. *In Memorium* is full of the opinions of Charles Darvon, the revolutionary, and Jeremy Bentham, who held that Pushkin was better than poetry. These opinions go without saying, and established Tennyson as "the poet of the purple" before his succession to the shrine of poet lariat in 1850. Meanwhile, the same W. H. Dryden, echoing Charles "Bobo" Olson's famous formula "the brain to the ear by way of bad breath," continued his examination of Tennyson's faculties by announcing that he had "the finest ear, perhaps of any English poet." To protect his ear against harm from the "strange fits" of Wordsworth, Tennyson early adopted Carlyle's "clothes philosophy." According to critic Barbara Herford Brown, author of *Poetic Tonsure*, this philosophy was based on Dr. Johnson's well-known quatrain:

> I put my hat upon my head
> And walked into the Strand,
> And there I met another man
> Whose hat was in his hand.

In his "Ears, Idle Ears," Tennyson acknowledges his debt to Johnson:

> Now crimson is the pate, now clothed the pate,
> In mink's or rabbit's fur, or soft velour;
> That ear which blushed sanguine or roseate,
> It shall not blush in public anymore.

The ornate style here is typical of this "loud of language." Tennyson, who accepted a porridge in 1884, died some years later.

Robert Barrett Browning's response to Carlyle's "clothes philosophy" was the following fierce diatribe directed against Johnson, "the sourpuss of Fleet Street":

> Churl, mark my hat—what, does't offend you—Say!
> The rakish tilt of it? The plume? Then what?
> What else to wear i'th' heat o'th' mid o'th' day?
> I bought it of Fra Cantaloupe just yesterday.
> Aye, Cantaloupe, San Marco's hattier.
> I paid—one, two, three four—four pounds for it.
> You think that high?—Not to a man of means.
> He said 'twould make a Borgia—Borgia!—blush.
> And so it would. Three steeple-sweeping chits
> With slingshot stones aimed at it: missed. Ha! Ha!
> —I'd guess you paid a shilling for your own.
> Two shillings? Hmmmm. Well, Faugh! A hat's a hat.
> I wear mine: la! you beg a pence with yours.
> You say that heav'n looks equally upon
> Poor hats and rich alike? So I concur.
> On earth the cap; in heav'n the perfect crown!

Like many of Robert Browning's dramatic monoliths, this one is replete with ideas borrowed from "the prose Browning," his wife Elizabeth, whose death inspired Browning to write his "Tradition and the Individual Tyrant" to Elizabeth's father. Browning followed this with *Andrea del Sartre*, the second existentialist materpiece after *Sartre Resartrus*. However, it was not poems like these that made Browning a byword at the various Browning Sodalities which sprang up in the latter part of the nineteenth century. Rather, it was the Browning who offered to his devoted readers the moral tonic water for which he has become famous in poems like "Paraseltzer," "Muckle-Mouth Mug," and "Seeing Cousin Syphilis Off." What these poems have in common (besides their foreshadowing the Cheese and Snack Poetry of the twentieth century) is grudging respect from Ezra Pound. Pound saw Browning as a literary profit and recognized in his monoliths the harsh disaccordions, unexpected juxtapollutions, and lack of personality that characterizes the work of "the bastards of the High Modernist Mode."

WILLIAM BLAKE
(1757-1827)

O have you caught the tiger?
And can you hold him tight?
And what immortal hand or eye
Could frame his fearful symmetry?
And does he try to bite?

Yes, I have caught the tiger,
And he was hard to catch.
O tiger, tiger, do not try
To put your tail into my eye,
And do not bite and scratch.

Yes, I have caught the tiger.
O tiger, do not bray!
And what immortal hand or eye
Could frame his fearful symmetry
I should not like to say.

And may I see the tiger?
I should indeed delight
To see so large an animal
Without a voyage to Bengal.
And mind you hold him tight.

Yes, you may see the tiger;
It will amuse you much.
The tiger is, as you will find,
A creature of the feline kind.
And mind you do not touch.

And do you feed the tiger,
And do you keep him clean?
He has a less contented look
Than in the Natural History book,
And seems a trifle lean.

Oh yes, I feed the tiger,
And soon he will be plump;
I give him groundsel fresh and sweet,
And much canary-seed to eat,
And wash him at the pump.

It seems to me the tiger
Has not been lately fed,
Not for a day or two at least;
And that is why the noble beast
Has bitten off your head.

—A.E. Housman

The Cry of the Child

I was angry with my cow:
I milked her not, my cow did low.
I was happy with my horse:
I milked him not, he was no worse.

My cow both day and night did low
Till at the last she burst with Pride.
My horse lowed not to see my cow
Dead by my infant child's side,

Where in the manger he did lay
Among the sweetly milken hay.
Then of my horse I thought the worse
When my small child did cry for nurse.

—William Zaranka

ROBERT BURNS
(1759-1796)

More Luck To Honest Poverty

More luck to honest poverty,
  It claims respect, and a' that;
But honest wealth's a better thing,
  We dare be rich for a' that.
    For a' that, and a' that,
      And spooney cant and a' that,
    A man may have a ten-pun note,
      And be a brick for a' that.

What though on soup and fish we dine,
  Wear evening togs and a' that,
A man may like good meat and wine
  Nor be a knave for a' that.
    For a' that, and a' that,
      Their fustian talk and a' that,
    A gentleman, however clean,
      May have a heart for a' that.

A prince can make a belted knight,
  A marquis, duke and a' that,
And if the title's earned, all right,
  Old England's fond of a' that.
    For a' that, and a' that,
      Their balderdash and a' that,
    A name that tells of service done,
      Is worth the wear for a' that.

Then let us pray that come it may,
  And come it will for a' that,
That common sense may take the place
  Of common cant and a' that.
    For a' that, and a' that,
      Who cackles trash and a' that,
    Or be he lord, or be he low,
      The man's an ass for a' that.

—Charles William Shirley Brooks

For A' That and A' That

"A man's a man," says Robert Burns,
"For a' that and a' that,"
But though the song be clear and strong,
It lacks a note for a' that.
The lout who'd shirk his daily work,
Yet claim his wage and a' that,
Or beg when he can earn his bread,
Is not a man for a' that.

If all who dine on homely fare
Were true and brave, and a' that;
And none whose garb is "hodden grey"
Was fool and knave and a' that;
The vice and crime that shame our time,
Would fade and fall and a' that;
And ploughmen be as good as kings,
And churls as earls, for a' that.

You see yon brawny, blustering sot,
Who swaggers, swears, and a' that;
And thinks, because his strong right arm
Might fell an ox, and a' that.
That he's as noble, man for man,
As duke or lord and a' that,
He's but a brute, beyond dispute,
And *not* a man for a' that.

A man may own a large estate,
Have palace, park, and a' that;
And not for birth, but honest worth,
Be thrice a man for a' that;
And Donald herding on the muir,
Who beats his wife and a' that,
Be nothing but a rascal boor,
Nor half a man for a' that.

It comes to this, dear Robert Burns,
The truth is old and a' that,
The rank is but the guinea's stamp,
The man's the gowd for a' that.
And though you put the minted mark
On copper, brass, and a' that,
The lie is gross, the cheat is plain,
And will not pass, for a' that.

For a' that and a' that
'Tis soul and heart, and a' that,
That makes the king a gentleman,
And not his crown, and a' that.
And man with man, if rich or poor,
The best is he, for a' that,
Who stands erect in self-respect,
And acts the man for a that.

—*Anonymous*

In Memory of Edward Wilson

Rigid Body (sings):

Gin a body meet a body
  Flyin' through the air,
Gin a body hit a body,
  Will it fly? and where?

Ilka impact has its measure,
  Ne'er a ane hae I,
Yet a' the lads they measure me,
  Or, at least, they try.

Gin a body meet a body
  Altogether free,
How they travel afterwards
  We do not always see.

Ilka problem has its method
  By analytics high;
For me, I ken na ane o' them,
  But what the waur am I?

—James Clerk Maxwell

Lilt Your Johnnie

Wi' patchit brose and ilka pen,
Nae bairns to clad the gleesome ken;
But chapmen billies, a' gude men,
  And *Doon* sae bonnie!
Ne'er let the scornfu' mutchit ben;
  But lilt your Johnnie!

For whistle binkie's unco'biel,
Wad haggis mak of ony chiel,
To jaup in luggies like the deil,
  O'er loop or cronnie:
You wadna croop to sic a weel;
  But lilt your Johnnie!

Sae let the pawkie carlin scraw,
And hoolie, wi' outlandish craw,
Kail weedies frae the ingle draw
  As blyth as honie;
Amang the thummart dawlit wa'
  To lilt your Johnnie.

—Anonymous

Roasted Sucking Pig

Cooks who'd roast a sucking-pig,
Purchase one not over big;
Coarse ones are not worth a fig
    So a young one buy.
See that he is scalded well
(That is done by those who sell).
Therefore on that point to dwell,
    Were absurdity.

Sage and bread, mix just enough,
Salt and pepper *quantum suff.*,
And the Pig's interior stuff,
With the whole combined.
To a fire that's rather high,
Lay it till completely dry;
Then to every part apply
Cloth, with butter lined.

Dredge with flour o'er and o'er,
Till the Pig will hold no more:
Then do nothing else before
'Tis for serving fit—
Then scrape off the flour with care:
Then a butter'd cloth prepare;
Rub it well; then cut—not tear—
Off the head of it.

Then take out and mix the brains
With the gravy it contains;
While it on the spit remains,
Cut the Pig in two.
Chop the sage, and chop the bread
Fine as very finest shred;
O'er it melted butter spread—
Stinginess won't do.

When it in the dish appears,
Garnish with the jaws and ears;
And when dinner-hour nears,
Ready let it be.
Who can offer such a dish
May dispense with fowl and fish;
And if he a guest should wish,
LET HIM SEND FOR ME!

—*Anonymous*

WILLIAM WORDSWORTH
(1770-1850)

The Aged Aged Man

I'll tell thee everything I can:
There's little to relate.
I saw an aged aged man,
A-sitting on a gate.
"Who are you, aged man?" I said.
"And how is it you live?"
And his answer trickled through my head
Like water through a sieve.

He said "I look for butterflies
That sleep among the wheat:
I make them into mutton-pies,
And sell them in the street.

I sell them unto men," he said,
"Who sail on stormy seas;
And that's the way I get my bread—
A trifle, if you please."

But I was thinking of a plan
To dye one's whiskers green,
And always use so large a fan
That they could not be seen.
So, having no reply to give
To what the old man said,
I cried "Come, tell me how you live!"
And thumped him on the head.

His accents mild took up the tale:
He said "I go my ways,
And when I find a mountain-rill,
I set it in a blaze;
And thence they make a stuff they call
Rowland's Macassar Oil—
Yet twopence-halfpenny is all
They give me for my toil."

But I was thinking of a way
To feed oneself on batter,
And so go on from day to day
Getting a little fatter.
I shook him well from side to side,
Until his face was blue:
"Come, tell me how you live," I cried,
"And what it is you do!"

He said "I hunt for haddocks' eyes
Among the heather bright,
And work them into waistcoat-buttons
In the silent night.
And these I do not sell for gold
Or coin of silvery shine,
But for a copper halfpenny,
And that will purchase nine."

"I sometimes dig for buttered rolls,
Or set limed twigs for crabs;
I sometimes search the grassy knolls
For wheels of hansom-cabs.
And that's the way" (he gave a wink)
"By which I get my wealth—
And very gladly will I drink
Your Honour's noble health."

I heard him then, for I had just
Completed my design
To keep the Menai bridge from rust
By boiling it in wine.
I thanked him much for telling me
The way he got his wealth,
But chiefly for his wish that he
Might drink my noble health.

And now, if e'er by chance I put
  My fingers into glue,
Or madly squeeze a right-hand foot
  Into a left-hand shoe,
Or if I drop upon my toe
  A very heavy weight,
I weep, for it reminds me so
Of that old man I used to know—
Whose look was mild, whose speech was slow,
Whose hair was whiter than the snow,
Whose face was very like a crow,
With eyes, like cinders, all aglow,
Who seemed distracted with his woe,
Who rocked his body to and fro,
And muttered mumblingly and low,
As if his mouth were full of dough,
Who snorted like a buffalo—
That summer evening long ago,
  A-sitting on a gate.

—*Lewis Carroll*

A Sonnet

Two voices are there: one is of the deep;
It learns the storm-cloud's thunderous melody,
Now roars, now murmurs with the changing sea,
Now bird-like pipes, now closes soft in sleep:
And one is of an old half-witted sheep
Which bleats articulate monotony,
And indicates that two and one are three,
That grass is green, lakes damp, and mountains steep:
And, Wordsworth, both are thine: at certain times
Forth from the heart of thy melodious rhymes,
The form and pressure of high thoughts will burst:
At other times—good Lord! I'd rather be
Quite unacquainted with the ABC
Than write such hopeless rubbish as thy worst.

—*J.K. Stephen*

The Everlasting Mercy

Ever since boyhood it has been my joy
To rove the hills and vales, the woods and streams,
To commune with the flowers, the beasts, the birds,
And all the humble messengers of God.
And so not seldom have my footsteps strayed
To that bare farm where Thomas Haythornthwaite
(Alas! 'tis now ten years the good old man
Is dead!) wrung turnips from the barren soil,
To keep himself and his good wife, Maria,
Whom I remember well, although 'tis now
Full twenty years since she deceased; and I
Have often visited her quiet grave
In summer and in winter, that I might
Place some few flowers upon it, and returned
In solemn meditation from the spot.
In the employment of this honest man

There was a hind, Saul Kane, I knew him well,
And oft-times 'twas my fortune to lament
The blackness of the youth's depravity.
For when I came to visit Haythornthwaite
The good old man, leaning upon this spade,
Would say to me, "Saul Kane is wicked, sir;
A wicked lad. Before he cut his teeth
He broke his poor old mother's heart in two.
For at the beer-house he is often seen
With ill companions, and at dead of night
We hear him loud blaspheming at the owls
That fly about the house. I oft have blushed
At deeds of his I could not speak about."
But yet so wondrous is the heart of man
That even Saul Kane repented of his sins—
A little maid, a little Quaker maid,
Converted him one day. "Saul Kane," she said,
"Dear Saul, I pray you will get drunk no more."
Nor did he; but embraced a sober life,
And married Mary Thorpe; and yesterday
I met him on my walk, and with him went
Up to the house where he and his do dwell.
And there I long in serious converse stayed,
Speaking of Nature and of politics,
And then turned homeward meditating much
About the single transferable vote.

—*J.C. Squire*

Only Seven

I marvelled why a simple child,
That lightly draws its breath,
Should utter groans so very wild,
And look as pale as Death.

Adopting a parental tone,
I ask'd her why she cried;
The damsel answered with a groan,
"I've got a pain inside!

"I thought it would have sent me mad
Last night about eleven."
Said I, "What is it makes you bad?
How many apples have you had?"
She answered, "Only seven!"

"And are you sure you took no more,
My little maid?" quoth I;
"Oh, please, sir, mother gave me four,
But they were in a pie!"

"If that's the case," I stammer'd out,
"Of course you've had eleven."
The maiden answered with a pout,
"I ain't had more nor seven!"

I wonder'd hugely what she meant,
And said, "I'm bad at riddles;
But I know where little girls are sent
For telling taradiddles.

"Now, if you won't reform," said I,
  "You'll never go to Heaven."
But all in vain; each time I try,
That little idiot makes reply,
  "I ain't had more nor seven!"

—*Henry S. Leigh*

Lucy Lake

Poor Lucy Lake was overgrown,
  But somewhat underbrained.
She did not know enough, I own,
  To go in when it rained.

Yet Lucy was constrained to go;
  Green bedding,—you infer.
Few people knew she died, but oh,
  The difference to her!

—*Newton Mackintosh*

There Lived Among the Untrodden Ways

There lived among the untrodden ways
  To Rydal Lake doth lead;
A bard whom there were none to praise
  And very few to read.

Behind a cloud his mystic sense,
  Deep hidden, who can spy?
Brightens the night when not a star
  Is shining in the sky.

Unread his works—his "Milk-white Doe"
  With dust is dark and dim;
It's still in Longman's shop, and O,
  The difference to him!

—*Hartley Coleridge*

James Rigg

On Tuesday morn at half-past six o'clock,
I rose and dressed myself, and having shut
The door o' the bedroom still and leisurely,
I walk'd downstairs. When at the outer-door
I firmly grasped the key that 'ere night-fall
Had turned the lock into its wonted niche
Within the brazen implement, that shone
With no unseemly splendour,—mellow'd light,
Elicited by touch of careful-hand
On the brown lintel; and the obedient door,
As at a potent necromancer's touch,
Into the air receded suddenly,
And gave wide prospect of the sparkling lake,
Just then emerging from the snow-white mist
Like angel's veil slow-folded up to heaven.
And lo! a vision bright and beautiful
Sheds a refulgent glory o'er the sand,
The sand and gravel of my avenue!

For standing silent by the kitchen-door,
Tinged by the morning sun, and in its own
Brown natural hide most lovely, two long ears
Upstretching perpendicularly, then
With the horizon levelled—to my gaze
Superb as horn of fabled Unicorn,
Each in its own proportions grander far
Than the frontal glory of that wandering beast,
Child of the Desert! Lo! a beauteous Ass,
With paniers hanging silent at each side!
Silent as cage of bird whose song is mute,
Though silent yet not empty, fill'd with bread
The staff of life, the means by which the soul
By fate obedient to the powers of sense,
Renews its faded vigour, and keeps up
A proud communion with the eternal heavens.
Fasten'd to a ring it stood, while at its head
A boy of six years old, as angel bright,
Patted its neck and to its mouth applied
The harmless thistle that his hand had pluck'd
From the wild common, melancholy crop.

—*James Hogg*

From THE RECLUSE

The Flying Tailor

If ever chance or choice thy footsteps lead
Into that green and flowery burial-ground
That compasseth with sweet and mournful smiles
The Church of Grasmere,—by the eastern gate
Enter—and underneath a stunted yew,
Some three yards distant from the gravel-walk,
On the left-hand side, thou wilt espy a grave,
With unelaborate headstone beautified,
Conspicuous 'mid the other stoneless heaps
'Neath which the children of the valley lie.
There pause—and with no common feelings read
This short inscription—"Here lies buried
The Flying Tailor, aged twenty-nine!"

Him from his birth unto his death I knew,
And many years before he had attained
The fulness of his fame, I prophesied
The triumphs of that youth's agility,
And crowned him with that name which afterwards
He nobly justified—and dying left
To fame's eternal blazon—read it here—
"The Flying Tailor!"

It is somewhat strange
That his mother was a cripple, and his father
Long way declined into the vale of years,
When their son Hugh was born. At first the babe
Was sickly, and a smile was seen to pass
Across the midwife's cheek, when, holding up
The sickly wretch, she to the father said,
"A fine man-child!" What else could they expect?
The mother being, as I said before,

A cripple, and the father of the child
Long way declined into the vale of years.
But mark the wondrous change—ere he was put
By his mother into breeches, Nature strung
The muscular part of his economy
To an unusual strength, and he could leap,
All unimpeded by his petticoats,
Over the stool on which his mother sat
When carding wool, or cleansing vegetables,
Or meek performing other household tasks.
Cunning he watched his opportunity,
And oft, as house affairs did call her thence,
Overleapt Hugh, a perfect whirligig,
More than six inches o'er the astonished stool!
What boots it to narrate, how at leap-frog
Over the breeched and unbreeched villagers
He shone conspicuous? Leap-frog do I say?
Vainly so named. What though in attitude
The Flying Tailor aped the croaking race
When issuing from the weed-entangled pool,
Tadpoles no more, they seek the new mown fields,
A jocund people, bouncing to and fro
Amid the odorous clover—while amazed
The grasshopper sits idle on the stalk
With folded pinions and forgets to sing.
Frog-like, no doubt, in attitude he was:
But sure his bounds across the village green
Seemed to my soul—(my soul for ever bright
With purest beams of sacred poesy)—
Like bounds of red deer on the Highland hill,
When, close environed by the tinchel's chain,
He lifts his branchy forehead to the sky,
Then o'er the many-headed multitude
Springs belling half in terror, half in rage,
And fleeter than the sunbeam or the wind
Speeds to his cloud-lair on the mountain top.

No more of this—suffice it to narrate,
In his tenth year he was apprenticed
Unto a Master Tailor, by a strong
And regular indenture of seven years,
Commencing from the date the parchment bore.
And ending on a certain day, that made
The term complete of seven solar years.
Oft have I heard him say, that at this time
Of life he was most wretched; for, constrained
To sit all day cross-legged upon a board,
The natural circulation of the blood
Thereby was oft impeded, and he felt
So numbed at times, that when he strove to rise
Up from his work, he could not, but fell back
Among the shreds and patches that bestrewed
With various colours, brightening gorgeously,
The board all round him—patch of warlike red
With which he patched the regimental suits
Of a recruiting military troop,
At that time stationed in a market-town
At no great distance—eke of solemn black
Shreds of no little magnitude, with which
The parson's Sunday coat was then repairing,
That in the new-roofed church he might appear

With fitting dignity—and gravely fill
The sacred seat of pulpit eloquence,
Cheering with doctrinal point and words of faith
The poor man's heart, and from the shallow wit
Of atheist drying up each argument,
Or sharpening his own weapons, only to turn
Their point against himself, and overthrow
His idols with the very enginery
Reared 'gainst the structure of our English Church.

Oft too, when striving all he could to finish
The stated daily task, the needle's point,
Slanting insidious from the eluded stitch,
Hath pinched his finger, by the thimble's mail
In vain defended, and the crimson blood
Distained the lining of some wedding-suit;
A dismal omen! that to mind like his,
Apt to perceive in slightest circumstance
Mysterious meaning, yielded sore distress
And feverish perturbation, so that oft
He scarce could eat his dinner—nay, one night
He swore to run from his apprenticeship,
And go on board a first-rate man-of-war,
From Plymouth lately come to Liverpool,
Where, in the stir and tumult of a crew
Composed of many nations, 'mid the roar
Of wave and tempest, and the deadlier voice
Of battle, he might strive to mitigate
The fever that consumed his mighty heart.

But other doom was his. That very night
A troop of tumblers came into the village,
Tumbler, equestrian, mountebank,—on wire,
On rope, on horse, with cup and balls, intent
To please the gaping multitude, and win
The coin from labour's pocket—small perhaps
Each separate piece of money, but when joined
Making a good round sum, destined ere long
All to be melted (so these lawless folk
Name spending coin in loose debauchery),
Melted into ale—or haply stouter cheer,
Gin diuretic, or the liquid flame
Of baneful brandy, by the smuggler brought
From the French coast in shallop many-oared,
Skulking by night round headland and through bay,
Afraid of the king's cutter, or the barge
Of cruising frigate, armed with chosen men,
And with her sweeps across the foamy waves
Moving most beautiful with measured strokes.

It chanced that as he threw a somerset
Over three horses (each of larger size
Than our small mountain-breed), one of the troop
Put out his shoulder, and was otherwise
Considerably bruised, especially
About the loins and back. So he became
Useless unto that wandering company,
And likely to be felt a sore expense
To men just on the eve of bankruptcy;
So the master of the troop determined
To leave him in the workhouse, and proclaimed

That if there was a man among the crowd
Willing to fill his place and able too,
Now was the time to show himself. Hugh Thwaites
Heard the proposal, as he stood apart
Striving with his own soul—and with a bound
He leapt into the circle, and agreed
To supply the place of him who had been hurt.
A shout of admiration and surprise
Then tore heaven's concave, and completely filled
The little field, where near a hundred people
Were standing in a circle round and fair.
Oft have I striven by meditative power,
And reason working 'mid the various forms
Of various occupations and professions,
To explain the cause of one phenomenon,
That, since the birth of science, hath remained
A bare enunciation, unexplained
By any theory, or mental light
Streamed on it by the imaginative will,
Or spirit musing in the cloudy shrine,
The penetralia of the immortal soul.
I now allude to that most curious fact,
That 'mid a given number, say threescore,
Of tailors, more men of agility
Will issue out, than from an equal show
From any other occupation—say
Smiths, barbers, bakers, butchers, or the like.
Let me not seem presumptuous, if I strive
This subject to illustrate; nor, while I give
My meditations to the world, will I
Conceal from it, that much I have to say
I learnt from one who knows the subject well
In theory and practice—need I name him?
The light-heeled author of the Isle of Palms,
Illustrious more for leaping than for song.

First, then, I would lay down this principle,
That all excessive action by the law
Of nature tends unto repose. This granted,
All action not excessive must partake
The nature of excessive action—so
That in all human beings who keep moving,
Unconscious cultivation of repose
Is going on in silence. Be it so.
Apply to men of sedentary lives
This leading principle, and we behold
That, active in their inactivity,
And unreposing in their long repose,
They are, in fact, the sole depositaries
Of all the energies by others wasted,
And come at last to teem with impulses
Of muscular motion, not to be withstood,
And either giving vent unto themselves
In numerous feats of wild agility,
Or terminating in despair and death.

Now, of all sedentary lives, none seems
So much so as the tailor's.—Weavers use
Both arms and legs, and, we may safely add,
Their bodies too, for arms and legs can't move
Without the body—as the waving branch

Of the green oak disturbs his glossy trunk.
Not so the tailor—for he sits cross-legged,
Cross-legged for ever! save at times of meals,
In bed, or when he takes his little walk
From shop to alehouse, picking, as he goes,
Stray patch of fustian, cloth, or cassimere,
Which, as by natural instinct, he discerns,
Though soiled with mud, and by the passing wheel
Bruised to attenuation 'gainst the stones.

Here then we pause—and need no farther go;
We have reached the sea-mark of our utmost sail.
Now let me trace the effect upon his mind
Of this despised profession. Deem not thou,
O rashly deem not, that his boyish days
Past at the shop-board, when the stripling bore
With bashful feeling of apprenticeship
The name of Tailor; deem not that his soul
Derived no genial influence from a life,
Which, although haply adverse in the main
To the growth of intellect, and the excursive power,
Yet in its ordinary forms possessed
A constant influence o'er his passing thoughts,
Moulded his appetences and his will,
And wrought out, by the work of sympathy
Between his bodily and mental form,
Rare correspondence, wondrous unity!
Perfect—complete—and fading not away.
While on his board cross-legged he used to sit,
Shaping of various garments to his mind,
An image rose of every character
For whom each special article was framed,
Coat, waistcoat, breeches. So at last his soul
Was like a storehouse, filled with images,
By musing hours of solitude supplied.
Nor did his ready fingers shape the cut
Of villager's uncouth habiliments
With greater readiness, than did his mind
Frame corresponding images of those
Whose corporal measurement the neat-marked paper
In many a mystic notch for aye retained.
Hence, more than any man I ever knew,
Did he possess the power intuitive
Of diving into character. A pair
Of breeches, to his philosophic eye,
Were not what unto other folks they seem,
Mere simple breeches, but in them he saw
The symbol of the soul-mysterious, high
Hieroglyphics! such as Egypt's Priest
Adored upon the holy Pyramid,
Vainly imagined tomb of monarchs old,
But raised by wise philosophy, that sought
But darkness to illumine, and to spread
Knowledge by dim concealment—process high
Of man's imaginative, deathless soul.
Nor, haply, in the abasement of the life
Which stern necessity had made his own,
Did he not recognize a genial power
Of soul-ennobling fortitude. He heard
Unmoved the witling's shallow contumely,
And thus, in spite of nature, by degrees

He saw a beauty and a majesty
In this despised trade, which warrior's brow
Hath rarely circled—so that when he sat
Beneath his sky-light window, he hath cast
A gaze of triumph on the godlike sun,
And felt that orb, in all his annual round,
Beheld no happier, nobler character
Than him, Hugh Thwaites, a little tailor boy.

Thus I, with no unprofitable song,
Have, in the silence of the umbrageous wood,
Chaunted the heroic youthful attributes
Of him the Flying Tailor. Much remains
Of highest argument, to lute or lyre
Fit to be murmured with impassioned voice;
And when, by timely supper and by sleep
Refreshed, I turn me to the welcome task,
With lofty hopes,—Reader, do thou expect
The final termination of my lay.
For, mark my words,—eternally my name
Shall last on earth, conspicuous like a star
'Mid that bright galaxy of favoured spirits,
Who, laughed at constantly whene'er they published,
Survived the impotent scorn of base Reviews,
Monthly or Quarterly, or that accursed
Journal, the Edinburgh Review, that lives
On tears, and sighs, and groans, and brains, and blood.

—James Hogg

Fragments

There is a river clear and fair,
'Tis neither broad nor narrow;
It winds a little here and there—

It winds about like any hare;
And then it holds as straight a course
As, on the turnpike road, a horse,
Or, through the air, an arrow.

The trees that grow upon the shore
Have grown a hundred years or more;
So long there is no knowing:
Old Daniel Dobson does not know
When first those trees began to grow;
But still they grew, and grew, and grew,
As if they'd nothing else to do,
But ever must be growing.

The impulses of air and sky
Have reared their stately heads so high,
And clothed their boughs with green;
Their leaves the dews of evening quaff,—
And when the wind blows loud and keen,
I've seen the jolly timbers laugh,
And shake their sides with merry glee—
Wagging their heads in mockery.

Fixed are their feet in solid earth
Where winds can never blow;

But visitings of deeper birth
Have reached their roots below.
For they have gained the river's brink,
And of the living waters drink.

There's little Will, a five years' child—
He is my youngest boy;
To look on eyes so fair and wild,
It is a very joy.

He hath conversed with sun and shower,
And dwelt with every idle flower,
As fresh and gay as them.
He loiters with the briar-rose,—
The blue-bells are his play-fellows,
That dance upon their slender stem.

And I have said, my little Will,
Why should he not continue still
A thing of Nature's rearing?
A thing beyond the world's control—
A living vegetable soul—
No human sorrow fearing.

It were a blessed sight to see
That child become a willow-tree,
His brother trees among.
He'd be four times as tall as me,
And live three times as long.

—*Catherine Maria Fanshawe*

SIR WALTER SCOTT
(1771-1832)

A Border Ballad

BY AN ENCHANTER UNKNOWN

The Scot, to rival realms a mighty bar,
Here fixed his mountain home: a wide domain,
And rich the soil, had purple heath been grain;
But what the niggard ground of wealth denied,
From fields more blest his fearless arm supplied.

—*Leyden*

The Scotts, Kerrs, and Murrays, and Deloraines all,
The Hughies o' Hawdon, and Wills-o'-the-Wall,
The Willimondswicks, and the hard-riding Dicks,
Are staunch to the last to their old Border tricks;
Wine flows not from heath, and bread grinds not from stone,
They must reeve for their living, or life they'll have none.

When the Southron's strong arm with the steel and the law
Had tamed the moss-troopers, so bonny and braw;
Though spiders wove webs in the rusty sword-hilt,
In the niche of the hall which their forefathers built;
Yet with sly paper credit and promise to pay,
They still drove the trade which the wise call convey.

They whitewashed the front of their old Border fort;
They widened its loopholes, and opened its court;
They put in sash-windows where none were before,
And they wrote the word 'Bank' o'er the new-painted door;
The cross-bow and matchlock aside they did lay,
And they shot the stout Southron with promise to pay.

They shot him from far and they shot him from near,
And they laid him as flat as their fathers laid deer:
Their fathers were heroes, though some called them thieves
When they ransacked their dwellings and drove off their beeves;
But craft undermined what force battered in vain,
And the pride of the Southron was stretched on the plain.

Now joy to the Hughies and Willies so bold!
The Southron, like Dickson, is bought and is sold;
To his goods and his chattels, his house, and his land,
Their promise to pay is as Harlequin's wand:
A touch and a word, and pass, presto, begone,
The Southron has lost, and the Willies have won.

The Hughies and Willies may lead a glad life;
They reap without sowing, they win without strife:
The Bruce and the Wallace were sturdy and fierce,
But where Scotch steel was broken Scotch paper can pierce;
And the true meed of conquest our minstrels shall fix
On the promise to pay of our Willimondswicks.

—*Thomas Love Peacock*

From WAT O' THE CLEUCH

Walsinghame's Song

O heard ye never of Wat o' the Cleuch?
The lad that has worrying tikes enow,
Whose meat is the moss, and whose drink is the dew,
And that's the cheer of Wat o' the Cleuch!
Wat o' the Cleuch! Wat o' the Cleuch!
Woe's my heart for Wat o' the Cleuch!

Wat o' the Cleuch sat down to dine
With two pint stoups of good red wine;
But when he look'd they both were dry;
O poverty parts good company!
Wat o' the Cleuch! Wat o' the Cleuch!
O for a drink to Wat o' the Cleuch!

Wat o' the Cleuch came down the Tine
To woo a maid both gallant and fine;
But as he came o'er by Dick o' the Side
He smell'd the mutton and left the bride.
Wat o' the Cleuch! Wat o' the Cleuch!
What think ye now of Wat o' the Cleuch?

Wat o' the Cleuch came here to steal,
He wanted milk and he wanted veal;
But ere he wan o'er the Beetleston brow
He hough'd the calf and eated the cow!
Wat o' the Cleuch! Wat o' the Cleuch!
Well done, doughty Wat o' the Cleuch!

Wat o' the Cleuch came here to fight,
But his whittle was blunt and his nag took fright,
And the braggart he did what I dare not tell,
But changed his cheer at the back of the fell.
　　Wat o' the Cleuch! Wat o' the Cleuch!
　　O for a croudy to Wat o' the Cleuch!

Wat o' the Cleuch kneel'd down to pray,
He wist not what to do or to say;
But he pray'd for beef, and he pray'd for bree,
A two-hand spoon and a haggis to pree.
　　Wat o' the Cleuch! Wat o' the Cleuch!
　　That's the cheer for Wat o' the Cleuch!

But the devil is cunning as I heard say,
He knew his right, and haul'd him away;
And he's over the Border and over the heuch,
An off to hell with Wat o' the Cleuch!
　　Wat o' the Cleuch! Wat o' the Cleuch!
　　Lack-a-day for Wat o' the Cleuch!

But of all the wights in poor Scotland,
That ever drew bow or Border brand,
That ever drove English bullock or ewe,
There never was thief like Wat o' the Cleuch.
　　Wat o' the Cleuch! Wat o' the Cleuch!
　　Down for ever with Wat o' the Cleuch!

—*James Hogg*

SAMUEL TAYLOR COLERIDGE
(1772-1834)

The Rime of the Auncient Waggonere

Part First

It is an auncient Waggonere,
　And hee stoppeth one of nine,
"Now wherefore dost thou grip me soe
　With that horny fist of thine?"

"The bridegroom's doors are opened wide,
　And thither I must walke;
Soe, by your leave, I must be gone,
　I have noe time for talke!"

Hee holds him with his horny fist—
　"There was a wain," quothe hee—
"Hold offe, thou raggamouffine tykke,"
　Eftsoones his fist dropped hee.

Hee satte him down upon a stone,
　With ruefulle looks of feare;
And thus began this tippsye manne,
　The red-nosed waggonere.

"The waine is fulle, the horses pulle,
  Merrilye did we trotte
Alonge the bridge, alonge the road,
  A jolly crewe, I wotte."
And here the tailore smotte his breaste,
  He smelte the cabbage potte!

"The night was darke, like Noe's arke,
  Our waggone moved alonge,
The hail poured faste, loude roared the blaste,
  Yet still we moved alonge;
And sung in chorus, 'Cease, loud Borus,'
  A very charming songe.

"'Bravoe, bravissimoe,' I cried,
  The sounde was quite elatinge;
But in a trice, upon the ice,
  We hearde the horses skaitinge.

"The ice was here, the ice was there,
  It was a dismale mattere
To see the cargoe, one by one,
  Flounderinge in the wattere!

"With rout and roare, we reached the shore,
  And never a soul did sinke;
But in the rivere, gone for evere,
  Swum our meate and drinke.

"At lengthe we spied a good grey goose,
  Through the snow it came;
And with the butte end of my whippe
  I hailed it in Goddhis name.

"It staggered as it had been drunke,
  So dexterous was it hitte;
Of brokene boughs we made a fire,
  Thomme Loncheone roasted itte."—

"Be done, thou tipsye waggonere,
  To the feaste I must awaye."
The waggonere seized him by the coatte,
  And forced him there to staye,
Begginge, in gentlemanlie style,
  Butte halfe-ane-hour's delaye.

Part Second

"The crimson sun was rising o'ere
  The verge of the horizon,
Upon my worde, as faire a sunne
  As ever I clapped eyes onne.

"'Twill bee ane comfortable thinge,"
  The mutinous crewe 'gan crye;
"'Twill be ane comfortable thinge
  Within the jaile to lye;
Ah! execrable wretche," saide they,
  "That caused the goose to die!

"The day was drawing near ittes close,
The sunne was well nighe settinge;
When lo! it seemed as iffe his face
Was veiled with fringe-warke-nettinge.

"Somme saide itte was ane apple tree,
Laden with goodlye fruite,
Somme swore itte was ane foreigne birde,
Some said it was ane brute;
Alas! it was ane bumbailiffe
Riding in pursuite!

"A hue and crye sterte uppe behind,
Whilke smote our ears like thunder,
Within the waggone there was drede,
Astonishmente and wonder.

"One after one, the rascalls rann,
And from the carre did jump;
One after one, one after one,
They felle with heavy thump.

"Six miles ane houre theye offe did scoure,
Like shippes on ane stormye ocean,
Their garments flappinge in the winde,
With ane short uneasy motion.

"Their bodies with their legs did flye,
Theye fled withe fears and glyffe;
Why star'st thoue soe?—With one goode blow,
I felled the bumbailiffe!"

Part Third

"I feare thee, auncient waggonere,
I feare thy hornye fiste,
For itte is stained with goose's gore,
And bailiff's blood I wist.

"I fear to gette ane fisticuffe
From thy leathern knuckles brown;"
With that the tailore strove to ryse—
The waggonere thrusts him down.

"Thou craven, if thou mov'st a limye,
I'll give thee cause for feare;"
And thus went on that tipsye man,
The red-billed waggonere.

"The bumbailiffe so beautiful!
Declared itte was no joke,
For, to his knowledge, both his legs
And fifteen ribs were broke.

"The lighte was gone, the nighte came on,
Ane hundrede lantherns' sheen
Glimmerred on the kinge's highwaye—
Ane lovelye sighte, I ween.

"'Is it he,' quoth one, 'is this the manne?
I'll laye the rascalle stiffe;'
With cruel stroke the beak he broke
Of the harmless bumbailiffe.

"The threatening of the saucye rogue
No more I coulde abide;
Advancing forthe my goode right legg
Three paces and a stride,
I sent my left foot dexterously
Seven inches through his side.

"Up came the second from the vanne;
We had scarcely fought a round,
When someone smote me from behind,
And I fell down in a swound:

"And when my head began to clear,
I heard the yemering crew—
Quoth one, 'This man hath penance done,
And penance more shall do'."

Part Fourth

"O Freedom is a glorious thing!
And, tailore, by the by,
I'd rather in a halter swing
Than in a dungeon lie.

"The jailere came to bring me foode,
Forget it will I never,
How he turned up the white o' his eye
When I stuck him in the liver.

"His threade of life was snapt: once more
I reached the open streete;
The people sang out 'Gardyloo'
As I ran down the streete.
Methought the blessed air of heaven
Never smelte so sweete.

"Once more upon the broad highwaye
I walked with feare and drede;
And every fifteen steppes I tooke
I turned about my heade,
For feare the corporal of the guarde
Might close behind me trede!

"Behold, upon the western wave
Setteth the broad bright sunne;
So I must onward, as I have
Full fifteen miles to runne.

"And should the bailiffes hither come
To aske whilke way I've gone,
Tell them I took the othere road,"
Said hee, and trotted onne.

The tailore rushed into the roome
O'erturning three or foure;
Fractured his skulle against the walle,
And worde spake never more!!

Morale.

Such is the fate of foolish men.
The danger all may see
Of those who list to waggonere,
And keepe bad companye.

—*William Maginn*

Isabelle

Can there be a moon in heaven to-night,
That the hill and the grey cloud seem so light?
The air is whitened by some spell,
For there is no moon, I know it well:
On this third day, the sages say,
('Tis wonderful how well they know),
The moon is journeying far away,
Bright somewhere in a heaven below.

It is a strange and lovely night,
A greyish pale, but not white!
Is it rain, or is it dew,
That falls so thick I see its hue?
In rays it follows, one, two, three,
Down the air so merrily,
Said Isabelle, so let it be!

Why does the Lady Isabelle
Sit in the damp and dewy dell
Counting the racks of drizzly rain,
And how often the Rail cries over again?
For she's harping, harping in the brake,
Craik, craik—Craik, craik.—
Ten times nine, and thrice eleven;—
That last call was an hundred and seven.
Craik, craik—the hour is near—
Let it come, I have no fear!
Yet it is a dreadful work, I wis,
Such doings in a night like this!

Sounds the river harsh and loud?
The stream sounds harsh, but not loud.
There is a cloud that seems to hover,
By western hill the churchyard over,
What is it like?—'Tis like a whale;
'Tis like a shark with half the tail,
Not half, but third and more;
Now 'tis a wolf, and now a boar;
Its face is raised—it cometh here;
Let it come—there is no fear.
There's two for heaven, and ten for hell,
Let it come—'tis well—'tis well
Said the Lady Isabelle.

What ails that little cut-tailed whelp,
That it continues to yelp, yelp?
Yelp, yelp, and it turns its eye
Up to the tree and half to the sky,
Half to the sky and full to the cloud,
And still it whines and barks aloud.
Why I should dread I cannot tell;
There is a spirit; I know it well!
I see it in yon falling beam—
Is it a vision or a dream?
It is no dream, full well I know,
I have a woeful deed to do!
Hush, hush, thou little murmurer;
I tell thee hush—the dead are near!

If thou knewest all, poor tailless whelp,
Well mightest thou tremble, growl, and yelp;
But thou knowest nothing, hast no part
(Simple and stupid as thou art)
Save gratitude and truth of heart.
But they are coming by this way
That have been dead for a year and a day;
Without challenge, without change,
They shall have their full revenge!
They have been sent to wander in woe
In lands of flame, and the lands of snow;
But those that are dead
Shall the greensward tread,
And those that are living
Shall soon be dead!
None to pity them, none to help!
Thou mayest quake, my cut-tailed whelp!

There are two from the grave
That I fain would save;
Full hard is the weird
For the young and the brave!
Perchance they are rapt in vision sweet,
While the passing breezes kiss their feet;
And they are dreaming of joy and love!
Well, let them go—there's room above.

There are three times three, and three to these,
Count as you will, by twos or threes!
Three for the gallows, and three for the wave,
Three to roast behind the stone,
And three that shall never see the grave
Until the day and the hour are gone!
For retribution is mine alone!
The cloud is redder in its hue,
The hour is near, and vengeance due;
It cannot, and it will not fail,—
'Tis but a step to Borrowdale!
Why shouldest thou love and follow me?
Poor faithful thing! I pity thee!

Up rose the Lady Isabelle,
I may not of her motion tell,
Yet thou mayest look upon her frame;
Look on it with a passing eye,
But think not thou upon the same,
Turn away and ask not why;
But if thou darest look again,
Mad of heart and seared of brain,
Thou shalt never look again!

What can ail that short-tailed whelp?
'Tis either behind or far before,
And it hath changed its whining yelp
To a shortened yuff—its little core
Seems bursting with terror and dismay,
Yuff, yuff—hear how it speeds away.
Hold thy peace, thou yemering thing,
The very night-wind's slumbering,
And thou wilt wake to woe and pain
Those that must never wake again.

Meet is its terror and its flight,
There's one on the left and two on the right!
But save the paleness of the face,
All is beauty and all is grace!
The earth and air are tinged with blue;
There are no footsteps in the dew;
Is this to wandering spirits given,
Such stillness on the face of heaven?
The fleecy clouds that sleep above
Are like the wing of beauteous dove,
And the leaf of the elm tree does not move!
Yet they are coming! and they are three!
Jesu! Maria! can it be!

The Conclusion

Sleep on, fair maiden of Borrowdale!
Sleep! O sleep! and do not wake!
Dream of the dance, till the foot so pale,
And the beauteous ankle shiver and shake;
Till thou shalt press, with feeling bland,
Thine own fair breast with lover's hand.
Thy heart is light as summer breeze,
Thy heart is joyous as the day;
Man never form of angel sees,
But thou art fair as they!
So lover ween, and so they say,
So thine shall weep for many a day!
The hour's at hand, O woe is me!
For they are coming, and they are three!

—*James Hogg*

The Wise Men of Gotham

Εκιᾶς 'όναρ
—Pindar

In a bowl to sea went wise men three,
On a brilliant night of June:
They carried a net, and their hearts were set
On fishing up the moon.

The sea was calm, the air was balm,
Not a breath stirred low or high,
And the moon, I trow, lay as bright below,
And as round as in the sky.

The wise men with the current went,
Nor paddle nor oar had they,
And still as the grave they went on the wave,
That they might not disturb their prey.

Far, far at sea, were the wise men three,
When their fishing-net they threw;
And at the throw, the moon below
In a thousand fragments flew.

The sea was bright with the dancing light
Of a million million gleams,
Which the broken moon shot forth as soon
As the net disturbed her beams.

They drew in their net: it was empty and wet,
And they had lost their pain,
Soon ceased the play of each dancing ray,
And the image was round again.

Three times they threw, three times they drew,
And all the while were mute;
And evermore their wonder grew,
Till they could not but dispute.

Their silence they broke, and each one spoke
Full long, and loud, and clear;
A man at sea their voices three
Full three leagues off might hear.

The three wise men got home again
To their children and their wives:
But touching their trip, and their net's vain dip,
They disputed all their lives.

The wise men three could never agree,
Why they missed the promised boon;
They agreed alone that their net they had thrown,
And they had not caught the moon.

I have thought myself pale o'er this ancient tale,
And its sense I could not ken;
But now I see that the wise men three
Were paper-money men.

'Rub-a-dub-dub, three men in a tub,'
Is a mystic burthen old,
Which I've pondered about till my fire went out,
And I could not sleep for cold.

I now divine each mystic sign,
Which robbed me oft of sleep,
Three men in a bowl, who went to troll,
For the moon in the midnight deep.

Three men were they who science drank
From Scottish fountains free;
The cash they sank in the Gotham bank,
Was the moon beneath the sea.

The breaking of the imaged moon,
At the fishing-net's first splash,
Was the breaking of the bank as soon
As the wise men claimed their cash.

The dispute which lasted all their lives,
Was the economic strife,
Which the son's son's son of every one
Will maintain through all his life.

The son's son's sons will baffled be,
As were their sires of old;
But they only agree, like the wise men three,
That they could not get their gold.

And they'll build systems dark and deep,
And systems broad and high;
But two of three will never agree
About the reason why.

And he who at this day will seek
The Economic Club,
Will find at least three sages there,
As ready as any that ever were
To go to sea in a tub.

—Thomas Love Peacock

Lines Written Near Linton, on Exmoor

By illness pent in lime-tree bower
And tossed upon the pains of sleep,
I gazed at lofty castle keep
With many a crenellated tower
On river-bank;—then, such a power
Poured through me, visionary, deep,
I seized my pen, in verse to keep
The revelation of that hour,

—But who beats oar so hard on oarlock,
Importunately shakes my doorlock,
Stands on doorsill tugging forelock?
Salesperson, scholiast, or warlock
Dissolves my dream, his task, and the name
Of the wretched place from whence he came...

—Daniel Hoffman

ROBERT SOUTHEY
(1774-1843)

The Friend of Humanity and the Knife Grinder

Friend of Humanity

"Needy Knife-grinder! whither are you going?
Rough is the road, your wheel is out of order—
Bleak blows the blast;—your hat has got a hole in't,
So have your breeches!

"Weary Knife-grinder! little think the proud ones,
Who in their coaches roll along the turnpike-
road, what hard work 'tis crying all day 'Knives and
Scissors to grind O!'

"Tell me, Knife-grinder, how you came to grind knives?
Did some rich man tyrannically use you?
Was it the squire? or parson of the parish?
Or the attorney?

"Was it the squire, for killing of his game? or
Covetous parson, for his tithes distraining?
Or roguish lawyer, made you lose your little
All in a lawsuit?

"(Have you not read the Rights of Man, by Tom Paine?)
Drops of compassion tremble on my eyelids,
Ready to fall, as soon as you have told your
Pitiful story."

Knife-Grinder

"Story! God bless you! I have none to tell, sir,
Only last night a-drinking at the Chequers,
This poor old hat and breeches, as you see, were
Torn in a scuffle.

"Constables came up for to take me into
Custody; they took me before the justice;
Justice Oldmixon put me in the parish-
Stocks for a vagrant.

"I should be glad to drink your Honour's health in
A pot of beer, if you will give me sixpence;
But for my part, I never love to meddle
With politics, sir."

Friend of Humanity

"I give thee sixpence! I will see thee damn'd first—
Wretch! whom no sense of wrongs can rouse to vengeance—
Sordid, unfeeling, reprobate, degraded,
Spiritless outcast!"

(*Kicks the Knife-grinder, overturns his wheel, and exit in a transport of Republican enthusiasm and universal philanthropy.*)

—George Canning and J.H. Frere

Father William

"You are old, Father William," the young man said,
"And your hair has become very white;
And yet you incessantly stand on your head—
Do you think, at your age, it is right?"

"In my youth," Father William replied to his son,
"I feared it might injure the brain;
But, now that I'm perfectly sure I have none,
Why, I do it again and again."

"You are old," said the youth, "as I mentioned before,
And have grown most uncommonly fat;
Yet you turned a back-somersault in at the door—
Pray, what is the reason of that?"

"In my youth," said the sage, as he shook his grey locks,
"I kept all my limbs very supple
By the use of this ointment—one shilling the box—
Allow me to sell you a couple?"

"You are old," said the youth, "and your jaws are too weak
For anything tougher than suet;
Yet you finished the goose, with the bones and the beak—
Pray, how did you manage to do it?"

"In my youth," said his father, "I took to the law,
And argued each case with my wife;
And the muscular strength, which it gave to my jaw,
Has lasted the rest of my life."

"You are old," said the youth, "one would hardly suppose
That your eye was as steady as ever;
Yet you balanced an eel on the end of your nose—
What made you so awfully clever?"

"I have answered three questions, and that is enough,"
Said his father. "Don't give yourself airs!
Do you think I can listen all day to such stuff?
Be off, or I'll kick you down stairs!"

—Lewis Carroll

THOMAS MOORE
(1779-1852)

'Twas Ever Thus

I never bought a young gazelle,
To glad me with its soft black eye,
But, when it came to know me well,
'Twas sure to butt me on the sly.

I never drilled a cockatoo,
To speak with almost human lip,
But, when a pretty phrase it knew,
'Twas sure to give some friend a nip.

I never trained a collie hound
To be affectionate and mild,
But, when I thought a prize I'd found,
'Twas sure to bite my youngest child.

I never kept a tabby kit
To cheer my leisure with its tricks,
But, when we all grew fond of it,
'Twas sure to catch the neighbor's chicks.

I never reared a turtle-dove,
To coo all day with gentle breath,
But, when its life seemed one of love,
'Twas sure to peck its mate to death.

I never—well I never yet—
And I have spent no end of pelf—
Invested money in a pet
That didn't misconduct itself.

—Anonymous

GEORGE GORDON, LORD BYRON
(1788-1824)

The Passing of Arthur

So all day long the noise of battle rolled
Among the mountains by the western sea,
Till, when the bell for evening service tolled,
Each side had swiped the other utterly;
And, looking round, Sir Bedivere the bold
Said, "Sire, there's no one left but you and me;
I'm game to lay a million to a fiver
That, save for us, there is not one survivor."

"Quite likely," answered Arthur, "and I'm sure
That I have been so hammered by these swine
To-morrow's sun will find us yet one fewer.
I prithee take me to yon lonely shrine
Where I may rest and die. There is no cure
For men with sixty-seven wounds like mine."
So Bedivere did very firmly grapple
His arm, and led him to the Baptist Chapel.

There he lay down, and by him burned like flame
His sword Excalibur: its massy hilt
Crusted with blazing gems that never came
From mortal mines; its blade, inlaid and gilt
And graved with many a necromantic name,
Still dabbled with the blood the king had spilt.
Which touching, Arthur said, "Sir Bedivere,
Please take this brand and throw him in the mere."

Bold Bedivere sprang back like one distraught,
Or like a snail when tapped upon the shell,
Was *this* the peerless prince for whom he'd fought,
A man who'd drop his cheque-book down a well?
Surely he must have dreamt the words, he thought.
Had the king spoken? Was it possible
To give so lunatic a proposal credit?...
And yet the king undoubtedly had said it.

He said it again in accents full serene:
"Go to the lake and throw this weapon in it,
And then come back and tell me what you've seen.
The business should not take you half a minute.
Off now. I say precisely what I mean."
"Right, sire!" But, *sotto voce*, "What a sin it
Would be, what criminal improvidence
To waste an *arme blanche* of such excellence!"

But Arthur's voice broke through his meditation,
"Why this delay? I thought I said 'at once'?"
"Yes, sire," said he, and, with a salutation
Walked off reflecting, "How this fighting blunts
One's wits. In any other situation
I should have guessed—'twere obvious to a dunce
That this all comes from Merlin's precious offices,
Why could he not confine himself to prophecies?"

Bearing the brand, across the rocks he went
  And now and then a hot impatient word
Witnessed the stress of inner argument.
  "Curse it," he mused, "a really sumptuous sword
Is just the very one accoutrement
  I never have been able to afford;
This beautiful, this incomparable Excalibur
Would nicely suit a warrior of my calibre.

"Could anything be madder than to hurl in
  This stupid lake a sword as good as new,
Merely because that hoary humbug Merlin
  Suggested that would be the thing to do?
A bigger liar never came from Berlin,
  I *won't* be baulked by guff and bugaboo;
The old impostor's take may call in vain for it
I'll stick it in a hole and come again for it."

So, having safely stowed away the sword
  And marked the place with several large stones
Sir Bedivere returned to his liege lord
  And, with a studious frankness in his tones,
Stated that he had dropped it overboard;
  But Arthur only greeted him with groans:
"My Bedivere," he said, "I may be dying,
But even dead I'd spot such barefaced lying.

"It's rather rough upon a dying man
  That his last dying orders should be flouted.
Time was when if you'd thus deranged my plan
I should have said, 'Regard yourself as outed,
I'll find some other gentleman who can.'
Now I must take what comes, that's all about it....
My strength is failing fast, it's very cold here.
Come, pull yourself together, be a soldier.

"Once more I must insist you are to lift
  Excalibur and hurl him in the mere.
Don't hang about now. You had better shift
  For all you're worth, or when you come back here
The chances are you'll find your master stiffed."
  Whereat the agonized Sir Bedivere,
His "Yes, Sire," broken by a noisy sob,
Went off once more on his distasteful job.

But as he walked the inner voice did say:
  "I quite agree with 'Render unto Caesar,'
But nothing's said of throwing things away
  When a man's king's an old delirious geezer,
You don't meet swords like this one every day.
  Jewels and filigree as fine as these are
Should surely be preserved in a museum
That our posterity may come and see 'em.

"A work of Art's a thing one holds in trust,
  One has no right to throw it in a lake,
Such Vandalism would arouse disgust
  In every Englishman who claims to take
An interest in Art. Oh no, I must
  Delude my monarch for my country's sake;
Obedience in such a case, in fact,
Were patently an anti-social act.

"It is not pleasant to deceive my king.
I had much rather humour his caprice,
But, if I tell him I have thrown the thing,
And, thinking that the truth, he dies in peace,
Surely the poets of our race will sing
(Unless they are the most pedantic geese)
The praises of the knight who lied to save
This precious weapon from a watery grave."

"He reached the margin of the lake and there
Until a decent interval had passed
Lingered, the sword once more safe in its lair.
Then to his anxious monarch hurried fast,
And, putting on a still more candid air,
Assured the king the brand had gone at last.
But Arthur, not deceived by any means,
Icily said: "Tell that to the marines.

"Sir Bedivere, this conduct won't enhance
Your reputation as a man of honour.
If you had dared to lead me such a dance
A week ago, you would have been a goner,
Listen to me! I give you one more chance;
And, if you fail again, I swear upon our
Old oath of fealty to the Table Round
I shall jump up and fell you to the ground."

So that sad soul went off alone once more.
Rebellion frowned no longer on his face;
His spirit was broken; when he reached the shore
He wormed the sword out of its hiding-place,
Excalibur, that man's eye should see no more,
And, fearing still a further lapse from grace,
Shut his eyes tight against that matchless jewel
And, desperately hissing, "This is cruel,"

Swung it far back; and then, with mighty sweep,
Hove it to southward as he had been bade.
And, as it fell, and arm did suddenly leap
Out of the moonlit wave, in samite clad,
And grasped the sword and drew it to the deep.
And all was still; and Bedivere, who had
No nerve at all left now, exclaimed, "My Hat!
I'll never want another job like that!"

Thus Bedivere at last performed his vow.
And Arthur, when the warrior bore in sight,
Read his success upon his gloomy brow.
"Done it at last," he murmured, "*that's* all right.
Well, Bedivere, and what has happened now?"
Demanded he; and the disconsolate knight
In a harsh bitter voice replied, "Oh, damn it all,
I saw a mystic arm, clothed in white samite all."

"Quite right," said Arthur, "better late than never;
Now, if you please, you'll take me for a ride,
Put me upon your back and then endeavour
To run top-speed unto the waterside.
Come, stir your stumps, you must be pretty clever,
Or otherwise I fear I shall have died
Before you've landed me upon the jetty,
And then the programme's spoilt: which were a pity."

What followed after this (although my trade is
  Romantic verse) is quite beyond my lay.
For automobile barges, full of ladies
Singing and weeping, never came my way.
Though, for that matter, I was once in Cadiz—
  But never mind. It will suffice to say
That in his final act our old friend Malory
Was obviously playing to the gallery.

—J. C. Squire

A Grievance

Dear Mr. Editor: I wish to say—
  If you will not be angry at my writing it—
But I've been used, since childhood's happy day,
  When I have thought of something, to inditing it;
I seldom think of things; and, by the way,
  Although this metre may not be exciting, it
Enables one to be extremely terse,
Which is not what one always is in verse.

I used to know a man, such things befall
  The observant wayfarer through Fate's domain
He was a man, take him for all in all,
  We shall not look upon his like again;
I know that statement's not original:
  What statement is, since Shakespere? or, since Cain,
What murder? I believe 'twas Shakespere said it, or
Perhaps it may have been your Fighting Editor.

Though why an Editor should fight, or why
  A Fighter should abase himself to edit,
Are problems far too difficult and high
  For me to solve with any sort of credit.
Some greatly more accomplished man than I
  Must tackle them: let's say then Shakespere said it;
And, if he did not, Lewis Morris may
(Or even if he did). Some other day,

When I have nothing pressing to impart,
  I should not mind dilating on this matter.
I feel its import both in head and heart,
  And always did,—especially the latter.
I could discuss it in the busy mart
  Or on the lonely housetop; hold! this chatter
Diverts me from my purpose. To the point:
The time, as Hamlet said, is out of joint,

And perhaps I was born to set it right,—
  A fact I greet with perfect equanimity.
I do not put it down to "cursed spite,"
  I don't see any cause for cursing in it. I
Have always taken very great delight
  In such pursuits since first I read divinity.
Whoever will may write a nation's songs
As long as I'm allowed to right its wrongs.

What's Eton but a nursery of wrong-righters,
A mighty mother of effective men;
A training ground for amateur reciters,
A sharpener of the sword as of the pen;
A factory of orators and fighters,
A forcing-house of genius? Now and then
The world at large shrinks back, abashed and beaten,
Unable to endure the glare of Eton.

I think I said I knew a man: what then?
I don't suppose such knowledge is forbid.
We nearly all do, more or less, know men,—
Or think we do; nor will a man get rid
Of that delusion, while he wields a pen.
But who this man was, what, if aught, he did,
Nor why I mentioned him, I do not know;
Nor what I "wished to say" a while ago.

—J.K. Stephen

Beer

In those old days which poets say were golden—
(Perhaps they laid the gilding on themselves:
And, if they did, I'm all the more beholden
To those brown dwellers in my dusty shelves,
Who talk to me "in language quaint and olden"
Of gods and demigods and fauns and elves,
Pan with his pipes, and Bacchus with his leopards,
And staid young goddesses who flirt with shepherds:)

In those old days, the Nymph called Etiquette
(Appalling thought to dwell on) was not born.
They had their May, but no Mayfair as yet,
No fashions varying as the hues of morn.
Just as they pleased they dressed and drank and ate,
Sang hymns to Ceres (their John Barleycorn)
And danced unchaperoned, and laughed unchecked,
And were no doubt extremely incorrect.

Yet do I think their theory was pleasant:
And oft, I own, my "wayward fancy roams"
Back to those times, so different from the present;
When no one smoked cigars, nor gave At-homes,
Nor smote a billiard-ball, nor winged a pheasant,
Nor "did" their hair by means of long-tailed combs,
Nor migrated to Brighton once a year,
Nor—most astonishing of all—drank Beer.

No, they did not drink Beer, "which brings me to"
(As Gilpin said) "the middle of my song."
Not that "the middle" is precisely true,
Or else I should not tax your patience long:
If I had said "beginning" it might do;
But I have a dislike to quoting wrong:
I was unlucky—sinned against, not sinning—
When Cowper wrote down "middle" for "beginning."

So to proceed. That abstinence from Malt
  Has always struck me as extremely curious.
The Greek mind must have had some vital fault,
  That they should stick to liquors so injurious—
(Wine, water, tempered p'raps with Attic salt)—
  And not at once invent that mild, luxurious,
And artful beverage, Beer. How the digestion
Got on without it, is a startling question.

Had they digestions? and an actual body
  Such as dyspepsia might make attacks on?
Were they abstract ideas—(like Tom Noddy
  And Mr. Briggs)—or men, like Jones and Jackson?
Then Nectar—was that beer, or whisky-toddy?
  Some say the Gaelic mixture, *I* the Saxon:
I think a strict adherence to the latter
Might make some Scots less pigheaded, and fatter.

Besides, Bon Gaultier definitely shows
  That the real beverage for feasting gods on
Is a soft compound, grateful to the nose
  And also to the palate, known as "Hodgson."
I know a man—a tailor's son—who rose
  To be a peer: and this I would lay odds on,
(Though in his Memoirs it may not appear,)
That that man owed his rise to copious Beer.

O Beer! O Hodgson, Guinness, Allsopp, Bass!
  Names that should be on every infant's tongue!
Shall days and months and years and centuries pass,
  And still your merits be unrecked, unsung?
Oh! I have gazed into my foaming glass,
  And wished that lyre could yet again be strung
Which once rang prophet-like through Greece, and taught her
Misguided sons that "the best drink was water."

How would he now recant that wild opinion,
  And sing—as would that I could sing—of you!
I was not born (alas!) the "Muses' minion",
  I'm not poetical, not even blue:
And he (we know) but strives with waxen pinion
  Whoe'er he is that entertains the view
Of emulating Pindar, and will be
Sponsor at last to some now nameless sea.

Oh! when the green slopes of Arcadia burned
  With all the lustre of the dying day,
And on Cithaeron's brow the reaper turned,
  (Humming, of course, in his delightful way,
How Lycidas was dead, and how concerned
  The Nymphs were when they saw his lifeless clay;
And how rock told to rock the dreadful story
That poor young Lycidas was gone to glory:)

What would that lone and labouring soul have given,
  At that soft moment, for a pewter pot!
How had the mists that dimmed his eye been riven,
  And Lycidas and sorrow all forgot!
If his own grandmother had died unshriven,
  In two short seconds he'd have recked it not;
Such power hath Beer. The heart which Grief hath canker'd
Hath one unfailing remedy—the Tankard.

Coffee is good, and so no doubt is cocoa;
  Tea did for Johnson and the Chinamen:
When "Dulce est desipere in loco"
  Was written, real Falernian winged the pen.
When a rapt audience has encored "Fra Poco"
  Or "Casta Diva", I have heard that then
The Prima Donna, smiling herself out,
Recruits her flagging powers with bottled stout.

But what is coffee, but a noxious berry,
  Born to keep used-up Londoners awake?
What is Falernian, what is Port or Sherry,
  But vile concoctions to make dull heads ache?
Nay stout itself (though good with oysters, very)—
  Is not a thing your reading man should take.
He that would shine, and petrify his tutor,
Should drink draught Allsopp in its "native pewter."

But hark! a sound is stealing on my ear—
  A soft and silvery sound—I know it well.
Its tinkling tells me that a time is near
  Precious to me—it is the Dinner Bell.
O blessed Bell! Thou bringest beef and beer,
  Thou bringest good things more than tongue may tell:
Seared is (of course) my heart—but unsubdued
Is, and shall be, my appetitie for food.

I go. Untaught and feeble is my pen:
  But on one statement I may safely venture:
That few of our most highly gifted men
  Have more appreciation of the trencher.
I go. One pound of British beef, and then
  What Mr. Swiveller called "a modest quencher";
That, home-returning, I may "soothly say",
"Fate cannot touch me: I have dined to-day."

—*Charles Stuart Calverley*

PERCY BYSSHE SHELLEY (1792-1822)

Ozymandias Revisited

I met a traveller from an antique land
Who said: Two vast and trunkless legs of stone
Stand in the desert. Near them on the sand
Half sunk, a shatter'd visage lies, whose frown
And wrinkled lip and sneer of cold command
Tell that its sculptor well those passions read
Which still survive, stamp'd on these lifeless things,
The hand that mocked them and the heart that fed;
And on the pedestal these words appear:
"My name is Ozymandias, king of kings!
Look on my works, ye Mighty, and despair!"
Also the names of Emory P. Gray,
Mr. and Mrs. Dukes, and Oscar Baer,
Of 17 West 4th Street, Oyster Bay.

—*Morris Bishop*

To a Bicycle

("Mr. Bushby said he could not convict a person of 'furiously driving' a bicycle under any clause of the Police Act, except in cases when the machine had been driven on the footway.")

Hail to thee, blithe roadster!—
Spurr'd thou never wert,
But *sans* stripe, or goad-stir,
Puttest on thy spurt,
In profuse rains, or unpremeditated dirt.

Nigher still and nigher
Down the hill thou springest;
Like a flash of fire,
O'er the ground thou wingest,
And "ting"-ing still dost speed, and speeding ever "ting"-est.

In the golden lightening
Of the sunken sun,
And when day is brightening
Thou dost rush and run,
Like a silk-bodied "jock" whose race is just begun.

The hale "peeler" even
Pelts from out thy flight,
Like a star of heaven
On a murky night,
Thou art unseen, but yet I hear thy bell's delight.

Swift as bow-sped arrow
Spins thy silver sphere,
Whose intense lamp, narrow,
'Twixt thy spokes hangs clear—
So that we, doubly, see and hear that thou art there.

All the earth and air
With a voice is loud
As, bebruised and bare,
Circled by a crowd,
A girl rains out her screams, and thou liest in the road.

We ache before and after
And pine for what is not;
Our sincerest laughter
With some pain is fraught;
Our deepest sighs are those that tell of some bruis'd spot.

Yet if we could scorn
Pain and pride and fear,
If we were things born
Not to shed a tear,
I know not how thy Bushby to us could be too dear.

Better than all measures
In the "Commons" found,
Better than all treasures
Here, or underground,
Thy wheel to pilot 'twere, thou scorner of the ground!

Teach me half their sadness
Who thy sore pain know—
Such outrageous badness
From my lips should flow
Moonshine'd not print me then, as it is printing now.

—Anonymous

JOHN KEATS
(1795-1821)

Ode on a Jar of Pickles

I

A sweet, acidulous, down-reaching thrill
Pervades my sense. I seem to see or hear
The lushy garden-grounds of Greenwich Hill
In autumn, where the crispy leaves are sere;
And odors haunt me of remotest spice
From the Levant or musky-aired Cathay,
Or from the saffron-fields of Jericho,
Where everything is nice.
The more I sniff, the more I swoon away,
And what else mortal palate craves, forego.

II

Odors unsmelled are keen, but those I smell
Are keener; wherefore let me sniff again!
Enticing walnuts, I have known ye well
In youth, when pickles were a passing pain;
Unwitting youth, that craves the candy stem,
And sugar plums to olives doth prefer,
And even licks the pots of marmalade
When sweetness clings to them.
But now I dream of ambergris and myrrh,
Tasting these walnuts in the poplar shade.

III

Lo! hoarded coolness in the heart of noon,
Plucked with its dew, the cucumber is here,
As to the Dryad's parching lips a boon,
And crescent bean-pods, unto Bacchus dear;
And, last of all, the pepper's pungent globe,
The scarlet dwelling of the sylph of fire,
Provoking purple draughts; and, surfeited,
I cast my trailing robe
O'er my pale feet, touch up my tuneless lyre,
And twist the Delphic wreath to suit my head.

IV

Here shall my tongue in otherwise be soured
Than fretful men's in parched and palsied days;
And, by the mid-May's dusky leaves embowered,
Forget the fruitful blame, the scanty praise.
No sweets to them who sweet themselves were born,
Whose natures ooze with lucent saccharine;
Who, with sad repetition soothly cloyed,
The lemon-tinted morn
Enjoy, and find acetic twilight fine.
Wake I, or sleep? The pickle-jar is void.

—Bayard Taylor

She Found Me Roots

She found me roots of relish sweet,
Doughnuts with jam and cream replete,
Dozens of oysters, pints of prawns,
Hams and tongues, terrines and brawns;

And honey wild and manna dew,
Syllabub and Irish stew,
Dover sole and lemon mousse,
Lobster, crab and Charlotte Russe

And sure in language strange she said
'Coq au vin, quiche aux courgettes,
Oeufs en cocotte, blanquette de veau,'
And then in husky murmur low

> *'I love thee true*
> Come nearer do...'
> But I cried, 'Stuff—
> I've had enough.'

—*R.W. Ransford*

THOMAS HOOD
(1799-1845)

Song of the Sheet

THE DRIPPING SHEET

This sheet wrung out of cold or tepid water is thrown around the body. Quick rubbing follows, succeeded by the same operation with a dry sheet. Its operation is truly shocking. Dress after to prevent remarks.

With nerves all shattered and worn,
  With shouts terrific and loud,
A patient stood in a cold wet sheet—
  A Grindrod's patent shroud.
Wet, wet, wet,
  In douche and spray and sleet,
And still, with a voice I shall never forget,
  He sang the song of the sheet.

"Drip, drip, drip,
  Dashing, and splashing, and dipping;
And drip, drip, drip,
  Till your fat all melts to dripping.
It's oh, for dry deserts afar,
  Or let me rather endure
Curing with salt in a family jar,
  If this is the water cure.

"Rub, rub, rub,
  He'll rub away life and limb;
Rub, rub, rub,
  It seems to be fun for him.
Sheeted from head to foot,
  I'd rather be covered with dirt;
I'll give you the sheet and the blankets to boot,
  If you'll only give me my shirt.

"Oh, men, with arms and hands,
Oh, men, with legs and shins,
It is not the sheet you're wearing out,
But human creature's skins.
Rub, rub, rub,
Body, and legs, and feet;
Rubbing at once with a double rub,
A skin as well as a sheet.

"My wife will see me no more—
She'll see the bone of her bone,
But never will see the flesh of her flesh,
For I'll have no flesh of my own.
The little that was my own,
They won't allow me to keep;
It's a pity that flesh should be so dear,
And water so very cheap.

"Pack, pack, pack,
Whenever your spirit flags,
You're doomed by hydropathic laws
To be packed in cold water rags;
Rolled up on bed or on floor,
Or sweated to death in a chair;
But my chairman's rank—my shadow I'd thank
For taking my place in there.

"Slop, slop, slop,
Never a moment of time;
Slop, slop, slop,
Slackened like mason's lime.
Stand and freeze and steam—
Steam or freeze and stand;
I wish those friends had their tongues benumbed,
That told me to leave dry land.

"Up, up, up,
In the morn before daylight,
The bathman cries 'Get up,'
(I wish he were up for a fight).
While underneath the eaves,
The dry snug swallows cling;
But give them a cold wet sheet to their backs,
And see if they'll come next spring.

"Oh! oh! it stops my breath,
(He calls it short and sweet),
Could they hear me underneath
I'll shout them from the street!
He says that in half an hour
A different man I'll feel;
That I'll jump half over the moon and want
To walk into a meal!

"I feel more nerve and power,
And less of terror and grief;
I'm thinking now of love and hope—
And now of mutton and beef.
This glorious scene will rouse my heart,
Oh, who would lie in bed?
I cannot stop, but jump and hop,
Going like needle and thread."

With buoyant spirit upborne,
With cheeks both healthy and red,
The same man ran up the Malvern Crags,
Pitying those in bed.
Trip, trip, trip,
Oh, life with health is sweet;
And still in a voice both strong and quick,
Would that its tones could reach the sick,
He sang the Song of the Sheet.

—*Anonymous*

Elegy

O spare a tear for poor Tom Hood,
Who, dazed by death, here lies;
His days abridged, he sighs across
The Bridge of Utmost Size.

His *penchant* was for punning rhymes
(Some lengthy, others—shorties);
But though his *forte* was his life,
He died within his forties.

The Muses cried: 'To you we give
The crown of rhymester's bay, Thos'.
Thos mused and thought that it might pay
To ladle out the pay-thos.

He spun the gold yet tangled yarn
Of sad Miss Kilmansegg;
And told how destiny contrived
To take her down a peg.

But now the weary toils of death
Have closed his rhyming toil,
And charged this very vital spark
To jump his mortal coil.

—*Martin Fagg*

RALPH WALDO EMERSON
(1803-1882)

Brahma

If the wild bowler thinks he bowls,
Or if the batsman thinks he's bowled,
They know not, poor misguided souls,
They, too, shall perish unconsoled.
I am the batsman and the bat,
I am the bowler and the ball,
The umpire, the pavilion cat,
The roller, pitch, and stumps, and all.

—*Andrew Lang*

All or Nothing

Whoso answers my questions
  Knoweth more than me;
Hunger is but knowledge
  In a less degree:
Prophet, priest, and poet
  Oft prevaricate,
And the surest sentence
  Hath the greatest weight.

When upon my gaiters
  Drops the morning dew,
Somewhat of Life's riddle
  Soaks my spirit through.
I am buskined by the goddess
  Of Monadnock's crest,
And my wings extended
  Touch the East and West.

Or ever coal was hardened
  In the cells of earth,
Or flowed the founts of Bourbon,
  Lo! I had my birth.
I am crowned coeval
  With the Saurian eggs,
And my fancy firmly
  Stands on its own legs.

Wouldst thou know the secret
  Of the barberry-bush,
Catch the slippery whistle
  Of the moulting thrush,
Dance upon the mushrooms,
  Dive beneath the sea,
Or anything else remarkable,
  Thou must follow me!

—Bayard Taylor

Mutton

If the fat butcher thinks he slays,
  Or he—the mutton—thinks he's slain,
Why, "troth is truth," the eater says—
  "I'll come, and cut and come again."

To hungry wolves that on him leer
  Mutton is cheap, and sheep the same,
No famished god would at him sneer—
  To famine, chops are more than fame.

Who hiss at him, him but assures
  That they are geese, but wanting wings—
Your coat is his whose life is yours,
  And baa! the hymn the mutton sings.

Ye curs, and gods of grander blood,
  And you, ye Paddies fresh from Cork,
Come taste, ye lovers of the good—
  Eat! Stuff! and turn your back on pork.

—Anonymous

ELIZABETH BARRETT BROWNING
(1806-1861)

In the Gloaming

In the gloaming to be roaming, where the crested waves are foaming,
And the shy mermaidens combing locks that ripple to their feet;
When the gloaming is, I never made the ghost of an endeavor
To discover—but whatever were the hour, it would be sweet.

"To their feet," I say, for Leech's sketch indisputably teaches
That the mermaids of our beaches do not end in ugly tails,
Nor have homes among the corals; but are shod with neat balmorals,
An arrangement no one quarrels with, as many might with scales.

Sweet to roam beneath a shady cliff, of course with some young lady,
Lalage, Naerea, Haidee, or Elaine, or Mary Ann:
Love, you dear delusive dream, you! Very sweet your victims deem you,
When, heard only by the seamew, they talk all the stuff one can.

Sweet to haste, a licensed lover, to Miss Pinkerton, the glover;
Having managed to discover what is dear Naerea's "size":
P'raps to touch that wrist so slender, as your tiny gift you tender,
And to read you're no offender, in those laughing hazel eyes.

Then to hear her call you "Harry," when she makes you fetch and carry—
O young men about to marry, what a blessed thing it is!
To be photograph'd—together—cased in pretty Russia leather—
Hear her gravely doubting whether they have spoilt your honest phiz!

Then to bring your plighted fair one first a ring—a rich and rare one—
Next a bracelet, if she'll wear one, and a heap of things beside;
And serenely bending o'er her, to inquire if it would bore her
To say when her own adorer may aspire to call her bride!

Then, the days of courtship over, with your WIFE to start for Dover
Or Dieppe—and live in clover evermore, what e'er befalls;
For I've read in many a novel that, unless they've souls that grovel
Folks *prefer* in fact a hovel to your dreary marble halls.

To sit, happy married lovers; Phillis trifling with a plover's
Egg, while Corydon uncovers with a grace the Sally Lunn,
Or dissects the lucky pheasant—that, I think, were passing pleasant,
As I sit alone at present, dreaming darkly of a Dun.

—C.S. Calverley

Gwendoline

'Twas not the brown of chestnut boughs
That shadowed her so finely;
It was the hair that swept her brows,
And framed her face divinely;
Her tawny hair, her purple eyes,
The spirit was ensphered in,
That took you with such swift surprise,
Provided you had peered in.

Her velvet foot amid the moss
And on the daisies patted,
As, querulous with sense of loss,
It tore the herbage matted.

"And come he early, come he late,"
  She saith, "it will undo me;
The sharp fore-speeded shaft of fate
  Already quivers through me.

"When I beheld his red-roan steed,
  I knew what aim impelled it.
And that dim scarf of silver brede,
  I guessed for whom he held it.
I recked not, while he flaunted by,
  Of Love's relentless vi'lence,
Yet o'er me crashed the summer sky,
  In thunders of blue silence.

"His hoof-prints crumbled down the dale,
  But left behind their lava;
What should have been my woman's mail
  Grew jellied as guava.
I looked him proud, but 'neath my pride
  I felt a boneless tremor;
He was the Beér, I descried,
  And I was but the Seemer!

"Ah, how to be what then I seemed,
  And bid him seem that is so!
We always tangle threads we dreamed,
  And contravene our bliss so,
I see the red-roan steed again!
  He looks as something sought he;
Why, hoity-toity!—*he* is fain,
  So *I*'ll be cold and haughty!"

—*Bayard Taylor*

HENRY WADSWORTH LONGFELLOW
(1807-1882)

Hiawatha's Photographing

From his shoulder Hiawatha
Took the camera of rosewood,
Made of sliding, folding rosewood;
Neatly put it all together.
In its case it lay compactly,
Folded into nearly nothing;
But he opened out the hinges,
Pushed and pulled the joints and hinges,
Till it looked all squares and oblongs,
Like a complicated figure
In the second book of Euclid.
  This he perched upon a tripod,
And the family in order
Sat before him for their pictures.
Mystic, awful, was the process.
  First, a piece of glass he coated
With Collodion, and plunged it
In a bath of Lunar Caustic
Carefully dissolved in water:

There he left it certain minutes.
    Secondly, my Hiawatha
Made with cunning hand a mixture
Of the acid Pyro-gallic,
And of Glacial Acetic,
And of Alcohol and water:
This developed all the picture.
    Finally, he fixed each picture,
With a saturate solution
Of a certain salt of Soda—
Chemists call it Hyposulphite.
(Very difficult the name is
For a metre like the present
But periphrasis has done it.)
    All the family in order,
Sat before him for their pictures.
Each in turn, as he was taken,
Volunteered his own suggestions,
His invaluable suggestions.
    First the Governor, the Father:
He suggested velvet curtains
Looped about a massy pillar;
And the corner of a table,
Of a rosewood dining-table.
He would hold a scroll of something,
Hold it firmly in his left-hand;
He would keep his right-hand buried
(Like Napoleon) in his waistcoat;
He would contemplate the distance
With a look of pensive meaning,
As of ducks that die in tempests.
    Grand, heroic was the notion:
Yet the picture failed entirely:
Failed, because he moved a little,
Moved, because he couldn't help it.
    Next his better half took courage;
She would have her picture taken.
She came dressed beyond description,
Dressed in jewels and in satin,
Far too gorgeous for an empress.
Gracefully she sat down sideways,
With a simper scarcely human,
Holding in her hand a nosegay
Rather larger than a cabbage.
All the while that she was taking,
Still the lady chattered, chattered,
Like a monkey in the forest.
"Am I sitting still?" she asked him.
"Is my face enough in profile?
Shall I hold the nosegay higher?
Will it come into the picture?"
And the picture failed completely.
    Next the Son, the Stunning-Cantab
He suggested curves of beauty,
Curves pervading all his figure,
Which the eye might follow onward,
Till they centered in the breast-pin,
Centered in the golden breast-pin.
He had learnt it all from Ruskin,
(Author of 'The Stones of Venice,'

'Seven Lamps of Architecture,'
'Modern Painters', and some others);
And perhaps he had not fully
Understood his author's meaning;
But, whatever was the reason,
All was fruitless, as the picture
Ended in an utter failure.
Next to him the eldest daughter:
She suggested very little;
Only asked if he would take her
With her look of 'passive beauty.'
Her idea of passive beauty
Was a squinting of the left-eye,
Was a drooping of the right-eye,
Was a smile that went up sideways
To the corner of the nostrils.
Hiawatha, when she asked him,
Took no notice of the question,
Looked as if he hadn't heard it;
But, when pointedly appealed to,
Smiled in his peculiar manner,
Coughed, and said it 'didn't matter,'
Bit his lip, and changed the subject.
Nor in this was he mistaken,
As the picture failed completely.
So in turn, the other sisters.
Last the youngest son was taken:
Very rough and thick his hair was,
Very round and red his face was,
Very dusty was his jacket,
Very fidgetty his manner.
And his overbearing sisters
Called him names he disapproved of:
Called him Johnny, 'Daddy's Darling,'
Called him Jacky, 'Scrubby Schoolboy.'
And, so awful was the picture,
In comparison the others
Might be thought to have succeeded—
To have partially succeeded.
Finally my Hiawatha
Tumbled all the tribe together,
('Grouped' is not the right expression,)
And, as happy chance would have it,
Did at last obtain a picture
Where the faces all succeeded:
Each came out a perfect likeness.
Then they joined and all abused it,
Unrestrainedly abused it,
As 'the worst and ugliest picture
They could possibly have dreamed of.
Giving one such strange expressions!
Sulkiness, conceit, and meanness!
Really any one would take us
(Any one that did not know us)
For the most unpleasant people!'
(Hiawatha seemed to think so,
Seemed to think it not unlikely.)
All together rang their voices,
Angry, loud, discordant voices,
As of dogs that howl in concert,

As of cats that wail in chorus.
But my Hiawatha's patience,
His politeness and his patience,
Unaccountably had vanished,
And he left that happy party.
Neither did he leave them slowly,
With the calm deliberation,
The intense deliberation
Which photographers aspire to:
But he left them in a hurry,
Left them in a mighty hurry,
Vowing that he would not stand it.
Hurriedly he packed his boxes:
Hurriedly the porter trundled
On a barrow all his boxes:
Hurriedly he took his ticket:
Hurriedly the train received him:
Thus departed Hiawatha.

—*Lewis Carroll*

Hiawatha Revisited

When he killed the Mudjokivis,
Of the skin he made him mittens,
Made them with the fur side inside,
Made them with the skin side outside,
He, to get the warm side inside,
Put the inside skin side outside;
He, to get the cold side outside,
Put the warm side fur side inside,
That's why he put the fur side inside.
Why he put the skin side outside,
Why he turned them inside outside.

—*George A. Strong*

The Metre Columbian

This is the metre Columbian. The soft-flowing trochees and dactyls,
Blended with fragments spondaic, and here and there an iambus,
Syllables often sixteen, or more or less, as it happens,
Difficult always to scan, and depending greatly on accent,
Being a close imitation, in English, of Latin hexameters—
Fluent in sound and avoiding the stiffness of blank verse,
Having the grandeur and flow of America's mountains and rivers,
Such as no bard could achieve in a mean little island like England;
Oft, at the end of a line, the sentence dividing abruptly
Breaks, and in accents mellifluous, follows the thoughts of the author.

—*Anonymous*

Excelsior

The swampy State of Illinois
Contained a greenish sort of boy,
Who read with idiotic joy—
"Excelsior!"

He tarried not to eat or drink,
  But put a flag of lightish pink,
  And traced on it in violet ink—
            Excelsior!

Though what he meant by that absurd,
  Uncouth, and stupid, senseless word,
  Has not been placed upon record—
            Excelsior!

The characters were very plain,
  In German text, yet he was fain
  With greater clearness to explain—
            Excelsior!

And so he ran, this stupid wight,
  And hollered out with all his might,
  (As to a person out of sight)—
            "Excelsior!"

And everybody thought the lad
  Within an ace of being mad,
  Who cried in accents stern and sad—
            "Excelsior!"

"Come to my arms," the maiden cried;
  The youth grinned sheepishly, and sighed,
  And then appropriately replied—
            "Excelsior!"

The evening sun is in the sky,
  But still the creature mounts on high
  And shouts (nor gives a reason why)
            "Excelsior!"

And ere he gains the topmost crag
  His feeble legs begin to lag;
  Unsteadily he holds the flag—
            Excelsior!

Now P.C. Nab is on his track!
  He puts him in an empty sack,
  And brings him home upon his back—
            Excelsior!

Nab takes him to a lumber store,
  They toss him in and lock the door,
  Which only makes him bawl the more—
            "Excelsior!"

—*Anonymous*

The Shades of Night

The shades of night were falling fast,
  And the rain was falling faster,
When through an Alpine village passed
  An Alpine village pastor:
A youth who bore mid snow and ice
  A bird that wouldn't chirrup,
And a banner with the strange device—
  "Mrs. Winslow's soothing syrup."

"Beware the pass," the old man said,
"My bold, my desperate fellah;
Dark lowers the tempest overhead,
And you'll want your umbrella;
And the roaring torrent is deep and wide—
You may hear how loud it washes."
But still that clarion voice replied:
"I've got my old goloshes."

"Oh, stay," the maiden said, "and rest
(For the wind blows from the nor'ward)
Thy weary head upon my breast—
And please don't think I'm forward."
A tear stood in his bright blue eye,
And he gladly would have tarried;
But still he answered with a sigh:
"Unhappily I'm married."

—A.E. Housman

The Day is Done

The day is done, and darkness
From the wing of night is loosed,
As a feather is wafted downward,
From a chicken going to roost.

I see the lights of the baker,
Gleam through the rain and mist,
And a feeling of sadness comes o'er me,
That I cannot well resist.

A feeling of sadness and longing
That is not like being sick,
And resembles sorrow only
As a brickbat resembles a brick.

Come, get for me some supper,—
A good and regular meal—
That shall soothe this restless feeling,
And banish the pain I feel.

Not from the pastry bakers,
Not from the shops for cake;
I would n't give a farthing
For all that they can make.

For, like the soup at dinner,
Such things would but suggest
Some dishes more substantial,
And to-night I want the best.

Go to some honest butcher,
Whose beef is fresh and nice,
As any they have in the city,
And get a liberal slice.

Such things through days of labor,
And nights devoid of ease,
For sad and desperate feelings,
Are wonderful remedies.

They have an astonishing power
To aid and reinforce,
And come like the "finally, brethren,"
That follows a long discourse.

Then get me a tender sirloin
From off the bench or hook.
And lend to its sterling goodness
The science of the cook.

And the night shall be filled with comfort,
And the cares with which it begun
Shall fold up their blankets like Indians,
And silently cut and run.

—*Phoebe Cary*

JOHN GREENLEAF WHITTIER
(1807-1892)

Mrs. Judge Jenkins

Maud Muller all that summer day
Raked the meadows sweet with hay;

Yet, looking down the distant lane,
She hoped the Judge would come again.

But when he came, with smile and bow,
Maud only blushed, and stammered, "Ha-ow?"

And spoke of her "pa," and wondered whether
He'd give consent they should wed together.

Old Muller burst in tears, and then
Begged that the Judge would lend him "ten";

For trade was dull, and wages low,
And the "craps," this year, were somewhat slow.

And ere the languid summer died,
Sweet Maud became the Judge's bride.

But on the day that they were mated,
Maud's brother Bob was intoxicated;

And Maud's relations, twelve in all,
Were very drunk at the Judge's hall.

And when the summer came again,
The young bride bore him babies twain;

And the Judge was blest, but thought it strange
That bearing children made such a change;

For Maud grew broad and red and stout,
And the waist that his arm once clasped about

Was more than he now could span: and he
Sighed as he pondered, ruefully,

How that which in Maud was native grace
In Mrs. Jenkins was out of place;

And thought of the twins, and wished that they
Looked less like the men who raked the hay

On Muller's farm, and dreamed with pain
Of the day he wandered down the lane.

And, looking down that dreary track,
He half regretted that he came back;

For, had he waited, he might have wed
Some maiden fair and thoroughbred;

For there be women fair as she,
Whose verbs and nouns do more agree.

Alas for maiden! alas for judge!
Add the sentimental,—that's one-half "fudge";

For Maud soon thought the Judge a bore,
With all his learning and all his lore;

And the Judge would have bartered Maud's fair face
For more refinement and social grace.

If, of all words of tongue and pen,
The saddest are, "It might have been,"

More sad are these we daily see:
"It is, but hadn't ought to be."

—*Bret Harte*

The Ballad of Hiram Hover

Where the Moosatockmaguntic
Pours its waters in the Skuntic,
Met, along the forest-side,
Hiram Hover, Huldah Hyde.

She, a maiden fair and dapper;
He, a red-haired, stalwart trapper,
Hunting beaver, mink, and skunk,
In the woodlands of Squeedunk.

She, Pentucket's pensive daughter,
Walked beside the Skuntic water,
Gathering, in her apron wet,
Snakeroot, mint, and bouncing-bet.

"Why," he murmured, loath to leave her,
"Gather yarbs for chills and fever,
When a lovyer, bold and true,
Only waits to gather you?"

"Go," she answered, "I'm not hasty;
I prefer a man more tasty:
  Leastways, one to please me well
  Should not have a beasty smell."

"Haughty Huldah!" Hiram answered;
"Mind and heart alike are cancered:
  Jest look here! these peltries give
  Cash, wherefrom a pair may live.

"I, you think am but a vagrant,
Trapping beasts by no means fragrant:
  Yet—I'm sure it's worth a thank—
  I've a handsome sum in bank."

Turned and vanished Hiram Hover;
And, before the year was over
  Huldah, with the yarbs she sold,
  Bought a cape, against the cold.

Black and thick the furry cape was;
Of a stylish cut the shape was,
  And the girls, in all the town,
  Envied Huldah up and down.

Then, at last, one winter morning,
Hiram came, without a warning:
  "Either," said he, "you are blind,
  Huldah, or you've changed your mind.

"Me you snub for trapping varmints,
Yet you take the skins for garments:
  Since you wear the skunk and mink,
  There's no harm in me, I think."

"Well," she said, "we will not quarrel,
Hiram; I accept the moral,
  Now the fashion's so, I guess
  I can't hardly do no less."

Thus the trouble all was over
Of the love of Hiram Hover;
  Thus he made sweet Huldah Hyde
  Huldah Hover as his bride.

Love employs, with equal favour
Things of good and evil savour;
  That, which first appeared to part,
  Warmed, at last, the maiden's heart.

Under one impartial banner,
Life, the hunter, Love the tanner,
  Draw, from every beast they snare,
  Comfort for a wedded pair!

—Bayard Taylor

EDWARD FITZGERALD
(1809-1883)

The Golfer's Rubaiyat

Wake! for the sun has driven in equal flight
The stars before him from the Tee of Night,
And holed them every one without a Miss,
Swinging at ease his gold-shod Shaft of Light.

Now, the fresh Year reviving old Desires,
The thoughtful Soul to Solitude retires,
Pores on this Club and That with anxious eye,
And dreams of Rounds beyond the Rounds of Liars.

Come, choose your Ball, and in the fire of Spring,
Your Red Coat and your wooden Putter fling;
The Club of Time has but a little while
To waggle, and the Club is on the swing.

A Bag of Clubs, a Silver Town or two,
A Flask of Scotch, a Pipe of Shag, and Thou
Beside me caddying in the Wilderness—
Ah, Wilderness were Paradise enow.

Myself, when young, did eagerly frequent
Jamie and His, and heard great argument
Of Grip, and Stance, and Swing; but evermore
Found at the Exit but a Dollar spent.

With them the seed of Wisdom did I sow,
And with mine own hand sought to make it grow;
And this was all the Harvest that I reap'd:
"You hold it in this Way, and you swing it So."

The swinging Brassie strikes; and, having struck,
Moves on; nor all your Wit or future Luck
Shall lure it back to cancel half a Stroke,
Nor from the Card a single Seven pluck.

No hope by Club or Ball to win the Prize;
The batter'd, blacken'd Remade sweetly flies,
Swept cleanly from the Tee; this is the Truth:
Nine-tenths is Skill, and all the rest is Lies.

And that inverted Ball they call the High,
By which the Duffer thinks to live or die,
Lift not your hands to It for help, for it
As impotently froths as you or I.

Yon rising Moon that leads us home again,
How oft hereafter will she wax and wane;
How oft hereafter rising, wait for us
At this same Turning—and for One in vain.

And when, like her, my Golfer, I have been
And am no more above the pleasant Green,
And you in your mild Journey pass the Hole
I made in One—ah, pay my Forfeit then!

—H.W. Boynton

EDGAR ALLAN POE
(1809-1849)

A Poe-'em of Passion

It was many and many a year ago,
  On an island near the sea,
That a maiden lived whom you mightn't know
  By the name of Cannibalee;
And this maiden she lived with no other thought
  Than a passionate fondness for me.

I was a child, and she was a child—
  Tho' her tastes were adult Feejee—
But she loved with a love that was more than love,
  My yearning Cannibalee;
With a love that could take me roast or fried
  Or raw, as the case might be.

And that is the reason that long ago,
  In that island near the sea,
I had to turn the tables and eat
  My ardent Cannibalee—
Not really because I was fond of her,
  But to check her fondness for me.

But the stars never rise but I think of the size
  Of my hot-potted Cannibalee,
And the moon never stares but it brings me nightmares
  Of my spare-rib Cannibalee;
And all the night-tide she is restless inside,
  Is my still indigestible dinner-belle bride,
In her pallid tomb, which is Me,
  In her solemn sepulcher, Me.

—*C.F. Lummis*

The Willows

The skies they were ashen and sober,
The streets they were dirty and drear;
It was night in the month of October,
  Of my most immemorial year.
Like the skies I was perfectly sober,
  As I stopped at the mansion of Shear,—
At the Nightingale,—perfectly sober,
  And the willowy woodland, down here.

Here, once in an alley Titanic
  Of Ten-pins, I roamed with my soul,—
  Of Ten-pins,—with Mary, my soul:
They were days when my heart was volcanic,
  And impelled me to frequently roll,
  And make me resistlessly roll,
Till my ten-strikes created a panic
  In the realms of the Boreal pole,
Till my ten-strikes created a panic
  With the monkey atop of his pole.

I repeat, I was perfectly sober,
But my thoughts they were palsied and sere,—
My thoughts were decidedly queer;
For I knew not the month was October,
And I marked not the night of the year,
I forgot that sweet *morceau* of Auber
That the band oft performèd down here,
And I mixed the sweet music of Auber
With the Nightingale's music by Shear.

And now as the night was senescent,
And the star-dials pointed to morn,
And car-drivers hinted of morn,
At the end of the path a liquescent
And bibulous lustre was born;
'Twas made by the bar-keeper present,
Who mixed a duplicate horn,—
His two hands describing a crescent
Distinct with a duplicate horn.

And I said: 'This looks perfectly regal,
For it's warm, and I know I feel dry,—
I am confident that I feel dry;
We have come past the emeu and eagle,
And watched the gay monkey on high;
Let us drink to the emeu and eagle,—
To the swan and the monkey on high,—
To the eagle and monkey on high;
For this bar-keeper will not inveigle,—
Bully boy with the vitreous eye;
He surely would never inveigle—
Sweet youth with the crystalline eye.

But Mary, uplifting her finger,
Said, 'Sadly this bar I mistrust,—
I fear that this bar does not trust.
O hasten! O let us not linger!
O fly,—let us fly—ere we must!'
In terror she cried, letting sink her
Parasol till it trailed in the dust,—
In agony sobbed, letting sink her
Parasol till it trailed in the dust,—
Till it sorrowly trailed in the dust.

Then I pacified Mary and kissed her,
And tempted her into the room,
And conquered her scruples and gloom;
And we passed to the end of the vista,
But were stopped by the warning of doom,—
By some words that were warning of doom;
And I said, 'What is written, sweet sister,
At the opposite end of the room?'
She sobbed as she answered, 'All liquors
Must be paid for ere leaving the room.'

Then my heart it grew ashen and sober,
As the streets were deserted and drear,—
For my pockets were empty and drear;
And I cried, 'It was surely October,
On this very night of last year,
That I journeyed,—I journeyed down here,—

That I brought a fair maiden down here,
On this night of all nights in the year.'
Ah! to me that inscription is clear;
Well I know now, I'm perfectly sober,
Why no longer they credit me here,—
Well I know now that music of Auber,
And this Nightingale, kept by one Shear.

—*Bret Harte*

The Promissory Note

In the lonesome latter years
(Fatal years!)
To the dropping of my tears
Danced the mad and mystic spheres
In a rounded, reeling rune,
'Neath the moon,
To the dripping and the dropping of my tears.
Ah, my soul is swathed in gloom,
(Ulalume!)
In a dim Titanic tomb,
For my gaunt and gloomy soul
Ponders o'er the penal scroll,
O'er the parchment (not a rhyme),
Out of place,—out of time,—
I am shredded, shorn, unshifty,
(Oh, the fifty!)
And the days have passed, the three,
Over me!
And the debit and the credit are as one to him and me!

'Twas the random runes I wrote
At the bottom of the note,
(Wrote and freely
Gave to Greeley)
In the middle of the night,
In the mellow, moonless night,
When the stars were out of sight,
When my pulses, like a knell,
(Israfel!)
Danced with dim and dying fays
O'er the ruins of my days,
O'er the dimeless, timeless days,
When the fifty, drawn at thirty,
Seeming thrifty, yet the dirty
Lucre of the market, was the most that I could raise!
Fiends controlled it,
(Let him hold it!)
Devils held for me the inkstand and the pen;
Now the days of grace are o'er,
(Ah, Lenore!)
I am but as other men;
What is time, time, time,
To my rare and runic rhyme,
To my random, reeling rhyme,
By the sands along the shore,
Where the tempest whispers, "Pay him!" and I answer,
"Nevermore!"

—*Bayard Taylor*

Ravings

The autumn upon us was rushing,
The Parks were deserted and lone—
The streets were unpeopled and lone;
My foot through the sere leaves was brushing,
That over the pathway were strown—
By the wind in its wanderings strown.
I sighed—for my feelings were gushing
Round Mnemosyne's porphyry throne,
Like lava liquescent lay gushing,
And rose to the porphyry throne—
To the filigree footstool were gushing,
That stands on the steps of that throne—
On the stolid stone steps of that throne!

I cried—'Shall the winter-leaves fret us?'
Oh, turn—we must turn to the fruit,
To the freshness and force of the fruit!
To the gifts wherewith Autumn has met us—
Her music that never grows mute
(That maunders but never grows mute),
The tendrils the vine branches net us,
The lily, the lettuce, the lute—
The esculent, succulent lettuce,
And the languishing lily, and lute;
Yes;—the lotos-like leaves of the lettuce;
Late lily and lingering lute.

Then come—let us fly from the city!
Let us travel in orient isles—
In the purple of orient isles—
Oh, bear me—yes, bear me in pity
To climes where a sun ever smiles—
Ever smoothly and speciously smiles!

Where the swarth-browed Arabian's wild ditty
Enhances pyramidal piles:
Where his wild, weird, and wonderful ditty
Awakens pyramidal piles—
Yes:—his pointless perpetual ditty
Perplexes pyramidal piles!

—Thomas Hood, the Younger

The Amateur Flute

Hear the fluter with his flute,
Silver flute!
Oh, what a world of wailing is awakened by its toot!
How it demi-semi quavers
On the maddened air of night!
And defieth all endeavors
To escape the sound or sight
Of the flute, flute, flute,
With its tootle, tootle, toot;
With reiterated tooteling of exasperating toots,
The long protracted tootelings of agonizing toots
Of the flute, flute, flute, flute,
Flute, flute, flute,

And the wheezings and the spittings of its toots.
Should he get that other flute,
Golden flute,
Oh, what a deeper anguish will his presence institoot!
How his eyes to heaven he'll raise,
As he plays,
All the days!
How he'll stop us on our ways
With its praise!
And the people—oh, the people,
That don't live up in the steeple,
But inhabit Christian parlors
Where he visiteth and plays,
Where he plays, plays, plays,
In the cruellest of ways,
And thinks we ought to listen,
And expects us to be mute,
Who would rather have the earache
Than the music of his flute,
Of his flute, flute, flute,
And the tootings of his toot,
Of the toots wherewith he tooteleth its agonizing toot,
Of the flute, flewt, fluit, floot,
Phlute, phlewt, phlewght,
And the tootle, tootle, tooting of its toot.

—*Anonymous*

Ravin's of Piute Poet Poe

Once upon a midnight dreary, eerie, scary,
I was wary, I was weary, full of worry, thinking of my lost Lenore,
Of my cheery, airy, faery, fiery Dearie—(Nothing more).
I was napping, when a tapping on the overlapping coping, woke me grapping, yapping, groping... toward the rapping. I went hopping, leaping... hoping that the rapping on the coping
Was my little lost Lenore.
That on opening the shutter to admit the latter critter, in she'd flutter from the gutter with her bitter eyes a-glitter;
So I opened the wide door, what was there? The dark weir and the drear moor,—or I'm a liar—the dark mire, the drear moor, the mere door and nothing more!

Then in stepped a stately raven, shaven like the bard of Avon; yes, a rovin' grievin' Raven, seeking haven at my door.
Yes, that shaven, rovin' Raven had been movin' (Get me Stephen) for the warm and lovin' haven of my stove an' oven door—
Oven door and nothing more.

Ah, distinctly I remember, every ember that December turned from amber to burnt umber;
I was burning limber lumber in my chamber that December, and it left an amber ember.
With a silken, sad, uncertain flirtin' of a certain curtain,
That old Raven, cold and callous, perched upon the bust of Pallas,
Just above my chamber door;
(A lusty, trusty, bust, thrust just
Above my chamber door.)
Had that callous cuss shown malice? Or sought solace, there on Pallas?

(You may tell us, Alice Wallace.)
Tell this soul with sorrow laden, hidden in the shade an' broodin',—
If a maiden out of Eden sent this sudden bird invadin'
My poor chamber; and protrudin' half an inch above my door.
Tell this broodin' soul (he's breedin' bats by too much sodden' readin'—
readin' Snowden's ode to Odin)
Tell this soul by nightmare's ridden, if (no kiddin') on a sudden
He shall clasp a radiant maiden born in Aidenn or in Leyden, or indeed
in Baden Baden—
Will he grab this buddin' maiden, gaddin' in forbidden Eden,

Whom the angels named Lenore?
Then that bird said: "Never more."

"Prophet," said I, "thing of evil, navel, novel, or boll weevil,
You shall travel, on the level! Scratch the gravel now and travel!
Leave my hovel, I implore"
And that Raven never flitting, never knitting, never tatting, never
spouting "Nevermore,"
Still is sitting (out this ballad) on the solid bust (and pallid)—
on the solid, valid, pallid bust above my chamber door:
And my soul is in the shadow, which lies floating on the floor,
Fleeting, floating, yachting, boating on the fluting of the matting,—
Matting on my chamber floor.

—C.L. Edson

From *To Allegra Florence in Heaven*

As an egg, when broken, never
Can be mended, but must ever
Be the same crushed egg forever—
So shall this dark heart of mine!
Which, though broken, is still breaking,
And shall nevermore cease aching
For the sleep which has no waking—
For the sleep which now is thine!

—Thomas Holly Chivers

ALFRED, LORD TENNYSON
(1809-1892)

The Higher Pantheism in a Nutshell

One, who is not, we see: but one, whom we see not, is;
Surely this is not that: but that is assuredly this.

What, and wherefore, and whence? for under is over and under;
If thunder could be without lightning, lightning could be without thunder.

Doubt is faith in the main: but faith, on the whole, is doubt;
We cannot believe by proof: but could we believe without?

Why, and whither, and how? for barley and rye are not clover;
Neither are straight lines curves: yet over is under and over.

Two and two may be four: but four and four are not eight;
Fate and God may be twain: but God is the same thing as fate.

Ask a man what he thinks, and get from a man what he feels;
God, once caught in the fact, shews you a fair pair of heels.

Body and spirit are twins: God only knows which is which;
The soul squats down in the flesh, like a tinker drunk in a ditch.

More is the whole than a part: but half is more than the whole:
Clearly, the soul is the body: but is not the body the soul?

One and two are not one: but one and nothing is two;
Truth can hardly be false, if falsehood cannot be true.

Once the mastodon was: pterodactyls were common as cocks;
Then the mammoth was God: now is He a prize ox.

Parallels all things are: yet many of these are askew.
You are certainly I: but certainly I am not you.

Springs the rock from the plain, shoots the stream from the rock.
Cocks exist for the hen: but hens exist for the cock.

God, whom we see not, is: and God, who is not, we see;
Fiddle, we know, is diddle: and diddle, we take it, is dee.

—*Algernon Charles Swinburne*

The Laureate

Who would not be
The Laureate bold,
With his butt of sherry
To keep him merry,
And nothing to do but to pocket his gold?

'Tis I would be the Laureate bold!
When the days are hot, and the sun is strong,
I'd lounge in the gateway all the day long
With her Majesty's footmen in crimson and gold.
I'd care not a pin for the waiting-lord,
But I'd lie on my back on the smooth greensward
With a straw in my mouth, and an open vest,
And the cool wind blowing upon my breast,
And I'd vacantly stare at the clear blue sky,
And watch the clouds that are listless as I,
Lazily, lazily!

And I'd pick the moss and the daisies white,
And chew their stalks with a nibbling bite;
And I'd let my fancies roam abroad
In search of a hint for a birthday ode,
Crazily, crazily!

Oh, that would be the life for me,
With plenty to get and nothing to do,
But to deck a pet poodle with ribbons of blue,
And whistle all day to the Queen's cockatoo,
Trance-somely, trance-somely!

Then the chambermaids, that clean the rooms,
Would come to the windows and rest on their brooms,
With their saucy caps and their crispéd hair,
And they'd toss their heads in the fragrant air,
And say to each other—"Just look down there,
At the nice young man, so tidy and small,
Who is paid for writing on nothing at all,
            Handsomely, handsomely!

They would pelt me with matches and sweet pastilles,
And crumpled-up balls of the royal bills,
Giggling and laughing, and screaming with fun,
As they'd see me start, with a leap and a run,
From the broad of my back to the points of my toes,
When a pellet of paper hit my nose,
            Teasingly, sneezingly!

Then I'd fling them bunches of garden flowers,
And hyacinths plucked from the Castle bowers;
And I'd challenge them all to come down to me,
And I'd kiss them all till they kissed me,
            Laughingly, laughingly.

Oh, would not that be a merry life,
Apart from care and apart from strife,
With the Laureate's wine, and the Laureate's pay,
And no deductions at quarter-day?
Oh, that would be the post for me!
With plenty to get and nothing to do,
But to deck a pet poodle with ribbons of blue,
And whistle a tune to the Queen's cockatoo,
And scribble of verses remarkably few,
And empty at evening a bottle or two,
            Quaffingly, quaffingly!

                'Tis I would be
                The Laureate bold,
                With my butt of sherry
                To keep me merry,
    And nothing to do but to pocket my gold!

—*William Aytoun*

Sir Eggnogg

Forth from the purple battlements he fared,
Sir Eggnogg of the Rampant Lily, named
From that embrasure of his argent shield
Given by a thousand leagues of heraldry
On snuffy parchments drawn. So forth he fared,
By bosky boles and autumn leaves he fared,
Where grew the juniper with berries black,
The sphery mansions of the future gin.
But naught of this decoyed his mind, so bent
On fair Miasma, Saxon-blooded girl,
Who laughed his loving lullabies to scorn,
And would have snatched his hero-sword to deck
Her haughty brow, or warm her hands withal,
So scornful she; and thence Sir Eggnogg cursed
Between his teeth, and chewed his iron boots

In spleen of love. But ere the morn was high
In the robustious heaven, the postern-tower
Clang to the harsh, discordant, slivering scream
Of the tire-woman, at the window bent
To dress her crispéd hair. She saw, ah, woe!
The fair Miasma, overbalanced, hurled
O'er the flamboyant parapet which ridged
The muffled coping of the castle's peak,
Prone on the ivory pavement of the court,
Which caught and cleft her fairest skull, and sent
Her rosy brains to fleck the Orient floor.
This saw Sir Eggnogg, in his stirrups poised.
Saw he and cursed, with many a deep-mouthed oath,
And, finding nothing more could reunite
The splintered form of fair Miasma, rode
On his careering palfrey to the wars,
And there found death, another death than hers.

—Bayard Taylor

Little Miss Muffet

Upon a tuffet of most soft and verdant moss,
Beneath the spreading branches of an ancient oak,
Miss Muffet sat, and upward gazed,
To where a linnet perched and sung,
And rocked him gently, to and fro.
Soft blew the breeze
And mildly swayed the bough,
Loud sung the bird,
And sweetly dreamed the maid;
Dreamed brightly of the days to come—
The golden days, with her fair future blent.
When one—some wondrous stately knight—
Of our great Arthur's "Table Round;"
One, brave as Launcelot, and
Spotless as the pure Sir Galahad,
Should come, and coming, choose her
For his love, and in her name,
And for the sake of her fair eyes,
Should do most knightly deeds.
And as she dreamed and softly sighed,
She pensively began to stir,
With a tiny golden spoon
Within an antique dish upon her lap,
Some snow-white milky curds;
Soft were they, full of cream and rich,
And floated in translucent whey;
And as she stirred, she smiled,
Then gently tasted them.
And smiling, ate, nor sighed no more.
Lo! as she ate—nor harbored thought of ill—
Nearer and nearer yet, there to her crept,
A monster great and terrible,
With huge, misshapen body—leaden eyes—
Full many a long and hairy leg,
And soft and stealthy footstep.
Nearer still he came—Miss Muffet yet,
All unwitting his dread neighborhood,
Did eat her curds and dream.
Blithe, on the bough, the linnet sung—
All terrestrial natures, sleeping, wrapt

In a most sweet tranquillity.
Closer still the spider drew, and—
Paused beside her—lifted up his head
And gazed into her face.
Miss Muffet then, her consciousness alive
To his dread eyes upon her fixed,
Turned and beheld him.
Loud screamed she, frightened and amazed,
And straightway sprung upon her feet,
And, letting fall her dish and spoon,
She—shrieking—turned and fled.

—*Anonymous*

The Three Voices

The First Voice

With hands tight clenched through matted hair,
He crouched in trance of dumb despair:
There came a breeze from out the air.

It passed athwart the glooming flat—
It fanned his forehead as he sat—
It lightly bore away his hat,

All to the feet of one who stood
Like maid enchanted in a wood,
Frowning as darkly as she could.

With huge umbrella, lank and brown,
Unerringly she pinned it down,
Right through the centre of the crown.

Then, with an aspect cold and grim,
Regardless of its battered rim,
She took it up and gave it him.

Awhile like one in dreams he stood,
Then faltered forth his gratitude,
In words just short of being rude:

For it had lost its shape and shine,
And it had cost him four-and-nine,
And he was going out to dine.

With grave indifference to his speech,
Fixing her eyes upon the beach,
She said 'Each gives to more than each.'

He could not answer yea or nay:
He faltered 'Gifts may pass away.'
Yet knew not what he meant to say.

'If that be so,' she straight replied,
'Each heart with each doth coincide.
What boots it? For the world is wide.'

And he, not wishing to appear
Less wise, said 'This Material Sphere
Is but Attributive Idea.'

But when she asked him 'Wherefore so?'
He felt his very whiskers glow,
And frankly owned 'I do not know.'

While, like broad waves of golden grain,
Or sunlit hues on cloistered pane,
'His colour came and went again.

Pitying his obvious distress,
Yet with a tinge of bitterness,
She said 'The More exceeds the Less.'

'A truth of such undoubted weight,'
He urged, 'and so extreme in date,
It were superfluous to state.'

Roused into sudden passion, she
In tone of cold malignity:
'To others, yes: but not to thee.'

But when she saw him quail and quake,
And when he urged 'For pity's sake!'
Once more in gentle tone she spake.

'Thought in the mind doth still abide;
That is by Intellect supplied,
And within that Idea doth hide.

'And he, that yearns the truth to know,
Still further inwardly may go,
And find Idea from Notion flow.

'And thus the chain, that sages sought,
Is to a glorious circle wrought,
For Notion hath its source in Thought.'

When he, with racked and whirling brain,
Feebly implored her to explain,
She simply said it all again.

Wrenched with an agony intense,
He spake, neglecting Sound and Sense,
And careless of all consequence:

'Mind—I believe—is Essence—Ent—
Abstract—that is—an Accident—
Which we—that is to say—I meant—'

When, with quick breath and cheeks all flushed,
At length his speech was somewhat hushed,
She looked at him, and he was crushed.

It needed not her calm reply:
She fixed him with a stony eye,
And he could neither fight nor fly,

While she dissected, word by word,
His speech, half guessed at and half heard,
As might a cat a little bird.

Then, having wholly overthrown
His views, and stripped them to the bone,
Proceeded to unfold her own.

So passed they on with even pace,
Yet gradually one might trace
A shadow growing on his face.

The Second Voice

They walked beside the wave-worn beach,
Her tongue was very apt to teach,
And now and then he did beseech

She would abate her dulcet tone,
Because the talk was all her own,
And he was dull as any drone.

She urged 'No cheese is made of chalk':
And ceaseless flowed her dreary talk,
Tuned to the footfall of a walk.

Her voice was very full and rich,
And, when at length she asked him 'Which?'
It mounted to its highest pitch.

He a bewildered answer gave,
Drowned in the sullen moaning wave,
Lost in the echoes of the cave.

He answered her he knew not what:
Like shaft from bow at random shot:
He spoke, but she regarded not.

She waited not for his reply,
But with a downward leaden eye
Went on as if he were not by.

Sound argument and grave defence,
Strange questions raised on 'Why?' and 'Whence?'
And weighted down with common sense.

'Shall Man be Man? And shall he miss
Of other thoughts no thought but this,
Harmonious dews of sober bliss?

'What boots it? Shall his fevered eye
Through towering nothingness descry
The grisly phantom hurry by?

'And hear dumb shrieks that fill the air;
See mouths that gape, and eyes that stare
And redden in the dusky glare?

'The meadows breathing amber light,
The darkness toppling from the height,
The feathery train of granite Night?

'Shall he, grown gray among his peers,
Through the thick curtain of his tears
Catch glimpses of his earlier years,

'And hear the sounds he knew of yore,
Old shufflings on the sanded floor,
Old knuckles tapping at the door?

'Yet still before him as he flies
One pallid form shall ever rise,
And, bodying forth in glassy eyes

'The vision of a vanished good,
Low peering through the tangled wood,
Shall freeze the current of his blood.'

Still from each fact, with skill uncouth
And savage rapture, like a tooth
She wrenched a slow reluctant truth.

Till, like some silent water-mill,
When summer suns have dried the rill,
She reached a full stop, and was still.

Dead calm succeeded to the fuss,
As when the loaded omnibus
Has reached the railway terminus:

When, for the tumult of the street,
Is heard the engine's stifled beat,
The velvet tread of porters' feet.

With glance that ever sought the ground,
She moved her lips without a sound,
And every now and then she frowned.

He gazed upon the sleeping sea,
And joyed in its tranquillity,
And in that silence dead, but she

To muse a little space did seem,
Then, like the echo of a dream,
Harped back upon her threadbare theme.

Still an attentive ear he lent,
But could not fathom what she meant:
She was not deep, nor eloquent.

He marked the ripple on the sand:
The even swaying of her hand
Was all that he could understand.

He left her, and he turned aside:
He sat and watched the coming tide
Across the shores so newly dried.

He wondered at the waters clear,
The breeze that whispered in his ear,
The billows heaving far and near;

And why he had so long preferred
To hang upon her every word;
'In truth,' he said, 'it was absurd.'

The Third Voice

Not long this transport held its place:
Within a little moment's space
Quick tears were raining down his face.

His heart stood still, aghast with fear;
A wordless voice, nor far nor near,
He seemed to hear and not to hear.

'Tears kindle not the doubtful spark:
If so, why not? of this remark
The bearings are profoundly dark.'

'Her speech,' he said, 'hath caused this pain;
Easier I count it to explain
The jargon of the howling main,

'Or, stretched beside some sedgy brook,
To con, with inexpressive look,
An unintelligible book.'

Low spake the voice within his head,
In words imagined more than said,
Soundless as ghost's intended tread:

'If thou art duller than before,
Why quittedst thou the voice of lore?
Why not endure, expecting more?'

'Rather than that,' he groaned aghast,
'I'd writhe in depths of cavern vast,
Some loathly vampire's rich repast.'

''Twere hard,' it answered, 'themes immense
To coop within the narrow fence
That rings *thy* scant intelligence.'

'Not so,' he urged, 'nor once alone:
But there was that within her tone
Which chilled me to the very bone.

'Her style was anything but clear,
And most unpleasantly severe;
Her epithets were very queer.

'And yet, so grand were her replies,
I could not choose but deem her wise;
I did not dare to criticise;

'Nor did I leave her, till she went
So deep in tangled argument
That all my powers of thought were spent.'

A little whisper inly slid;
'Yet truth is truth: you know you did—'
A little wink beneath the lid.

And, sickened with excess of dread,
Prone to the dust he bent his head,
And lay like one three-quarters dead.

Forth went the whisper like a breeze;
Left him amid the wondering trees,
Left him by no means at his ease.

Once more he weltered in despair,
With hands, through denser-matted hair,
More tightly clenched than then they were.

When, bathed in dawn of living red,
Majestic frowned the mountain head,
'Tell me my fault,' was all he said.

When, at high noon, the blazing sky
Scorched in his head each haggard eye,
Then keenest rose his weary cry.

And when at eve the unpitying sun
Smiled grimly on the solemn fun,
'Alack,' he sighed, 'what *have* I done?'

But saddest, darkest was the sight,
When the cold grasp of leaden Night
Dashed him to earth, and held him tight.

Tortured, unaided, and alone,
Thunders were silence to his groan,
Bagpipes sweet music to its tone:

'What? Ever thus, in dismal round,
Shall Pain and Misery profound
Pursue me like a sleepless hound,

'With crimson-dashed and eager jaws,
Me, still in ignorance of the cause,
Unknowing what I brake of laws?'

The whisper to his ear did seem
Like echoed flow of silent stream,
Or shadow of forgotten dream;

The whisper trembling in the wind:
'Her fate with thine was intertwined,'
So spake it in his inner mind:

'Each orbed on each a baleful star,
Each proved the other's blight and bar,
Each unto each were best, most far:

'Yea, each to each was worse than foe,
Thou, a scared dullard, gibbering low,
And she, an avalanche of woe.'

—*Lewis Carroll*

ROBERT BROWNING
(1812-1889)

The Cock and the Bull

You see this pebble-stone? It's a thing I bought
Of a bit of a chit of a boy i' the mid o' the day—
I like to dock the smaller parts-o'-speech,
As we curtail the already cur-tail'd cur
(You catch the paronomasia, play 'po' words?)
Did, rather, i' the pre-Landseerian days.
Well, to my muttons. I purchased the concern,
And clapt it i' my poke, having given for same
By way o' chop, swop, barter or exchange—
"Chop" was my snickering dandiprat's own term—
One shilling and fourpence, current coin o' the realm.
O-n-e one and f-o-u-r four
Pence, one and fourpence—you are with me, sir?—
What hour it skills not: ten or eleven o' the clock,
One day (and what a roaring day it was
Go shop or sight-see—bar a spit o' rain!)
In February, eighteen sixty-nine,
Alexandrina Victoria, Fidei
Hm—hm—how runs the jargon? being on throne.

Such, sir, are all the facts, succinctly put,
The basis or substratum—what you will—
Of the impending eighty thousand lines.
"Not much in 'em either," quoth perhaps simple Hodge.
But there's a superstructure. Wait a bit.
Mark first the rationale of the thing:
Hear logic rivel and levigate the deed.
That shilling—and for matter o' that, the pence—
I had o' course upo' me—wi' me say—
(*Mecum's* the Latin, make a note o' that)
When I popp'd pen i' stand, scratch'd ear, wiped snout,
(Let everybody wipe his own himself)
Sniff'd—tch!—at snuffbox; tumbled up, he-heed,
Haw-haw'd (not hee-haw'd, that's another guess thing:)
Then fumbled at, and stumbled out of, door,
I shoved the timber ope wi' my omoplat;
And *in vestibulo*, i' the lobby to wit,
(Iacobi Facciolati's rendering, sir,)
Donn'd galligaskins, antigropeloes,
And so forth; and, complete with hat and gloves,
One on and one a-dangle i' my hand,
And ombrifuge (Lord love you!) case o' rain,
I flopp'd forth, 'sbuddikins! on my own ten toes,
(I do assure you there be ten of them),
And went clump-clumping up hill and down dale
To find myself o' the sudden i' front o' the boy.
Put case I hadn't 'em on me, could I ha' bought
This sort-o' kind o'-what-you-might-call toy,
This pebble-thing, o' the boy-thing? Q.E.D.
That's proven without aid from mumping Pope,
Sleep porporate or bloated Cardinal.
(Isn't it, old Fatchaps? You're in Euclid, now.)
So, having the shilling—having i' fact a lot—
And pence and halfpence, ever so many o' them,
I purchased, as I think I said before,

The pebble (lapis, lapidis, -di,-dem,-de—
What nouns 'crease short i' the genitive, Fatchaps, eh?)
O' the boy, a bare-legg'd beggarly son of a gun,
For one-and-fourpence. Here we are again.

Now Law steps in, bigwigg'd, voluminous-jaw'd
Investigates and re-investigates.
Was the transaction illegal? Law shakes head.
Perpend, sir, all the bearings of the case.

At first the coin was mine, the chattel his.
But now (by virtue of the said exchange
And barter) *vice versa* all the coin,
Per juris operationem, vests
I' the boy and his assigns till ding o' doom;
In *soecula soeculo-o-o-orum*;
(I think I hear the Abate mouth out that.)
To have and hold the same to him and then...
Confer some idiot on Conveyancing.
Whereas the pebble and every part therof,
And all that appertaineth thereunto,
Quodcunque pertinet ad eam rem,
(I fancy, sir, my Latin's rather pat)
Or shall, will, may, might, can, could, would or should,
(*Subandi coetera*—clap me to the close—
For what's the good of law in a case o' the kind?)
Is mine to all intents and purposes.
This settled, I resume the thread o' the tale.

Now for a touch o' the vendor's quality.
He says a gen'lman bought a pebble of him,
(This pebble i' sooth, sir, which I hold i' my hand)—
And paid for't *like* a gen'lman, on the nail.
"Did I o'ercharge him a ha'penny? Devil a bit
Fiddlepin's end! Get out, you blazing ass!
Gabble o' the goose. Don't bugaboo-baby *me*!
Go double or quits? Ya! tittup! what's the odds?'
—There's the transaction view'd i' the vendor's light.

Next ask that dumpled hag, stood snuffling by,
With her three frowsy blowsy brats o' babes,
The scum o' the kennel, cream o' the filth-heap—Faugh!
Aie, aie, aie, aie! *orororororor*
('Stead which we blurt out Hoighty toighty now)—
And the baker and the candlestickmaker, and Jack and Jill,
Blear'd Goody this and queasy Gaffer that.
Ask the schoolmaster. Take schoolmaster first.

He saw a gentleman purchase from a lad
A stone, and pay for it *rite*, on the square,
And carry it off *per saltum*, jauntily,
Propria quae maribus, gentleman's property now
(Agreeably to the law explain'd above),
In proprium usum, for his private ends.
The boy he chuck'd a brown i' the air, and bit
I' the face the shilling: heaved a thumping stone
At a lean hen that ran cluck clucking by,
(And hit her, dead as nail i' post o' door,)
Then abiit—what's the Ciceronian phrase?—
Excessit, evasit, erupit—off slogs boy;

Off like bird, *avi similis*—(you observed
The dative? Pretty i' the Mantuan!)—*Anglice*,
Off in three flea skips. *Hactenus*, so far,
So good, *tam bene. Bene, satis, male*—,
Where was I with my trope 'bout one in a quag?
I did once hitch the syntax into verse:
Verbum personale, a verb personal,
Concordat—ay, "agrees", old Fatchaps—*cum*
Nominativo, with its nominative,
Genere, i' point o' gender, *numero*,
O' number, *et persona*, and person. *Ut*,
Instance: *Sol ruit*, down flops sun, *et* and
Montes umbrantur, out flounce mountains. Pah!
Excuse me, sir, I think I'm going mad.
You see the trick on 't though, and can yourself
Continue the discourse *ad libitum*.
It takes up about eighty thousand lines,
A thing imagination boggles at:
And might, odds-bobs, sir! in judicious hands,
Extend from here to Mesopotamy.

—*Charles Stuart Calverley*

Angelo Orders His Dinner

I, Angelo, obese, black-garmented,
Respectable, much in demand, well fed
With mine own larder's dainties,—where, indeed,
Such cakes of myrrh or fine alyssum seed,
Thin as a mallow-leaf, embrowned o' the top,
Which, cracking, lets the ropy, trickling drop
Of sweetness touch your tongue, or potted nests
Which my recondite recipe invests
With cold conglomerate tidbits—ah, the bill!
(You say,) but given it were mine to fill
My chests, the case so put were yours, we'll say,
(This counter, here, your post, as mine to-day,)
And you've an eye to luxuries, what harm
In smoothing down your palate with the charm
Yourself concocted? There we issue take;
And see! as thus across the rim I break
This puffy paunch of glazed embroidered cake,
So breaks, through use, the lust of watering chaps
And craveth plainness: do I so? Perhaps;
But that's my secret. Find me such a man
As Lippo yonder, built upon the plan
Of heavy storage, double-navelled, fat
From his own giblets' oil, an Ararat
Uplift o'er water, sucking rosy draughts
From Noah's vineyard,—crisp, enticing wafts
Yon kitchen now emits, which to your sense
Somewhat abate the fear of old events,
Qualms to the stomach,—I, you see, am slow
Unnescessary duties to forgo,—
You understand? A venison haunch, *haut goût*,
Ducks that in Cimbrian olives mildly stew,
And sprigs of anise, might one's teeth provoke
To taste, and so we wear the complex yoke
Just as it suits,—my liking, I confess,
More to receive, and to partake no less,

Still more obese, while through thick adipose
Sensation shoots, from testing tongue to toes
Far-off, dim-conscious, at the body's verge,
Where the froth-whispers of its waves emerge
On the untasting sand. Stay, now! a seat
Is bare: I, Angelo, will sit and eat.

—*Bayard Taylor*

From *The Puss and the Boots*

Put case I circumvent and kill him: good.
Good riddance—wipes at least from book o' th' world
The ugly admiration-note-like blot—
Gives honesty more elbow-room by just
The three dimensions of one wicked knave.
But then slips in the plaguy After-voice.
'Wicked? Holloa! my friend, whither away
So fast? Who made you, Moses-like, a judge
And ruler over men to spare or slay?
A blot wiped off forsooth! Produce forthwith
Credentials of your mission to erase
The ink-spots of mankind—t' abolish ill
For being what it is, is bound to be,
Its nature being so—cut wizards off
In flower of their necromantic lives
For being wizards, when 'tis plain enough
That they have no more wrought their wizardship
Than cats their cathood.' Thus the plaguy Voice,
Puzzling withal not overmuch, for thus
I turn the enemy's flank: 'Meseems, my friend,
Your argument's a thought too fine of mesh,
And catches what you would not. Every mouse
Trapped i' the larder by the kitchen wench
Might reason so—but scarcely with effect.
Methinks 'twould little serve the captured thief
To plead, "The fault's Dame Nature's, guiltless I.
Am I to blame that in the parcelling-out
Of my ingredients the Great Chemist set
Just so much here, there so much, and no more
(Since 'tis but question, after all is said,
Of mere proportion 'twixt the part that feels
And that which guides), so much proclivity
To nightly cupboard-breaking, so much lust
Of bacon-scraps, such tendency to think
Old Stilton-rind the noblest thing on earth?
Then the *per contra*—so much power to choose
The right and shun the wrong; so much of force
Of uncorrupted will to stoutly bar
The sensory inlets of the murine soul,
And, when by night the floating rare-bit fume
Lures like a siren's song, stop nostrils fast
With more than Odusseian sailor-wax:
Lastly so much of wholesome fear of trap
To keep self-abnegation sweet. Then comes
The hour of trial, when lo! the suadent scale
Sinks instant, the deterrent kicks the beam,
The heavier falls, the lighter mounts (as much
A thing of law with motives as with plums),
And I, forsooth, must die simply because

Dame Nature, having chosen so to load
The dishes, did not choose suspend for me
The gravitation of the moral world.'
How would the kitchen-wench reply? Why thus
(If given, as scullions use, to logic-fence
And keen retorsion of dilemmata
In speeches of a hundred lines or so):
"Grant your plea valid. Good. There's mine to hear.
'Twas Nature made you? well: and me, no less;
You she by forces past your own control
Made a cheese-stealer? Be it so: of me
By forces as resistless and her own
She made a mouse-killer. Thus, either plays
A rôle in no wise chosen of himself,
But takes what part the great Stage Manager
Cast him for, when the play was set afoot.
Remains we act ours—without private spite,
But still with spirit and fidelity,
As fits good actors: you I blame no whit
For nibbling cheese—simply I throw you down
Unblamed—nay, even morally assoiled,
To pussy there: blame thou not me for that.'
Or say perhaps the girl is slow of wit,
Something inapt at ethics—why, then thus.
"Enough of prating, little thief! This talk
Of 'fate, free-will, foreknowledge absolute,'
Is hugely out of place! What next indeed,
If all the casuistry of the schools
Be prayed in aid by every pilfering mouse
That's caught i' th' trap? See here, my thieving friend,
Thus I resolve the problem. We prefer
To keep our cheeses for our own behoof,
And eat them with our proper jaws; and so,
Having command of mouse-traps, we will catch
Whatever mice we can, and promptly kill
Whatever mice we catch. *Entendez vous?*
Aye, and we *will*, though all the mice on earth
Pass indignation votes, obtest the faith
Of gods and men, and make the welkin ring
With world-resounding dissonance of squeak!"

But hist! here comes my wizard! Ready then
My nerves—and talons—for the trial of strength!
A stout heart, feline cunning, and—who knows?

—*Henry Duff Traill*

Old King Cole

Who smoke-snorts toasts o' My Lady Nicotine,
Kicks stuffing out of Pussyfoot, bids his trio
Stick up their Stradivarii (that's the plural
Or near enough, my fatheads; *nimium*
Vicina Cremonoe; that's a bit too near.)
Is there some stockfish fails to understand?
Catch hold o' the notion, bellow and blurt back "Cole"?
Must I bawl lessons from a horn-book, howl,
Cat-call the cat-gut "fiddles"? Fiddlesticks!

—*G.K. Chesterton*

The Flight of the Bucket

Pre-admonisheth the writer:
H'm, for a subject it is well enough!
Who wrote "Sordello" finds no subject tough.

Well, Jack and Jill—God knows the life they led
(The poet never told us, more's the pity)
Pent up in some damp kennel of their own,
Beneath the hillside; but it once befell
That Jack and Jill, niece, cousin, uncle, aunt
(Some one of all the brood), would wash and scour,
Rinse out a cess-pit, swab the kennel floor,
And water (*liquor vitae*, Lawson calls,
But I—I hold by whisky. Never mind;
I did n't mean to hurt your feelings, sir,
And missed the scrap o' blue at buttonhole),
Spring water was the needful at the time,
So they must climb the hill for't. Well and good.
We all climb hills, I take it, on some quest,
Maybe for less than stinking (I forgot!
I mean than wholesome) water.... Ferret out
The rotten bucket from the lumber shed,
Weave ropes and splice the handle—off they go
To where the cold spring bubbles up i' the cleft,
And sink the bucket brimful in the spate.
Then downwards—hanging back? (You bet your life
The girl's share fell upon Jack's shoulders.) Down,
Down to the bottom—all but—trip, slip, squelch!
And guggle-guggle goes the bucketful
Back to the earth, and Jack's a broken head,
And swears amid the heather does our Jack.
(A man would swear who watched both blood and bucket,
One dripping down his forehead, t' other fled
Clinkety-tinkle, to the stones below,
A good half-hour's trudge to get it back.)
Jack, therefore, as I said, exploded straight
In brimstone-flavored language. You, of course,
Maintain he bore it calmly—not a bit.
A good bucolic curse that rent the cliffs
And frightened for a moment quaking Jill
Out of the limp, unmeaning girl's tee-hee
That womankind delight in.... Here we end
The first verse—there's a deal to study in 't.

So much for Jack—but here's a fate above,
A cosmic force that blunders into right,
Just when the strained sense hints at revolution
Because the world's great fly-wheel runs aslant—
And up go Jill's red kibes. (You think I'm wrong;
And Fate was napping at the time; perhaps
You're right.) We'll call it Devil's agency
That sent the shrieking sister on her head,
And knocked the tangled locks against the stones.
Well, down went Jill, but was n't hurt. Oh, no!
The Devil pads the world to suit his own,
And packs the cards according. Down went Jill
Unhurt. And Jack trots off to bed, poor brute,
Fist welted into eyeball, mouth agape
For yelling,—your bucolic always yells,

And out of his domestic pharmacy
Rips forth the cruet-stand, upsets the cat,
And ravages the store-room for his balm.
Eureka!—but he did n't use that word—
A pound of candles, corpse-like, side by side,
Wrapped up in his medicament. Out, knife!
Cut string, and strip the shrouding from the lot!
Steep swift and jam it on the gaping cut;
Then bedward—cursing man and friends alike.

Now back to Jill. She was n't hurt, I said,
And all the woman's spite was up in arms.
So Jack's abed. She slips, peeks through the door,
And sees the split head like a luggage-label,
Halved, quartered, on the pillow. "Ee-ki-ree,
Tee-hee-hee-hee," she giggles through the crack,
Much as the Roman ladies grinned—don't smile—
To see the dabbled bodies in the sand,

Appealing to their benches for a sign.
Down thumbs, and giggle louder—so did Jill.
But mark now! Comes the mother round the door,
Red-hot from climbing up the hill herself,
And caught the graceless giggler. Whack! Flack! Whack!
Here's Nemesis whichever way you like!
She did n't stop to argue. Given a head
Broken, a woman chuckling at the door,
And here's your circumstantial evidence complete.
Whack! while Jack sniffs and sniggers from the bed.
I like that horny-handed mother o' Jill.
The world's best women died, sir, long ago.
Well, Jack's avenged; as for the other, gr-r-r-r!

—*Rudyard Kipling*

The Last Ride Together

FROM HER POINT OF VIEW

When I had firmly answered "No,"
And he allowed that that was so,
I really thought I should be free
For good and all from Mr. B.,
        And that he would soberly acquiesce.
I said that it would be discreet
That for awhile we should not meet;
I promised that I would always feel
A kindly interest in his weal;
I thanked him for his amorous zeal;
        In short, I said all I could but "yes."

I said what I'm accustomed to;
I acted as I always do.
I promised he should find in me
A friend,—a sister, if that might be;
        But he was still dissatisfied.
He certainly was most polite;
He said exactly what was right,
He acted very properly,
Except indeed for this, that he
Insisted on inviting me
        To come with him for "one more last ride."

A little while in doubt I stood:
A ride, no doubt, would do me good;
I had a habit and a hat
Extremely well worth looking at;
        The weather was distinctly fine.
My horse, too, wanted exercise,
And time, when one is riding, flies;
Besides, it really seemed, you see,
The only way of ridding me
Of pertinacious Mr. B.;
        So my head I graciously incline.

I won't say much of what happened next;
I own I was extremely vexed.
Indeed I should have been aghast
If any one had seen what passed;
        But nobody need ever know
That, as I leaned forward to stir the fire,
He advanced before I could well retire;
And I suddenly felt, to my great alarm,
The grasp of a warm, unlicensed arm,
An embrace in which I found no charm;
        I was awfully glad when he let me go.

Then we began to ride; my steed
Was rather fresh, too fresh indeed,
And at first I thought of little, save
The way to escape an early grave,
        As the dust rose up on either side.
My stern companion jogged along
On a brown old cob both broad and strong.
He looked as he does when he's writing verse,
Or endeavoring not to swear and curse,
Or wondering where he has left his purse;
        Indeed it was a sombre ride.

I spoke of the weather to Mr. B.,
But he neither listened nor spoke to me.
I praised his horse, and I smiled the smile
Which was wont to move him once in a while.
        I said I was wearing his favorite flowers,
But I wasted my words on the desert air,
For he rode with a fixed and gloomy stare.
I wonder what he was thinking about.
As I don't read verse, I shan't find out.
It was something subtle and deep, no doubt,
        A theme to detain a man for hours.

Ah! there was the corner where Mr. S.
So nearly induced me to whisper "yes;'
And here it was that the next but one
Proposed on horseback, or would have done,
        Had his horse not most opportunely shied;
Which perhaps was due to the unseen flick
He received from my whip; 'twas a scurvy trick,
But I never could do with that young man,—
I hope his present young woman can.
Well, I must say, never, since time began,
        Did I go for a duller or longer ride.

He never smiles and he never speaks;
He might go on like this for weeks;
He rolls a slightly frenzied eye
Towards the blue and burning sky,
    And the cob bounds on with tireless stride.
If we are n't home for lunch at two
I don't know what papa will do;
But I know full well he will say to me,
"I never approved of Mr. B.;
It's the very devil that you and he
    Ride, ride together, forever ride."

—J.K. Stephen

How I Brought the Good News from Aix to Ghent (or Vice Versa)

I sprang to the rollocks and Jorrocks and me,
And I galloped, you galloped, he galloped, we galloped all three...
Not a word to each other; we kept changing place,
Neck to neck, back to front, ear to ear, face to face;
And we yelled once or twice, when we heard a clock chime,
"Would you kindly oblige us, *Is that the right time?*"
As I galloped, you galloped, he galloped, we galloped, ye galloped, they two shall have galloped; *let us trot.*

I unsaddled the saddle, unbuckled the bit,
Unshackled the bridle (the thing didn't fit)
And ungalloped, ungalloped, ungalloped, ungalloped a bit.
Then I cast off my bluff-coat, let my bowler hat fall,
Took off both my boots and my trousers and all—
Drink off my stirrup-cup, felt a bit tight,
And unbridled the saddle: it still wasn't right.

Then all I remember is, things reeling round
As I sat with my head 'twixt my ears on the ground—
For imagine my shame when they asked what I meant
And I had to confess that I'd been, gone and went
And *forgotten the news* I was bringing to Ghent.

Though I'd galloped and galloped and galloped and galloped and galloped And galloped and galloped and galloped. (Had I not would have been galloped?)

Envoi

So I sprang to a taxi and shouted "To Aix!'
And he blew on his horn and he threw off his brakes,
And all the way back till my money was spent
We rattled and rattled and rattled and rattled and rattled
And rattled and rattled—
And eventually sent a telegram.

—R.J. Yeatman and W.C. Sellar

EMILY BRONTE
(1818-1848)

It was far in the night and the bairnies grat
The mither beneath the mools heard that
There were swalies flinkin in the damson sky
Wad swook adoon sharp and plurt yeer eye.

Ony bairnie roarin' when the swalies preek
Gets peripoll's snort come Lammas week
For the swalies bide i' the cauld, cauld kirk
Where the chinlies tubble and the goblins plerk.

Sae shiel' yeer bairnies frae the jonkle-quigs
By a-melishing brae-fresh myrtle twigs
Then chant ye the sacred Vinselplune
While sneckling pluffs neath a lemon moon.

It's up an' doon an' aboon they slant
Wi' shallimax wings they flamp and rant.
When it's far in the night and the bairnies grat
The mither beneath the mools knows *that*.

—*Gerry Hamill*

PRINCE ALBERT
(1819-1861)

Ballad by Hans Breitmann

Der noble Ritter Hugo
Von Schwillensaufenstein,
Rode out mit shpeer and helmet,
Und he coom to de panks of de Rhine.

Und oop dere rose a meermaid,
Vot hadn't got nodings on,
Und she say, 'Oh, Ritter Hugo,
Vhere you goes mit yourself alone?'

And he says, 'I rides in de creenwood,
Mit helmet und mit shpeer,
Till I cooms into ein Gasthaus,
Und dere I trinks some beer.'

Und den outshpoke de maiden
Vot hadn't got nodings on:
'I ton't dink mooch of beoplesh
Dat goes mit demselfs alone.

'You'd petter coom down in de wasser,
Vhere dere's heaps of dings to see,
Und hafe a shplendid tinner
Und drafel along mit me.

'Dere you sees de fisch a schwimmin',
   Und you catches dem efery von:'—
So sang dis wasser maiden
   Vot hadn't got nodings on.

'Dere ish drunks all full mit money
   In ships dat vent down of old;
Und you helpsh yourself, by dunder!
   To shimmerin' crowns of gold.

'Shoost look at dese shpoons and vatches!
   Shoost see dese diamant rings!
Coom down and fill your bockets,
   Und I'll giss you like efery dings.

'Vot you vantsh mit your schnapps und lager?
   Coom down into der Rhine!
Der ish pottles der Kaiser Charlemagne
   Vonce filled mit gold-red wine!'

Dat fetched him—he shtood all shpell pound;
   She pooled his coat-tails down,
She drawed him oonder der wasser,
   De maiden mit nodings on.

—C.G. Leland

QUEEN VICTORIA
(1819-1901)

The Water-Drinker

Oh! water for me! Bright water for me!
And wine for the tremulous debauchee!
It cooleth the brow, it cooleth the brain,
It maketh the faint one strong again;
It comes o'er the sense like a breeze from the sea,
All freshness, like infant purity.
Oh! water, bright water for me, for me!
Give wine, give wine to the debauchee!

Fill to the brim! Fill, fill to the brim!
Let the flowing crystal kiss the rim!
For my hand is steady, my eye is true,
For I, like the flowers, drink nought but dew.
Oh! water, bright water's a mine of wealth,
And the ores it yieldeth are vigour and health.
So water, pure water for me, for me!
And wine for the tremulous debauchee!

Fill again to the brim! again to the brim!
For water strengtheneth life and limb!
To the days of the aged it addeth length,
To the might of the strong it addeth strength.
It freshens the heart, it brightens the sight,
'Tis like quaffing a goblet of morning light!
So, Water! I will drink nought but thee,
Thou parent of health and energy!

When o'er the hills, like a gladsome bride,
Morning walks forth in her beauty's pride,
And, leading a band of laughing hours,
Brushes the dew from the nodding flowers;

Oh! cheerily then my voice is heard,
Mingling with that of the soaring bird,
Who flingeth abroad his matins loud,
As he freshens his wing in the cold gray cloud.

But when Evening has quitted her sheltering yew,
Drowsily flying and weaving anew
Her dusky meshes o'er land and sea—
How gently, O sleep! fall thy poppies on me;
For I drink water, pure, cold, and bright,
And my dreams are of heaven the livelong night;
So, hurrah! for thee, Water! hurrah, hurrah!
Thou art silver and gold, thou art riband and star!
Hurrah! for bright Water! hurrah, hurrah!

—*Edward Jonson*

WALT WHITMAN
(1819-1892)

Jack and Jill

I celebrate the personality of Jack!
I love his dirty hands, his tangled hair, his locomotion blundering.
Each wart upon his hands I sing,
Paeans I chant to his hulking shoulder blades.
Also Jill!
Her I celebrate.
I, Walt, of unbridled thought and tongue,
Whoop her up!
Her golden hair, her sun-struck face, her hard and reddened hands;
So, too, her feet, hefty, shambling.
I see them in the evening, when the sun empurples the horizon, and through the darkening forest aisles are heard the sounds of myriad creatures of the night.
I see them climb the steep ascent in quest of water for their mother.
Oh, speaking of her, I could celebrate the old lady if I had time.
She is simply immense!

But Jack and Jill are walking up the hill.
(I didn't mean that rhyme.)
I must watch them.
I love to watch their walk,
And wonder as I watch;
He, stoop-shouldered, clumsy, hide-bound,
Yet lusty,
Bearing his share of the 1-lb bucket as though it were a paperweight.
She, erect, standing, her head uplifting,
Holding, but bearing not the bucket.
They have reached the spring.
They have filled the bucket.
Have you heard the "Old Oaken Bucket"?
I will sing it:—

Of what countless patches is the bed-quilt of life composed!
Here is a piece of lace. A babe is born.
The father is happy, the mother is happy.
Next black crêpe. A beldame "shuffles off this mortal coil."
Now brocaded satin with orange blossoms.
Mendelssohn's "Wedding March," an old shoe missile,

A broken carriage window, the bride in the Bellevue sleeping.
Here's a large piece of black cloth!
"Have you any last words to say?"
"No."
"Sheriff, do your work!"
Thus it is: from "grave to gay, from lively to severe."

I mourn the downfall of my Jack and Jill.
I see them descending, obstacles not heeding.
I see them pitching headlong, the water from the pail outpouring, a noise from leathern lungs out-belching.
The shadows of the night descend on Jack, recumbent, bellowing, his pate with gore besmeared.
I love his cowardice, because it is an attribute, just like
Job's patience or Solomon's wisdom, and I love attributes.
Whoop!!!

—*Charles Battell Loomis*

Home Sweet Home with Variations

I

You over there, young man with the guide book red-bound, covered flexibly with red linen,
Come here, I want to talk with you; I, Walt, the Manhattanese, citizen of these States, call you.
Yes, and the courier, too, smirking, smug-mouthed, with oiled hair; a garlicky look about him generally; him, too, I take in, just as I would a coyote, or a king, or a toadstool, or a ham sandwich, or anything or anybody else in the world.
Where are you going?
You want to see Paris, to eat truffles, to have a good time; in Vienna, London, Florence, Monaco, to have a good time; you want to see Venice.
Come with me. I will give you a good time; I will give you all the Venice you want, and most of the Paris.
I, Walt, I call to you. I am all on deck! Come and loaf with me! Let me tote you around by your elbow and show you things.
You listen to my ophicleide!
Home!
Home, I celebrate! I elevate my fog-whistle, inspir'd by the thought of home.
Come in!—take a front seat; the jostle of the crowd not minding; there is room enough for all of you.
This is my exhibition—it is the greatest show on earth—there is no charge for admission.
All you have to pay me is to take in my romanza.

II

1. The brownstone house; the father coming home worried from a bad day's business; the wife meets him in the marble-paved vestibule; she throws her arms about him; she presses him close to her; she looks him full in the face with affectionate eyes; the frown from his brow disappearing.

   Darling, she says, *Johnny has fallen down and cut his head; the cook is going away and the boiler leaks.*
2. The mechanic's dark little third-story room, seen in a flash from the Elevated Railway train; the sewing machine in a corner; the small cook stove; the whole family eating cabbage around a kerosene lamp; of the clatter and roar and groaning wail of the Elevated Train unconscious; of the smell of the cabbage unconscious.

   Me, passant, in the train, of the cabbage not quite so unconscious.

3. The French flat; the small rooms, all right angles, unindividual; the narrow halls; the gaudy cheap decorations everywhere.
   The janitor and the cook exchanging compliments up and down the elevator shaft; the refusal to send up more coal, the solid splash of the water upon his head, the language he sends up the shaft, the triumphant laughter of the cook, to her kitchen retiring.
4. The widow's small house in the suburbs of the city; the widow's boy coming home from his first day down town; he is flushed with happiness and pride; he is no longer a schoolboy, he is earning money; he takes on the airs of a man and talks learnedly of business.
5. The room in the third class boarding-house; the mean little hard-coal fire, the slovenly Irish servant-girl making it, the ashes on the hearth, the faded furniture, the private provender hid away in the closet, the dreary backyard out the window; the young girl at the glass, with her mouth full of hair-pins, doing up her hair to go downstairs and flirt with the young fellows in the parlour.
6. The kitchen of the old farm-house; the young convict just returned from prison—it was his first offense, and the judges were lenient to him.
   He is taking his first meal out of prison; he has been received back, kiss'd, encourag'd to start again; his lungs, his nostrils expand with the big breaths of free air; with shame, with wonderment, with a trembling joy, his heart, too, expanding.
   The old mother busies herself about the table; she has ready for him the dishes he us'd to like; the father sits with his back to them, reading the newspaper, the newspaper shaking and rustling much; the children hang wondering around the prodigal—they have been caution'd: *Do not ask where our Jim has been; only say you are glad to see him.*
   The elder daughter is there, pale-fac'd, quiet; her young man went back on her four years ago; his folks would not let him marry a convict's sister. She sits by the window, sewing on the children's clothes, the clothes not only patching up; her hunger for children of her own, invisibly patching up.
   The brother looks up; he catches her eye, he, fearful, apologetic; she smiles back at him, not reproachfully smiling, with loving pretence of hope, smiling—it is too much for him; he buries his face in the folds of his mother's black gown.
7. The best room of the house, on the Sabbath only open'd; the smell of horse-hair furniture and mahogany varnish; the ornaments on the what-not in the corner; the wax-fruit, dusty, sunken, sagged-in, consumptive-looking, under a glass globe; the sealing-wax imitation of coral; the cigar boxes with shells plastered over; the perforated card-board motto.
   The kitchen; the housewife sprinkling the clothes for the fine ironing to-morrow—it it Third-day night, and the plain things are already iron'd, now in cupboards, in drawers, stowed away.
   The wife waiting for the husband—he is at the tavern, jovial, carousing; she, alone in the kitchen sprinkling clothes—the little red wood clock with peaked top, with pendulum wagging behind a pane of gaily painted glass, strikes twelve.
   The sound of the husband's voice on the still night air,—he is singing: *We won't go home till morning!*—the wife arising, toward the woodshed hastily going, stealthily entering, the voice all the time coming nearer, inebriate, chantant.
   The wood-shed; the club behind the door of the woodshed; the wife annexing the club; the husband approaching, always inebriate, chantant.
   The husband passing the door of the wood-shed; the club over his head, now with his head in contact; the sudden cessation of song; the temperance pledge signed the next morning; the benediction of peace over the domestic foyer temporarily resting.

III

I sing the soothing influences of home.
You young man, thoughtlessly wandering, with courier, with guidebook wandering.
You hearken to the melody of my steam-calliope.
Yawp!

—*H.C. Bunner*

Old King Cole

Me clairvoyant,
Me conscious of you, old camarado,
Needing no telescope, lorgnette, field-glass, opera-glass, myopic pince-nez,
Me piercing two thousand years with eye naked and not ashamed;
The crown cannot hide you from me;
Musty old feudal-heraldic trappings cannot hide you from me,
I perceive that you drink.
(I am drinking with you. I am as drunk as you are.)
I see you are inhaling tobacco, puffing, smoking, spitting
(I do not object to your spitting),
You prophetic of American largeness,
You anticipating the broad masculine manners of these States;
I see in you also there are movements, tremors, tears, desire for the melodious,
I salute your three violinists, endlessly making vibrations,
Rigid, relentless, capable of going on for ever;
They play my accompaniment; but I shall take no notice of any accompaniment;
I myself am a complete orchestra.
So long.

—*G.K. Chesterton*

"A Classic Waits for Me"

A classic waits for me, it contains all, nothing is lacking,
Yet all were lacking if taste were lacking, or if the endorsement of the right man were lacking.
O clublife, and the pleasures of membership,
O volumes for sheer fascination unrivalled.
Into an armchair endlessly rocking,
Walter J. Black my president,
I, freely invited, cordially welcomed to membership,
My arm around John Kieran, Hendrick Willem van Loon, Pearl S. Buck,
My taste in books guarded by the spirit of William Lyon Phelps
(From your memories, sad brothers, from the fitful risings and callings I heard),
I to the classics devoted, brother of rough mechanics, beauty-
parlor technicians, spot welders, radio-program directors
(It is not necessary to have a higher education to appreciate these books),
I, connoisseur of good reading, friend of connoisseurs of good reading everywhere,
I, not obligated to take any specific number of books, free to reject any volume, perfectly free to reject Montaigne, Erasmus, Milton,
I, in perfect health except for a slight cold, pressed for time, having only a few more years to live,
Now celebrate this opportunity.
Come, I will make the club indissoluble,
I will read the most splendid books the sun ever shone upon,

I will start divine magnetic groups,
With the love of comrades,
With the lifelong love of distinguished committees.

I strike up for an old Book.
Long the best-read figure in America, my dues paid, sitter in armchairs everywhere, wanderer in populous cities, weeping with Hecuba and with the late William Lyon Phelps,
Free to cancel my membership whenever I wish.
Turbulent, fleshy, sensible,
Never tiring of clublife,
Always ready to read another masterpiece provided it has the approval of my president, Walter J. Black,
Me imperturbe, standing at ease among writers,
Rais'd by a perfect mother and now belonging to a perfect book club,
Bearded, sunburnt, gray-neck'd, astigmatic,
Loving the masters and and the masters only
(I am mad for them to be in contact with me),
My arm around Pearl S. Buck, only American woman to receive the Nobel Prize for Literature,
I celebrate this opportunity.
And I will not read a book nor the least part of a book but has the approval of the Committee,
For all is useless without that which you may guess at many times and not hit, that which they hinted at,
All is useless without readability.
By God! I will accept nothing which all cannot have their counterpart of on the same terms ($.89 for the Regular Edition or $1.39 for the De Luxe Edition, plus a few cents postage).
I will make inseparable readers with their arms around each other's necks,
By the love of classics,
By the manly love of classics.

—E.B. White

Narcissus in Camden

A CLASSICAL DIALOGUE OF THE YEAR 1882

("In the course of his lecture Mr.——— remarked that the most impressive room he had yet entered in America was the one in Camden town where he met ——— ———. It contained plenty of fresh air and sunlight.... On the table was a simple cruse of water."...)

Paumanokides. Narcissus.

Paumanokides.
Who may this be?
This young man clad unusually, with loose locks, languorous, glidingly toward me advancing.
Toward the ceiling of my chamber his orbic and expressive eyeballs uprolling,
As I have seen the green-necked wild-fowl, the mallard, in the thundering of the storm,
By the weedy shore of Paumanok my fish-shaped island.
Sit down, young man!
I do not know you, but I love you with burning intensity.
I am he that loves the young men, whosoever and wheresoever they are or may be hereafter, or may have been any time in the past,
Loves the eye-glassed literat, loves also and probably more the vender of clams, raucous-throated, monotonous-chanting,
Loves the Elevated Railroad employee of Mannahatta, my city;
I suppress the rest of the list of the persons I love, solely because I love you,
Sit down, élève, I receive you!

Narcissus
O clarion, from whose brazen throat
  Strange sounds across the seas are blown,
Where England, girt as with a moat,
  A strong sea-lion, sits alone!
A pilgrim from that white-cliffed shore,
  What joy, large flower of Western land!
To seek thy democratic door,
  With eager hand to clasp thy hand!

Paumanokides
Right you are!
Take then the electric pressure of these fingers. O my Comrade!
I do not doubt you are the one I was waiting for, as I loaf'd here enjoying my soul,
Let us two under all and any circustances stick together from this out!

Narcissus
Seeing that isle of which I spake but late
  By ignorant demagogues is held in fee,
  The grand Greek limbs of young Democracy
Beckoned me thence to this ideal State,
Where maiden fields of life Hellenic wait
  For one who in clear culture walks apart
  (Avoiding all rude clamors of the mart
That mar his calm) to sow the seeds of great
  Growths yet to be—the love of sacred Art,
And Beauty, of this breast queen consecrate,
Whose throne mean Science seeks to violate;
  The flawless artist's lunacy serene,
His purely passionate and perfect hate
  And noble scorn of all things Philistine.

Paumanokides
Hold up there, Camerado!
Beauty is all very good as far as it goes, and Art the perpetuator of Beauty is all very good as far as it goes, but you can tell your folks,
Your folks in London, or in Dublin, or in Rome, or where the Arno flows, or where Seine flows,
Your folks in the picture-galleries, admiring the Raphaels, the Tintorettos, the Rubenses, Vandycks, Correggios, Murillos, Angelicos of the world,
(I know them all, they have effused to me, I have wrung them out, I have abandoned them, I have got beyond them,)—

Narcissus (aside with tenderness)
Ah, Burne-Jones!

Paumanokides
Tell them that I am considerably more than Beauty!
I, representing the bone and muscle and cartilage and adipose tissue and pluck of the Sierras, of California, of the double Carolinas, of the Granite State, and the Narragansett Bay State, and the Wooden Nutmeg State!
I, screaming with the scream of the bald-headed bird, the eagle, in the primitive woods of America my country, in the hundred and sixth year of these States!

Dear son, I have learned the secret of the Universe,
I learned it from my original *bonne*, the white-capped ocean,
I learned it from the Ninth-Month Equinoctial, from the redwood tree, and the Civil War, and the hermit-thrush, and the telephone, and the Corliss engine,

The secret of the Universe is not Beauty, dear son, nor is it Art the perpetuator of Beauty,
The secret of the Universe is to admire one's self.
Camerado, you hear me!

Narcissus
Ah, I too loitering on an eve of June
Where one wan narciss leaned above a pool,
While overhead Queen Dian rose too soon,
And through the Tyrian clematis the cool
Night airs came wandering wearily, I too,
Beholding that pale flower, beheld Life's key at last, and knew

That love of one's fair self were but indeed
Just worship of pure Beauty; and I gave
One sweet, sad sigh, then bade my fond eyes feed
Upon the mirrored treasure of the wave,
Like that lithe beauteous boy in Tempe's vale,
Whom haples Echo loved—thou know'st the Heliconian tale!

And while heaven's harmony in lake and gold
Changed to a faint nocturne of silvern-gray,
Like rising sea-mists from my spirit rolled
The grievous vapors of this Age of Clay
Beholding Beauty's re-arisen shrine,
And the white glory of this precious loveliness of mine!

Paumanokides
I catch on, my Comrade!
—You allow that your aim is similar to mine, after all is said and done.
Well, there is not much similarity of style, and I recommend my style to you.
Go gaze upon the native rock-piles of Mannahatta, my city,
Formless, reckless,
Marked with the emerald miracle of moss, tufted with the unutterable wonder of the exquisite green grass,
Giving pasture to the spry and fearless-footed quadruped, the goat,
Also patched by the heaven-ambitious citizens with the yellow handbill, the advertisement of patent soaps, the glaring and vari-colored circus poster:
Mine, too, for reasons, such arrays;
Such my unfettered verse, scorning the delicatesse of dilettantes.
Try it, I'll stake you my ultimate dollar you'll like it.

Narcissus (*gracefully waiving the point*)
Haply in the far, the orient future, in the dawn we herald like the birds,
Men shall read the legend of our meeting, linger o'er the music of our words;

Haply coming poets shall compare me then to Milton in his lovely youth,
Sitting in the cell of Galileo, learning at his elder's lips the truth.

Haply they shall liken these dear moments, safely held in History's amber clear,
Unto Dante's converse bland with Virgil, on the margin of that gloomy mere!

Paumanokides
Do not be deceived, dear son;
Amid the choruses of the morn of progress, roaring, hilarious, those names will be heard no longer.
Galileo was admirable once, Milton was admirable,
Dante the *I*-talian was a cute man in his way,
But he was not the maker of poems, the Answer!
I, Paumanokides, am the maker of poems, the Answerer.

And I calculate to chant as long as the earth revolves,
To an interminable audience of haughty, effusive, copious, gritty,and chipper Americanos!

Narcissus
What more is left to say or do?
Our minds have met; our hands must part.
I go to plant in pastures new
The love of Beauty and of Art.
I'll shortly start.
One town is rather small for two
Like me and you!

Paumonikides
So long!

—Helen Gray Cone

MATTHEW ARNOLD
(1822-1888)

The Dover Bitch

A CRITICISM OF LIFE

for Andrews Wanning

So there stood Matthew Arnold and this girl
With the cliffs of England crumbling away behind them,
And he said to her, 'Try to be true to me,
And I'll do the same for you, for things are bad
All over, etc., etc.'
Well now, I knew this girl. It's true she had read
Sophocles in a fairly good translation
And caught that bitter allusion to the sea,
But all the time he was talking she had in mind
The notion of what his whiskers would feel like
On the back of her neck. She told me later on
That after a while she got to looking out
At the lights across the channel, and really felt sad,
Thinking of all the wine and enormous beds
And blandishments in French and the perfumes.
And then she got really angry. To have been brought
All the way down from London, and then be addressed
As a sort of mournful cosmic last resort
Is really tough on a girl, and she was pretty.
Anyway, she watched him pace the room
And finger his watch-chain and seem to sweat a bit,
And then she said one or two unprintable things.
But you musn't judge her by that. What I mean to say is,
She's really all right. I still see her once in a while
And she always treats me right. We have a drink
And I give her a good time, and perhaps it's a year
Before I see her again, but there she is,
Running to fat, but dependable as they come.
And sometimes I bring her a bottle of *Nuit d'Amour.*

—Anthony Hecht

Arcades Ambo

Why are ye wandering aye 'twixt porch and porch,
  Thou and thy fellow—when the pale stars fade
At dawn, and when the glowworm lights her torch,
  O Beadle of the Burlington Arcade?
  —Who asketh why the Beautiful was made?
A wan cloud drifting o'er the waste of blue,
  The thistledown that floats above the glade,
The lilac-blooms of April—fair to view,
And naught but fair are these; and such, I ween, are you.

Yes, ye are beautiful. The young street boys
  Joy in your beauty. Are ye there to bar
Their pathway to that paradise of toys,
  Ribbons and rings? Who'll blame ye if ye are?
  Surely no shrill and clattering crowd should mar
The dim aisle's stillness, where in noon's midglow
  Trip fair-hair'd girls to boot-shop or bazaar;
Where, at soft eve, serenely to and fro
The sweet boy-graduates walk, nor deem the pastime slow.

And O! forgive me, Beadles, if I paid
  Scant tribute to your worth, when first ye stood
Before me robed in broadcloth and brocade
  And all the nameless grace of Beadlehood!
  I would not smile at ye—if smile I could
Now as erewhile, ere I had learn'd to sigh:
  Ah, no! I know ye beautiful and good,
And evermore will pause as I pass by,
And gaze, and gazing think, how base a thing am I.

—*Charles Stuart Calverley*

Softly The Evening

'Softly the evening descends,
Violet and soft. The sea
Adds to the silence, below
Pleasant and cool on the beach
Breaking; yes, and a breeze
Calm as the twilight itself
Furtively sighs through the dusk,
Listlessly lifting my hair,
Fanning my thought-wearied brow.
  Thus I stand in the gloom
Watching the moon-track begin
Quivering to die like a dream
Over the far sea-line
To the unknown region beyond.

  'So for ages hath man
Gazed on the ocean of time
From the shores of his birth, and, turning
His eyes from the quays, the thronged
Marts, the noise and the din
To the far horizon, hath dreamed
Of a timeless country beyond.

Vainly: for how should he pass,
Being on foot, o'er the wet
Ways of the unplumbed waves?
How, without ship, should he pass
Over the shipless sea
To the timeless country beyond?

'Ah, but once—once long ago,
Came there a ship white-sailed
From the country beyond, with bright
Oarsmen, and men that sang;
Came to Humanity's coasts,
Called to the men on the shore,
Joyously touched at the port.
Then did time-weary man
Climb the bulwarks, the deck
Eagerly crowding. Anon
With jubilant voices raised,
And singing, "When Israel came
Out of Egypt," and whatso else
In the psalm is written, they passed
Out of the ken of the land,
Over the far sea-line,
To the unknown region beyond.

'Where are they now, then—they
That were borne out of sight by the ship—
Our brothers, of times gone by?
Why have they left us here
Solemn, dejected, alone,
Gathered in groups on the shore?
Why? For we, too, have gazed
O'er the waste of waters, and watched
For a sail as keenly as they.
Ah, wretched men that we are!
On our haggard faces and brows
Aching, a wild breeze fawns
Full of the scents of the sea,
Redolent of regions beyond.
Why, then, tarries the ship?
When will her white sail rise
Like a star on the sea-line? When?

'When?—And the answer comes
From the sailless face of the sea,
"Ah, vain watchers, what boots
The calm of the evening?
Have ye not watched through the day
Turbulent waves, the expanse
Endless, shaken with storm,
And ask ye where is the ship?
Deeper than plummet can dive
She is bedded deep in the ooze,
And over her tall mast floats
The purple plain of the calm."

'Yes—and never a ship
Since this is sunken, will come
Ever again o'er the waves—
Nay, not even the craft with the fierce

Steersman, him of the marsh
Livid, with wheels of flame
Circling his eyes, to smite
The lingering soul with his oar.
—Not that even. But we
Drop where we stand one by one
On the shingles and sands of time,
And cover in taciturn gloom,
With only perhaps some tear,
Each for his brother the hushed
Heart and the limitless dreams
With a little gift of sand.'

—W. H. Mallock

From *The Steam-Engine*

I dream'd I walk'd, in raptures high,
Through realms of sunny clime,
Not of this earth; they seem'd to lie
Beyond the bourne of time.

Nor did they seem all heav'nly fair,
But happy fields between
This lowly earth of vexing care
And the celestial scene....

No labour long and hard oppress'd
The happy human race,
Save pleasing tasks with bracing rest,
In this exalted place.

No beast, throughout its breadth and length,
Was e'er compell'd to toil;
For POWERS of superhuman strength
Gave culture to the soil.

The chariots here, in gorgeous train,
Sped swift in pageant tours;
And vessels on the rolling main,
Moved by these MIGHTY POWERS....

I'd seen these god-like POWERS before
On this our lowly earth;
Was present at th'auspicious hour,
When they received their birth:

Yet here I miss'd the vexing cares,
The avarice and pride,
The loud contentions, angry jars,
Which man from man divide.

My wonder deep one standing near
At once deign'd to explain;
"Behold," he said, "the destined sphere
Of GREAT MESSIAH'S reign!

"He slavish toil and care destroy'd,
By aid of THESE VAST POWERS;
While bliss, like Eden's, is enjoy'd
In this bright land of ours!

"And strangled by HIS mighty hold
Are vice and sin and woe;
As holy prophets had foretold
Some thousand years ago!"

Th' advancing day's tumultuous noise
My happy slumber broke;
From raptures of celestial joys,
To real scenes I woke;

Not without hopes the time would come,
When earth would be renew'd,
With all such glories in their bloom,
As I in vision view'd!

—*T. Baker*

DANTE GABRIEL ROSSETTI
(1828-1882)

Cimabuella

Fair-tinted cheeks, clear eyelids drawn,
In crescent curves above the light
Of eyes, whose dim, uncertain dawn
Becomes not day: a forehead white
Beneath long yellow heaps of hair:
She is so strange she must be fair.

Had she sharp, slant-wise wings outspread,
She were an angel; but she stands
With flat dead gold behind her head,
And lilies in her long thin hands:
Her folded mantle, gathered in,
Falls to her feet as it were tin.

Her nose is keen as pointed flame;
Her crimson lips no thing express;
And never dread of saintly blame
Held down her heavy eyelashes:
To guess what she were thinking of,
Precludeth any meaner love.

An azure carpet, fringed with gold,
Sprinkled with scarlet spots, I laid
Before her straight, cool feet unrolled:
But she nor sound nor movement made
(Albeit I heard a soft, shy smile,
Printing her neck a moment's while);

And I was shamed through all my mind
For that she spake not, neither kissed,
But stared right past me. Lo! behind

Me stood, in pink and amethyst,
Sword-girt and velvet-doubleted,
A tall, gaunt youth, with frowzy head,

Wide nostrils in the air, dull eyes,
Thick lips that simpered, but, ah me!
I saw, with most forlorn surprise,
He was the Thirteenth Century!
I but the Nineteenth: then despair
Curdled beneath my curling hair.

O, Love and Fate! How could she choose
My rounded outlines, broader brain,
And my resuscitated Muse?
Some tears she shed, but whether pain
Or joy in him unlocked their source,
I could not fathom which, of course.

But I from missals, quaintly bound,
With either and with clavichord
Will sing her songs of sovran sound:
Belike her pity will afford
Such faint return as suits a saint
So sweetly done in verse and paint.

—Bayard Taylor

Sonnet for a Picture

That nose is out of drawing. With a gasp,
She pants upon the passionate lips that ache
With the red drain of her own mouth, and make
A monochord of colour. Like an asp,
One lithe lock wriggles in his rutilant grasp.
Her bosom is an oven of myrrh, to bake
Love's white warm shewbread to a browner cake.
The lock his fingers clench has burst its hasp.
The legs are absolutely abominable.
Ah! what keen overgust of wild-eyed woes
Flags in that bosom, flushes in that nose?
Nay! Death sets riddles for desire to spell,
Responsive. What red hem earth's passion sews,
But may be ravenously unripped in hell?

—Algernon Charles Swinburne

The Poster Girl

The blessed Poster girl leaned out
From a pinky-purple heaven.
One eye was red and one was green;
Her bang was cut uneven;
She had three fingers on her hand,
And the hairs on her head were seven.

Her robe, ungirt from clasp to hem,
No sunflowers did adorn,
But a heavy Turkish portière
Was very neatly worn;
And the hat that lay along her back
Was yellow, like canned corn.

It was a kind of wobbly wave
That she was standing on,
And high aloft she flung a scarf
That must have weighed a ton;
And she was rather tall—at least
She reached up to the sun.

She curved and writhed, and then she said,
Less green of speech than blue:
"Perhaps I *am* absurd—perhaps
I *don't* appeal to you;
But my artistic worth depends
Upon the point of view."

I saw her smile, although her eyes
Were only smudgy smears;
And then she swished her swirling arms,
And wagged her gorgeous ears.
She sobbed a blue-and-green-checked sob,
And wept some purple tears.

—*Carolyn Wells*

After Dilettante Concetti

"Why do you wear your hair like a man,
Sister Helen?
This week is the third since you began."
"I'm writing a ballad; be still if you can,
Little brother.
(*O Mother Carey, mother!*
What chickens are these between sea and heaven!)"

"But why does your figure appear so lean,
Sister Helen?
And why should you dress in sage, sage green?"
"Children should never be heard, if seen,
Little brother!
(*O Mother Carey, mother!*
What fowls are a-wing in the stormy heaven!)"

"But why is your face so yellowy white,
Sister Helen?
And why are your skirts so funnily tight?"
"Be quiet, you torment, or how can I write,
Little brother?
(*O Mother Carey, mother!*
How gathers thy train to the sea from heaven!)"

"And who's Mother Carey, and what is her train,
Sister Helen?
And why do you call her again and again?"
"You troublesome boy, why that's the refrain,
Little brother.
(*O Mother Carey, mother!*
What work is toward in the startled heaven?)"

"And what's a refrain? What a curious word,
Sister Helen!
Is the ballad you're writing about a sea-bird?"
"Not at all; why should it be? Don't be absurd,
Little brother.
(*O Mother Carey, mother!*
Thy brood flies lower as lowers the heaven.)"

(*A big brother speaketh:*)
"The refrain you've studied a meaning had,
Sister Helen!
It gave strange force to a weird ballad.
But refrains have become a ridiculous 'fad,'
Little brother.
And *Mother Carey, mother,*
Has a bearing on nothing in earth or heaven.

"But the finical fashion has had its day,
Sister Helen.
And let's try in the style of a different lay
To bid it adieu in poetical way,
Little brother.
So Mother Carey, mother!
Collect your chickens and go to—heaven."

(*A pause. Then the big brother singeth accompanying himself in a plain-tive wise on the triangle:*)

"Look in my face. My name is Used-to-was;
I am also called Played-out and Done-to-death,
And It-will-wash-no-more. Awakeneth
Slowly, but sure awakening it has,
The common sense of man; and I, also!
The ballad-burden trick, now known too well,
Am turned to scorn, and grown contemptible—
A too transparent artifice to pass.

"What a cheap dodge I am! The cats who dart
Tin-kettled through the streets in wild surprise
Assail judicious ears not otherwise;
And yet no critics praise the urchin's 'art,'
Who to the wretched creature's caudal part
Its foolish empty-jingling 'burden' ties."

—Henry Duff Traill

EMILY DICKINSON
(1830-1886)

Emily's Haunted Housman

I taste a Draught Beer never brewed—
From Noggins graved in Smile—
And smoothlipped Meissen Mugs—that sweat
The Tears—of Crocodile—

Dun Dugs—of Lady Succor—dry—
Yield—a chary Curd—
Love's Wine is aged in Skins so thin—
Vinegar at a Word!

As Lads—we all press round the Punchbowl—
Then reel away—though I'm
Like most—Thirst raging at the Call
HURRY UP PLEASE IT'S TIME—

This Wassail wets the Whistle—dark—
Damps to Sigh the Reed—
Be Quick to name your Poison—Lads—
The Brand is on the Seed!

—*David Cummings*

Feathered Friends

A splendid Fellow in the Grass
Occasionally rides—
I know you've seen him—did you not
His clucking noisy is—

The Grass divides as with a Comb—
His glossy Feathers quaver—
He beaks his Biddy's little Comb
And shoves it to her Liver—

He likes her secret Parts—
They are so sweet and soupy—
And when he's through and doth withdraw—
His tiny Shaft is juicy—

Most of Nature's feathered Friends
I know, and they know me—
I feel for them a transport—
Of erotic Cordiality—

Except for this randy Fellow—
Old Chanticleer the Bold—
He leaves me tighter breathing—
And quivering with Cold.

—*Robert Peters*

Because I Could Not Dump

Because I could not Dump the Trash—
Joe kindly stopped for Me—
The Garbage Truck held but Ourselves—
And Bacterial Colonies—

We slowly drove—Joe smelled of Skunk—
Yet risking no delay
My hairdo and composure too,
Were quickly Fumed away—

We passed a School, where Dumpsters stood
Recycling—in the Rain—
We picked up Yields of Industry—
Dead Cats and Window Panes—

Or rather—Joe picked up—
Seeing maggot-lined cans—I recoiled—
When heir to smelly Legacies,
What sort of Woman—Spoils?

We paused before a Dump that seemed
A Swelling of the Ground—
The Soil was scarcely visible—
Joe dropped—his Booty—down.

Since then—'tis a fortnight—yet
Seems shorter than the Day
I first set out the Old Fish Heads—
And hoped Joe'd come my Way—

—Andrea Paterson

CHRISTINA ROSSETTI
(1830-1894)

Remember

Remember it, although you're far away—
Too far away more fivers yet to land,
When you no more can proffer notes of hand,
Nor I half yearn to change my yea to nay.
Remember, when no more in airy way,
You tell me of repayment sagely planned:
Only remember it, you understand!
It's rather late to counsel you to pay;
Yet if you should remember for awhile,
And then forget it wholly, I should grieve;
For, though your light procrastinations leave
Small remnants of the hope that once I had,
Than that you should forget your debt and smile,
I'd rather you'd remember and be sad.

—Anonymous

Ding Dong

Ding dong, Ding dong,
There goes the Gong,
Dick, come along,
'Tis time for dinner.
Wash your face,
Take your place,
Where's your grace,
You little sinner?

"Like an apple?"
"Yes, I should,
Nice, nice, nicey!
Good, good, good!"
"Manners miss,
Please behave,
Those who ask,
Shan't have."

"Those who don't
  Don't want.
I'll eat it,
  You shan't."

Baby cry,
Wipe his eye.
Baby good,
Give him food,
Baby sleepy,
Go to bed.
Baby naughty,
Smack his head!

Poor little thrush,
Found dead in a bush!
When did he die?
He is rather high.
Bury him deep,
He won't keep.
Bury him well,
Or he'll smell.

What have horns?
Cows and moons.
What have crests?
Cocks and spoons.
What are nice?
Ducks and peas.
What are nasty?
Bites of fleas.
What are fast?
Tides and times.
What are slow?
Nursery Rhymes.

—*Arthur Clement Hilton*

WILLIAM McGONAGALL
(1830-1902)

The Albion Battleship Calamity

'Twas in the year of 1898, and on the 21st of June,
The launching of the Battleship Albion caused a great gloom,
Amongst the relatives of many persons who were drowned in the River Thames,
Which their relatives will remember while life remains.

The vessel was christened by the Duchess of York,
And the spectators' hearts felt as light as cork
As the Duchess cut the cord that was holding the fine ship,
Then the spectators loudly cheered as the vessel slid down the slip.

The launching of the vessel was very well carried out,
While the guests on the stands cheered without any doubt,
Under the impression that everything would go well;
But, alas! instantaneously a bridge and staging fell.

Oh! little did the Duchess of York think that day
That so many lives would be taken away
At the launching of the good ship Albion,
But when she heard of the catastrophe she felt woebegone.

But accidents will happen without any doubt,
And often the cause thereof is hard to find out;
And according to report, I've heard people say,
'Twas the great crowd on the bridge caused it to give way.

Just as the vessel entered the water the bridge and staging gave way,
Immersing some three hundred people which caused great dismay
Amongst thousands of spectators that were standing there,
And in the faces of the bystanders, were depicted despair.

Then the police boats instantly made for the fatal spot,
And with the aid of dockyard hands several people were got,
While some scrambled out themselves, the best way they could—
And the most of them were the inhabitants of the neighborhood.

Part of them were the wives and daughters of the dockyard hands,
And as they gazed upon them they in amazement stands;
And several bodies were hauled up quite dead.
Which filled the onlookers' hearts with pity and dread.

One of the first rescued was a little baby,
Which was conveyed away to a mortuary;
And several were taken to the fitter's shed, and attended to there
By the firemen and several nurses with the greatest care.

Meanwhile heartrending scenes were taking place,
Whilst the tears ran down many a Mother and Father's face,
That had lost their children in the River Thames,
Which they will remember while life remains.

Oh, Heaven! it was horrible to see the bodies laid out in rows,
And as Fathers and Mothers passed along, adown their cheeks the tears flows,
While their poor, sickly hearts were throbbing with fear.

A great crowd had gathered to search for the missing dead,
And many strong men broke down because their heart with pity bled,
As they looked upon the distorted faces of their relatives dear,
While adown their cheeks flowed many a silent tear.

The tenderest sympathy, no doubt, was shown to them,
By the kind hearted Police and Firemen;
The scene in fact was most sickening to behold,
And enough to make one's blood run cold,
To see tear-stained men and women there
Searching for their relatives, and in their eyes a pitiful stare.

There's one brave man in particular I must mention,
And I'm sure he's worthy of the people's attention.
His name is Thomas Cooke, of No. 6 Percy Road, Canning Town,
Who's name ought to be to posterity handed down,
Because he leapt into the River Thames, and heroically did behave,
And rescued five persons from a watery grave.

Mr. Wilson, a young Electrician, got a terrible fright,
When he saw his mother and sister dead—he was shocked at the sight,
Because his sister had not many days returned from her honeymoon,
And in his countenance, alas! there was a sad gloom.

Her Majesty has sent a message of sympathy to the bereaved ones in distress,
And the Duke and Duchess of York have sent 25 guineas I must confess.
And £1000 from the Directors of the Thames Ironworks and Shipbuilding
Company,
Which I hope will help to fill the bereaved one's hearts with glee.

And in conclusion I will venture to say,
That accidents will happen by night and by day;
And I will say without any fear,
Because to me it appears quite clear,
That the stronger we our houses do build,
The less chance we have of being killed.

—*William McGonagall*

On First Looking Into Chapman's Homer

Much have I travelled in East Lothian and Dundee,
Many fine buildings and bridges for to see.
I have even journeyed as far as Arran,
Though sad to say it is rather barren.

Frequently of another expanse had I been told,
Described by Homer, the Greek writer of old.
But only when I read Mr. Chapman's translation
Did I have a very strong sensation.

An amateur astronomer was what I felt like,
When he sees a new planet or comet late at night;
Or a fat Spaniard who is to become quite famous,
Looking at the sea and wondering what its name is.

—*W.S. Brownlie*

La Belle Dame Sans Merci

O, what can be the matter with thee, Knight-at-arms,
Alone, loitering and with a very pale face,
The sedge has withered as it will do in winter
And no birds at all sing about the place.

O, perhaps you have a chill, Knight-at-arms,
Your eyes are red and your nostrils dripping?
The squirrel's filled his little tree larder
And you look as if into a depression you were slipping.

Your brow is as white as a lily,
Sprouting with sweat drops like dew;
And your cheeks which were as ruddy as a pillar box
Are becoming as white as a lily too.

I met a lady in the meadow behind the allotments,
As pretty as any actress on the stage;
And that is why I stand about here with my nostrils streaming,
Looking twice my age.

—*T. Griffiths*

Do Not Go Gentle

Do not go gentle into Death's esteemed vale,
Elderly persons should try to hang on when the body starts to fail;
Though, of course, one day it naturally transpires,
That everyone's membership of the human race expires.
And even if life wasn't spent in clover,
When the finger points—I'm afraid it's over.
Then the fun-lover sees his wasted chances—
And wishes he'd kept away from dances;
Or the sober man whose books were his treasures,
Finds his thoughts turning to coarser pleasures.
And you, Father, on the very brink as it were,
Where the world must seem little more than a blur,
Can still get angry and show real fight—
e.g. your rage when I switched off the light!

—Tim Hopkins

The Soldier

Oh! if by any unfortunate chance I should happen to die,
In a French field of turnips or radishes I'll lie.
But thinking of it as really Scottish all the time
Because my patriotic body will impart goodness to the slime.
For I've been brought up by the bonnie country of Scotland
Which I like very much indeed with its lochs and its plots of land
And many other picturesque sites which any tourist can see
So long as he is able to pay British Rail the requisite fee.

And you might give a thought too to my decomposing body
As it lies, poor dead thing, under the frog soddy.
For it will be thinking too of my very nice home country
And its weather which is anything but sultry,
And all the exceedingly jocund times I enjoyed there
And frolicked when I was able to in the soggy Scottish air.

—J.Y. Watson

Gather Ye Rosebuds

Although Michaelmas Daisies bloom for a very long time
Especially in soil which has been treated with horse-manure and lime
It is very important and you should all be told,
Fellow citizens, to pick them before they grow too old.

By looking up at that noble ball known as the sun,
Warming us up at Greenwich Mean Time half past one,
Our Nation's Scientists can truthfully aver
That it is going to set, whatever may be the time of the year.

Also consider, gentlemen, the truest word I ever spoke
Is that tossing the caber with a hernia is no joke.
For Highland Games and other things you must be young
For that makes you healthy in kidney and also in lung.

So when you see a beautiful woman, indigent or rich,
Let the marriage celebrations proceed without a hitch.
For if you do not follow the natural instincts of a rabbit
I must earnestly warn you that you will eventually lose the habit.

—Laurence Fowler

WILLIAM MORRIS
(1834-1896)

Jubilee Before Revolution

"Tell me, O Muse of the Shifty, the Man who wandered afar,"
So have I chanted of late, and of Troy Burg wasted of war—
Now of the sorrows of Menfolk that fifty years have been,
Now of the Grace of the Commune I sing, and the days of a Queen!
Surely I curse rich Menfolk, "the Wights of the Whirlwind" may they—
This is my style of translating, Αρπυιαι—snatch them away!
The Rich Thieves rolling in wealth that make profit of labouring men,
Surely the Wights of the Whirlwind shall swallow them quick in their den!
O baneful, O wit-straying, in the Burg of London ye dwell,
And ever of Profits and three per cent. are the tales ye tell,
But the stark, strong Polyphemus shall answer you back again,
Him whom "No man slayeth by guile and not by main."
(By "main" I mean "main force," if aught at all do I mean.
In the Greek of the blindfold Bard it is simpler the sense to glean.)
You Polyphemus shall swallow and fill his mighty maw,
What time he maketh an end of the Priests, the Police, and the Law,
And then, ah, who shall purchase the poems of old that I sang,
Who shall pay twelve-and-six for an epic in Saga slang?
But perchance even "Hermes the Flitter" could scarcely expound what I mean,
And I trow that another were fitter to sing you a song for a Queen.

—*Andrew Lang*

Rondel

Behold the works of William Morris,
 Epics, and here and there wall-papery,
 Mild, mooney, melancholy vapoury
A sort of Chaucer *minus* Horace.

Spun out like those of William Loris,
 Who wrote of amourous red-tapery,
Behold the works of William Morris,
 Epics, and here and there wall-papery!

Long ladies, knights, and earles and choris-
 ters in the most appropriate drapery,
 Samite and silk and spotless napery,
Sunflowers and apple blossoms and orris,
Behold the works of William Morris!

—*Anonymous*

ALGERNON CHARLES SWINBURNE
(1837-1909)

Octopus

Strange beauty, eight limbed and eight handed,
 Whence camest to dazzle our eyes?
With thy bosom bespangled and banded
 With the hues of the seas and the skies;

Is thy home European or Asian,
O mystical monster marine?
Part molluscous and partly crustacean,
Betwixt and between.

Wast thou born to the sound of sea trumpets?
Hast thou eaten and drunk to excess
Of the sponges—thy muffins and crumpets,
Of the seaweed—thy mustard and cress?
Hast thou nurtured in caverns of coral,
Remote from reproof or restraint?
Art thou innocent, art thou immoral,
Sinburnian or Saint?

Lithe limbs curling free as a creeper
That creeps in a desolate place,
To enrol and envelop the sleeper
In a silent and stealthy embrace;
Cruel beak craning forward to bite us,
Our juices to drain and to drink,
Or to whelm us in waves of Cocytus,
Indelible ink!

Oh breast that 'twere rapture to writhe on!
Oh arms 'twere delicious to feel
Clinging close with the crush of the Python
When she maketh her murderous meal!

In thy eight-fold embraces enfolden
Let our empty existence escape,
Give us death that is glorious and golden,
Crushed all out of shape!

Ah thy red lips, lascivious and luscious,
With death in their amorous kiss!
Cling round us and clasp us, and crush us,
With bitings of agonised bliss;

We are sick with the poison of pleasure,
Dispose us the potion of pain;
Ope thy mouth to its uttermost measure,
And bite us again!

—*Arthur Clement Hilton*

Nephelidia

From the depth of the dreamy decline of the dawn through a notable nimbus of nebulous noonshine,
Pallid and pink as the palm of the flag-flower that flickers with fear of the flies as they float,
Are they looks of our lovers that lustrously lean from a marvel of mystic miraculous moonshine,
These that we feel in the blood of our blushes that thicken and threaten with throbs through the throat?
Thicken and thrill as a theatre thronged at appeal of an actor's appalled agitation,
Fainter with fear of the fires of the future than pale with the promise of pride in the past;
Flushed with the famishing fullness of fever that reddens with radiance of rathe recreation,

Gaunt as the ghastliest of glimpses that gleam through the gloom of the gloaming when ghosts go aghast?
Nay, for the nick of the tick of the time is a tremulous touch on the temples of terror,
Strained as the sinews yet strenuous with strife of the dead who is dumb as the dust-heaps of death:
Surely no soul is it, sweet as the spasm of erotic emotional exquisite error,
Bathed in the balms of beatified bliss, beatific itself by beatitude's breath.
Surely no spirit or sense of a soul that was soft to the spirit and soul of our senses
Sweetens the stress of suspiring suspicion that sobs in the semblance and sound of a sigh;
Only this oracle opens Olympian, in mystical moods and triangular tenses—
'Life is the lust of a lamp for the light that is dark till the dawn of the day when we die.'
Mild is the mirk and monotonous music of memory, melodiously mute as it may be,
While the hope in the heart of a hero is bruised by the breach of men's rapiers, resigned to the rod;
Made meek as a mother whose bosom-beats bound with the bliss-bringing bulk of a balm-breathing baby,
As they grope through the grave-yard of creeds, under skies growing green at a groan for the grimness of God.
Blank is the book of his bounty beholden of old, and its binding is blacker than bluer:
Out of blue into black is the scheme of the skies, and their dews are the wine of the bloodshed of things;
Till the darkling desire of delight shall be free as a fawn that is freed from the fangs that pursue her,
Till the heart-beats of hell shall be hushed by a hymn from the hunt that has harried the kennel of kings.

—*Algernon Charles Swinburne*

The Manlet

In stature, the Manlet was dwarfish—
No burly big Blunderbore he:
And he wearily gazed on the crawfish
His Wifelet had dressed for his tea.
"Now reach me, sweet Atom, my gunlet,
And hurl the old shoelet for luck:
Let me hie to the bank of the runlet,
And shoot thee a Duck!"

She has reached him his minikin gunlet:
She has hurled the old shoelet for luck:
She is busily baking a bunlet,
To welcome him home with his Duck.
On he speeds, never wasting a wordlet,
Though thoughtlets cling, closely as wax,
To the spot where the beautiful birdlet
So quietly quacks.

Where the Lobsterlet lurks, and the Crablet
So slowly and sleepily crawls:
Where the Dolphin's at home, and the Dablet
Pays long ceremonious calls:
Where the grublet is sought by the Froglet:
Where the Frog is pursued by the Duck:
Where the Ducklet is chased by the Doglet—
So runs the world's luck!

He has loaded with bullet and powder:
His footfall is noiseless as air:
But the Voices grow louder and louder,
And bellow, and bluster, and blare.
Thy bristle before him and after,
Thy flutter above and below,
Shrill shriekings of lubberly laughter,
Weird wailings of woe!

They echo without him, within him:
They thrill through his whiskers and beard:
Like a teetotum seeming to spin him,
With sneers never hitherto sneered.
"Avengement," they cry, "on our Foelet!
Let the Manikin weep for our wrongs!
Let us drench him, from toplet to toelet,
With Nursery-Songs!

"He shall muse upon 'Hey! Diddle! Diddle!'
On the Cow that surmounted the Moon:
He shall rave of the Cat and the Fiddle,
And the Dish that eloped with the Spoon:
And his soul shall be sad for the Spider,
When Miss Muffet was sipping her whey,
That so tenderly sat down beside her,
And scared her away!

"The music of Midsummer-madness
Shall sting him with many a bite,
Till, in rapture of rollicking sadness,
He shall groan with a gloomy delight:
He shall swathe him, like mists of the morning,
In platitudes luscious and limp,
Such as deck, with a deathless adorning,
The Song of the Shrimp!

"When the Ducklet's dark doom is decided,
We will trundle him home in a trice:
And the banquet, so plainly provided,
Shall round into rose-buds and rice:
In a blaze of pragmatic invention
He shall wrestle with Fate, and shall reign:
But he has not a friend fit to mention,
So hit him again!"

He has shot it, the delicate darling!
And the Voices have ceased from their strife:
Not a whisper of sneering or snarling,
As he carries it home to his wife:
Then cheerily champing the bunlet
His spouse was so skilful to bake,
He hies him once more to the runlet,
To fetch her the Drake!

—*Lewis Carroll*

A Melton Mowbray Pork-Pie

Strange pie that is almost a passion,
    O passion immoral for pie!
Unknown are the ways that they fashion,
    Unknown and unseen of the eye.
The pie that is marbled and mottled,
    The pie that digests with a sigh:
For all is not Bass that is bottled,
    And all is not pork that is pie.

Richard Le Gallienne

The Twentieth Century

1912:	Pound issues "Harriet Monroe Doctrine."
1914-1918:	Rupert Bridges drowns in watershed of European civilization.
1918:	Hopkins's windoeuvre published.
1921:	Yeast's "The Second Camembert," first Cheese Poem.
1922:	Eliot seeks "objective Coriolanus" in Hamlet.
1922:	Joyless publishes *Harold Bloom.*
1938:	Lowell leaves Harvard for Kenya.
1949:	*Parmesan Cavilcantos* awarded Bowling Green Prize.
1950:	Olson advocates "composition by fool."
1954:	Breakfast of Campions poet Hoffman wins the Yale Younger Poets' Cereal Award.
1965:	Eliot dies of faberous tumor.
1965:	Plath's *Aerial* called "unacknowledged antenna of mankind"
1969:	*Naked Lunch Poetry* unclothes couplet.
1972:	Strange publishes *Dumber*, first Dumb-Imagist anthology.
1972:	"Il miglior fabliaux" dies.
1975:	Tennis Court Oaf wins National Bull Award.
1980:	Snack philanthropist James Muncher funds Iowa Cheese-Doodlers.
1981:	William Zaranka raised to obscurity.

THE TWENTIETH CENTURY MAYONNAISE

The poet Stephen Spenser relates an anecdote about the English Department store, Herod's, which once tried to induce Arnold Bennett (Pound's "cash-Nixon"), H. M. S. Wells, and George Bernhardt Shaw to write in its behalf. All three declined in gentlemanly fashion, with regret.

The anecdote may be pointless, yet it is not without significance. One cannot imagine asking a Pound or an Eliot to take part in such an anecdote. This is because of the "negative capability" which set in on the heels of Pater's great "Conclusion to the Runonsentence," the chief document of the Art Fart's Sake Movement, after which artists sought to burn with jamlike flames and became burnt-out cases. In other words, Arnold's brooch between the poets and the fillibusters widened and later resulted in the "alien corn of the artist," a terrible spiritual mayonnaise which included fragmentary isolation, personal solollipopsism, and self-insemination. Eliot and Pound, of course, were engaged in the so-called "Boor War" against just such middle- and low-boors as those who frequented Herod's. This trench-coat warfare between high-boor and low-boor gave rise to the sausage ironies of Vidal Sassoon, who replaced Rupert Bridges as England's favorite war poet after Bridges drowned in the watershed of European Civilization. Other casualties of the Boor War were Edmund Spender, replaced by John Hunter Donne as the poet of the sixteenth/seventeenth century, and Alfred North Tennyson, replaced by Gerard Manfred Hopkins ("Old Hippety-Hopkins of the accents") as the poet of the Victorian Age. Hopkins' claim is flimsy, for his terrible sonnets are marked by careless prosodomy, crippling instep, and sponge-sole rhythm, reminding the reader of nothing so much as the club-foot meter of Lord Byron. Nor are we helped by Hopkins's system of scansion, nor by his use of strong stretch-marks followed by "hangars" or "outriggers" (short syllables which can be measured in terms of inches or tads). Yet for all his faults, the knowledgable reader cannot help but agree with Bridges, who published the whole of Hopkins's windoeuvre posthumorously in 1918, that Hopkins is an important poet—if only for his spirited use of obliteration, onomato potato, and smegma in his verse.

THE MADAME AND THE MASSAGE

Once the war had subsided and Eliot had ascended to the literary dictatorship of England, the poet once again busied himself with an old preoccupation: searching for an "Objective Coriolanus" in Shakespeare's *Hamlet.* Eliot never found this level-headed alternative to Hamlet's emotional friend Horace, and never got over the disappointment. Indeed, it was Eliot who earlier had conned the term "discombobulation of sensibility" to describe the symptoms of the ill penseroso, John Milton. Yet Eliot might as well have been describing the same symptoms—acclerated grimace, dry salivations, and little giddings—in himself,as well as in other Disease Poets such as Conrad Aching and Edna St. Vincent Malaise. In "Titillation and the Individual Tyrant," his rewriting of Browning's biography of his father-in-law, Eliot dismisses the problems of sensibility by eschewing personality. According to Eliot, the artist has not a personality to express, but a madame. Here Eliot is acknowledging his debt to Madame LaForgue, who along with Stephane Mallomar, Arthur Rainbow, and Frankie Verlaine, influenced the method of *The Waste Land*, which is replete with illusions and other French phalluses of imitative form. Without a doubt, *The Waste Land* is the most influential document of the Modernist Movement, which includes such important works as James Joyless's mollycoddling *Harold Bloom* (a novel written in the stream-of-concubines technique of Homer's *Ulysses*) and Joyless's other book *Finnegan's Wok*, in which Western and Accidental philosophies are juxtaposed in much the same way as they are in Eliot's "The Fire Semen," written to Eliot's lover Paul Valery.

Since the anxiety of Eliot's influence has been traced by a host of critics, including John Crowe Ronsard, William Epsom, F.R. Livid, and others, suffice to say that by the time of his death of a faberous tumor in 1965, Eliot had established himself, in Pound's phrase, as the "unacknowledged antenna of mankind."

MAKING IT NEWARK

Another unacknowledged antenna is sometime Cheese poet Ezra Pound, whom critic Anthony Perkins has called perhaps the greatest of "the bastards of the High Modernist Mode." Born in 1885, Pound emigrated from his native Idaho to escape the potato feminists and study Romance sandwiches at the University of Pennsylvania. There he profoundly influenced William Tennessee Williams (inventor of the "variable foot" of Laura in *The Glass Menage a Trois*, and author of *Floyd Paterson*). Having influenced Williams, Pound went abroad and became a permanent expatriarch. His "Harriet Monroe Doctrine" spelled out in no uncertain terms the three tenants of the early "Amygist Movement":

1. No ideas, budding things;
2. Katydids, no metronomes;
3. The eyes by way of the nose to the buttercup.

Pound's unabashed call for a flower-centered Romanticism struck a responsive curd in Cheese philosopher David Hulme, whose call for "the word infinite in every other line" seemed to advocate a return to the quiet bucauliflowers (Bowdlaire's term for flowers of the forest primeval) of the Georgians (and other Southern Temptress Fugitives from Edwardian fleshiness). It was toward this end that Pound, Eliot's "ill miglior fabliaux," began "breeding lilacs" out of Eliot's *The Waste Land*, pruning Yeats's "Secret Rose" and tending Frost's "Subverted Flower." In 1949, Pound was awarded the Bowling Green Prize for his *The Parmesan Cavilcantos* (part of *The Guido Cavilcantos*, his life's work), even though he was at the time carcinogenic for treason. In 1972, Pound belied his prediction that "a tawdry *ladra*/Shall outlast our days" by dying, but not before becoming what Eliot has called "the spokesman of his Gerontion."

"AN OLD BIRCH GONE IN THE TEETH"

One accomplishment of Robert Frost was his use of the "luggage really used by men." In this respect, Frost is the child of Wordsworth and the father of Williams as well as of many contemporary champions of "the poetry which speech bred." In "Birches," one of his most famous poems, we find the lines,

> For an old birch gone in the teeth,
> For a birched civilization...

In the first line Frost is referring to his wife Elinor, while in the second his use of slant-eye rhyme suggests that he is referring to the yellow peril of his "momentary stays against Confucius." The amazing thing is that he is able to link the personal and the universal in accents unmistakably those of speech class. Frost achieved these colloquial effects while at the same time observing traditional form, and simple scansion using stretch marks will show that although Frost's poetry sounds like blank talk it is actually highly crafted blank verse which is often unrhymed and which makes use of a predictable Caesar in the middle of each line [see Prosodomy]. Suspicious of so-called "free verse," Frost modified Whitman's famous smellie to read "Free verse is like playing tennis without a hairnet," and continued to write blankly until the end of his days. No chicken farmer, Frost nevertheless garnered three Pullet Prizes before his death of local cholera in 1963.

MODERNISM AND THE MILK OF HUMANKINDNESS

Does Modernist Poetry lack the milk of humankindness? Is art Modern insofar as it does not resemble the human, as Ortega y Gasket suggests? Perhaps Donald Davie Daiches is right when he criticizes Eliot's poetry for lacking "scope and [human] sympathy." On the other hand, the work of William Bluster Yeast seems overflowing with milk. In such poems as "The Man Who Dreamed of Dairyland" and "The Second Camembert," Yeast writes:

> Churning and churning in the widening Gruyere,
> Surely the Second Camembert is at hand.

Here Yeast is echoing the sentiment expressed by Hardy's Tess in "Neuter Tones," where occurs the famous smellie:

> And the sun was white as though cheddar of God.

Both poets, of course, owe a debt to the Milton of *Samsoe Agonistes*, and to Wordsworth, whose "The Ruined Cottage Cheese," like much of the poetry of Frost, takes place in the luggage really used by men. Milton and Wordsworth set the standard for gerontions of Cheese (and later, Snack) Poets, including John Hausman, author of "Loveliest of Cheese, the Cheshire Now" and "With Rue My Heart is Leyden," Wallace Stevens, author of "Anecdote of the Jarlsberg" and "The Emperor of Cream Cheese," and Robert Graves, author of "The White Gouda" (cf. Robinson's "Minerva Cheesy" and "Muriel Rukase." But it is to the mature Yeast, whose career spans the end of one fin de siecle, the nineteenth, and the beginning of another, the twentieth, we must go for the greatest Cheese poems in the English language (the Greek poet Constantine Havarti is recognized as the world's most important). Most of these poems were composed during the Boston Celtic Twilight which Yeast, indisputably the greatest English poet in Ireland, immobilized forever. The most frequently anthologized of these, and therefore the best, is the poem Yeast dedicated to the aging naturalist Maud Gorgonnezola, with whom he was in love most of his life. It is, of course, "Liederkranz and the Swan" composed under Ben Bulben,

> where all the Lieders start,
> In the foul wine-and-cheese shop of the heart.

Surely, here is poetry possessed of all the milk of humankindness a reader could wish.

POST-MODERN AND CONTEMPORARY: FROM THE FORMAL TO THE INFERNAL

Ironically, the modern already seems to have fled before the onslaught of the post-modern, which even as we speak is being overrun by what Breakfast of Campions poet Daniel Hoffman, winner of the Yale Younger Poets Cereal Award, has called the "Balakianization of contemporary poetry" and its attendant acrimonies. In all the welter, the career of Robert Lowell stands out as exemplary of the movement of contemporary poetry from the formal to the infernal.

Lowell began his career under the influence of so-called traditional "Temptress Fugitives" like John Crowe Ronsard, David Jansen, and James Tate, with whom Lowell studied in Kenya. The early poems of *Land of Unlikeness* revealed a sensibility stooped in Milton. These poems were replete with rhetorical flushies, epic smellies, excremental repetition, and violent endjabments of the feminine end. Lowell soon grew tired of Kenya, and wrote in "Colloquy in Black Rock" of being "rattled screw and foosball" by its "nigger-brass perdidition," and of being seduced one Christmas Eve under a statue by a hooker. Shaken by having "planted the serpent's seeds of delight," thereby losing his virginity, the highly Catholic Lowell returned to Boston to confess his sins and turn over a new life. Lowell collected the poems of this penitent period in the influential *Life Smutties*, itself influenced by petfood enthusiast W.D. Snodgrass's *Hartz Noodle*, the Beet Poetry of vegetarian Alan Ginsberg, and the autobiological poetry of San Francisco's Hell's Anglos, Anne Sextons, and Wandering Jutes. Lowell's rejection of traditional meter and established forms in favor of a more generic verse idiom—the verse that speech bred—is a miniature watershed in literary history, and echoes minimal poet Robert Creeley's famous formula, "form is never more than an excretion of content," which was seconded by the author of *Sorrow Dunce* Denise Nemerov (also of the Bald Mountain School). Accordingly, poets like W.S. Moron, Wolfgang von Roethke, John Ashberyman, and Howeard Levertov, who had begun their careers as University Warts (academic footnodes to contemporary belly-litters), threw off the shackles of preconceited forms and became either rheumatic primitivists like Charles "Bobo" Olson and Gary Snodgrass, pedestrians like William Stafford and Marvin Bull, or Beets like Ginsberg and Diane Bukowski.

THE UMP OF THE PERVERSE

As important as the formal revolution *Life Smutties* engendered was the so-called "Confessional School" it inspired. Lowell's unabashed revelations of his own bouts of alcoholic insanity, sexual inadequacy and spitefulness to animals (the poet once drowned thirty-three turtles in a garden urn—were new in contemporary poetry, although Alan Larkin's obsessive "Church Goring" (of the Papal Bull) provides Lowell some stiff confessional competition. Equally competitive were Sylvia Plath, wife of Langston "Ted" Hughes, and Tennis Court Oaf John Ashberyman, husband of the tenth muse. The deferred dream of suicide nurtured by both these poets was finally fulfilled posthumorously in 1963 and 1972, respectfully. According to Lowell, the narcotic Ashberyman "used the language as if he spoke it," which is high phrase for the author of *His Tool, His Dram, His Roost* and charter member of the Kneejerk School, while Lowell's introduction to Plath's *Aerial* foreshadows Jack Kroll's study of Plath as a mythological heroine dealer of collosal proportions, a larger-than-*Life Smutties* figure out of Greek tragedy. This is supported by critic Margerie Perloff's reading of the poems, which makes use of nasal lineation and sharp throbs and sloshes of Acropolyptic imagery. On the strength of *Aerial* alone, the critic Rosenthal has tarted Plath, along with Pound and Eliot, as one of the unacknowledged antennae of mankind.

THE POETRY RETCH

Another sometime confessional poet is fisher queen Adrienne Rich, whose *Diving into the Retch* inspired the "deep image" theories of Robert Bly and James Wright, and the closely related "dumb image" theories of W.S. Moron, Mark Strange, and Charles Similac. According to Bly, the poet must dive deep down into his own pisces in order to find Jung's mother. Once found, she must be celebrated in only the most nerudimentary language, a notion supported by Wright's "Lying to a Haddock at William Duffy's Farm in Pine Island, Minnesota." In this poem, brief, evocative aspergilloses precede a stunning last sentence, "I have wasted my line," which, like Ranier Maria Roethke's beat elegy, "Corso, An Archaic Apollo," is a sorrowful elegy of lament over the loss of "the one that got away" into the retch of individual consciousness. In *Slippers Joining Hands*, Bly advocates a feet-first rather than headfirst leap into the retch, where the "teeth-mother" (Joyce Carol Ogre), a not-too-distant relation to the toothfairy, lurks in wait for the unwary poet. This is an atypical approach for Bly, whose magazine *The Fifties* changes its name each decade, presumably to confuse unborn textual critics.

DEEP IMAGE VS. DUMB IMAGE

It was perhaps fear and anxiety over Bly's "teeth-mother" that first provoked the so-called "dumb images" of Mark Strange, author of *Reasons for Mewling* and *Dumber*, and those of Charles Similac, author of *Return to a Place Lit by a Glass of Milk*, first published in Brazil because of its lack of adhesives in this country. Since then, Similac has gained fame at the hands of such champions as George Kayak, editor of the influential *Hitchcock* magazine, and Dogged Wagoner, editor of *North by Northwest*, while Strange has been tarted by other supporters of the fine hearts such as Richard Howard Moss of *The Kneejerker*, Stephen Bug of the *The American Poetry Rebuke*, and John Frederick Nimitz of *Poultry* (Chicago).

FATHER TO NIGHTINGHOULS

While Bly may be said to be the father of such poets as Strange and Similac, and perhaps even of Russell Edsel, author of *The Intuitive Gerbil*, it may be stretching matters somewhat to attribute paternity in the case of Galway Charnell, author of *The Avenue Bearing the Ignatow of Christ into the New Wodwo* and *The Book of Nightinghouls* (with Langston "Ted" Hughes). Here the adjectives "deep" and "dumb" seem scarcely to apply. Rather, it is this poet's chilling vision of the union of nightinghoul and wodwo into the single *ignatow* which Anne Sexton has said "will last for gerontions." The primitivist impulse to fill the cultural vacuum of our century's lingering watershed with a new mythology—unsparing in its brutality and violins, yet at the same time tender and even domestic—is most obvious in Charnell's treatment of the birth of his dogger, who is compared most strikingly to "a peck of stunned pork."

THE TENNIS COURT OAFS

Hardly related to Bly, except perhaps as a cousin of the language in which they both write, is Marilyn Hackman, winner of the National Bic Award for *Presentation Puss* and, recently, *The French-Kiss Connection.* The latter has been unsuccessfully parodied by Tennis Court Oaf Kenneth Kook in his *Sleeping With Wimpies.* Other Tennis Court Oafs include Flank O'Hara, author of *Peronism*, and Andre Kostelanatz, author of *Beware The Poetry MFA!*, both of whom have been affectionately dubbed "Kneejerk" poets by John Ashberyman, head of the so-called Kneejerk School. These poets pride themselves on owing nothing to the free-verse example of Robert Frost, and still less to Eliot's *Tradition and the Individual Tyrant.* The poetry of the Kneejerk School, little understood and highly overpraised, has nevertheless been tarted not only by Kneejerk groupies such as David Shapiro, but also by more thoughtful crickets such as Willie Lehman, whose book *Beyond Amusement*, despite its pretentions, seems unlikely to earn its editor complete Tennis Court Oaf status.

POETRY OF SNACK OR PERISHABLE POEM?

Young and promising poets are few among post-contemporaries since Bly, with the exception of the so-called Snack Poets such as Felix Stefanile, author of *East River Knackwurst*, Olga Braunschweiger, author of *Beginning With Mayo*, Marvin Baloney, author of *Residue Of Sausage*, and Robert Pork, author and director of the Bread Loaf Writers Conference in Vermont. Pork's work derives, of course, from Victorian easyist Thomas Carlyle's "On Hero Sandwiches" and on Cheese Poet William Yeast's reputed remark on the death of Swinburne, that he was "king of the coldcuts." Yet Pork is not averse to inviting other Snack Poets to that prestigious gathering. Past conferees have included Dip Poets such as Daniel (*Life Among Hoagies*) Haluepino and Carol Mustard, Hors d'oeuvres Poets such as David Jelly Smith, author of *Cucumber Station*, Confection Poets such as Judith Muffin and Linda Pastry, Before-Dinner-Drink Poets such as Lawrence Raab-Roy and Harvey Shapiro, and finally, After-Dinner Drink Poets such as Kelly Cherry, Norman Drambuie, and Coffee Awoonor. Indeed, the Bread Loaf Conference may be said to provide a full intercourse meal for anyone with an appetite for poetry. Anyone without such an appetite may look elsewhere, perhaps in the direction of Bly's brainchild, the "perishable poem," which has inspired a myriad of post-contemporary poets to consign their works and eventually their names to oblivion.

THOMAS HARDY
(1840-1928)

He Sports by Himself

On Christmas morn awake did I,
And stare at the murkèd sodden sky,
The sodden sky.
I said: "On Poldon Top the rime
Makes silvern fretwork. 'Tis no crime
To seek the haunts of former time.
All here's awry."

Past Yellham Hill I vamped my way,
And as I stalked I bore a tray,
A dinted tray,
My arm beneath, of metal made,
Britannia called. For naught I stayed,
Though dull brats gaped and sheep-dogs bayed
And an ass did bray.

I sweated much on Poldon Top;
I loosed the scarf which I had wrop,
Grimly had wrop
My neck around. Not as whilom,
Though doggedly, the hill I'd clomb.
My boot heels, clogged with frozen loam,
Made dismal plop.

Scowling, upon my tray I perched;
To right and left I swung and lurched,
Wanzing I lurched.
The frore wind caused my nose to drip;
A ruthless bough bruised chest and hip;
My stomach heaved as on a ship;
My heart I searched.

I said: "Not now as days of yore,
As merry days of heretofore,
Long heretofore;
For once ten yelling blithe-eyed wights,
With muscles taut and joyous sprites,
Tobogganed here, and sailed their kites;
Nine nevermore."

The moon was up as home I tramped,
Not as at day-break I had vamped,
Had sturdily vamped;
For my agèd bones were aching sore;
My tree-scratched face was caked with gore;
Night mists had chilled me to the core;
My sprite was damped.

Each of that laughing circle, save
One, now lies mouldering in his grave,
Worm-riddled grave.
I only live to bear my tray
To Poldon Top this Christmas day,
And with nine phasms zestless play
That grin and rave.

—*Susan Miles*

The Darkling Chicken

I look into the henyard
And view the squatting hen
Inviting the cock to mount her
In the far muddy corner of the pen.

With blast-beruffled plume
And pinions opened wide
The yellow cockerel balances
And keeps an even ride.

The hen receives her pleasure.
He thrids her in a dream.
And mounting high and higher
Emits a bird-like scream.

His ecstasy eludes me.
There trembles in the air
Some chicken-bliss whereof he knows
And I am unaware.

—*Robert Peters*

GERARD MANLEY HOPKINS
(1844-1889)

The Wreck of the Deutschland

A boat-load of emigrant Huns
Including five doom-destined nuns
Came to grief on a shoal—
But since heaven's our goal,
The dead were the fortunate ones.

—*David Annett*

Breakfast with Gerard Manley Hopkins

'Delicious heart-of-the-corn, fresh-from-the-oven flakes are sparkled and spangled with sugar for a can't-be-resisted flavour.'

—*Legend on a packet of breakfast cereal*

Serious over my cereals I broke one breakfast my fast
With something-to-read-searching retinas retained by print on a packet;
Sprung rhythm sprang, and I found (the mind fact-mining at last)
An influence Father-Hopkins-fathered on the copy-writing racket.

Parenthesis-proud, bracket-bold, happiest with hyphens,
The writers stagger intoxicated by terms, adjective-unsteadied—
Describing in graceless phrases fizzling like soda siphons
All things, crisp, crunchy, malted, tangy, sugared and shredded.

Far too, yes, too early we are urged to be purged, to savour
Salt, malt and phosphates in English twisted and torn,
As, sparkled and spangled with sugar for a can't-be-resisted flavour,
Come fresh-from-the-oven flakes direct from the heart of the corn.

—*Anthony Brode*

SIR EDMUND GOSSE
(1849-1928)

To a Gosse

If thou didst feed on western plains of yore;
Or waddle wide with flat and flabby feet
Over some Cambrian mountain's plashy moor;
Or find in farmer's yard a safe retreat
From gypsy thieves, and foxes sly and fleet;
If thy grey quills, by lawyer guided, trace
Deeds big with ruin to some wretched race,
Or love-sick poet's sonnet, sad and sweet,
Wailing the rigour of his lady fair;
Or if, the drudge of housemaid's daily toil,
Cobwebs and dust thy pinions white besoil,
Departed Gosse! I neither know nor care.
But this I know, that we pronounced thee fine,
Seasoned with sage and onions, and port wine.

—*Robert Southey*

OSCAR WILDE
(1854-1900)

Quite the Cheese

There was once a maiden who loved a cheese;
Sing, hey! potatoes and paint!
She could eat a pound and a half with ease
Oh, the odorous air was faint!

What was the cheese that she loved the best?
Sing, hey, red pepper and rags!
You will find it out if you read the rest;
Oh, the horrors of frowning crags!

Came lovers to woo her from ev'ry land—
Sing, hey! fried bacon and files!
They asked for her heart, but they meant her hand,
Oh, the joy of the Happy Isles.

A haughty old Don from Oporto came;
Sing, hey! new carrots and nails!
The Duke of Gorgonzola, his famous name,
Oh, the lusciously-scented gales!

Lord Stilton belonged to a mighty line!
Sing, hey! salt herrings and stones!
He was "Blue" as chine—his taste divine!
Oh, the sweetness of dulcet tones.

Came stout Double Glo'ster—a man and wife,
Sing, hey! post pillars and pies!
And the son was Single, and fair as fate;
Oh, the purple of sunset skies!

De Camembert came from his sunny France,
Sing, hey! pork cutlets and pearls!
He would talk sweet nothings, and sing and dance,
Oh, the sighs of the soft sweet girls.

Came Gruyère so pale! a most hole-y man!
Sing, hey! red sandstone and rice!
But the world saw through him as worldings can,
Oh, the breezes from Isles of Spice.

But the maiden fair loved no cheese but one!
Sing, hey! acrostics and ale!
Save for Single Glo'ster she love had none!
Oh, the roses on fair cheeks pale!

He was fair and single—and so was she!
Sing, hey! tomatoes and tar!
And so now you know which it is to be!
Oh, the aid of a lucky star!

They toasted the couple the livelong night,
Sing, hey! cast iron and carp!
And engaged a poet this song to write.
Oh, the breathing Aeolian harp!

So he wrote this ballad at vast expense!
Sing, hey! pump-handles and peas!
And, though you may think it devoid of sense,
Oh, he fancies it QUITE THE CHEESE!

—H.C. Waring

A Maudle-in Ballad

TO HIS LILY

My lank limp lily, my long lithe lily,
My languid lily-love fragile and thin,
With dank leaves dangling and flower-flap chilly,
That shines like the shin of a Highland gilly!
Mottled and moist as a cold toad's skin!
Lustrous and leper-white, splendid and splay!
Art thou not Utter and wholly akin
To my own wan soul and my own wan chin,
And my own wan nose-tip, tilted to sway
The peacock's feather, *sweeter than sin*,
That I bought for a halfpenny yesterday?

My long lithe lily, my languid lily,
My lank limp lily-love, how shall I win—
Woo thee to wink at me? Silver lily,
How shall I sing to thee, softly or shrilly?
What shall I weave for thee—what shall I spin—
Rondel, or rondeau, or virelai?
Shall I buzz like a bee with my face thrust in
Thy choice, chaste chalice, or choose me a tin
Trumpet, or touchingly, tenderly play
On the weird bird-whistle, *sweeter than sin*,
That I bought for a halfpenny yesterday.

My languid lily, my lank limp lily,
My long lithe lily-love, men may grin—
Say that I'm soft and supremely silly—
What care I while you whisper stilly;
What care I while you smile? Not a pin!
While you smile, you whisper—'T is sweet to decay?

I have watered with chlorodine, tears of chagrin,
The churchyard mould I have planted thee in,
Upside down in an intense way,
In a rough red flower-pot, *sweeter than sin*,
That I bought for a halfpenny yesterday.

—*Punch*

A.E. HOUSMAN
(1859-1936)

What, Still Alive

What, still alive at twenty-two,
A clean upstanding chap like you?
Sure, if your throat 'tis hard to slit,
Slit your girl's, and swing for it.

Like enough, you won't be glad,
When they come to hang you, lad:
But bacon's not the only thing
That's cured by hanging from a string.

So, when the spilt ink of the night
Spreads o'er the blotting pad of light,
Lads whose job is still to do
Shall whet their knives, and think of you.

—*Hugh Kingsmill*

When Lads Have Done

When lads have done with labor
in Shropshire, one will cry,
"Let's go and kill a neighbor,"
and t'other answers "Aye!"

So this one kills his cousins,
and that one kills his dad;
and, as they hang by dozens
at Ludlow, lad by lad,

each of them one-and-twenty,
all of them murderers,
the hangman mutters: "Plenty
even for Housman's verse."

—*Humbert Wolfe*

The Shropshire Lad's Cousin

AN EVEN GLOOMIER FELLOW THAN HIS CELEBRATED RELATIVE

I

When I was one and twenty,
My ills were in their prime,
With aches and pains aplenty,
And gout before my time;
I had the pyorrhea,
And fever turned me blue—
They said that I would be a
Dead man at twenty-two.

Now I am two and twenty,
The aches and pains I thought
Were miseries aplenty,
Compared to these, are naught;

And even these are bubbles,
That scarce can worry me,
When I regard the troubles
I'll have at twenty-three.

2

With rue my heart is laden
For many a lass I had,
For many a rouge-lipped maiden,
That's got a richer lad.

In rooms too small for leaping
Such lads as I are laid,
While richer boys are keeping
The girls that do not fade.

3

Comrade, never take a bath,
For you'll tread the selfsame path;
For you'll do the selfsame work,
Where the dust and cinders lurk.

Comrade, cast aside your hope
Of the benefits of soap:
Though you scrub the morn away,
You'll be soiled at close of day.

4

Along the street as I came by,
A cinder hit me in the eye;
When I went walking in the field,
I stepped upon a snake concealed;
When in the woods I took a stroll,
A she-bear nipped my arm off whole;
When I went swimming in the creek,
A porpoise bit me in the cheek;
And so it goes, from dawn to dusk;
There's never corn; there's only husk.

When famished, I sit down to eat,
The cook has always burned the meat;
When I would rest my weary head,
A score of mice are in my bed;
When cheerful friends I do desire,
Their houses ever are on fire.

There's nothing good, there's only ill:
In winter, hot; in summer, chill;
And when my time is come to die,
There will not be a grave to buy.

5

When I go to the circus,
My heart is full of woe,
For thinking of the people
Who used to see the show,
And now are laid below.

They stood beneath the tent-cloth,
And heard the lion roar;
They saw the striped hyena
Revolve upon the floor;
And now they are no more.

I think of all the corpses
Worm-eaten in the shade;
I cannot chew my peanuts
Or drink my lemonade:
Good God, I am afraid!

I see the grave-worms feeding
Upon the tigers' tails;
I see the people quiet
As prisoners in jails,
Because they're dead as nails.

Then what's the good of watching
The horses and trapeze,
The big show and the little,
And the menageries?—
We're all a lot of fleas.

6

I had three friends in Gotham,
And one of them is dead,
And one of them has palsy
And cannot leave his bed.

And now I know the other
Will soon desert me too,
And end his days in Sing Sing,
For something he will do.

7

Northward wing the happy swallows
To their olden haunts again,
And the poison ivy follows,
And the quinsy and the rain.

Soon the lovers will be walking
In the raw, malicious air,
Through catarrhal noses talking
Slush no mortal man can bear.

8

"Terence, this is fearful rot,
Putting poison in the pot;
All your song is measles, mumps,
Cramps and colic and the dumps;
Terence, you are rather frayed—
Go and have your teeth X-rayed."

Go ahead, my lad, and talk,
While your legs are fit to walk;
While your hair is on your head:
You'll not talk when you are dead.

Scorn, at will, my gloomy stuff;
You'll regret it soon enough.
Wait a year or two, and see
What a sorry sight you'll be;
Your liver and your eyes will fail;
You'll be languishing in jail;
You'll be run over by a cart,
And get a lesion on your heart;
Stir not till I have my say:
The girl you love will run away,
But she'll not stay away for good
And leave you to your solitude;
To her lad she'll not be true—
She'll come back and marry you;
And the kind of life you'll lead
Will make your bones and marrow bleed.
Wait a minute, I'm not through
With the things in store for you:
All you'll get to eat will be
Lettuce, nuts and hominy;
This much, too, I can foretell:
You'll get ill and won't get well;
Neither will you die, my lad;
Worse for you, and that's but bad;
You'll not die of mortal ache:
They will hang you by mistake;
They'll discover it too late,
Which is just the usual fate.
So I sing this doleful song
Just to dull your sense of wrong.
When you've read my verses through,
Not a thing can make you blue;
You will be prepared for all
Fearful things that will befall.
Fare you well, lad; on your way:
You'll break a leg ere close of day.

—*Samuel Hoffenstein*

From THE PROSE POEMS OF A.E. HOUSMAN

Loveliest of Counties, Shropshire Now

Colour it cherry-red and call it Death-Wish Valley—that's the message as Spring comes to the sleepy county of Shropshire.

Cherry trees blossom as murder and suicide rates spiral and hundreds of young men join the Forces daily.

Shrewbury's recruiting officer said yesterday:
'Many applicants say they will sign on only if they can be posted to Crossmaglen.'

They blame the local girls. 'The birds bugger us about,' one disgruntled Shropshire lad told me in Ludlow's swinging Land of Lost Content disco last night. 'Playing blokes off against each other and that. There's knife fights here every night.'

With so many young Salopians murder of suicide victims, serving life sentences or away in the Forces, the birth rate has fallen dramatically.

Shropshire may soon be known as the Deserted County.

—*Ian Sainsbury*

Come Live With Me

Ron Endaway, shepherd of the hills at Malvern, looked very sheepish as he stood in the dock yesterday, charged with rape.

Miss X, aged 14, denies having made sheeps' eyes at him. She told the court Endaway had lured her to some rocks with sweet talk.

'He said he wanted me to live with him and be his love, but he was only after the one thing.'

Ron, she alleged, had tried to pull the wool over her eyes with a flock of promises. These included fragrant posies, a straw belt with amber studs and a table made of solid ivory. He also said he would make her an embroidered kirtle.

But he didn't do any of these things, according to Miss X. Instead, she alleges, Ron proved to be a bit of a ram.

The case continues.

—*Naomi Marks*

On the Vanity of Earthly Greatness

The tusks that clashed in mighty brawls
Of mastodons, are billiard balls.

The sword of Charlemagne the Just
Is ferric oxide, known as rust.

The grizzly bear whose potent hug
Was feared by all, is now a rug.

Great Caesar's bust is on the shelf.
And I don't feel so well myself!

—*Arthur Guiterman*

RUDYARD KIPLING
(1865-1936)

Municipal

"Why is my District death-rate low?"
Said Binks of Hezabad.
"Well, drains, and sewage-outfalls are
"My own peculiar fad.
"I learnt a lesson once. It ran
"Thus," quoth that most veracious man:—

It was an August evening and, in snowy garments clad,
I paid a round of visits in the lines of Hezabad;
When, presently, my Waler saw, and did not like at all,
A Commissariat elephant careering down the Mall.

I couldn't see the driver, and across my mind it rushed
That that Commissariat elephant had suddenly gone *musth*.
I didn't care to meet him, and I couldn't well get down,
So I let the Waler have it, and we headed for the town.

The buggy was a new one and, praise Dykes, it stood the strain.
Till the Waler jumped a bullock just above the City Drain;
And the next that I remember was a hurricane of squeals,
And the creature making toothpicks of my five-foot patent wheels.

He seemed to want the owner, so I fled, distraught with fear,
To the Main Drain sewage-outfall while he snorted in my ear—
Reached the four-foot drain-head safely and, in darkness and despair,
Felt the brute's proboscis fingering my terror-stiffened hair.

Heard it trumpet on my shoulder—tried to crawl a little higher
Found the Main Drain sewage-outfall blocked, some eight feet up, with mire;
And, for twenty reeking minutes, Sir, my very marrow froze,
While the trunk was feeling blindly for a purchase on my toes!

It missed me by a fraction, but my hair was turning grey
Before they called the drivers up and dragged the brute away.
Then I sought the City Elders, and my words were very plain.
They flushed that four-foot drain-head and—it never choked again!

You may hold with surface-drainage, and the sun-for-garbage cure,
Till you've been a periwinkle shrinking coyly up a sewer.
I believe in well-flushed culverts....
This is why the death-rate's small;
And, if you don't believe me, get *shikarred* yourself.
That's all.

—Rudyard Kipling

To R.K. (1891)

As long as I dwell on some stupendous
And tremendous (Heaven defend us!)
Monstr'-inform'-ingens-horrendous
Demoniaco-seraphic
Penman's latest piece of graphic.
—Browning

Will there never come a season
Which shall rid us from the curse
Of a prose that knows no reason
And an unmelodious verse:
When the world shall cease to wonder
At the genius of an Ass,
And a boy's eccentric blunder
Shall not bring success to pass;

When mankind shall be delivered
From the clash of magazines,
And the inkstands shall be shivered
Into countless smithereens:
When there stands a muzzled stripling,
Mute, beside a muzzled bore:
When the Rudyards cease from Kipling
And the Haggards Ride no more?

—J.K. Stephen

A Ballad

As I was walkin' the jungle round, a-killin' of tigers an' time;
I seed a kind of an author man a writin' a rousin' rhyme;
'E was writin' a mile a minute an' more, an' I sez to 'im, "Ooare you?"
Sez 'e "I'm a poet—'er majesty's poet—soldier an' sailor, too!"
An 'is poem began in Ispahan an' ended in Kalamazoo,
It 'ad army in it, an' navy in it, an' jungle sprinkled through,
For 'e was a poet—'er majesty's poet—soldier an' sailor, too!

An' after, I met 'im all over the world, a doin' of things a host;
'E 'ad one foot planted in Burmah, an' one on the Gloucester coast;
'E's 'alf a sailor an' 'alf a whaler, 'e's captain, cook, and crew,
But most a poet—'er majesty's poet—soldier an' sailor too!
'E's often Scot an' 'e's often not, but 'is work is never through,
For 'e laughs at blame, an' 'e writes for fame, an' a bit for revenoo,—
Bein' a poet—'er majesty's poet—soldier an' sailor too!

'E'll take you up to the Ar'tic zone, 'e'll take you down to the Nile,
'E'll give you a barrack ballad in the Tommy Atkins style,
Or 'e'll sing you a Dipsy Chantey, as the bloomin' bo'sums do,
For 'e is a poet—'er majesty's poet—soldier an' sailor too!
An' there is n't room for others, an' there's nothin' left to do;
'E 'as sailed the main from the 'Arn to Spain, 'e 'as tramped the jungle through,
An' written up all there is to write—soldier an' sailor, too!

There are manners an' manners of writin', but 'is is the *proper* way,
An' it ain't so hard to be a bard if you'll imitate Rudyard K.;
But sea an' shore an' peace an' war, an' everything else in view—
'E 'as gobbled the lot!—'er majesty's poet—soldier an' sailor,too.
'E's not content with 'is Indian 'ome, 'e's looking for regions new,
In another year 'e'll have swept 'em clear, an' what'll the rest of us do?
'E's crowdin' us out!—'er majesty's poet—soldier an' sailor too!

—*Guy Wetmore Carryl*

WILLIAM BUTLER YEATS
(1865-1939)

Old King Cole

Of an old King in a story
From the grey sea-folk I have heard,
Whose heart was no more broken
Than the wings of a bird.

As soon as the moon was silver
And the thin stars began,
He took his pipe and his tankard,

And three tall shadows were with him
And came at his command;
And played before him for ever
The fiddles of fairyland.

And he died in the young summer
Of the world's desire;
Before our hearts were broken
Like sticks in a fire.

—*G.K. Chesterton*

Mavrone

ONE OF THOSE SAD IRISH POEMS, WITH NOTES

From Arranmore the weary miles I've come
An' all the way I've heard
A Shrawn[1] that's kep' me silent, speechless, dumb,
Not sayin' any word.
An' was it then the Shrawn of Eire[2], you'll say,
For him that died the death of Carrisbool?
It was not that, nor was it, by the way,
The sons of Garnim[3] blitherin' their drool,
Nor was it any Crowdie of the Shee,[4]
Or Itt, or Himm, nor wail of Barryhoo[5]
For Barrywhich that stilled the tongue of me;
'Twas but my own heart cryin' out for you,
Magraw![6] Bulleen, Shinnanigan, Boru,
Arron, Machree, Aboo![7]

—*Arthur Guiterman*

The Celtic Lyric

Seven dead men, Brigit,
Came from the sea,
(Mist on the waters
And sorrow in the tree).

Seven pallid men, Brigit,
Cold from the sea,
And each with his strange eyes
Whispered to me:

"O, sad voyagers,
Wither are ye faring?
Do ye bring a tale of grief
For desolate Eirinn?"

"Oisinn and Dubb we be,
And Cucutullitore,
And Fish and Fash and Fingall,"
They spoke never more.

1. A shrawn is a pure Gaelic noise, something like a groan, more like a shriek, and most like a sigh of longing.
2. Eire was daughter of Carne, King of Connaught. Her lover, Murdh of the Open Hand, was captured by Greatcoat Mackintosh, King of Ulster, on the plain of Carrisbool, and made into soup. Eire's grief on this tragic occasion has become proverbial.
3. Garnim was second cousin to Manannan MacLir. His sons were constitutionally sad about something. There were twenty-two of them, and they were always unfortunate in love at the same time, just like a chorus at the opera. "Blitherin' their drool" is about the same as "dreeing their weird."
4. The Shee (or "Sidhe" as I should properly spell the word if you were not so ignorant) were the regular, conservative, organization fairies of Erin. The Crowdie was their annual convention, at which they made melancholy sounds. The Itt and Himm were the irregular or independent fairies. They made still more melancholy sounds because they *never* got any offices or patronage. Cf., MacAlester,*Polity of the Sidhe of West Meath*, page 985 et seq.
5. The Barryhoo is an ancient Celtic bird about the size of a mavis, with lavender eyes and a black crepe tail. It continually mourns its mate (Barrywhich, feminine form), a gentle creature with an hereditary predisposition to an early and tragic demise,that invariably dies first.
6. Magraw, a Gaelic term of endearment, often heard on the baseball fields of Donnybrook.
7. These last six words are all that tradition has preserved of the original incantation by means of which Irish rats were rhymed to death. (See Shakespeare and his contemporaries). Thereby hangs a good Celtic tale which I should be delighted to recount, but being prosed to death is at least as bad as being rhymed to death,and I don't think that you'll stand for any more.

But each wove a warp, a warp,
And each wove a weft
Of lost stars and suns forlorn
And moons bereft.

—*J.C. Squire*

Numerous Celts

There's a grey wind wails on the clover,
And grey hills, and mist around the hills,
And a far voice sighing a song that is over,
And my grey heart that a strange longing fills.

A sheen of dead swords that shake upon the wind,
And a harp that sleeps though the wind is blowing
Over the hills and the seas and the great hills behind,
The great hills of Kerry, where my heart would be going.

For I would be in Kerry now where quiet is the grass,
And the birds are crying in the low light,
And over the stone hedges the shadows pass,
And a fiddle weeps at the shadow of the night.

With Pat Doogan
Father Murphy
Brown maidens
King Cuchullain
The Kine
The Sheep
Some old women
Some old men
And Uncle White Sea-gull and all.

(*Chorus*) And Uncle White Sea-gull and all.

—*J.C. Squire*

Parachuting Thoor Ballylee

Atop a tower I pitched a silken thing,
Pale as Plato's shroud, a half-rood square,
That my wife's soul and mine might once take wing,
And our guyed flesh perne gyres in Irish air.
What though she balk the leap? What though she wring
Her trembling hands? That blindman's ditch down there
Was not so fearsome after all. Meanwhile,
All Ballyleeans mocked our sweat and toil.

I hold an unintellectual scorn the worst.
And yet, what scorn outstays a swan or saint?
A swan she was; and hagiography would first
Rewrite itself before it dare to paint
A ditch with my wife's blood. And Tom be curst,
Tom Monahan who made a drunken rant,
And brought against my plan some habeas writ,
Mocked my grand scheme and made a ruin of it.

Or some such writ, because Tom thought to think
A parachute the devil's very toy,
And heard the woman shriek upon the brink
Of Scott's remodeled stones, and seized that toy,
And spread it in the ditch's mire and stink.
Then sixty of Tom's vulgar spawn and fry
Forced her down the winding stair of Thoor,
Who were like harlots comforting a whore.

That emblem of the soul, and what of that?
I saw it shred in youth, now shred again,
Because some Monahan, some blacksmith autocrat,
Ordered it spread under his horse. Those ten
And fifty, spilled of brains, would fill one hat,
One hat or beggar's cup. If those were men,
Then all is gone to smash, gone utterly—
Heart, star, rood, rose, swan, gyre, and Ballylee.

—*William Zaranka*

The Cult of the Celtic

When the eager squadrons of day are faint and disbanded,
  And under the wind-swept stars the reaper gleans
The petulant passion flowers—although, to be candid,
  I haven't the faintest notion what that means—

Surely the Snow-White Bird makes melody sweeter
  High in the air than skimming the clogging dust.
(Yes, there's certainly something queer about this metre,
  But, as it's Celtic, you and I must take it on trust.)

And oh, the smile of the Slave as he shakes his fetters!
  And oh, the Purple Pig as it roams afar!
And oh, the—something or other in capital letters—
  As it yields to the magic spell of a wind-swept star!

And look at the tricksy Elves, how they leap and frolic,
  Ducking the Bad Banshee in the moonlit pool,
Celtic, yet fully content to be 'symbolic',
  Never a thought in their head about Home Rule!

But the wind-swept star—you notice it has to figure,
  Taking an average merely, in each alternate verse
Of every Celtic poem—smiles with a palpable snigger,
  While the Yellow Wolf-Hound bays his blighting curse,

And the voices of dead desires in sufferers waken,
  And the voice of the limitless lake is harsh and rough,
And the voice of the reader, too, unless I'm mistaken,
  Is heard to remark that he's had about enough.

But since the critics have stated with some decision
  That stanzas very like these are simply grand,
Showing 'a sense of beauty and intimate vision',
  Proving a 'Celtic Renaissance' close at hand;

Then, although I admit it's a terrible tax on
  Powers like mine, yet I sincerely felt
My task, as an unintelligent Saxon,
  Was, at all hazards, to try to copy the Celt!

—*Anthony C. Deane*

Crazy Bill to the Bishop

I swear by what the sages spoke
Round the Macrobiotic Lake:
That Shelley's Witch of Atlas knew
Proclaimed and set the cocks a-crow.

Here's the gist of what they meant:
Swear by those hens, by women
Whose double-yolked eggs prove superhuman.
Out of the shell at wintry dawn
Came Castor and Pollux, their passions gone,
Robbed by the rooster, that bird
Who thrust his muscle strong
Midst Leda's thighs, like death
Turning for another breath,
A copulation song
Of wattles and chicken-dung,
Of warrior twins untimely wronged.

Make fowl fill their incubators tight.
Penis-measurement will set things right.

A rooster's glans, a hen's canal
Defy our randy-laughter.
Gyres run on, and we poor souls
Hurry after.

—*Robert Peters*

EDGAR LEE MASTERS
(1868-1950)

Birdie McReynolds

I kept the house on the corner of Linden and Pineapple Streets,
Down in the district.
And a lively house it was, too,
For a burg like Fork River.
I liked the business,
And that's why I went in it.
Nobody has to do anything he doesn't want to.
How else could I have stuck it out in that hick town?
Imagine me a Fork River housewife,
With a Fork River husband,
The kind that used to come down to my house—
Me, Birdie McReynolds!
Don't make me swallow some dirt.
I never lost my virtue.
Don't think it!
I gave it away for a while,
And then I sold it,
And I had a good time both ways.
I knew everybody,
And everybody liked me.
I kept the judge in his place,
The Mayor, the Sheriff, and the Councilmen,
Or the town couldn't have held them.

They needed somebody like me to tone them down,
The poor, swell-headed, small-town fish,
And it's usually a Birdie McReynolds that does it.
I could read a man's character
By the kind of suspenders he wore;
The old sports went in for white silk ones
With "Fireman" or "Policeman" engraved on the buckles.
It made them feel virile,
The poor saps!
Don't think you'll get a sob-story out of me, Eddie Masters;
I wasn't that kind of a jezebel.
There ain't any, anyhow.
It's the good women must weep
While the men work.
We like them to work—
They spend more.
Now go away and let me sleep;
That's one thing I never got enough of
In my business,
Or I wouldn't be here.

—*Samuel Hoffenstein*

EDWIN ARLINGTON ROBINSON
(1869-1935)

Miniver Cheevy, Jr.

Miniver Cheevy, Jr., child
Of Robinson's renowned creation,
Also lamented and reviled
His generation.

Miniver similarly spurned
The present that so irked his pater,
But that langsyne for which he yearned
Came somewhat later.

Miniver wished he were alive
When dividends came due each quarter,
When Goldman Sachs was 205,
And skirts were shorter.

Miniver gave no hoot in hell
For Camelot or Troy's proud pillage:
He would have much preferred to dwell
In Greenwich Village.

Miniver cherished fond regrets
For days when benefits were boundless;
When radios were crystal sets,
And films were soundless.

Miniver missed the iron grills,
The whispered word, the swift admission,
The bath-tub gin, and other thrills
Of prohibition.

Miniver longed, as all men long,
To turn back time (his eyes would moisten),
To dance the Charleston, play mah jong
And smuggle Joyce in.

Miniver Cheevy, Jr., swore,
Drank till his health was quite imperiled,
Miniver sighed, and read some more
F. Scott Fitzgerald.

—David Fisher Parry

Rambuncto

Well, they're quite dead, Rambuncto; thoroughly dead.
It was a natural thing enough; my eyes
Stared baffled down the forest aisles, brown and green,
Not learning what the marks were... still, who knows?
Not I, who stooped and picked the things that day,
Scarlet and gold and smooth, friend—smooth enough!
And she's in a vault now, old Jane Fotheringham,
My mother-in-law; and my wife's seven aunts,
And that cursed bird who used to sit and croak
Upon their pear tree... they threw scraps to him...
My wife, too... Lord, that was a curious thing!
Because—"I don't like mushrooms much," I said;
So they ate all I picked.... And then they died.
But—well, who knows it isn't better that way?
It's quieter, anyhow.... Rambuncto—friend—
Why, you're not going? Well... it's a stupid year,
And the world's very useless.... Sorry.... Still
The dusk intransience that I much prefer
Leaves room for little hope and less regret.
I don't suppose he'd care to stay and dine
Under the circumstances.... What's life for?

—Margaret Widdemer

Relativities

What wisdom have we that by wisdom all
Sources of knowledge which the years suggest,
Hidden in rubric, stone or palimpsest,
Will turn and answer us because we call?
About us planets rise and systems fall
Where, lost to all but matter, Newtons rest;
And who are we to label worst and best
While all of force is gravitational?

Held by a four-dimensional concern,
He gropes among the atoms to beseech
A swifter sublimation that may reach
A little further than the funeral urn.
And we, who always said that we could teach,
Have nothing much to say and more to learn.

—Louis Untermeyer

WALTER DE LA MARE
(1873-1956)

... Makes the Little Ones Dizzy

1

When winking stars at dusk peep through
Pin-holes in the tent of blue,
Nurse puts spectacles on nose
And points them out to Little Lou.

With sad distempers all awry,
She stares with a myopic eye,
And mumbles names of stars and spheres
As they were letters in the sky.

Orion, Great Bear, Dipper—she
Cons them with a cracked "Tee, hee!"
While wretched Little Lou must keep
Nose to the pane unwillingly.

While ants crawl up and down his back,
She ties him to the zodiac,
And feeds him his astronomy
With many a salty pinch or whack.

Hour by hour goes slowly past;
The stars, like measles, fade at last;
Nurse goes upstairs, but Little Lou
Is to the window frozen fast.

2

When the Great Captain Sun goes home
And calls his spearsmen from the dome,
Sheep-bells, cow-bells, goat-bells and ram-bells
Tinkle and jangle in the gloam.

Pastures that were pistachio green,
In the slate dusk can scarce be seen,
And now are empty, where but late
Quick goats, slow cows, dumb sheep have been.

Then elves, that make the barn their house,
And in the bins and mangers browse,
Bob up and down in oats and hay
And bleat like sheep and moo like cows.

3

Speckled with glints of star and moonshine,
The house is dark and still as stone,
And Fido sleeps in the dogwood kennel
With forlegs over his mutton bone.

Then out of the walnut wood, the squirrels
Peep, with their bushy tails upreared,
And the oak on the wood's-edge stretches his branches,
And combs with his roots his mossy beard.

Then ninnies and oafs and hook-nosed zanies,
And rabbits bred in the realm of Wales,
Dance and scream in the frosty starlight,
Swinging the squirrels by the tails,

Till out of the wood, Grandfather Nightmare
Rides in a chariot of Stilton cheese,
And eats the ninnies, the oafs and zanies,
The rabbits, the oak and the walnut trees.

—*Samuel Hoffenstein*

The Last Bus

Nid-nod through shuttered streets at dead of night
  Soundless the last grey motor-bus went home;
Hailed it no watcher in its phantasm flight;
  Up the steep belfry stair no passenger clomb.

Mute as a mammet, bowed above the wheel
  The driver. His moustache was green with moss
Cobwebs about him had begun to steal;
  Deafer than dammit the conductor was.

Red rust was on the gear chain. Hung long trails
  Of bugloss and bindweed from the bonnet's crown;
Charlock and darnel cluttered up the rails;
  The destination boards were upside down.

Yet still the bus moved, billowy with grass,
  Tottered and laboured, spurted, swayed and slowed;
Stock still the constable beheld it pass;
  Bunched sat the cat and feared to whisk the road.

Doom-loud the vegetable transport train
  Thundered their hallos, ground the earth to grit;
Scavengers turned to wave and wave again,
  Night revellers screamed "Toot-a-loot" to it.

And still no sound. Only a murmur, a sigh
  Showed it not all a thing of shadow and gleam;
Fled the tall soap-works, fled the brewery by,
  Fled the municipal baths as though in a dream.

None knew whence came this shadowy motor-bus,
  What it was doing, why, and whither away
It sped on into the night adventurous,
  Covered with lichens and all a-shake with hay.

Aye, but the forms within! What face was that
  Glassily seen—and that one, mild yet mum?
There—with the pink petunia in her hat!
  There—with the purple pelargonium!

And some have parcels of meat and fish and tea,
  And some eat aniseed from paper bags,
And some with sightless eyes scan momently
  Novels—yet turn no page—and fictional mags.

Fares are not asked. Time here is all withdrawn;
  A tenderness is here most tranquil and sweet;
As the still bus incessantly sails on
  Nobody stamps on anybody's feet.

Till see! They are out beyond the shuttered streets,
Beyond the edge of the pavement and the trams.
A wonderful change! The ghosts stir in their seats.
Dawn glints. The first grey light shows fields of lambs.

Lollops a coney; peeps from tangled hedge
Bright eye of weasel (so unvexed the route):
Sits tit and sways on perilous blossom's edge;
Squabbles a squirrel; ululates a coot.

Bluebells start up, fantastically long,
Cowslip and cuckoo pint; all round the wheels
Dactyls wave arms and extra syllables throng
Looping the felloes. Topples the bus and heels.

And now an amazing sense of freedom from care
Deliciously moves their hearts as out they get.
This is the terminus. Rose-sweet the air,
Although underfoot the ground is still quite wet.

Leaves his sad perch the driver. Laughing and gay,
Lands the conductor a friendly slap on the snout;
They bind the engine anew with a twist of hay;
All breathe, dance, skip, take breakfast, scamper about.

—E.V. Knox (Evoe)

AMY LOWELL
(1874-1925)

On Hearing Prokofieff's Grotesque For Two Bassoons, Concertina and Snare-drums

A sulphur-yellow chord of the eleventh
Twitches aside the counterpane.
Blasts of a dead chrysanthemum,
Blur.
Whispers of mauve in a sow's ear;
Snort of a daffodil,
Bluster of zinnias hurtling through nasal silences,
Steeplejack in a lace cassock
Pirouetting before a fly-blown moon.
Soap-bubble groans where the wheezing planets
Abandon the jig.

—Louis Untermeyer

From MICE AND MANDRAGORA

Wallflower to a Moonbeam

In the pause
When you first came
The stillness rang with the clashing of wine-cups.
You spoke—
And jonquil-trumpets blew dizzy bacchanals.
You smiled—

And drunken laughter
Spilled over the edges of the gauffered night.
Now you have gone,
The dusk has lost its sparkle;
My days are trickling water,
Tepid and tasteless.
But I am no longer thirsty.

—*Louis Untermeyer*

Oiseaurie

Glunk!
I toss my heels up to my head...
That was a bird I heard say glunk
As I walked statelily through my extensive, expensive English country estate
In a pink brocade with silver buttons, a purple passementerie cut withpanniers, a train, and faced with watered silk:

But it
Is dead now!
(The bird)
Probably putrescent
And green....

I scrabble my toes...
Glunk!

—*Margaret Widdemer*

ROBERT FROST
(1874-1963)

Mending Sump

"Hiram, I think the sump is backing up.
The bathroom floor boards for above two weeks
Have seemed soaked through. A little bird, I think
Has wandered in the pipes, and all's gone wrong."
"Something there is that doesn't hump a sump,"
He said; and through his head she saw a cloud
That seemed to twinkle. "Hiram, well," she said,
"Smith is come home! I saw his face just now
While looking through your head. He's come to die
Or else to laugh, for hay is dried-up grass
When you're alone." He rose, and sniffed the air,
"We'd better leave him in the sump," he said.

—*Kenneth Koch*

The Sagging Bough

There, where it was, we never noticed how,
Flirting its tail among the smoothed-off rocks,
The brook would spray the old, worm-eaten bough,
That squeaked and scratched like puppies in a box.

Whether the black, half-rotted branch leaned down,
  Or seemed to lean, for love, or weariness
Of life too long lived out, or hoped to drown
  Its litter of last year's leaves, we could not guess.

Perhaps the bough relaxed as though it meant
  To give its leaves their one taste of depravity;
Or, being near the grave itself, it bent
  Because of nothing more than gravity.

—*Louis Untermeyer*

Medical Aid

Doctor Bottom was preparing to leave
After a visit to the Sykes farm.
Sid Sykes was down with a cold and fever.
The Doctor wasn't sure just what
It might develop into.
So he instructed Mrs. Sykes to keep a close watch.
Since the farm was five miles from the village
He didn't want to come again that day.
He gave Mrs. Sykes a clinical thermometer
And told her to take Sid's temperature
Toward night, and then, if it showed a rise,
To call him on the party wire.
—If I don't hear from you, Mis' Sykes,
I'll come up in the morning.

Mrs. Sykes had never seen any thermometer
Except the faded one that hung
Outside the kitchen door.
It had taken her some time to understand
The Doctor's explanation,
And even then she was uncertain.

The next morning, after his village calls,
The Doctor drove out to the Sykes farm.
Having heard nothing he supposed all was well.
The door into the bedroom was open
And as the Doctor came into the sitting room
He could see that the bed was empty.
It was made up all fresh and smooth
And there was no sign of Sid or of anyone else.
Bewildered, he crossed the sitting room
And went into the kitchen.
There he heard the regular swish of a washing machine
And the uneven puff of the gasoline engine.

—Wall, as I was sayin'! Mrs. Sykes leaned against the tub,
—I ketched m'foot and dropped that glass tube.
Then I WAS in a pickle.
Then I recollected that round thing with a face on it
That them city boarders gave Sid.
It hed a tube like the one you gave me
Only I couldn't get the whole thing
Into Sid's mouth.
She wiped her face with her apron and went on.

—So I laid it onto Sid's chest.
'Twa'n't long afore that hand pinted t' "Very Dry."
I went down cellar and fetched up a pi'cher o' cider
And gave it t' Sid.
She waved her hand toward the meadow.
—And he's out there mowin' now.

—Walter Hard

Robert Frost's Left-Leaning TRESPASSERS WILL BE SHOT Sign

I stood and watched him dig one hole all day.
He finally got it deep enough to sink
A post of rotten oak, then wedge it in
With rocks he chose out of the pile he'd made.
He'd need ten years of digging for one fence
With that small spade he used, all bent and splined
Like a fork a tractor mowed.
"Friend," I said,
"I own a post-hole digger. Own it clear.
And you can buy one cheap at Murphy's store."

He nodded and he looked me in the eye,
The kind of proud-flesh nod or wince or shrug
A horse makes when it's lashed across the snout,
Then started counting off the steps between
My property and his, where with his rotten posts
He'd fence us off. Then he came back and winked,
The kind of desperate wink a hired man winks
When asked to read a letter he can't read:

"Last thing I need's a post-hole digger, friend."

"The soil is stingy here, it will not yield,"
I said, "except to men with sense enough
To use the proper tool to make it yield.
You aim to dig a fence, you need to use
The proper tool. If anything, it's that
Which separates us from the savages,
The way we men with bigger brains use tools
To dig our holes and save our fingernails."

He puzzled and he sniffed his fingernails.
"You got a point. I need an oil rig."

I held a chuckle down. "But why an oil rig?"
"Well, I don't know. Except it smells like oil.
It feels like oil. Bet you it even burns."

He was so poor, so threadbare hopeful poor,
This man smelling his thumbs on my front porch,
He thought that all he had to do was dig
One hole and out gushed oil, or plant one seed
And up an apple or a cherry orchard sprang.
"You say that you struck oil?" I challenged him.

"The map I got says oil. The well's supposed
To run just my side of the boundary line.
Just lookit how them swallows veer away
From it. Them swallows know there ain't no bugs
To catch and eat on oil-bearin' land."

"It's hard to tell which way a swallow veers.
That's motor-oil," I challenged him again.

"Well, I don't own no tractor nor no truck,"
He snapped, and turned his heel, and walked away.

I called to him: "You say you've got a map?"

He grinned and shrugged: "Well, I ain't sayin'," he said.
You know how digging holes all night can be.
Something there is that makes you want to quit,
To take your post-hole-digger and go home
And light a candle. Birds are all asleep,
Except the owl who flashes, talons first,
Out of the nightmare dark to pince a mouse,
And shred it back upon his branch again.
Accomplishing one hole, and then the next,
And then the next: why, that's the only thing
That keeps you going almost until dawn,
Except if it's a newborn sense of pride
In helping a new neighbor who needs help,
But who's too proud to ask you for some help.

At noon I heard a knock.
"Come take a look,"
He said, pointing at the post-holes I had dug.
"Somebody tried to steal my oil last night."

There are some men who'd rather point a thief
Than admit a charity in their behalf.
And so I let him have his little wrath.
The poor illusion of his need was what
He needed most. I didn't say a word.

"They must of dug all night, and whatya think?
That map's a fluke. There ain't one drop of oil.
I guess I'll put me up a little fence."

He sunk his posts. He strung two barbed-wire lines
Between his shingle-blasted house and mine.
The last thing that he did that day was nail
A sign onto the post of rotten oak:
TRESPASSERS WILL BE SHOT ON SIGHT, it read.

There are no cattle here. None to keep off.
That barbed wire is the spirit of the man
Strung out and gleaming like a set of teeth.
At night it sings like bow-string in the wind.

I call to him each day,
"That sign of yours,
It leans a little too much to the left,
Onto my property."
And he agrees,
But not to make it right, or take it down.

—*William Zaranka*

CARL SANDBURG
(1878-1967)

Dry

Take away the stuff!
Haul it out o' my sight, dump it into the Chicago River, clean the streets with it, let the fat-bellied rich wash down their frogs' legs with it.
I won't traffic with it; it's poison; it drives you crazy; it give you the D.T.'s and the willies, and I'm not the only one that can prove it—
Not by a damsite; not by a long shot; not by the purple jowls of the brewers and the distillers—God strike 'em dead with their stiff shirts on!
There are ten million wives and widows can prove it; yes, twenty million; thirty million; thirty-seven million, five hundred thousand, in the forty-eight States and some Territories—
And some of the wives have children, and some of the widows have orphans, all legitimate and registered, and entitled to decent treatment, and a fine mess booze has made of them, including those who will grow up to be Presidents of the United States.
Think of them, forty years from now, sitting in the Blue Room of the White House, recalling their rotten childhoods—spoiled and embittered because their fathers came home blind drunk, smelling like a municipal budget, and raised hell and sang drivelling songs, and fell asleep with their clothes on, anywhere from the sink to the ceiling—
What kind of Presidents do you think they'll make?
Go among the Hunkies, the Wops, the Micks, the Californians—the workers and foreigners, who dig the coal and the ditches and furnish the stuff for the Sunday rotogravure supplements—
I except the Kikes, who prefer gambling and women—
And you'll see what John Barleycorn has put over; you'll get your booze-facts straight from the shoulder, so help me God, you will, I'm telling you till I sweat.
And the same holds for native Americans, as hard-drinking a race as ever licked their chops in front of a bar, or in a side-room, or sat down on a curb-stone to wait for the cop or Xmas.
I hate the stuff.
When you say saloon, I see red buffaloes charging along the plains like a bloody hurricane;
I want to pull the hair out of my chest, and brandish it like a torch in the faces of the anti-prohibitionists, the bootleggers, the scofflaws and the big corporations.
Take it out o' my sight; don't tempt me; I wouldn't taste it for the stockyards— all right, I'll take a swig, but it won't change me, mind; I'm agin it!
Cripes! but I'm agin it!

—Samuel Hoffenstein

JOHN MASEFIELD
(1878-1967)

Sea-Chill

When Mrs. John Masefield and her husband, the author of "I Must Go Down to the Seas Again," arrived here on a liner, she said to a reporter, "It was too uppy-downy, and Mr. Masefield was ill."

—News item

I must go down to the seas again, where the billows romp and reel,
So all I ask is a large ship that rides on an even keel,
And a mild breeze and a broad deck with a slight list to leeward,
And a clean chair in a snug nook and a nice, kind steward.

I must go down to the seas again, the sport of wind and tide,
As the gray wave and the green wave play leapfrog over the side.
And all I want is a glassy calm with a bone-dry scupper,
A good book and a warm rug and a light, plain supper.

I must go down to the seas again, though there I'm a total loss,
And can't say which is worst, the pitch, the plunge, the roll, the toss.
But all I ask is a safe retreat in a bar well tended,
And a soft berth and a smooth course till the long trip's ended.

—Arthur Guiterman

Jack and Jill

A whistle shrilled; the farm hands left the stack;
Down in the byre the bucketeers arose,
Jilly the milkmaid, and the cowherd Jack,
And swung out on the old well path that goes
On to the summit, where the well-shaft shows—
Jack leading with a yodeler's pride of limb,
And Jilly, admiring, lightly following him.

They reached the well, and soon the bucket brimmed;
But he had turned to the wells her eyelids cover,
And knew he saw there his soul's fellow limned;
And then, manoeuvring to play the lover,
Forgot the bucket, and fell kicking it over.
She leaned to clutch him as he left the level:
She missed.... He cracked his crown—and brain, poor devil.

She followed after, more in flight than fall,
Skimming the slope, as swallows skim the mere,
And, lighting softly, stooped, softly to call,
"It's Jilly, Jacky. Speak to Jilly, dear.
Oh, Jacky, little love, he cannot hear."
Sudden there came a crazy laugh: "Oh, chuck it.
It will go on," he said, "I've kicked the bucket."

And then they took and shut him up in cells,
Where, biding his Sovereign's pleasure and his own pain,
He kept on kicking buckets filled at wells
And seeing milkmaids clutch at him in vain.
And Jilly murmured, "He will come again."
Whereat the farm hands, pity in their laughter,
"There, too, the simple wench will follow after."

—Charles Powell

The Cheerful Chilterns

Old man Brown
   Lived near Hampden,
He hated the town
   And often damned en.

Brown had a son
   Who—a boy's habit—
Kept one
   Buck rabbit.

Saturday night
  Home from Wycombe
Brown rolled tight,
  With merry hiccup.

He'd had a wet;
  Reeling and dribbling
He eyed Tommy's pet,
  A lettuce nibbling.

And being far
  Gone in strong waters,
Laid his cigar
  On the buck's quarters.

It happened so
  In remote Chiltern
Not long ago.
  But worms will turn.

Tommy was angered,
  He could not bear it,
Squared to the drunkard,
  And tapped his claret.

Fury seized Brown,
  Like sparks in tinder,
He knocked Tommy down,
  Kicked the buck outer window.

Tommy took a knife,
  Lay ready for supper,
Let the rich life
  Out of his papa.

Death is so clean,
  Life is so dirty.
Life at eight fifteen,
  Death at eight thirty.

From Brown's lips
  Drooled a curse,
In last eclipse
  He spoke worse

Than ever before.
  "Tom, good-bye.
Death opens a door.
  O grand to die."

And Tommy said,
  "Life is not fair,
I'll soon be dead,
  Dancing on air.

While the horned herds
  Crop the sweet vetches,
And slim brown birds
  Mouse in the hedges."

* * *

Because he failed
 To curb his knife,
Tom got gaoled
 For life.

Dead now the boy,
 Dead his progenitor.
Life has no joy,
 Death is man's mentor.

Dead the buck rabbit
 In remote Bucks.
Life is so vapid,
 Death reconstructs.

The east wind whistles
 Over the high hill.
Nettles, docks, thistles;
 Praeterea nihil.

—Frank Sidgwick

WALLACE STEVENS
(1879-1955)

13 Ways of Eradicating Blackbirds

I
Reason with them. Speak softly. Hide your stick.
II
Buy them off. Six ton of feed corn, old wheat
and rusty sorghum ought to turn the trick.
III
Drop brochures of Capistrano, complete
with winter rates. Tell them they are swallows.
IV
Frighten their children with authentic stuffed owls.
V
Stand in a field and threaten. Stop, bellow
like nincompoop. Point and shout, Pow! Pow!
VI
Declare a park. Hire them to pick up trash.
When they call in sick, relocate the park.
VII
Dye yourself black. Whirl about wildly, thrash,
flap, chirp, and tweet like a demented lark.
VIII
Set out tanks of discount peanut butter.
Verily, it gloms to the roof of their beaks.
IX
Take a million hostages. Then mutter
about one death a day. Ignore their shrieks.
X
Convert the Super Dome to micro-wave.
Tell them it's a pie. The dumb butts can't count.
XI
Build a monstrous runway near their roost. Pave
it with bird brains. Black feather the airport.

XII

Give them to Three. To Ten. To a Thousand.
O.K. Call the Marines. Show the bastards.

XIII

Napalm their asses! Flame throw em! Douse em
in lead! Waste em! Hose them with the last word
in death. Laser them and defoliate.
Blast and butt stroke. Gouge, rack off their dark wings.
Pop out those beady inscrutable eyes.
Pound them to soup. Win! Win! Win! Die! Die! Die!

—Mark DeFoe

A High-Toned Old Fascist Gentleman

I

To treat the thing directly, Ezra Pound,
Nor any metronomes tink tonk tink tonk
A word winked out smiles its own contribution.

II

A plague, the plied pentameter of swans.
The heave that perished them hove and they sighed,
Droning the glottals of the epicene.
To mean the infinite in every line,
Not every other, they all strove. So-la.
For in their cold companioning was not
The honking thing itself but honking self.

III

Life's a wincing rowboat on a lake.
O riddanced patriots and sacristans
Of sun, lay down your swan-mirroring poems!
A violent disorder scrubs the dock
Of throttled plumage and old isinglass,
Brisance of windpipes stooping in the sun.
Incarnadine, the carnage of the swans.

—William Zaranka

Sunday Service

Call the seller of used cars,
The crapulent one, and let him spin
His pitch to Mamma at the dishwater
Wasting her young life feeding peanut butter
To His Nibs the little holy man,
The human garbage can.
The only pontiff is the pontiff of candy bars.

Take from the man of steel,
If you can pry him from his wars,
One swollen oracle:
Well, it is OK, even the stars
Had mothers. All is well.
The suns come reeling in great shaken spheres.
The only pontiff is the pontiff of candy bars.

—Michael Heffernan

VACHEL LINDSAY
(1879-1931)

John L. Sullivan Enters Heaven

TO BE SUNG TO THE TUNE OF "HEAVEN OVERARCHES YOU AND ME"

Sullivan arrived at the very lowest Heaven
Which is sometimes mistaken for the very highest Hell,
Where barkeeps, pugilists, jockeys, and gamblers
And the women corresponding (if there are any) dwell.
They done queer things, but they done 'em on the level,
And thus they escape the jurisdiction of the Devil.

Sullivan felt, and he couldn't find his ticket.
He thought for a moment he would have to go to Hell.
But the gatekeeper told him, "You don't need a ticket:
Everybody knows you: Your name's John L.
There's a lot of fighting characters been setting up waiting
To see if you were up to your mundane rating."

Sullivan asked, "They've been setting up to see me?"
And the gatekeeper answered, "They have like Hell!
They've been setting up to try you, and see if they can lick you,
And settle who's who in the Fields of Asphodel.
So you may as well be ready to take them all on—
Hercules and Pollux and the whole doggone

"Fraternity of sluggers, I mean the first-raters
(We send the second-raters to entertain Hell).
I seen Herc's hands all wound with lead and leather
Till they looked like the balls on a great dumb-bell.
He's mad because the deeds you matched his with
Were sound printed facts, while his were just myth."

Sullivan said "I guess I'm in for trouble."
He cracked the gate a little and then said "Hell!
I hope I ain't expected to take all them together.
If I take them in succession I'll be doing damn well.
I wish I'd staid in Boston or Chelsea, and would of
If I'd had the least encouragement to think I could of."

The gatekeeper said "You don't need to worry;
The way to do's to rush them and give them sudden Hell.
They've been so purged of earthliness they don't weigh nothing
While you weigh something, and will for a spell.
They've nothing to sustain them but their jealousy of you,
While you still feel the good of Boston beans, you do."

Sullivan burst into heaven roaring.
The devils beyond the board fences of Hell
Put the whites of their eyes to crannies and knotholes
To see who was driving the angels pell-mell.
They said 'twas the greatest punch of all times.
Ring the bells of Heaven! Sound the gladsome chimes!

—*Robert Frost*

Mr. Vachel Lindsay Discovers Radio

In nineteen hundred and twenty-two,
A son of Italy,
A short, swart son-of-a-gun from Italy
Broke right through—
Broke through the ether with a bang and a crash,
Broke through the ether with a flip and a flash;
Yes, he did,
Sure, he did,
Did!
Did!
Did!
Crashed into the ether and broke right through
From Kennebunkport to Kalamazoo;
From Kalamazoo to San Francisco;
Broke right through
And invented raio;
Crashed through the air
Like a zim-zam Zbysco,
From Kennebunkport to San Francisco;
Tied up Cohen and Shultz and Harrigan,
From Portland, Maine, to Portland, Oregon—
Tied them up in knots of air—
Hey, you, Marconi, are you there?
Bill Marconi,
Son of Italy,
Say, you, Marconi, are you there?
I'll say you're there!
There,
There,
There!
Crashing through the air
Without any wire;
I'll say you're there
Like a prairie fire;
Radio,
Radio,
Radio,
Radio!
Right through space with a crash like Zbysco,
From Salem, Mass., to San Francisco!
Hey, there, Buffalo,
Get that soprano!
Hey, there, Idaho,
Get that piano!
Get Paderewski pounding the piano!
X Y Z
W J G
P Q D

Hey, Pennsylvania,
Do you know
That California
Had an inch of snow?
Oklahoma is cloudy and cool,
And they're putting on their rubbers
When they send their kids to school.
Did you hear about the drop
In Minnesota,

And the bumper crop
In South Dakota?—
The bumper, bumper, bumper crop!
Listen in,
You son of sin,
Amalgamated Indigo took another flop;
Flop,
Flop,
Flop!
The ships on the ocean
Beat a retreat;
They're scared to death;
They hold their breath;—
There's a commotion down on the Street;
The bulls and the bears, and the bears and the bulls,
Tear one another's hair by the hard handfuls;—
The bulls and the bears
Are at one another's throats;
The bulls and the bears
Get one another's goats!
Radio,
Radio,
Radio,
Radio!
Hey, there, Bill,
Marconi Bill,
Hold 'em still,
While the news is crashed,
While the news is hurled,
Right through the centre of the bloomin' world!

W O P
F T G—
Shoot the news from every station,
Let it flash through all the nation!
Spark on spark,
Spark on spark,
Fiery needlepoints in the dark;
A million, billion, trillion, quadrillion,
Sextillion needlepoints hitting their mark.
The panther in the jungle,
The ostrich on the sand,
Is listening in
On Sousa's band;
The yak in the zoo
Is saying to the gnu,
"What's on the radio,
Gnu, what's new?"
The otter says
To the simple seal,
"I otter get
An ottermobile;
I heard all the prices,
At the latest show;
I heard all the prices
On the rad-i-o."
The lion and the tiger
Are jazzing on the sand,
They're jazzing on the Niger

To a Broadway band;—
Hey, there, Mischa,
Tune up your fiddle;
The Sphinx is getting ready
To unravel her riddle;
It's radio, radio, everywhere,
To the lamb in the meadow
And the llama at prayer—
Radio, radio, everywhere.

In the days when messages
Went by pony—
Those were the slow days, westward-ho days,
Those were the watch-your-step-as-you-go days—
Who would have thought that a guy like Marconi,
Nothing but a Dago
From across the foam,
A bloomin' Roman
Out of Rome;
Yes, he is;
Sure, he is;
Your teacher will tell you if she knows her biz;
Your father and your mother,
The corner cop,
Your sister and your brother
Will tell you he's a Wop—
Who would have thought that a guy like that
Would have the radio under his hat?
Well, he did;
Sure, he did;—
What does it matter if it's Dago or it's Yid?
Whoever did is the Kandy Kid;—
Yes, he is;
Sure, he is;
What does it matter where he got his phiz?
Radio,
Radio,
Radio,
Radio!
There's a guy who knew his biz!
There's a boy
Who stirred up things;
Who plays a fiddle without any strings;
Who taught us how to fly
Without any wings.
Hats off to you, Bill;
Hats off, boy;
From Pekin, China,
To Peoria, Illinois.
Radio!
Radio!
X Y Z!
Skips over mountains
And scoops up the sea;—
Who would have thought that a guy like that
Had the radio under his hat?

—*Samuel Hoffenstein*

WILLIAM CARLOS WILLIAMS
(1883-1963)

Variations on a Theme by William Carlos Williams

1

I chopped down the house that you had been saving to live in next summer. I am sorry, but it was morning, and I had nothing to do and its wooden beams were so inviting.

2

We laughed at the hollyhocks together
and then sprayed them with lye.
Forgive me. I simply do not know what I am doing.

3

I gave away the money that you had been saving to live on for the next ten years.
The man who asked for it was shabby
and the firm March wind on the porch was so juicy and cold.

4

Last evening we went dancing and I broke your leg.
Forgive me. I was clumsy, and
I wanted you here in the wards, where I am a doctor.

—*Kenneth Koch*

Final Soliloquy on a Randy Rooster (in a Key of Yellow)

After the rooster falls from the hen
We return to plain things. It is as if
Our imaginations end,
Inanimate in the rooster's end.

A vibrant *savoir*. The noun eludes me.
I feel a nameless sadness, a dull cold.
My nose becomes a flooded house.
My vas deferens has a lessened floor.

The hen-roost badly needs new paint.
The walls were whitewashed fifty years ago.
The roof slants. A fantastic effort
Has failed to be imagined. The rooster's
Sexual pond is plain sense, without reflections.
Mud, offal, dirty glass, expressing silence.

My silence is a rat come forth to see
The great hen-yard and its waste of eggs,
His whiskers tickle some inevitable knowledge
As he strums a yellow guitar and whistles
Through his teeth—as necessity requires.

—*Robert Peters*

EZRA POUND
(1885-1972)

August

August!
How long
Gongula?

—*Robert Frost*

You Call That a Ts'ing: A Letter

When I was a girl I sat with the old men.
Or watching my cherry blossom
I would play with your ts'ing.[1]
When the birds flew westward
I came to the Province of So Ho
Where no cherry is to be found.
But the old men turned up.
They rose like carp to the feeding hand.
Now after too many months I sit alone.
I mark the days on my calendar.
When you read these words
Clasp your ts'ing and come.

—*Jedediah Barrow*

A Study in Aesthetics

The very small chickens in tattered feathers
Being smitten with emotional anemia
Stopped in their pecking as I passed them
And chirped
Ch'e be'a. (How beautiful she is.)

Three minutes after this
I heard young Ez, whose middle name I do not know—
Speaking ancient Chinese to a fresh catch of squid,
And his elders
Were packing them in great plastic pails
For the market in Sirmione, and he
Leapt about, grabbing at the squirting squid
And when the elders
Would not let him pack the creatures in the pails
He stood there and stroked them
Murmuring, and stroking his groin,
Ch'e be'a.

1.An instrument similar to a d'ong but smaller.
(trans.)

My boredom was perverse.
This is the end of good breeding.

—*Robert Peters*

Rainuv: A Romantic Ballad From the Early Basque

...so then naturally
This Count Rainuv I speak of
(Certainly I did not expect you would ever have heard of him;
You are American poets, aren't you?
That's rather awful... I am the only American poet
I could ever tolerate... well, sniff and pass....)
Therefore... well, I knew Rainuv.
(My P.G. course at Penn, you'll remember;
A little Anglo-Saxon and Basuto,
But Provencal, mostly. Most don't go in for that....
You haven't, of course... What, no Provencal?
Well, of course, I know
Rather more than you do. That's my specialty.
But then—*Omnis Gallia est divisa*—but no matter.
Not fit, perhaps you'd say, that, to be quoted
Before ladies.... That's your rather amusing prudishness....)
Well, this Rainuv, then,
A person with a squint like a flash
Of square fishes... being rather worse than most
Of the usual *literati*
Said, being carried off by desire of boasting
That he knew all the mid-Victorians
Et ab lor bos amics:
(He thought it was something to boast of.)

We'll say he said he smoked with Tennyson,
And—deeper pit—*pax vobiscum*—went to vespers
With Adelaide Anne Procter; helped Bob Browning elope
With Elizabeth and her lapdog (said it bit him)
Said he was the first man Blake told
All about the angels in a pear-tree at Peckham Rye
Blake drew them for him, he said; they were grackles, not angels—
(Blake's not a mid-Victorian, but you don't know better)
So... we come, being slightly irritated, to facing him down.
"...And George Eliot?" we ask lightly.
"*Roomed with him,*" nodded Rainuv confidently,
"*At college!*"... Ah, *bos amic! bos amic!*
Rainuv is a king to you....
Three centuries from now (you dead and messy) men whispering insolently
(Eeni meeni mini mo...) will boast that their great-grand-uncles
Were kicked by me in passing....

—*Margaret Widdemer*

Homage

And so depart into dark
long in limbo, hornet-stung and following battered flags
and manufacturing various hells for his own enemies
all stamped EZRA POUND
(Phoebus, what a name
to swill the speaking trump, *gloriae futuris*)
though ole T.S.E. proclaimed his maestro
and in *such* prose, my God
constipated but dignified like an elderly cat
"trying his technique so that it will be ready like a well-oiled fire—
engine when the moment comes to strain it to the ut-
most," ooh, my God, *splendeur Dex!*

But the *Criterion* folded
(good old *Criterion* many a happy hour
have I spent at the bar watching the lovelies
shantih
shantih?
No, 'e shan't!)
and the cantos went not with a bang but a fizzle
didn't even get ther ber-luddy reviews
and the expatriate adorers all came running back to mamma's womb
so there was no one left to visit the shrine....

We have observed, quoth Plinius, that sacrifices hitherto popular in
many provinces of the empire have now almost ceased, to the great
impoverishment of butchers, graziers, and the like. Dabam Romae
prid. III Kal. Iul.: that's June 1, buddy, in their dago lingo....

And there sat the well-oiled fire-engine
all ready to strain its gutmost
eek ow ouf honk honk
unable to think, but ready to quote and paraphrase in six languages
including Provencal
ei didl didl
li chat e li fidl
it took a man like Ezra to kill Provencal poetry
for us....

And he learnt all he could
not a hell of a lot
—sterile bulls, that was a good one, Canto I
a significant bit of bull
Cimbrorumque Minas—Welsh coal mines, meant to be funny,
maybe?
pretty damn funny, anyway
QUAINT like all his Chinese and Greeks and Romans
they appear QUAINT to Homer Pound's boy from the
backwoods
The Idaho poeta....

And his temper was never good, you get eccentric living in Rapallo
and loving
BEAUTY
the emperor is at Ko
but No
silken strings shiver no longer, clashing of smilax, dark nuts
on the dry bough, nuts on wet earth, nuts
it's lonesome, too, being the only one who understands
Caius Properzius,
'Alkaios,
Li Pu,
all great guys,
an' I *know* 'em, see?
Uncle Ezry on the Acropopopoulos, the rube at the grocery
stove
gignetei colon
:
SO?
So he took to damning his own country, living in Rapallo and Rome
among the blackshirted brownbottomed yellowhearted
Heroes
the gallant macaronis that ran from the Greeks, 3 to 1 aera!
aera!!
whoosh!!/
sure, Ezra loved 'em:
the lover of the third-rate loving fascist Italia e l'IMPERO
pfft
the bogus aristocrat wanting Discipline and no Lower
Classes

So Ezra attacked the ole USA and pluto-bolsho-Britain
Jews, & negroes, & Roosevelt, & armament trusts, & usurers
melodious swill-pipe for Goebbels
(Frank Sullivan says Gayda is the only newspaper that
can write the way a Pekinese barks... He shd read Ezra's
XIVth Canto....
tender...
like a centaur's asphodel...)

And so to his own hell, the last hell, the ninth hell, Antenora
of ice
for traitors
teeth gnashing like the chattering of storks

—*Gilbert Highet*

H.D. (Hilda Doolittle)
(1886-1961)

Wind Gardens

Where now
are time and space,
frailer than clove-pinks,
or sprays of dittany,
or citron-flowers or myrrh
from the smooth sides of Erymanthus.

Rigid and heavy,
the three dimensions press against us.
But what of a fourth?
Can myrrh-hyacinths blossom within it,
or violets with bird-foot roots;
can nereids lose themselves
in its watery forests,
can wood-daemons splash through a surf
of silver saxifrage
and dogwood petals?

Here is no beauty.
There is no scent of fruit
nor sound of broken music,
sharp and astringent,
in this place.
For this light,
colder than frozen marble,
thin and constricted,
is light without heat.

O fire, descend on us,
cut apart these theories;
shower us with breath of pine
and freesia buds.

—*Louis Untermeyer*

T.S. ELIOT
(1888-1965)

Chard Whitlow

MR. ELIOT'S SUNDAY EVENING POSTSCRIPT

As we get older we do not get any younger.
Seasons return, and today I am fifty-five,
And this time last year I was fifty-four,
And this time next year I shall be sixty-two.
And I cannot say I should care (to speak for myself)
To see my time over again—if you can call it time,
Fidgeting uneasily under a draughty stair,
Or counting sleepless nights in the crowded Tube.

There are certain precautions—though none of them very reliable—
Against the blast from bombs, or the flying splinter,
But not against the blast from Heaven, *vento dei venti*,
The wind within a wind, unable to speak for wind;
And the frigid burnings of purgatory will not be touched
By any emollient.
I think you will find this put,
Better than I could ever hope to express it,
In the words of Kharma: 'It is, we believe,
Idle to hope that the simple stirrup-pump
Can extinguish hell.'
Oh, listeners,
And you especially who have turned off the wireless,
And sit in Stoke or Basingstoke, listening appreciatively to the silence,
(Which is also the silence of hell) pray, not for yourselves but your souls.

And pray for me also under the draughty stair.
As we get older we do not get any younger.

And pray for Kharma under the holy mountain.

—Henry Reed

The Love Song of J. Alfred Prufrock

An angst-ridden amorist, Fred,
Saw sartorial changes ahead.
His mind kept on ringing
With fishy girls singing,
Soft fruit also filled him with dread.

—J. Walker

The Eumenides at Home

AUDIENCE AT SEA

It does not worry me that this verse has three stresses,
Why should it since the glass in my car is triplex?
One must move with the times,
As an old maid said in the musical comedy
On meeting a young gent Oxonianly debagged.
Nor does it worry me that this verse does not tinkle.
I do not expect modern art to sound nice.
Or even to look nice...
What does worry me about this play is something altogether different—
The sneaking suspicion that I may not be intellectually up to it.
Il est si facile, said Balzac, de nier ce que l'on ne comprend pas.
Meaning that the fool sees not the same tree that the wise man sees.
Perhaps it might be easier if I had the Eumenides nearer my finger-tips,
In which case I should know whether moaning becomes Agatha as mourning
becomes Electra...

Chorus

Twice two are four
But twice three are not five
Cows neigh in the byre
Herb-o'-grace looks for Sunday
Octaves wilt
Fifths grow consecutive
Moon and green cheese
Have come to terms
Fog horns summon
The household to supper
The bones of the majordomo
Rap out curses
Methylated spirits
Wait around the corner...

Will someone, for example, tell me exactly where
Harry is going to when he puts on Johnson's overcoat?
Is he for the police station to give himself up,
Or lankly starting on an introspective, cis-Jordanian trek?
Where, where, where, where, where, where?
And as the author didn't know,
Nor Aeschylus nor even the Libraries,
We in the audience must pretend to be wabe-conscious,
Some gyred, others gimbled. I did neither.
But nothing could stop foyer-cluttered Bloomsbury
From explaining *en deux mots* what the play was all about.
It baffled me but did not in the least baffle them
To read a B.C. cross-word by an A.D. light.
Yet try as I would I, a modern Englishman, could not see why
Because a man's aunt ought to have been his mother
He must push his wife overboard
And I just could not accept the explanation
That it was all because Harry's soul
Had got mixed up with the Wishwood drains.
And here I have to say quite firmly
That what was good enough for Aeschylus is by no means
Good enough for me!

—*James Agate*

Myself When Young

Myself when young did eagerly frequent
Streets that followed like a tedious Argument;
And merry-make; and the cold Lip I kissed;
Came out by the same Door as in I went.

After the Skirts that trail along the Floor,
As the Cock crew, those who stood before
The Tavern shouted, 'How his Hair is growing thin
And once departed may return no more!'

Those restless Nights, the one-night cheap Hotel,
They robbed me of my Robe of Honour-well,
I am not the Sultan Mahmud nor was meant to be,
And Thou art fresher than the Goods they sell.

So come, let old Khayyam presume to reach
For the silken Tassel of thy Purse... or pluck this Peach?
That is not what you meant at all?
Well, there are other Mermaids on the Beach.

—*Tom Donnelly*

It Always Seems

It always seems to me that Thomas Gray
In praise of lowly folk was led astray.
'Some *mute inglorious* Milton?' I prefer
The scholar Milton, who had much to say.

Then as to politics—the proper thing
I should have thought, was loyalty to a King:
Republicans and Democrats are dull,
But *Royalist* now! That has a noble ring.

Despite my early infidelity
I now am wedded to the C. of E.
Like Rome, she has tradition, and you know
Without tradition we are all at sea.

In short, though born and bred in USA
Like James, I feel a pressing need to stay
Among the people who have honoured me—
'More English than the English'—if I may.

—*A.M. Sayers*

Awake!

Awake! For Sweeney in Pyjamas bright
Has struck the Match that makes the Gas to light.
Odours of Breakfast: nephric, fungiform,
And Tesco stirs the Wells of Appetite.

The Unknown Hand that wields the Coffee-Spoon,
With a deft Stroke upon the Hour of Noon,
Two Fingers shows with dirty Fingernails
That warn the Guest he has got up too soon.

A Slice of Toast beside the *Daily Mail*,
A Rind of Scrambled Egg (grown slightly stale)
And Sweeney pungent in the Kitchenette!
Grishkin revokes. The Sausages are pale.

And hushed the Voices of the Crowds that wait
(Viviparous, heresiarch, oblate).
One Thing is certain, and the Rest is Dust:
The Train that runs on Time is never late.

—*Jack Black*

Sweeney, Old and Phthisic, Among the Hippopotami

Cum loca reppereris, quae tangi femina gaudet,
None obstet, tangas quo minus illa, pudor.
—Ovid

Redbummed Sweeney bolts the gate,
Hunkers in the public stall
(Coconut will constipate);
Strains for one hard turd to fall.

A thrill, a peristaltic start;
But then the dread mudbelly moan,
The headwind of a hippo fart.
And Sweeney's hopes are overthrown.

Bladderburst of 'potamus!
Sweeney flushes, girds for war:
Chafing in the Band-Steel truss,
Looses a catarrhal roar

Which spending in a gargled oath
Springs a bubble to his lips,
Popping pink across the both
(Panicking the girded hips).

Red clouds, hypertrophic, tear
Heaving heavenward fit vibrations;
The glottals of a Sweeney prayer
Are drowned in great expectorations.

—David Cummings

Sweeney in Articulo

The Voice of Sweeney

Sunday is the dullest day, treating
Laughter as a profane sound, mixing
Worship and despair, killing
New thought with dead forms.
Weekdays give us hope, tempering
Work with reviving play, promising
A future life within this one.
Thirst overtook us, conjured up by Budweisserbrau
On a neon sign: we counted our dollar bills.
Then out into the night air, into Maloney's Bar,
And drank whiskey, and yarned by the hour.
Das Herz ist gestorben,[1] swell dame, echt Bronx.
And when we were out on bail, staying with the Dalai Lama,
My uncle, he gave me a ride on a yak,
And I was speechless. He said, Mamie.
Mamie, grasp his ears. And off we went
Beyond Yonkers, then I felt safe.
I drink most of the year and then I have a Vichy.

Where do we go from here, where do we go,
Out of the broken bottles? Pious sot!

1. Schiller, *Das Mädchens Klage.*

You have no guide or clue for you know only
Puce snakes and violet mastodons, where the brain beats,
And a seltzer is no answer, a vomit no relief,
And the parched tongue no feel of water. Only
There is balm in this YMCA
(Claim now the balm inside this YMCA),
And you will see that there is more in life than
Those vigils at the doors of pubs in the morning,
Or bootings from the doors of pubs at closing-time.
I will show you fear in a pile of half-bricks.
Wer reitet so spät
Durch Nacht Und Wind?
Es ist der Vater mit seinem Kind.[2]
"You called me 'Baby Doll' a year ago;
You said that I was very nice to know,"
Yet when we came back late from that Wimbledon dance-hall,
Your arms limp, your hair awry, you could not
Speak, and I likewise, we were neither
Living nor dead, and we knew nothing,
Gazing blankly before us in the carriage.
"Bank Station! All change! *Heraus! Heraus!*"

(Cloax is the vilest drink, gouging
Pockets out of your giblets, mixing
Frenzy and remorse, blending
Rot-gut and white-ants.
Jalap has a use, laundering
Colons with refreshing suds, purging
The lower soul with gentle motion.)

Count Cagliostro,[3] famous impostor,
Often in gaol, nevertheless
Enjoyed a great career, adored by the ladies.
Sold them love and youth elixirs. Said he,
Take this powder, "Lymph of Aphrodite,"
("In delay there lies no plenty."[4] See!)
Made with belladonna, that lightens up your eyes,
Enhances your fascinations.
Much more than this, now listen, it gives you power
To peep into the past and future, crystalline bright.
Just a pinch, you witness the fall of ancient Troy,
Another small pinch, a deep breath, before your eyes
The Apocalypse! Just watch *me* taste.
Lo! The Four Horsemen and the Beast, as plain as the stars!
Goodbye, Marquise. If you see her Majesty the Queen,
Tell her I have the Diamond Necklace,[5]
It's hidden in my *cabinet de toilette.*

Earthly Limbo,
Chilled by the raw mist of a January day,
A crowd flowed down King's Parade, so ghostly,
Mowed down by the centuries, so ghostly.
You barely heard the gibbering and the squeaks
As each man gazed in front with staring eyes,

2. Goethe. *Erlkönig.*
3. Count Cagliostro (1743-95), Italian alchemist, whose real name was Giuseppe Balsamo. (See Note 5 below.)
4. Shakespeare, *Sweet and Twenty.*
5. The Affair of the Diamond Necklace (1778-86). A mysterious incident which involved Marie Antoinette. In the sensational trial which ensued, Cagliostro was acquitted.
Here Cagliostro figures as the Prophet of the Age of Unreason, which he foretold would begin in earnest in 1922.

Flowed past Caius Insurance Offices
To where the clock in Trinity Great Court
Marked off the hours with male and female voice.
There I saw one I knew, and hailed him shouting, Muravieff-Amursky!
You who were with me up at Jesus,
And fought in my battalion at Thermopylae!
Your brain-box stopped an arrow, you old cadaver.
Are you Hippolytus,[6] killed by your horses' hoofs,
Revivified by Aesculapius?
"I sometimes think there never blows so red
The Rose as where some buried Caesar bled."[7]
"If Winter comes can Spring be far behind?"[8]

Narrator

His words are very indistinct—perhaps it's atmospherics?
He's quoting from the *Daily Telegraph*, and now there's a piece that sounds as if it might be Herrick's—
Ah, there he is once more, completely audible again,
Summing up his views, I think, though he seems to be in pain!

The Voice of Sweeney

This is the vacant mind,
This is the barren mind,
Empty, bereft of intellect,
Can nothing fill the yawning void?
Is there no voodoo, charm, or pious platitude
To save the world from thought?
. . . . .
But you must believe in *some*thing!
Can't you see it's only alle*gor*ical!
And what would happen to so*ci*ety?
. . . . .
Indica me. Deus, et discérne causam meam de gente non sancta: ab hômine iníquo, et dolóso érue me.[9]
Boomalay, boomalay, boomalay, boom![1]
L'Erèbe les eût pris pour ses coursiers funèbres.[2]

聖人因而與制不事心焉 [3]

[illegible] [4]

• • • — — — • • • [5]

[illegible] [6]

6. Hippolytus, son of Theseus by Hippolyta, Queen of the Amazons. He was falsely suspected of having attempted the dishonour of Theseus' second wife, Phaedra. Poseidon, at the instigation of Theseus, sent forth a bull from the water at which the horses drawing Hippolytus' chariot took fright, overturned the chariot, and dragged Hippolytus along the ground until he was dead. Artemis, however, induced Aesculapius to restore him to life again.

Originally a Vegetation Myth, but here, for the sake of poetical consistency, Aesculapius administers arsenic instead of elixir to Hippolytus.

7. FitzGerald. *Omar Kháyyam.* "The Rose"=Pernicious Anaemia.

8. Shelley, *Ode to the West Wind.* For "Winter" read "Spring" and vice versa.

9. Roman Catholic *Liturgy of the Mass.* Here read in Anglican (or "Pickwickian") sense.

1. Vachel Lindsay, *The Congo.* Last words of St. Mumbo Jumbo.

2. Baudelaire, *Les Chats.* Euphony only (no relevance).

3. From *Lü* Shih Ch'un Ch'iu. "The Sage follows Nature in establishing social order, and does not invent principles out of his own head."

Since this is a rational statement in authentic Chinese it is thought to have slipped in by mistake for a quotation from Mr. Pound.

4. From an ancient Egyptian inscription. Literally, "Thy breath of life is sweet in my nostril."

"Life" here is an occult symbol for death.

5. The famous Morse signal of distress sent out by the Titanic on 14 April 1912. Here it is sent out by the inhabitants of the "Unreal City." No one answers it.

6. "Hydor," water, short for "Ariston Men Hydor," i.e. "Take more water with it." A message in manual code from Microcephalos, the deaf-and-dumb soothsayer of Thebes, to Tiresias (who was blind anyway) on the morning after a feast. Here it signifies the Seven Types of Ambiguity.

"Love thy neighbour as thyself,"
"Couldn't you bring better weather with you?" and,
Above all,
"Please adjust your dress before leaving."[7]

—Myra Buttle

Little Pudding

Afternoon is the snack's own seasoning.
Suspended in time between lunch and dinner
the soul's stomach growls at the gummy pudding,
the pennycandy firetrucks surrounding the bowl
and dripping as the little pudding defrosts. Between
freezing and melting, we starve in the afternoon,
this unimaginable ZERO
of an afternoon.

There are ashes on the pudding, never
and always edible, like candy clocks.
I met one walking and, with scrutiny, asked:
"What! Are *you* here?" The cold friction of his concern
was speech, so speech compelled us to address
the little pudding whole in the bowl
and in the ingredients of its parts.

This is the use of the mammary:
for lactation. And the idea milked
beyond desire. Quick now, here, now, always—
the pudding a complete simplicity,
and we shall be filled without
even eating, when the pudding thaws
to reality, when the idea of eating
and the idea of pudding
are one.

—Mary M. Roberts

Shantih shantih shantih
It's only a shantih in old
Shantih town.

—Edward Pygge

CONRAD AIKEN
(1889-1973)

The Dance of Dust

So, to begin with, ghosts of rain arise
And blow their muffled horns along the street...
Who is it wavers through this nebulous curtain,
Floating on watery feet?

7. Reproduced by permission of the Westminster City Council.

Wind melts the walls. A heavy ray of starlight,
Weighed down with languor, falls. Black trumpets cry.
The dancers watch a murder. Cool stars twinkle.
In a broken glass, three faded violets die.

And so, says Steinlin, the dust dissolves,
Plots a new curve, strikes out tangentially,
Builds its discordant music in faint rhythms
Under a softly crashing sea.

"I am the one," he cries, "who stumbles in twilight,
I am the one who tracks the anfractuous gleam"...
The futile lamps go out. The night is a storm of silence....
What do we wait for? Is it all a dream?

—Louis Untermeyer

EDNA ST. VINCENT MILLAY
(1892-1950)

... Says Something Too

I

I want to drown in good-salt water,
I want my body to bump the pier:
Neptune is calling his wayward daughter,
Crying, "Edna, come over here!"

I hate the town and I hate the people;
I hate the dryness of floor and pave;
The spar of a ship is my tall church-steeple;
My soul is wet as the wettest wave.

I'm seven-eighths salt and I want to roister
Deep in the brine with the submarine;
I speak the speech of the whale and oyster;
I know the ways of the wild sardine.

I'm tired of standing still and staring
Across the sea with my heels in dust:
I want to live like the sober herring,
And die as pickled when die I must.

2

My neighbor is a goose girl
And tends her silly geese;
But I love a rakish earl
And hunt the golden fleece.

My neighbor lives on bread and milk
And shuts her door on show;
But I would rather fall in silk
Than rise in calico.

My neighbor goes to bed at eight
And never sees the moon;
But I never stir till late,
And go to bed at noon.

My neighbor, fearful of a fall,
Was wed before her prime;
But I never wed at all
And have a better time.

What do I care if people stare
Or care what people say?
The golden dogs I'm going to
Are handsome dogs and gay.

—Samuel Hoffenstein

ARCHIBALD MacLEISH
(1892-)

Ar(chibald')s Poetica

"... mute/as a globed fruit...
A poem should not mean/But be"
A. MacLeish

A poem may boast bravado
Like a muted avocado

Shriek
Like old razor blades to the cheek

Resound like the moss-grown casements
Of flooded basements

But a poem to be laudable
Must be inaudible

* * *

A poem should be hushed
As a bowl of mush

Leaving as the mush is swallowed
Mouthful by mouthful the spoon-entangled hollow

Leaving as the mush goes down
Memories of the lack of sound

A poem should be hushed
As a bowl of mush

* * *

A poem like a proper child
Should not be wild

Should clean its face
Should not mean all over the place

Should not be particularly present, should avoid
The regions of Cupid

Should be
A little bit stupid

—Alan Ribback

HUGH MACDIARMID (C.M. Grieve)
(1892-)

To His Coy Mistress

Gin ye hae'd corneich airth an' time,
Yon flauchters queanie wadna' coont a crime.
We sit oor seifu' doups an' think the like
O' hae tae jonk yon gausty rumple-fyke?
Ye bidin' nigh yon Ganges bonny braes
Wad ken red skinklan blinterin'; in the sprays
O' freathy Humber I'd be crockats up the noo;
Be eisenin' a fu' decade afore yon blinnin' stew
An' should air sibness turn a' widdifow
Until a' semites burn wi' Kirk o' Scotland's lowe,
My mochiness tae ye wad thow an' get
Mair dwamin' than empires, an' mair switherin' yet.

—*Gerry Hamill*

E.E. CUMMINGS
(1894-1962)

Horse & Rider

The rider
Is fat
As that( )
Or wider( )
In torso
Of course
The horse
Is more so ( )

—*Wey Robinson*

ROBERT GRAVES
(1895-)

To His Coy Mistress

Though your prerogative is to disdain
Those lovers ordered by the sun's chronometer,
Your liberties confirmed in lunar no-time;
And though your beauty is allowed to be
As secret as the cloud inside your opal,
What huntress can deny the stag's allegiance
Whose triple trees are caught among her thickets?
Ride down, bare heeled, hair dark as thunder,
So we, sworn foes to amity and custom,
By such exchange may run time widdershins:
Veteran and novice hold their oath unbroken
Should trolls chumble and the rain strike upward.

—*Peter Scupham*

STEVIE SMITH
(1902-1971)

To His Coy Mistress

Nobody loves you Chloe, you sly minx,
Procrastinating:
You'd be much better off now with me
And not waiting but mating.

If we had the time to spare we could
Just mildly dally
Along the Ganges shore, but let's instead
Be far more pally.

Oh, no, no, no, no, don't stand here in Hull
Still hesitating.
Now, now, now, is the day we should be
Not waiting but mating.

—Edward Bird

JOHN BETJEMAN
(1906-)

Death, Don't be Boring

Death you are a dreadful fellow,
Death you are a frightful bore.
While you lurk I'll stay mellow,
Dreaming what you have in store.
You may think you're proud and mighty,
For me you'll be a welcome snooze.
Beyond you stands eternal Blighty,
Schoolgirls I can never lose.
I am coming home Miranda,
To silver birches and the moon,
To lounge upon a warm verandah:
Death, be a chum and make it soon.

—Roy Kelly

Busy Old Fool

Oh, *do* buzz off, you bumptious Sun:
The night, it seems, has scarce begun
Before its blissful course is run...
Now, after brekker,
I snatch my brolly from the stand
And flee our nest so fondly planned
Out here in smiling Metroland—
A daily trekker
To eight hours clerking at the 'Pru',
Ten hours in all bereft of you,
My darling girl! I hurry through
Those *grinding* hours

Till sunset brings the crowded train
That speeds me home to my Elaine,
To supper, Horlicks—bed again
And love that flowers . . ."

—Ian Kelso

Hello There

When we played in the nursery till seven
Drank cocoa, and fought, and cried 'Pax',
Did we dream of this amorous heaven—
You in Arpege, and me in my Daks?
The world jets about in a hurry,
While pundits and media-men fuss.
Our concorde's a bedroom in Surrey:
Very Sanderson, very us.
So pass the Rice Krispies, my honey,
And let's listen in to *Today*,
For our love is as solid as money
And sound as this egg on my tray.

—Brian S. Salome

Death Again

O John 'Doctor' Donne, O John 'Doctor' Donne,
The dance so soon over, the race nearly run;
In life's fearful twilight when Death lays his hand,
You smile at the hourglass wherein falls the sand.
Can you be such a dreamer you fear not life's end?
It is true that you look upon Death as a friend?
Are you right to insist your demise might be fun?—
Or is it mere sophistry, John 'Doctor' Donne?

—T. Hope

And Again

Fate on the left hand, and Death on the right,
And me in the middle to get through the night,
A bottle of whisky, a handful of pills,
What a simple solution to most of my ills.
Death on a tandem without any brakes,
Death in a tea-shop without any cakes,
Death as a joke with the punch-line forgot,
As a film without end, a suburban gavotte.
Where's your sting, little death?
Where's your pride? Where's your power?
I'll wake up by and by
And play squash for an hour.

—Humphrey Evans

To His Coy Mistress

Had we but world enough, and time,
I'd write some verse that didn't rhyme,
And then we'd wander, hand in hand,
Through what is left of Metroland,
And nightly haunt the gaslit Techs
Of half-forgotten Middlesex.

But ever at my back I hear
Destruction's bulldozers draw near,
And soon a balding Laureate's lust
Will vanish in a cloud of dust;
So quick before it is too late,
Let's fix on a convenient date.
And though we cannot make the sun
Stand still, I'll make Joan Hunter Dunn.

—*Stanley J. Sharpless*

W.H. AUDEN
(1907-1973)

To His Coy Mistress

A mistress allows an average lover,
working slowly,
to roll her over in an afternoon.

Such physical compassion
may not guarantee a marriage
but it helps.

Time watches from the shadow
and coughs when I would show
my faithless hand.

Let's yoke our bodies at your liquid centre
in the tiny world of lovers' arms and
challenge time.

—*John Flood*

Travellers Turning Over Borders

Travellers turning over borders like riffled pages
In slave states where policeman patrols the museums
And all *burglich* elderly ministers open a vein,
Carried by waves to sandy archipelagos,
Or in bookstores hearing the times of the nautical hero,
Now publish the way of the future, expertly mapped
For the alive gland and the urgent lovable rocket,
Sing like a lesson the surgical joy of the watcher
Dazzled by stars, woken and willing, not drugged
By rugger or nurses, the boy who has burned his blazer
And the man who won't stay at home with his wireless,
Explore strategic passes in mountains where hope
Fills the ammunition-belt, enjoy while you can
The view from the rocks burrowed by sensitive tunnels.

—*Basil Ransome*

Ode to a Nightingale

Dreamy in a darkling bar,
idly sipping Southern Bourbon,
remembering an evening star,
half-forgetting urban boredom.

Nightingales who sang in childhood
can't be heard on this night street.
Here there is no magic wildwood,
still, cornmash liquor is warm and sweet.

Time has taken me and shook me,
left me with these dying boozers.
Though we all are rich and look free,
all except the years are losers.

Only language can escape time.
Only words and childhood birdsong.
Immortal, they may rest sublime,
though beauty burns and love goes wrong.

—*Roy Kelly*

Quicksands

If it form the one landscape that looks as bad
 As it smells, this is more or less because
Water, when it stagnates, looks and smells rotten.
 Mark this diarrhoeic fetor with its
Mantle of brown scum, and beneath, imagine
 The upright corpses, blind mouths full of muck,
Ears so clogged it is doubtful that any one
 Of them heard his hearbeat stop when he'd thrashed
His last; examine this natural outhouse
 Where one would think a God had stopped to dump:
Say what could be more like the mudpie you made
 As a child by accident from what Spot,
Your cocker spaniel, had reared up to and kicked
 Sand on, but hadn't wholly buried; whose poop
Had the consistency of pap? It is glop
 From which a man, who ordinarily
Does not take shortcuts, once immersed, would never
 Want to return to a clean, aproned wife
Patiently waiting their first anniversary
 Dinner on his arrival with the champagne.

Watch, then, the band of rich dowagers set down
 In the rank jungle by a gunrunner
With matinee voice and a deep, romantic scar;
 Accustomed to ne'er-do-wells with soft spots
For nuns, they have never had to contend with
 The mongrel eyes and rough locutions
Of a thug without scruples or a mother
 Himself; born promoters of the civic
Brunch, loathe to condemn a human being on purely
 Ethnic grounds, yet unable to conceive
Of a country where low-down rapscallions
 Fly planes, they deplane with a bump, grey heads
Buzzing with a wowser to tell back home; used
 To a white suburb where no one gets lost,
They've never understood the term "parasite"
 To mean anything more than a duffer
On welfare, or a "leech" mean anyone but
 Fred's brother; finally, driven mad by
Incessant munching of omnivorous pupae,
 Stings that leave bumps big as boils, rashes,
The runs, and something that looked like a tiger,
 They break into a trot and go under

In the only flat place that looked safe and paved,
  Which could happen to us...
                That's why, I dare say,
"Sylvan" means something more to me than forest
  Primeval, and plains always make me puke,
And even the sight of a flat-chested girl
  Is known to make me shudder, disgusted;
Which may be to say I'd hate being absorbed
  By anything for too long, especially
A faultless love, however faultlessly men love
  To sink into the smell of their own farts.

—*William Zaranka*

Ode on a Grecian Urn

This is a nice vase that's so very Greek;
It's plenty to say although it can't speak.

Some figures play pipes, whilst others play drums.
Whatever the music, they'll stay as the dumbs.

Some men are hunters, the women pursuing;
I cannot but wonder what they are doing.

Their love is lasting, unlike us poor quick;
When real passion ends, it makes people sick.

On this side of the jar, a priest takes a bow;
Are those people watching him killing a cow?

Did they come from that city and leave its streets dead?
Their secret's still secret, for nothing is said.

This Hellenic pot's a permanent token,
Outlasting the living, unless it is broken.

Its splendour will live; that's true, you'll agree;
Thus, truth equals beauty; that's proved. Q.E.D.

—*E.O. Parrott*

On First Looking into Chapman's Homer I

O I had been to sunny Spain
And I had been to Rome,
I'd been to Majorca again and again,
New York was as good as home,
But the scholars they spoke of a golden land
Described by an ancient Greek;
Yet all I got was Blackpool sand
Till I heard Chapman speak.
O he was like a big pools win
Or a dance by Legs and Co.
O he was as good as an hour of sin
With a hostess in Soho,
And I felt like Cortez when he saw
The sea from a Darien peak—
'Cos Pope does a lot but Chapman more
(If you can't read Homer in Greek).

—*T. Griffiths*

On First Looking into Chapman's Homer II

In Chapman's day poets had to write about Gods
and Heroes using capital letters and high-flown verses ad libitum
in the opinion of good judges;
I shall not read him again; for now we deprecate all
manifestations of heroism at whatever level,
and prefer verse that trudges.

In any event, I have never been interested
in well chosen epithets and rhetorical flourishes,
preferring to penetrate all disguise;
in this resembling Odysseus' dog—what was his name, then?—
who from his dunghill was the only
one his returning master
actually to recognize.

—Peter Peterson

THEODORE ROETHKE
(1908-1963)

... Foots It

The shape of a Roethke?
Like a Goethe,
Less than a bear,
But biggern a flea,
And goes in more directions
Than a knee.

Can he weep like a minnow,
Can he tremble?
Laughing turn more flips
Than a thimble?

Odd man out,
Odd man in,
Out he weeps,
In he grins.

Finders weepers,
Losers keepers,
Teddy follows his feet
Like a sneaker.

—D.C. Berry

CHARLES OLSON
(1910-1970)

I, Lessimus, of Salt Lake City

I am drunk of the pot.
I have been gone so long.
My nets are bloody. My
stick is bloody. My head

is bleeding too. I want
Edith Hamilton, Walter Pater,
and H.D. Kitto to rescue
me.

(the soul
is in the body, in the
Homeric body. The dead
swims around the living,
is as much of the living
as the living, is drunk
of the pot too, is really
not enigmatic, although it
eludes us a lot

(the spleen
floats in the pancreas;
the heart is certainly the
lungs; the glans is really
the vitreous humor; the
anal sphincter a delicate
brown rose

I don't envy everybody!

I prefer Hector and Ulysses
to Sam Huston (and I here
thumb my arse at daddy Carlos,
hold him responsible that I
don't have more depth than I
do, that there's not enough
mythic honey to make my verses
sunny).

—*Robert Peters*

Meeting Mick Jagger

AT PANNA GRADY'S PARTY, LONDON, SUMMER 1967

I. The Reading, Queen Elizabeth Hall

This poet is
7 feet tall, mainly bald
with tendrils around his skull
whitmanic tendrils blonde
which he strokes and plays upon.

A lengthy cough, a drink, a
belly pat, a sigh and a swing
as his fingers flutter, his
skull sags forward. He reads:
projective chant, lament.
A fly
buzzing inside
over there!
in the open field, frosted
with a lilt.

II: Commentary, by C. Olson

Gary, how is it in Japan? Philip and
John, what's doing in New York?
Whom do I want to touch in Afghanistan,
Peru?

But No
No
where to go, my old captain, *whit* (what)
man? to everport? to trip-is-done?
to gloucester, to camden?

I proclaim the oceans! all of them!
choice windhovers and morning minions!
Let us lash with the best lash first, or,
let us lash with the worst lash first!

I have forgotten to buy margarine again.
The coffee boils over. Embrace the seven seas!
the seas, sailed upon by Argonauts and Medes
coming from Troy (or was it Samothrace?)
retrieving abducted queens....

O haunt me, Matthew Arnold! Undo my corded bales—
as I disrupt my nobel-self.

I must see Creeley again,
inquire after... what are you really doing
on that beach, Mat, with Miss Grating Roar?
downtheircarvednamestheraindropplows (T Hardy).

I pause.

I drink water, display my tendrils more,
feel Greek, drink water from a well dug by David
under Jonathan's gaze. Oh, Medes and Persians,
we are all one (though
in between we are someone else
apart we stand.

I want to drink from Neruda's pitcher, Ensenzberger's
blue bottle, Ungaretti's old flask! I want to be a
beatle on a rock, a lordly satyr of verse, a
rolling stone!

III: Panna Grady's Party

Beneath the portico and columns
facing Regent's Park, well after
dark: food demolished in an hour
by poets from British and American
scenes. I was there and you were
there and he was there and she was there
and who was not there wandering from
stair to stair?

The witching hour. Jagger and Marian
appear. Ginsberg clicks his bells; and
Empson, Hughes, Montgomery, (Auden
absent hosting the ghost of MacNiece),
Henri, Hecht, Picard, McSweeney,
Patten, Dorn...

How are you, Mick? We meet at last.
forces of contemporary art, etcetera.
Great scene, Mick. Mick? I'm standing
here. here. I must speak. don't
divert your gaze. The cataclysmic moment,
verse or song, does not last long.

—Robert Peters

J.V. CUNNINGHAM
(1911-)

...Gets Hung up on a Dirty, of All Things, Joke

Love, I have lain awake by night
And tried to get the punch line right,

And tried to keep, with fierce intent,
A firm grasp of my instrument;

Though words are scarce and thought is thick
My flawless grammar is the trick

By which, though I am short of wit
And slow to make my couplets fit,

I shall explain, with love and luck,
Three Chinese sailors and a duck.

—Henry Taylor

Great Fleas

Great fleas have little fleas upon their back to bite 'em.
And little fleas have lesser fleas, and so *ad infinitum.*
The great fleas themselves in turn have greater fleas to go on,
While these again have greater still, and greater still, and so on.

—Anonymous

HENRY REED
(1914-)

Naming of Private Parts

This perspex model is what you might call a perfect replica
Except of course for the perspex, of a typical shelter,
If such a thing as typical exists. The first thing to notice
Is the door, and this long thing is the radiation reflector,
Which in your case you have not got. This little room here
Is the same as the little room in every house and under it
Is the water recycling device, which again you have not got.
I see some of you are looking alarmed and a lady in the back
Has fainted but there is no need to panic because this is
Only a model and I assure you that in the real thing
That little room I showed you is not made of perspex.

—John Lloyd Williams

JOHN BERRYMAN
(1914-1972)

Faces

Psss, the beard is a bit too long,
snip, there, that's better ain't it?
And the moustache too,
Mr. Bones. The peepers look wrong;
cut them out with the snippers.
Mr. Bones be no fool.

Part this way the hair or that.
Cut it you lower your ears.
That's better, Mr. Bones.
But if you the ears lower that
means no more black glasses
you've had too long.

Mr. Bones I gets rid of them
teeths, too—face up to a new face,
chomp, chomp.
And if you can't finish this picture in
the final solution, then, presto grace,
yourselves jump.

—D.C. Berry

Ode

—Mistah Berrybones, you daid?
Wherefore was Hindley in his graveshock laid
adown. Now twice-retired is his pen, his blouse of hair,
and jockey underwear.
O, that we had a quart of Hindley's semen
to impregnate our women!

—Mistah Berrybones, you *still*
believes youse really Jesus Christ?
Well, nearly: martyr in an age of Iacocca, overkill
and an awful zeitgeist,
Hindley "Used the language as if he made it."
End of quote. To whit,

one each of second comings to a customer.
Hindley botched things. Wherein did he err?
we ask, and also ask
you, hypocrite poseur, behind the mask,
you, blackface cad:
—De man's immortal, but de poems is *baad.*

—William Zaranka

DAVID IGNATOW
(1914-)

Alluding to the One-Armed Bandit

Be sure you paint
me with three hands,
one between the eyes
to flip through
the sets of eyes
to find just the ones for you,
then to flip through each
of you to find the right one
for the look in me.

This may take time.
Nothing says the third hand
will work together.

—D.C. Berry

WILLIAM STAFFORD
(1914-)

Cosmogony

For a forehead: Kansas skies.
For mouth and cheeks: plains.
For eyes: the horizon.

The chin is where you fall off
When I look at my shoes.

—D.C. Berry

Stafford in Kansas

Every morning
Before anyone else
Is weak enough to get up
These poems come to me:
I only write them down—
Mostly to get published.

That's when I go back,
Really, am taken back,
To Hutchinson, Kansas,
Where my father's Wooly
Hat is a long shadow
In these good gutters.

Now, naturally, everyone
Follows me for I am
The Father even though
They can't see my Wooly
Hat, for its tenacious band

Cuts deep. Following, also
My wife:
        Also four boys
        Also our same old dog.
The baby carriage wheels
Squeak messages.

In the Hutchinson streets everyone
Else goes past in the opposite
Direction: we have shields
On our backs;
They have shields
On their backs.
In Hutch everyone is Greek.

These good sidewalks become
Roads which lead to a strange place:
I recognize the place because
I am writing this poem:
The very same farmyard,
It is, where all of us began.

Weeds still there,
Clouds are gates opening
Overhead. Our old dog
Is still there, remembers us.

Why, I know that door!
The new people who open
The door are just like we were:
Stare kindly, say "Don't want
Any today" and we understand
They already have their Wooly
Hats and—somewhere—their shields.

At that moment, which has
Happened before and will
Recur in some future poem,
Everyone understands everything.

We huddle beside the road:
I look for a deer
To kick in the guts.
But all the deer have fled:
It's Hutch, pressing
Our backs to these invisible
Walls, even out here, somewhere.

Overhead we hear something United:
Flight 42, headed for Denver.
The boys stare into the speaking
Silence, and because I say so
They bow down.

Well, all of us from Oregon
And also from California
Are all going East, to Washington.
All of us, and especially me,
Need to see the awful stone pinions

Of power, to see them often,
But only, of course, to honor Robert Frost.

In haste we slam the car
Doors, head East, to do some Good.

If war comes, try Waldport, Oregon:
We gathered there last time, prayed.
And our side won, I think.

—James B. Hall

ROBERT LOWELL
(1917-1977)

Memories of Aunt Maria-Martha

No longer to lie reading Strauss's *Life*
Of Jesus near the duck-blind where my aunt
Maria-Martha—nicknamed "Mother"—wife
Of Uncle Joe, on Christmas day would hunt
Purgation's mallard, alternating shots
With beers, until duck flippers and duck guts
Rained on my page like Milton's Huguenots,
"Mother with infant on the rocks." Her mutts,
Cerberus and Scylla, ranged the bog,
While Charon's rowboat tugged upon the rope
Lashed to my toe until, nobody's dope,
I skidded like a lubber from my log
Splash! down into that cold, baptismal fen,
To drink the brack that Ahab spit at heaven.

—William Zaranka

Dog

The jawbone is a platter for the face,
the chin knocked sideways by a grin,
the forehead a knuckling pate skint back,
knocked down by history running
like a licking dog up under my heels,
tumbling me Ichabod crazy,
my eyes peeping out like jack-in-the-boxes
at the licking dog howling "the next, now, now,"
my nose the thumb in a fist-face to steady
the carving on the platter. Don't get the ears
mixed up with the nose like I do, the three
rolling around like loaded dice in the cup.
Throw them platter and all to the licking dog.

—D.C. Berry

Notes for a Sonnet

Stalled before my metal shaving mirror
With a locked razor in my hand I think of Tantalus
Whose lake retreats below that fractured lower lip
Of my will. Splinter the groined eyeballs of our sin,
Ford Maddox Ford: you on the Quaker golf-course
In Nantucket double-dealt your practised lies
Flattering the others and me we'd be great poets.
How wrong you were in their case. And now Nixon,
Nixon rolls in the harpoon ropes and smashes with his flukes
The frail gunwales of our beleaguered art. What
Else remains now but your England, Ford? There's not
Much Lowell-praise left in Mailer but could be Alvarez
Might still write that book. In the skunk-hour
My mind's not right. But there will be
Fifty-six new sonnets by tomorrow night.

—Edward Pygge

Revised Notes for a Sonnet

On the steps of the Pentagon I tucked my skull
Well down between my knees, thinking of Cordell Hull
Cabot Lodge Van du Plessis Stuyvesant, our gardener,
Who'd stop me playing speedway in the red-and-rust
Model A Ford that got clapped out on Cape Cod
And wound up as a seed-shed. Oh my God, my God,
How this administration bleeds but will not die,
Hacking at the rib-cage of our art. You were wrong, R.P.
Blackmur. Some of the others had our insight, too.
Though I suppose I had endurance, toughness, faith,
Sensitivity, intelligence and talent. My mind's not right,
With groined, sinning eyeballs I write sonnets until dawn
Is published over London like a row of books by Faber—
Then shave myself with Uncle's full-dress sabre.

—Edward Pygge

Notes for a Revised Sonnet

Slicing my head off shaving I think of Charles I
Bowing to the groined eyeball of Cromwell's sinning will.
Think too of Orpheus, whose disembodied head
Dumped by the Bacchants floated singing in the river,
His love for Eurydice surviving her dumb move
By many sonnets. Decapitation wouldn't slow me down
By more than a hundred lines a day. R.P. and F.M.F.
Play eighteen holes together in my troubled mind,
Ford faking his card, Blackmur explicating his,
And what is love? John Berryman, if you'd had what it took
We could have both blown England open. Now, alone,
With a plush new set-up to move into and shake down,
I snow-job Stephen Spender while the liquor flows like lava
In the parlour of the Marchioness of Dufferin and Ava.

—Edward Pygge

CHARLES BUKOWSKI
(1920-)

You Don't Know What Love Is

AN EVENING WITH CHARLES BUKOWSKI

You don't know what love is Bukowski said
I'm 51 years old look at me
I'm in love with this young broad
I got it bad but she's hung up too
so it's all right man that's the way it should be
I get in their blood and they can't get me out
They try everything to get away from me
but they all come back in the end
They all come back to me except
the one I planted
I cried over that one
but I cried easy in those days
Don't let me get onto the hard stuff man
I get mean then
I could sit here and drink beer
with you hippies all night
I could drink ten quarts of this beer
and nothing it's like water
But let me get onto the hard stuff
and I'll start throwing people out windows
I've done it
But you don't know what love is
You don't know because you've never
been in love it's that simple
I got this young broad see she's beautiful
She calls me Bukowski
Bukowski she says in this little voice
and I say What
But you don't know what love is
I'm telling you what it is
but you aren't listening
There isn't one of you in this room
would recognize love if it stepped up
and buggered you in the ass
I used to think poetry readings were a copout
Look I'm 51 years old and I've been around
I *know* they're a copout
but I said to myself Bukowski
starving is even more of a copout
So there you are and nothing is like it should be
That fellow what's his name Galway Kinnell
I saw his picture in a magazine
He has a handsome mug on him
but he's a *teacher*
Christ can you imagine
But then you're teachers too
here I am insulting you already
No I haven't heard of him
or him either
They're all termites
Maybe it's ego I don't read much anymore
but these people who build
reputations on five or six books
termites

Bukowski she says
Why do you listen to classical music all day
Can't you hear her saying that
Bukowski why do you listen to classical music all day
That surprises you doesn't it
You wouldn't think a crude bastard like me
would listen to classical music all day
Brahms Rachmaninoff Bartok Telemann
Shit I couldn't write up here
Too quiet up here too many trees
I like the city that's the place for me
I put on my classical music each morning
and sit down in front of my typewriter
I light a cigar and I smoke it like this see
and I say Bukowski you're a lucky man
Bukowski you've gone through it all
and you're a lucky man
and the blue smoke drifts across the table
and I look out the window onto Delongpre Avenue
and I see people walking up and down the sidewalk
and I puff on the cigar like this
and then I lay the cigar in the ashtray like this
and take a deep breath
and I begin to write
Bukowski this is the life I say
it's good to be poor it's good to have hemorrhoids
it's good to be in love
But you don't know what it's like
You don't know what it's like to be in love
If you could see her you'd know what I mean
She thought I'd come up here and get laid
She just knew it
She told me she knew it
Shit I'm 51 years old and she's 25
and we're in love and she's jealous
Jesus it's beautiful
She said she'd claw my eyes out if I came up here and got laid
Now that's love for you
What do any of you know about it
Let me tell you something
I've met men in jail who had more style
than the people who hang around colleges
and go to poetry readings
They're bloodsuckers who come to see
if the poet's socks are dirty
or if he smells under the arms
Believe me I won't disappoint em
But I want you to remember this
there's only one poet in this room tonight
only one poet in this town tonight
maybe only one real poet in this country tonight
and that's me
What do any of you know about life
What do any of you know about anything
Which of you here has been fired from a job
or else has beaten up your broad
or else has been beaten up by your broad
I was fired from Sears and Roebuck five times
They'd fire me then hire me back again
I was a stockboy for them when I was 35
and then got canned for stealing cookies

I know what it's like I've been there
I'm 51 years old and I'm in love
This little broad she says
Bukowski
and I say What and she says
I think you're full of shit
and I say baby you understand me
She's the only broad in the world
man or woman
I'd take that from
But you don't know what love is
They all come back to me in the end too
everyone of em came back
except that one I told you about
the one I planted
We were together seven years
We used to drink a lot
I see a couple of typers in this room but
I don't see any poets
I'm not surprised
You have to have been in love to write poetry
and you don't know what it is to be in love
that's your trouble
Give me some of that stuff
That's right no ice good
That's good that's just fine
So let's get this show on the road
I know what I said but I'll have just one
That tastes good
Okay then let's go let's get this over with
only afterwards don't anyone stand close
to an open window

—*Raymond Carver*

RICHARD WILBUR
(1921-   )

Occam's Razor Starts in Massachusetts

Occam's Razor starts in Massachusetts
Yet in time the Pitti Palace is unravelled,
An old moon re-arising as the new sets
To show the poet how much he has travelled.

Laforgue said missing trains was beautiful
But Wittgenstein said words should not seduce;
Small talk from him would at the best be dutiful—
And news of trains from either man, no use.

Akhmatova knew of Akhnaten,
The consonants they shared *a fortiori*
Yoked them in the same *Gemusegarten*
Though Alekhine might tell a different story.

They all of them together share this lyric
Where learning deftly intromits precision:
The shots are Parthian, the victories Pyrrhic.
Banquo's ghost was not so pale a vision.

But still you must concede this boy's got class.
His riddles lead through vacuums to a space
Where skill leans on the parapet of farce
And sees Narcissus making up his face.

—Edward Pygge

Conceit Upon the Feet

Feet at their loveliest are like two hands
That hang from arms caparisoned in hose,
White, Naireid arms crossed at the elbow; bands
Of hair, like wedding-gold, adorn the toes

Of feet, whose heels are like the fleshy balls
From which the thumbs protrude; the soles are palms;
Corns, warts; and so on, till the mind recalls
Those greater, metric feet, without which, poems

Would languish fallen-arched and in despair
Beside the road, like journeymen who swear
A foot in mouth gives safisfaction rare
As two left feet belied with false compare.

—William Zaranka

KINGSLEY AMIS
(1922-)

What About You?

When Mrs. Taflan Gruffyd Lewis left Dai's flat
She gave her coiffe a pat
Having straightened carefully those nylon seams
Adopted to fulfil Dai's wicked dreams.
Evans didn't like tights.
He liked plump white thighs pulsing under thin skirts in packed pubs on warm nights.

That's that, then, thought Evans, hearing her Jag start,
And test-flew a fart.
Stuffing the wives of these industrial shags may be all
Very well, and *this* one was an embassy bar-room brawl
With Madame Nhu.
Grade A. But give them that fatal twelfth inch and they'll soon take their cue

To grab a yard of your large intestine or include your glans
Penis in their plans
For that Rich, Full Emotional Life you'd thus far ducked
So successfully.
Yes, Evans was feeling... Mucked
-up sheets recalled their scrap.
Thinking barbed thoughts in stanza form
after shafting's a right sweat. Time for a nap.

—Edward Pygge

PHILIP LARKIN
(1922-)

Leavings

It would be nice to simply melt away,
For, after all, you can't do yourself in;
The world's a load of crap, like some backyard
Full of fag-ends and ragwort. Father's dead;
Two months, or less, and he was twice the man
My uncle is—Satchmo to Harry James—
And he looked after mum (this memory hurts!)
And she hung around him as if the sun
Shone out of his backside: and yet so soon
Before those new, slightly outmoded, shoes
She wore that morning to the cemetery
Showed signs of wear, she shacked up with my uncle,
While those obscene mascara runs still showed;
Too quick after her oats: too close to home.
It can't be right; but my affronted heart
I'll hide beneath my waistcoat. Mum's the word.

—*Gerard Benson*

High Wonders

When I see some kid from Norway
Getting ready for a scrap
And not giving a sod for consequences,
I know I'm full of crap.

What's the point of being alive
If all a man's got to do
Is sleep a third of his life away
And stuff himself and screw?

The thing is, we make excuses
For dropping out when the going's hard;
We tell ourselves we're being sensible
But really we're shit-scared.

Here's me, with Dad done in
And Mum behaving like a brass
And what do I do about it? Fuck-all.
It's time I got off my arse.

—*Naomi Marks*

ANTHONY HECHT
(1923-)

Peruke of Poets

No. Merely to have writ
Verse influenced somewhat by Pope,
Somewhat by Hugh Auden, above all by Marvell,
Is not (such as read modern books of verse can tell)
To have writ well. And yet I hope
I have a pretty wit.

In Brooklyn once I wrote
A garden poem, and later made
Another in the Italian city of Rome.
Wherefrom that humble mix of moss, manure, and loam
Such intellectual nightshade
Bloomed, as made me gloat

To think of Lowell or of Tate
Spading their poor sod, in periwigs.
What though some neo-Blackwood's hack dismiss my toil
As "clever, mannered, lighweight stuff"? Spleen marks a fool,
Keats knew, who cast his pearls at pigs.
Yet he habits with the great.

In Rochester I thrive
But labor now under the load
Of weighty themes: man's inhumanity to man
(As imaged in my recent flayed-Valerian)
For one. And I swear unto my God
I live hard hours to live.

But I am clever, yes,
And write "a fine, decisive line"
(Two critics called it), in both idioms, and thus
Am gathered to Yeats' bosom, where the Muses muss
My hair, and as it were divine
This peruked prettiness.

—*William Zaranka*

JAMES DICKEY
(1923-)

The Boy; or, Son of Rip-Off

In the summer heat and fever crackling
the backs of the hills like driven napalm I saw him
floating in the top of the sycamore the solitary
tree on Billy Bob's farm a boy thin as the first
ice in the clay-rut puddles in the logging road
that chiseled at the edges of Pea-Vine Ridge. No one
knew how he sprang there his head a wart-eaten
balloon or how he fell from the star-ridden
moon some astronaut's sucking toy or practical joke
on poor farmers huddling under the hay bales
skinned and flailed by a nameless fright But there
he was shank fur and nail a child of the boiling
tub of our moon-carved dreams a child we fathered
all of us guilty as a plow-rip at the roots
of the river-trunked tree He the accuser
whining, whining
My stones are the starlike prick-balls
of this sycamore seed-heavy
in my hand I come to you
with thorns in my feet an orphan
of a long-forgotten squash court
the only pride I had hammered thin
I hover here carrion dead

words like pebbles in my mouth
yet yet alive still breathing
my nostrils flared like coiling
leaves alive to tell you
tell you,
I will come again at night higher
than U-2 my eyes blazing with sterno
to watch you work your woman into
griddle-cake batter with your powerful
hands your harrowing discs plows
and balers. I will watch you eat
the wounds of lust in the box-camera
dark and at the apogee of your
sunstorm-falling I will rip off
the shivering roof of your farmhouse
and scream *Your moves are right*
for water clod or stone I know you
when you come, blind eyes, blind eyes,
you motherfucking SAVAGE!

—Malcolm Glass

The Cropdusting

—Ja, die Kanzel ist fur der
Selbstbefleckung nicht der Platz.

—Baron von Schnapsig

Grasshoppers beware.
Twenty-five years strafing alfalfa,
Corn wheat
The staffs of life,
And soon a field is a field
At a hundred feet or a thousand.
And before that,
Before corn dreamt in the dark surrounding
Shucks
A month from harvest moon combine Iowan barnshade
And silo
was Okinawa.

All phyla masticated in chorus
That afternoon:
hopper, worm, spider,
Clovermite, locust,
a division of ephemera
An emperor would be rid of
stopped: sighed
Hit the deck
under the rising sun of Okinawa.

Now, in the vast, swift shadow
Of my renovated Stuka
raining death
down,
It is much the same death: all are victims
In the cloud of Nox-on eating at tanks,
Two tanks hundreds of pressurized gallons

Arrays of nozzles
under one thumb.
O merciless
Cloud-fall, burst dike
Of myself expending gas
and law to larvae
Pruning a little of the world
For life,
life enthralled by a yellow cloud
Eclipsing family trees
Of dung-beetles, stink-bugs, lice:
To whom I say only
forgive
Nothing of the deaths
Of children born
Misshapen,
each of a thousand blind eyes
Straining
three o'clock high for light,
Children without limbs
mandible-less knotted
of antennae
Broken and delirious
with yellow smog, face-down
On the delirious island of Iowa.

Forgive... what?
In this business, reputation is all.
It is all, and

"We Deliver."

—*William Zaranka*

In Orbit

The darkness is closing around us
And the loudspeaker calls out the hours
In seconds of waiting.
High in my tower of steel and fuel
Which points to the stars,

Bravely phallic,
I lie strapped to my seat
In a spacesuit.

The instruments cluster around me.
I give each of them one final handshake.
I close my eyes when the time comes,
Nestling down in my long chair.
As the weight of my body presses

Down into me, the colors
Pass in front of my eyes,
The glorious purple of Heaven.
The thunder of engines enraged
Makes the tower quiver in terror.

I rise, I float from the ground,
Into the heavenly purple.
For the moment, there is nothing
But darkness.
But the rocket knows what it is doing,
And it bends its course in a circle.
I look through the electrical eyes
And I see my green earth below me.
I shout three green cheers for myself.

The black sky resounds with my joy.
The stars, incredibly bright,
Shine through the blackness toward me.
In the blue of my joy I salute them.
Re-entry into the earth's air
Begins after my third tour of the sky.

I start my brave plunge to the ocean,
Exulting in the thunder of sun,
Of engines no longer enraged,
But burnt out.
My happy comrades are waving

From the deck of the ship that awaits me.
I shout as I crash into the sea.
I feel the capsule slow down,
And bob back up to the surface.
Blackness closes around me.

I hear the voice of my captain
Come over the loudspeaker toward me.
The blastoff has been postponed again.
There is weather over the ocean.

I greet the sad face of my captain,
And I smile.
His sadness does not disturb me.
I climb down from my tower in triumph:
Tonight I have marched through the heavens.
I shout three green cheers for myself.

—Henry Taylor

DENISE LEVERTOV
(1923-)

Dead Bird

A dead bird
in a cage is not
depressing, for I,
delicate, spooky
woman that I am,
can imagine songs
the bird ought to have sung,
had he been given
the gift—my gift.

I give it now,
transforming him perfectly.
I hope he knows now
why I had to wring
his inadequate neck.

—David R. Slavitt

MAXINE KUMIN
(1925-)

That Everything Moves Its Bowels

That everything moves its bowels and bleeds, and then
dies and is buried or is eaten, or frequently both,
is pastoral and marvelous. O the country
is full of such wisdom: fields and stables are
abattoirs where the mallet of truth whomps
between my eyes. In the back of my pick-up truck
is a dead horse, my birthday present, alive
with maggots and flies, busy as any city.
When I'm sad or out of sorts, I beat its bloat,
beat the dead horse, and the air hums, shines,
primitive, convincing, disgustingly real.

—David R. Slavitt

DAVID WAGONNER
(1926-)

Is There a Voice

Is there a voice of the Turtle
In the land? Of course: it is in
The cadence of our idiomatic Snake,
Our Owl, our eloquent Trout.
Think of it, you who speak
Nothing but guttural Fortran,
You with your broken Payroll, your pidgin Suffrage:
There are featherless bipeds out here
Beyond your hearing,
Collecting folk songs of the Spotted Thrush,
Howling in native Wolf as if your lives
Depended on this message:
The end of the mantic Muskrat and the Seal
Is the end of you, my inarticulate friends.

—Philip Appleman

A.R. AMMONS
(1926-   )

Try

Try wading in sand,
you will see
    that History is the craft
of life seen backwards, Order
available at last because
    events are dead
as the crust of a picked crab—forms,
definitions, erected over our acts
    like country gravestones.
The mind, I used to think—my mind—
is a mirror, not a magnifier;
    today
        I find it more
a refractive medium, a little sky
making sunsets in the dust
of living—in any case,
no microscope.
History? Movements? Find
    a caress in the curve
        of a tern, the risk of death
in the dainty step of herons—the mind,
refracting, paints it all:
    where we have been,
        where we are going,
all we need.
Tomorrow
I shall see it differently.

—Philip Appleman

Coming Down To It

The water has to start
somewhere. Upland, I
suppose, and then with dart
and drive it cuts down

through rock, log, moss,
and root like a persistent
syllogism intruding
its conclusion into the loss

and ending all our lives
come down to. Well, we all
go this way, wearing our
way down sure as knives

growing dull on stone, or
logic wearing channels
in the corpuscles of strength.
It's still and still a bore,

no matter what discourse
pools in valley ground
or lumps up like fool's gold.
Philosophers have found

nothing. Though dressed in metaphor,
abstract celebration's still a bore.

—Malcolm Glass

JAMES MERRILL
(1926-)

It is Enough

It is enough; time presses, we are thrifty
Now with fire and gold, with scorn and praise
Of Progress, of all Movements: these are the days
Of 1976, and I am fifty.

The cupola on Water Street's in motion,
Panning past World War II, past Rilke dead,
Past mad King George trumpeting *Off with their heads*
At traitors snitching land across his ocean.

Does it matter now? To whom? Is mine the freak
Vision, focusing Water Street, solemn
In fog, gray gulls, the grim Doric columns
Of George's reign, pretending to be Greek,

Fooling no one? No more than all that stuff
About the Wars, the Movements, the Depression:
Interesting, perhaps, but a digression.
I'm fifty. I am fifty. It's enough.

—Philip Appleman

ROBERT CREELEY
(1926-)

...Also Watches

The portrait is where you
put it, where it is,
did you, for example, that

large tank there, silvered,
with the white church along
side, lift the house

with the portrait there,
to what purpose? How
heavy the slow

world is with
everything put
in place.

A leaf of
yellow is
going to fall.

and while you are
watching, I too,
slowly.

—D.C. Berry

. . . Listens, Too

There is no portrait
but what painting makes
it less tangible. The hand
fast as it goes, loses

pace, puts in place of it
lines, sketches,
for a way only to
hopefully come back to

where it cannot. It
fades. My hand sinks.
I leave on the canvas such weight
it is only my knuckles popping.

—D.C. Berry

When

When they sd to me this
is the way it all
unravels, the loose ends
of history,

I heard the indifferent rain
falling
into somebody else's
ambition

and I sd look, if you sing
in a minor key
they'll call you
a minor poet.

—Philip Appleman

Buying a Record

There are records. Do not
mistake me. If you

want some, prove that you
get them from a store

a popular discount house
in the suburbs, take a

remote chance, of course, that the
one you want may be out

of stock, that buying a record is
bartering my love. I

may sell it to you, and
I may not.

—*Robert Peters*

In The Ladies' Room at The Bus Terminal

In the only free
toilet there
she sat.
Should I

politely
excuse myself
or not. Dare I
break that calm water,

that silence. Must I
turn unceremonious
on my heel and out
of your life

lady, and apotheosis
of lady
who had been gracious
and never so

embarrassed
before by a man cocking
one eye, tipping
his hat

in a place like that.

—*William Zaranka*

ALLEN GINSBERG
(1926-)

Squeal

I saw the best minds of my generation
Destroyed—Marvin
Who spat out poems; Potrzebie
Who coagulated a new bop literature in fifteen
Novels; Alvin
Who in his as yet unwritten autobiography
Gave Brooklyn an original *lex loci.*
They came from all over, from the pool room,

The bargain basement, the rod,
From Whitman, from Parkersburg, from Rimbaud
New Mexico, but mostly
They came from colleges, ejected
For drawing obscene diagrams of the Future.

They came here to L.A.,
Flexing their members, growing hair,
Planning immense unlimited poems,
More novels, more poems, more autobiographies.

It's love I'm talking about, you dirty bastards!
Love in the bushes, love in the freight car!
I saw them fornicating and being fornicated,
Saying to Hell with you!

America.
America is full of Babbitts.
America is run by money.

What was it Walt said? Go West!
But the important thing is the return ticket.
The road to publicity runs by Monterey.
I saw the best minds of my generation
Reading their poems to Vassar girls,
Being interviewed by *Mademoiselle.*
Having their publicity handled by professionals.
When can I go into an editorial office
And have my stuff published because I'm weird?
I could go on writing like this forever...

—Louis Simpson

...Leaps Over the Aisle of Syllogism

Let Allen's eyes be a jukebox of light plugged into the navel of Whitman's verb,
Whose forehead is an anecdote of skid marks sliding through the stanzas of San Francisco,
Whose hair in ecstasy is a halo of blackbirds scratching this way this way this way to the flop houses of Selah,
Whose mouth is a vase a Ming a cup of vowel and the holy grail of Iambic Couplet,
Whose tongue is the red red rose of Orlovsky's rhapsodic thorn,
Whose nose jumped off the Golden Gate Bridge this really happened July 9, 1951, 1:20 p.m. and walked back to his flat unknown not one free beer atta boy or pat on the rump,
Whose ears are strippers on the saxophones of Houston jazz and the back of the greyhound,
Whose teeth line up ring around the rosy and scoop velvet mushrooms out of the fog,
Whose upper lip and nether lip in cahoots cook up a pederasty of hiccups,
Whose cheeks are the shores where bottles with notes inside from Burroughs wash up from Tangiers, heah Allen what the hell I bought the last round,
Whose butt hole is the last chance between Madison Square Garden and Prague then take two lefts and a right to the pinks of Cezanne,
Whose knees are temples for the footloose complete with prayer pads made in Japan on the outskirts of love,
Whose stomach is the lawn of morning the veil of evening, the Alpha and Omega of a hairy pear,
Whose arms like ex-cons threw their elbows into the gutters of N.C.'s Denver and went straight,

Whose elbows patiently wait at the Salvation Army located at the intersection of the western wind,
Whose dong during the last Synod rose to preeminence,
Whose balls in the midst of all the hub bub were uplifted,
Whose ankles and wrists are full of loaded dice rolling the moment into the Ultimate Eternity of Craps,
Whose back has been up against the wall more than a humping tom cat or Harvard ivy,
Whose hands are ten sweet sisters and brothers of the silque mouth and the latest publication of fingernails,
Whose hips leap over the aisle of syllogism and sit smack on the front row of Nirvana,
Whose feet he has on loan from the tracks left in the snow outside Ferlinghetti's walk-up.

—D.C. Berry

Blessing a Bride and Groom: A Wedding Night Poem

I enter, jingling hindu temple bells, deodorant ears laughing and happiness-fulfillment lips breathing
towards stretched-out nakedbody sandwich, happy bride and mayonnaise bridegroom on hot cupcake sheets
cool icecream pillows, shuddering alpha and omega lips and eyes glinting holy messages, spuming from holes (ascetic
orifices of general love), myself garbed simply, pilgrim almost, alphabet soup of virtues, pubic albatrosses, sweetbutter
hairy tangles—all under a loving overhead lightbulb as these lovers avoiding me grind glorious thickpressure
fuckskins, forcing me, outcast, St. Anthony giggles assaulting my crayfish loins, tender vinegar crabs unhouseled, weird
seaweed veins, to do it myself this time, onanistic, choking it off, caressing, archer-shooting, spurting, draft of
moisture weeping nightbreeze, nude ghost, rectile, from shuddering Blakean cockspaces, hungering, till I point
forefinger at tormented Christian bed tossing, endlessly rocking itching from head to asshole. The bride wails, sheets swirl,
bridegroom in pinkcream chambered nautilus rocking, hard honeyself not yet flaccid, sees me in flourescent shadow
gaiety of fat neck above and below, cock waving, going over, depositing armlets, hairbraids & anklets
on the floor, I crawl in between sexy nutrient sandwich, elephant happiness tears flow, crocodile-snapping muskmists,
intricate practiced lovegestures from me, me, itinerant epithalamium-maker, as the redundant bride unsheathes her
turpentine claws, rakes bleeding trail of sexhatred down my anus-shuddering spine.

—Robert Peters

Amurrika!

Give me the wretched refuse of your teams: pitchers with sore elbows, tackles with slipped disks, geriatric jocks, Unitas, DiMaggio, Riggs—
I WANT HEROES! Boxers with rubber legs, Wimbledon champs with redhot tennis-elbows—all speckled, spotted, brindled bigshots—give me billiards kings with D.T.'s, famous jockeys gone to fat, Soap-Box Derby finalists over the hill in grad schools—
Kerouac! Burroughs!—I want your 30's idols, Cary Grant, Robert Taylor, John Payne—Sages, Archangels, show me their wrinkles, their flab,
and I'll give them a Karma they never found on the Silver Screen: San Francisco! Denver! Katmandu!—give me your aging failures, Universe,

listen to me—I'm sick of pushing 50 a hero to kids who can't remember Dean Rusk—
give me the Golden Oldies, the best torsos of my generation, men with cataract eyes glaring at the abyss of oblivion, the guts sucked out of them—
none of your Noble Causes, all of us hanging in there gutless in our hallucinating daisychain chanting
Give me your tired blood, your poor circulation, your huddled quarterbacks retired in '53—send these to me because
I AM AMURRIKA
and I'll kiss every one of their grimy toes, Amurrika, and your true history will begin in the year of that Lightning Eternal Paradise Epiphany Apocalypse!

—Philip Appleman

A Pizza Joint in Cranston

What thoughts I have of you tonight, Walt Whitman, for I work late at Ernie's Pizza and Grinders with a headache self-conscious looking at the bulge under my apron.

In my hungry fatigue, and cooking for images, I've been fondling tomatoes, dreaming of your recipes!

What sauce and combinations! Whole families eating together! Mouths oozing pizza! Wives gorging mushrooms! Babies stuck under mozzarella!—and you, Garcia Lorca, What do you mean it needs more oregano?

I saw you, Walt Whitman, childless, lonely old grubber, poking among the olives and eyeing the sub rolls.

I saw you sneaking samples of each: Who pays I ask? You smile, salami in your beard.

I wander in and out of bins of chopped onions and anchovies following you, and followed in my imagination by Ernie himself.

We strode down by heaps of dough in our solitary fancy tasting my special dressing, possessing the key to the coke machine, and never passing the cashier.

Where are we going, Walt Whitman? The oven shuts down in an hour. Where will the salami drop off your beard tonight?

(I touch your book and dream of oddyssey in the men's room and feel absurd.)

Will we walk all night through the solitary streets? The trees add shade to shade, lights out in the houses, we'll both be lonely and burp pizza.

Will we stroll dreaming of super combinations of the ultimate sandwich, home to our silent cottage?

Ah dear father, crudbeard, lonely old cooking teacher, what bicarbonate did you have when Ernie quit poling his ferry and started this franchise leaving you with stomach cramps on the black streets of Cranston?

—Craig Weeden

FRANK O'HARA
(1926-1966)

In Blue

It's 12:21 in New York a Thursday
one day after April fool's day, yes
it is the year of our Lord and I go get

my shirt out of the 1-day
because I am meeting the blonde at
1:30 and want to look sharp

and a guy with a frame and a dog
wants to do a picture of me so okay
I step inside the frame and he asks
me to just stand there a minute until the sun comes
back out so he can get the eyes just right
specifically blue and then it starts
to rain and the dog starts smelling
and my shirt is losing its crease

and the blonde is walking up to say
hi but I'm afraid if I speak I'll ruin
the picture and the blonde is walking away now
and the guy and the dog are too

and I'm ringing the blonde's
door bell my eyes are just right

—D.C. Berry

In the Gazebo

In the gazebo we were flipping
piastres, fighting off outraged
parakeets, insisting
Bosch would have loved us all:
salamanders, Moors,
avaricious philosphers—this
is getting serious—rain
rams the lattice work
like hired goons. Escape from History?
We flip for it—two out of three?
Sudden death:
I say, split for the Indy 500,
They say, a week on Fire Island.
Piastres fall like rain:
I lose. Goodbye Broadway,
Hello Rilke.

—Philip Appleman

ROBERT BLY
(1926-)

More

More than leaves, more than flakes
Of snow in Minnesota,
Words fall through the darkness,
Drifting into poems:
In the Oval Office, the Man shuffles, Ankle-deep in poems—he kicks away
Allusions to Jefferson, calls Kissinger,
Demanding to know where the hell all the poems
Are coming from, why the Minute Men are not
Blasting them down as they float in,

The CIA not thowing them into dungeons—how
Are they getting through, miring the National Guard,
Marching on the Pentagon?
No answer, only wheezing, like the oom-
Pah-pah of a beer-hall band. The Man fidgets,
Calls New York: why is the Market
Glutted with poems, it's all
On TV, a scandal! Another scandal!
The Chase National Bank
Goes militant, sics its bulls
And bears on villanelles,
Sends out stockholders armed
With push-brooms, sweeping poems
Into heaps for bonfires—nothing
Helps: the Man chokes on a lyric, panics
Pushes the red button.
His ultimate weapon fires—billion-dollar rockets,
Maddened by poems,
Scream off to burn huts in Asia:
In a fine frenzy of National Defense
We bomb ourselves back
To the stone age.

—Philip Appleman

...Says Something, Too

I

I wake to find myself lying in an open field.
About my head the ends of grasses
Wave softly in the wind.

II

I raise my head and turn on my side
And see a horse's tail swishing at flies.
It is attached to the end of a horse.

III

In my way I love to consider things I love—
Oh, often even in summer in this kind of field
I think I should be covered up with snow!

—Henry Taylor

Walking Through a Cornfield in the Middle of Winter I Stumble Over a Cow Pie and Think of the Sixties Press

Blue toads are dying all over Minnesota
among the cantaloupes, the ripening waists
of the banana republics.

The horses brush flies with their tails.
The flies are Literary Establishment flies,
Trujillo flies, Franco flies, General Motors flies.
The horses love each other
but do not know what to do about it.
They nuzzle the fence posts affectionately.
The fence posts grow larger and fill up the whole horizon
in a sea of turning eagles.

I shall print my friends on a Thursday, in Paris,
in the rain, from an untouchable cave
behind my Guggenheim.
And watch the Wops scribble all over the statues
beside the Villa d'Este.

All the Shell stations are bathed in a luminous film
iridescent with gas.

It is also good to be poor, and live in the hen house
with the droppings of last year's chickens
blazing into magazines under my feet.

—*Barbara Harr*

...Finds Something in New Jersey

I

I love the stream flowing endlessly
All day between the long cat tails covered with sunlight,
Carrying beer cans down to the sea
As if it is infinite.

II

The cockroach is carrying joy on his antennae;
The rat is lifting tiny bits of food in his mouth;
The shapeless amoebae are hungry
Like old men without coats.

III

I am driving; it is dawn; New Jersey.
The shining black water beetle obeys something—
Perhaps covered by something else—
And it is hard and eternal.

—*Carol Poster*

PAUL BLACKBURN
(1926-)

La Misère

La misère existe : that is all
it is a very
Zen
experience / this life.
It is midnight : it is Xmas
it is Xmas midnight.
Why
do you never / listen?

THERE IS NO SUCH THING
as Relevance

in the
hallways
Nemesis
is
thumping
on
snare-drums.

I am thinking
of angels
I am thinking
of L.A.
I am thinking
of what comes after
the ninth inning :

it is a very
Zen
experience / this death

—*Philip Appleman*

STANLEY MOSS
(1926-)

My Friend

My friend, you don't understand,
You with your clear Engagement;
For us it's all shift, mutation,
A matter of slant vision:
We see with the eyes
We sleep with. Why do you suppose
Pope pronounced couplets as if
Infallible, Frost saw the world
As a snowy woods? Why
Does Lowell speak only to God?
We bend light around ourselves, our looking
Makes funhouse rainbows. Movements?
Why, everything moves: look around,
Can't you see it all shimmering, quivering,
Velvet-green—this landscape perfectly
Moss?

—*Philip Appleman*

W.D. SNODGRASS
(1926-)

So What

So what did you expect,
To get younger every year?
As everything else went sere
And yellow, we'd resurrect?

Of course our teeth are rarer
Each decade, our dark hair flecked
With grizzle—whose blank check
Is made out *Pay to Bearer*?

We all bring with us toward
The grave, or incinerator
The guilt of the creator
Of nothing. Nothing but words

There's fear in every flower,
Shame on all horizons:
Neighbor, choose your poison;
We tasted, then chose ours.

—*Philip Appleman*

JOHN WOODS
(1926-)

Maples

Maples bleed themselves dry:
Mother Nature has changes of life, too;
It hasn't been fatal yet. Don't
Kid yourself—if you're really up
On Movements, you'll feel the smoke
Slithering out of November bonfires,
The first feather of snow
Melting on your cheek. Depression?
It's the opposite of April,
Darling buds of May in cold
Storage, hot flashes in a freezing month, War
To the last chrysanthemum.
You should be asking,
Why is it that after fifty years of marriage,
I'm still faithful to spring,
Never look at another season, wait,
Through Depressions and Wars,
For that witching every year,
When April tickles the palm of my hand
And I flower green and yellow...
What's that?
Spring? Listen:
If you have to ask,
You can't afford it.

—*Philip Appleman*

JOHN ASHBERY
(1927-)

Suite for Celery and Blind Date

Impatient with the enigmatic, Al Capone
let that one pass. *Le petit mal*
is only a fedora you hang in a friend's closet
while Scheherazade beplumed with agitation
among the mangroves and tepidity sighs
as the tire is reinflated.

"After all," as Voltaire is apt to have remarked,
"it's never the heat." Take *Le Bon Dieu*
if you will. But the suburbs are alert with
nylon zippers and some notable disappointments.
One has in the aformentioned Patrimony
too much time, Time that is, too many choices, intrigues:
God did provide an excess of birds.

Our species more or less of cockatoo
would not have undermined his specious case
sub specie aeternitatas for existence.
Seduction is a diversion like milk bottle caps
gaily aloft towards a partly opened dormer window.
Capone let that pass too. Alimony
diverted among the asters
or is it astral somewhat short of the horizon.

Can you be sure that a pirouette
doesn't leave the parquet out of line
here in the Grand Salon where the orphan
presupposes triumph as her alter ego
fills his winsome cube with a faithful *arf*?
The eye may also render a glissando
there to the cornice and recall the vague
as corms and umbels, just as a thoroughbred
rounds the stretch not coming from behind.
Yet other considerations remain. The lilac
sheathed thigh adjacent the pinstripes,
whose hauteur as he thought was
less of a fulcrum than she thought:

So it had become nineteen twenty-eight already
and Voltaire kept cropping up behind his pseudonym
to prove nothing or (considering the inefficacious
in such commerce between tongues) Everything.
"What difference does it make," God wept.

That as we all know is the crinoline rose
in the garter, coruscating and intent.
It insists on raising its ugly little head
among the discussants. Nonetheless the committee
issues its acclamations like leit-motifs
among the neutral and humid beyonds.

The zoom-lens has dissipated its novelties
among the lianas where the Star
is glossed with steadfast precision:
Capone among the primates. In a canvas chair,
Arouete riffles the pages, deleting,
and Buster Crabbe catches his breath of incipience.

That was Saturday afternoon
where the Cambridge Anthropologists
pounded the tom-toms and in the upper balcony
the Encyclopedic leered with his one-eye
and dropped his delicate fingers
into the lap of Andy Breton's putative bride.

Clay pigeon are a comfort and
temporary like remembrance.
A saving grace and its dividends.

—*Philip Dow*

Synthesizing Several Abstruse Concepts With an Experience

At the window, you look out
On the abstractions of heliotrope
Clouds touched by the declining twilight
Through the soot flakes.
The black crystalline forms realize
Pre-existent predicates. Why must it be like this?
Grasped between your index finger and opposing thumb,
The yellow cord of the shadeless lamp
Was yanked and fell off. This wealth of coincidence
Was indeed rich in interwoven allusions
As the heterogenous river carries photosynthetic organs.
Existence, no doubt, precedes essence, but things
Became worse when the roof caved in.

—Carol Poster

W.S. MERWIN

(1927-)

Forehead Dead-Ends Half-Way Through the Poem

The smile
A. One gull wing flying alone

The eyes
A. Like lightless stars keep on going out

The ears
A. Echo, repeating no sound
The eyes, really
A. Two half-pints the morning after

The forehead
A. Dead-end either way

The cheek bones
A. Blessed are the silent gates

The nose
A. Aims the face this way no this way

The chin
A. Chariot

The hair
A. What the spine does when it sprouts

What
A. A skull cap

—D.C. Berry

JAMES WRIGHT
(1927-1980)

Depressed by the Death of the Horse that He Bought from Robert Bly

Never have I seen the sky more clear
Than in Montana. Birds with eyes
Inside my bones confuse this clarity.
I stand here in this Montana field
Remembering when things were as they were,
And watch the silent eyes of a horse
Which I recently bought from a friend.

Small creatures are talking among themselves
In the grass around my shoes.
I discover, to my surprise
(For lack of a better word),
That the horse did not belong to my friend
In the first place.

Alone, alone, I sink to my knees
In the grass by an ownerless horse
And weep for all students of Spanish.
Minnesota is what I meant to say,
And they may never know.

—Henry Taylor

Imitations Based on the American

1

I have drifted in silence
to this place.
It is the grave stone of James Wright,
a poem half-sunken
in the twilight, the mud of twilight.
I will not hitch my horse
and stay long. A feather floats
down from the sky,
and it is autumn in Lumbago, Minnesota.
I feel it in my bones.
That my love is dead.

2

I have written translations
of the poems of poets
I have not known,
until I have learned to write
my own poems
to sound like translations
of the poems of a poet
I have not known.
In the meantime, I have done my work on Bly's farm.
I hold my breath an hour at a time.
Outside the window, Bly is up to his neck
in snow. He is silent.
His face is red as an apple.
I told him. It must have been 20 feathers
of breath ago I told him
the weather forecast in Manitoba.

Oh Jesus Christ, the Brazilians
are drunk again slipping
into the shit pits of Bremerhaven.

3

Now is the longest day of the year,
summer solstice, northern
hemisphere, midwest American wind
like a yawn, warm, human.
It comes to me,
we're all spaced out on the farm.
I turn and see
three tomato plants. To my left,
an onion seed is deep
in the earth,
beating.
I lean back. I dream of the Pampas,
the green sweet grass
of the Argentine,
and all those mustachioed gauchos
fucking sheep.
I have wasted my life.

—*Frank Polite*

GALWAY KINNELL
(1927-)

The Skunk

1

Bloated
on rotten eggs,
glutted with goose grease,
stuffed with sourgrass, gorged
on frijoles, fermenting
from beer, the skunk
vamooses.

2

In character
he resembles me in seven ways:
he avoids bathing
he thinks himself distinctly an essence
he's a gas on the tennis courts
he turns his back on danger
and takes heart in his privates
he ceases being bothersome if stripped of certain glands
he shits on the run (touche)
he is tamed to give vicarious thrills to middle-aged girls

3

Highway fatality, handy
epithet: you give us what we loathe
in ourselves—

He would fumigate
the world of civility, our artifice
cloaking our good animal musk
masking our lust with disgust—

Ultra-Poe-like demon!

4

Fire
for some higher
flight
light-
ens these limbs: I
grow giddy. I
aspire—
This poor manflesh
does not flinch
from the fate of Icarus

5

(whose human wings
still can stir
in us
whistles angelic, ir-
resistible to the poet's inner
ear).

6

I grow web feet, I waddle.
Heaven lies in every puddle.

7

This carnal cloak
(or cosmic joke)
I pray not shirk—
but, drunk
with grace (from gliding in the drink),
transcend: become Man
-Drake!
and beg not lay but golden eggs.
But I hack him dead.
With proper ritual
I skin the creature, and eat
until my senses are woozing
then wrap his hide on my head
and snooze.

8

Beginning to dream
my quest's a success—though I take
much gas for the raw
stuff of my art, I've amber grease
for a whale of a poem—
I awaken
on all fours.

—Philip Dow

ANNE SEXTON
(1928-1974)

From the Brothers Grimm to Sister Sexton to Mother Goose: One Transmogrification

As sure as shooting
a Serpent will come
to the Garden
like the cutworm
or urban developer,

blighting the green
and simple dream.

He is the Trespasser
whose trespasses
we do not forgive.
That old story.
The Confidence Man
with an eye-opening deal
in black market produce
for the curious helpmate,
that blood mother of Faust,
who tiring of the Delicious
and believing she knew a bargain
bit.
That old story of a bad apple
come to this.
Every ruddy pippin
cankered at the core.

He is the hit man
in a space suit
with a contract
on the Man in the Moon.

The Britannica man,
on the spoor of innocence
like a harrier,
has found out
the ivied cottage in the hollow,
has already one Florsheimed cloven foot
in the door,
peddling death
in red morocco
and easy monthly payments.

Wheedler, panderer, pusher,
he deals in the passion pinks
and rosebud and cherry reds
of carcinogenic lipsticks.
In the heart stopping purity
that can be ours
for keeping faith
in Hexachlorophene.

In the giant discount store
we know him by his Dale Carnegie smile
in children's wear.
He is arranging the rack,
the new line of party dresses from Hong Kong,
each a bewitching Medea creation
of hand-stitched napalm,
fashioned to flare
and melt the heart of the wearer.

He buries a surprise
in every hermetic box
of BHT-embalmed
Post Toasties,
this one a toy death's head on a pin,
no bigger than an eyeball,

to wear like a Cub Scout badge
or Jocasta's brooch.

He is the Fixer
of any bleat or belt.
He lets us ride the white horse
into the high country.
We keep his surety,
a monkey.

Once
there was a blue-eyed maid,
little Ms. Muffet,
an Adelle Davis sunflower child
that Wordsworth would have called Lucy,
who one morning
was sitting pretty on her tuffet,
a dandy do-it-yourself hassock of new hay,
eating from an earthenware cup
her curds and whey.
A kind of yogurt, you might say,
a Bulgarian culture.

It was a pastoral for shawms and pipes.
It was an idyll for a watercolor by Pissarro.
It was a Mother Earth breakfast to warm the maw and cockles.

But down out of the blue
swung a big spider,
like Buster Crabbe on the ubiquitous vine,
to a soft eight-point landing
on of all places the dear tuffet!
A real hairy, bandy-legged arachnid.
An intimidator.

He was an advance man
for the Dairymen's Association
and the Battle Creek boys,
and threw an awful fright into Ms. Muffet,
spinning scare stories
about the Bulgarians,
their curds and whey,

decrying "commie comestibles."
He was also one of those,
a phrasemonger of the Agnewian school.

He declared her breakfast
every bit as un-American
as jugged hare,
Scottish bap,
kasha,
or raw embryo wheat germ.
And even impugned the tuffet,
its georgic cut and character,
as Yugoslavian.

He cozened Ms. Muffet
on the distinct romantic advantages,
according to Masters & Johnson laboratory tests,
of the national breakfast—

cooked eggs, uncoddled,
hot curls of bacon,
melting bricks of butter on toasted Wonder Bread,
and the *pièce de résistance,*
a sweet swamp of flakes and cream
called The Breakfast of Champions.
He rolled all eight eyes
like a gang of Grouchos,
then winked the right bank
in learing promise:
a someday prince of a fellow to come
again and again.
Mark my word, he cried, a tireless Jack-in-the-box!

For Ms. Muffet
it was the burning bush
and Apollo revealed.
An all-American vision of Armstrong.

She upchucked the curds, the whey,
kicked over the tuffet
and all arcadian traces,
and lit out for the supermarket.

It was another idyll in ruin.
It was another fall from grace.
It was another defeat for the apostles
of a cheap but nutritious Mother Earth breakfast.

Ms. Muffet?
You have seen her.
The Renoir special.
The *boule de suif.*
The dimpled dumpling.
That one.

The belligerent snacker.
The Dairy Queen hanger on.
The sweetheart of Boston Cream Pie.
That one.

The wench dawdles
in a languor of saturates
and lickerish sighs,
Bartlett breasts overblown
to ripe honeydews,
a once modest bum
cheeky with pneumatic promise
like a Goodyear Power Cushion.
She laps up cream
and schoolboy oglings
like a randy Angora.

In the night
she keeps a Coleman lantern vigil,
huffing desire
like the Little Blue Engine,
firebox aglow,
and rehearses the dream of his Coming,
the muscular One,
Armstrong,

whipping in her kitchen cup
concupiscent curds.

So much for the blue girls, their dance of grace.
So much for the blighters who pipe them down.
So much for the breakfast, shot out of guns over the graves of the Cholesterol dead.
So much for this fable, snatched from nursery, rooked of rhyme.
So much for the Mothers Goose and Earth.

—*David Cummings*

DONALD HALL
(1928-)

Reflecting on the Aging-Process

I have seen bus depots
in fifty states.
I remember only the empty stools
at the far end of the
lunch counters I did not
know, the tight-faced
waitresses hoping for
assignations and a cut
of my rat money.
O water, dark, and smog.
I cannot see
for all the shine of darkness
the thorns of life
on which I fall
but do not bleed.
My mood
wanders. I know the drain
is plugged. Drains are made
of steel, I think; or is
it wood?
I suffer along, and sing;
for I have kept moving—
despite temptation: that
I have done, have kept
moving, waiting for
nothing much to occur,
expecting less—a touch
of whimsy in a corner,
a prick at the end of my
thumb, a cornea endangered,
the dull plain fact of
someone in my family
rocking on the front porch
swing, grunting, belching,
passing wind, also alone.
I wait for a stroke
of bilious gas to pass.

I take out
grandpa's watch-fob. I know,
without looking at the face
that I am older, am no longer
twenty-five am fat and
turning to stone.

—Robert Peters

ADRIENNE RICH
(1929-)

The Griefs of Women

The griefs of women are quiet; rustle
like crinoline or whisper like
the tearing of old silk;

hum like appliances, give off the sharp sweet smell
of burnt out motors; tap like typewriter keys.
The strengths of women are quiet,
but hardy as the weed that finds its cranny
between the concrete block of the sidewalk
and the concrete slab of the wall, and grows there,
and blooms there.
Men are bums.
We're really better than they are.

—David R. Slavitt

THOM GUNN
(1929-)

I Enter by the Darkened Door

I enter by the darkened door
From simple night to the great floor
Where cirling couples pick their way
By nature's soft sufficiency.
Mere habit swells the music's din
Till blood and muscle drink it in.

Haphazard richness in the hall,
The will can never compass all.
I seek the clean, ungrasping sense
Of purposeless munificence,
Where music, dance and man's desires
Mingle and burst like sudden fires.

—Jenny King

GEORGE GARRETT
(1929-)

Getting at the Root of the Matter

Once, walking in the woods,
I came to a clump of Jack-in-
the-Pulpits, dancing in the breeze,
shaken by the Spirit, shouting from
under their canopies Are You Saved.
I pulled one up. The root a bulb.

I cut a little piece of it with
my knife and tasted it. Lay
on my tongue like raw potato,
then, after a time, took fire, burned
my tongue as pepperoni never did
in Rome, or artillery fire in Trieste.

Let someone else decide why
such a root held down that
holy figure. All I know is,
I walked for miles before
I found a spring, and cold
clear water tasted good.

—Henry Taylor

PETER PORTER
(1929-)

To His Coy Mistress

And yet the driving mirror shows me plain
Death sharking up the overtaking lane;
While out ahead the Mortalway reels in
The Vermicelli Junction feeder line.
A shroud will not, I think, help turn men's eyes
(May even cut my poems down to sighs).
The holy cleft you rest your virtue on
Will gape hip-wide in your flayed skeleton—
Perhaps to hold a rugby ball at Barts
Alongside jars of my cold pickled parts.
It gives no pleasure—learn it now or later—
To be on heat in the incinerator.

—W.J. Webster

GARY SNYDER
(1930-)

Having Eaten Breakfast

We're all at home:
Kai fooling around outside,
Gen finger painting,
Masa walks into the hot August sun

Standing in the room. We've eaten breakfast
                    oranges and I'll sit
For this. Assumed a yoga position.
Arms shanking down ribs
Hands across ankles
                    rest—
Wearing starched worn out button down shirt
Slowly breathe, silent,
Beads of sweat on lip, but brush scratching,
Heard Kai crying, then lookt out
                    a strawberry on knee
A red seepage down the dark leg.
Now dressed with swabs. Finally.
                    On the ragged tten-year-
Ago home-made rug
Of the Kyoto days,
Meditated,
                    Masa painted

—*D.C. Berry*

Melon-Slaughterer, Or,
A Sick Man's Praise for a Well Woman

Because you once beat me up
blackened my eye and bit off
my left tit, drunk,
lying out flat on yurt or frame,
Game of Go, Smash the Bottle,
Moon Trance, or *Smear*
                    I know
that it tends to this:
you want to make up.
But I avoid your karma
kitchen & stay drunk
you make me want to
decorate myself:
woodpunk, oysters
kelp around my balls
hemlock up my nose
                    You
are madder than me   you
prancing naked
"smalle foules maken melodye"
lips open, wrists slack
head tossed back
breasts quivering like
calcutta gelatin

I found you
in a dentist's chair
in Baluchistan
your bright teeth set
your cheeks frozen tight
by peace corps novocain.

you are
my astral Circe
spurting milk
over fertile islands
carob trees.

O, Deva!
your sweet
panchatantra cunt
moist
below the tiny golden
belt you wear...
O my Deva!
O dragon tongue &
black snag tooth of
Deva!

I'd slaughter
melons with my cock
for you.

—*Robert Peters*

TED HUGHES
(1930-)

Crow Resting

I sit at the top of the tree,
My mouth closed. I have been sitting here
Since the beginning of Time.
I am going to carry on sitting here
And if anybody tries to stop me sitting here
I will remove his head;
A single-mind-sized bite will do it.
I will eat his head and with a stab, a jerk
A bounce I'll have his bowels, balls,
Big toes, his colon and his semi-colon.
I will drink his blood from the goblet
Of his skull, his thin giblets
From the platter of his pelvic bone. And
I will spread his shit with generosity.
In other words forget it.
I was here first, I was here long ago.
I was here before you. And I will be here
Long after you have gone. What Superbard says
Goes. I am going to keep things like this.

—*Edward Pygge*

SYLVIA PLATH
(1932-1963)

Godiva

I wear a cobra's black bonnet,
A granite
Grin,

With an acetylene
Tongue
Behind the row of headstones.

Don't touch, Herr...
Just look.
Look. Look. Look.

A jacket of ashes,
Ragged umbrellas for hands,
The shadow of this lip a pit,

Just look at it.
Good God!
A mole in a spotlight of knives,

A puppet with no strings
Attached. Nothing.
Lady Godiva on a nag, nag, nag.

Suck this living doll's
Last tear if you will,
But beware

I eat in
Like Hiroshima ash.
I sizzle,

Herr Love, Herr Lucifer,
Your flash
In the pan.

—*D.C. Berry*

Ragout

What a trick—
Your prick instead of a carrot.
O pinch of pepper lover,
My soprano man,

Once a week I try it, I do,
Whetting the carving knives,
Making a stew,
A stew of the privates of you.

Dashed with paprika, it's you.
Blue on the butcher-block, you.
A less Fascist, tenderized you.

Come into my ticklish kitchen!
Where the toil is,
Where the tinfoil is,
And the balls are ground live
In the blender.

Ich, ich, ich, yum, yum, yum:
A ragout.
And it tastes like nobody but you.

—*William Zaranka*

MARK STRAND
(1934-)

Up Against The Wall

In the painting
I am the absence
of canvas.

As usual
I'm what's missing.

On your wall
this canvas is the absence
of the wall.

If you
want your wall
whole, get
rid of this.

—D.C. Berry

MICHAEL BENEDIKT
(1935-)

Air

Inventor of the geodesic domes
honeycombed
in beer foam. O air
who've been everywhere
and back (in hiccups
or farts) wafting fragrance
and laughter; gestalt
exalting lovers, their sighs
and lies, yielding arenas
for high dives, tickle-tensor
of skyplaces, you
are the Great Hyphenator: your very name
on an envelope connects us quicker.

Ambassador at large, you ring
the Earth like the white
of an egg
clear and viscuous, you stick
to everything, O

Air chameleonic

Innersphere of the child's ball
outwhere it zips in

(your sister, Silence; your lover, Wind)

You put out your red carpet
for frivolity

stringing along, Potentate of kites
our childish perspectives
galloping deception, giving us visions
hysteric

—Philip Dow

DIANE WAKOSKI
(1937-)

Broads

If I were the kind of man I want
you to be, I'd be
beating the shit out of you
because I like toughs, and
because I'm too sensitive/sensible
to put up with your double
knit Orange county
leisure suits & yr
hideous tan shoes.

But if you were the kind
of unkind man I want
you to be you'd
beat the shit out of me
or just beat it,
because of my stringy hair,
my tacky Goodwill/Illwill dress,
but most of all because of
my poems, poems like these
you'll never understand.

—David R. Slavitt

CHARLES SIMIC
(1938-)

Putting on My Shoes I Hear the Floor Cry Out Beneath Me

I was all night at this.

The wolves in the bedroom
Scampered at first like fawns
In a Disney forest,
Then they were chunks of granite
With eyes made of mica
Staring out to sea.

You stirred in your sleep.
I watched your shoulder
Rise on the dark like the hump
Of the last of the buffalo

Folding himself to breathe
The last of his breath in the tall grass
While bees with faces
Like Bippo the Clown swam by
Out of ancient kelp-beds
Drifting the fossil currents.

Then I remembered my shoes.

Slowly they settled
To the ocean floor
To be found in stone years after.

—Michael Heffernan

JAMES TATE
(1943-)

Naked War

The swarthy little statue
Of Emiliano Guzmann
stood by the greensward
beckoning, beckoning.

Fart, mad ducks, fart!
I manfully exhorted.
Then all about us rose
the reft applause of ducky angelus.

Walruses idled in the estuaries.

—Michael Heffernan

AI (Florence Anthony)
(1947-)

Dried Fruit

He stands in the door
against the flare of smudge pots.
I don't pretend sleep.
Hey, Babe, Duke done whiped that greaser's ass!
hooo-eeeeeee——
his fist explodes against the door
like a shotgun,
the trailer jars.
Dark again, the baby cries.
I blend it with the dehydrator,
whine of a forklift.
I taste the blood on his mouth
and on his body.
The woman he had.
He comes home to be made clean by me.
I am his bath. His wallow.

Water he dirties. I think of him
in the tub, his cock bobbing
at the surface like a frog
but puckered, dead.
It will come up again.
In me.
Each time
I will make it shrivel.

—*Philip Dow*

RUSSELL EDSON
(ca. 20th c.)

The Snack

Oh my God, screamed Mommy, You went and ate the Baby.
What baby? asked Daddy. You know that's just the last of the leftover donkey.
Donkey my ass! said Mommy with some sentience. Do you think I don't recognize my own baby? Why I can still see his little privates caught in the gap between your front teeth. How many times have I told you to take only what's on the *top* two shelves of the freezer?
But there wasn't a thing to eat, cried Daddy. And am I not the master of my own
Nothing to eat? What about the elephant testicles in aspic that I put up for you just last week in the ball jar? Our very first baby, too, wailed Mommy, that I was saving for Christmas dinner.
Testicles, testicles, said Daddy. A man gets tired of testicles.

—*L.L. Zeiger*

Prosodomy

Verse may be distinguished from *prose* not only by its spelling, but also by its high compression and *rhythm method*. The study of this rhythm method, or *meter*, is commonly referred to as *prosodomy*. Prosodomy is an inexact—indeed, almost a backward—science; therefore, it deals primarily with the *irregularities* or *aberrations* of rhythm method to which poets are subjected. The four major aberrations perpetrated by poets of all ages are meaningless unless their relationship to the traditional division of English lines into *feet* and *meters*, and American poetry into *inches* and *tads*, is understood. Quite simply, the English iambic foot contains a tad more than two American inches, the second of which is generally longer than the first, whereas in the trochaic foot the first inch is generally longer than the second. *Scansion* is used to determine the longer of the two, and is usually indicated by means of strong and weak *stretch marks*. Petty nationalism aside, the English foot is normally perceived as longer and grander than the American, hence the invention of the two *left feet* of three inches in length, the *apoplectic* and the *ducktylic*. The poet Robert Burns, one of the "Sons of Stephen Duck," has written:

Nine inch will please a lady.

The line is an undisguised attack on the classical apoplectic barometer line, which contained 29.65 inches and contented itself with the measurement of deviations from the status quo vadis, and a call for the unabashedly Romantic iambic tachometer line, which boasted nine inches and promised revolution.

If scansion is the grammar of prosodomy in both English and American poetry, stretch marks are the determinant of the degree of *prosthesis* in the metrical line. It is to prosthesis, or *substitute feet*, that the Wesleyan poet Richard Wilbur is referring in these lines from his "Conceit Upon the Feet":

Untíl the mind recalls
Those greater, metric feet, without which poems

Would languish fallen arched and in despair
Beside the road, like journeymen who swear
A foot in mouth gives satisfaction rare
As two left feet belied with false compare.

Likewise, when Eliot's "il miglior fabliaux," Ezra Pound, writes

And he ate all that night, inch by inch, for his art,
Half a foot of her sausage, of her small beer a quart.

he is illustrating once again the close relationship between inches and feet and the accumulation of those inches and feet into stanzas.

Stanzas come in as many sizes as shapes. Among the most pleasing of stanzaic shapes is the *clothed couplet* with the *feminine end.* Because of the immediately recognizable shape of the clothed couplet, and the natural temptation male poets of all ages have felt toward *endjabment* of the feminine end, such couplets are said to be *end-stooped.* The following, from Herrick's "Upon Julia,"

It gaped, and would have made a dead Man skip
To see it mump and wag its upper Lip.

is one such couplet, quite obviously end-stooped. When two such couplets are joined, as in Blake's "The Chimney Sweepstakes" below, the result is *copulation*, and we refer to the union as a *foursome*, or *squatrain*:

Have you not in a Chimney seen
A sullen Faggot wet and green,
How coyly it receives the Heat,
And at both Ends does fume and sweat?

Further union results in the sexain, octavius, and quinine. Spender's lovely "Amoretto" is a sexain:

A knight delights in hardy Deeds of arms;
Perhaps a Lady loves sweet Musick's Charms;
Rich Men in Store of Wealth delighted be;
Infants love dandling on the Mother's knee.
Coy Maids love something, Nothing I'll express,
Keep the first letters of these Lines, and guess.

Perhaps the most famous octavius in the language is Milton's renunciation of his blindness. This is described in *Go Down, Samson*, where the ill penseroso writes:

Tell me, abandon'd miscreant, prithee tell
What damned Power, invok'd and sent from Hell
(If Hell were bad enough) did thee inspire
To write, what Fiends, asham'd wou'd blushing hear?

Hast thou of late embrac'd some *Succubus*,
And us'd the lewd Familiar for a Muse?
Or didst thy Soul by Inch of Candle fell,
To gain the glorious Name of Pimp to Hell?

Masculine ends, unlike feminine ends, are found exclusively in the *fixed forms*. Among the fixed forms is the *Pederastic Ode*, named after the Greek Peter. It is an exalted lyric with a serious massage, popular in Greece and gaining in England and America. In his poem, "The Scholar Pipsqueak," Matthew Arnold laments in lyric fashion the loss of his beloved Glanvill:

Lost it too soon, and learnt a stormy note
Of men contention tossed, of men who groan,
Which tasked thy pipe too sore, and tired thy throat—
It failed, and thou wast mute!

Another of the fixed forms is the *sonnet*, of which there are two kinds, the *Shakespearean* and the *Petrarchan*, or *Whopper*. Shakespeare's sonnets are the finest produced during the age, and may be distinguished from those of Petrarch by their superior structure. While Petrarch's whoppers divide naturally into an eight-line *proposition* followed by a six-line *sexpot*, Shakespeare's proposition takes longer (twelve lines) and the sexpot is replaced by a *capulet*. The latter may be varied to achieve special effects, as in Milton's "I Saw Last Night My Late Expung'd Snot":

She was a heaven (of a kind);
She held salvation in her eyes;
'Twas grace abounding, her behind,
And purgatory were her thighs.
There reigned a Lord in her right breast,
All-knowing and all-powerful;
The left one hung south by southwest,
And rendered Godhead plurable.

Alas, that heaven hath been lost,
And closéd is that hairy gate;
Then of thy wives, men, make the most,
But if thou canst not, masturbate,
Or take a whore, and treat her well,
Else thou may burn for, but not enter Hell.

Other fixed forms which are used only rarely in our language are the *siesta*, a six-stanza poem which makes use of terminal words and a concluding three-line *envy*; The *villain*, a French poem composed of five *turd-sets* and a final *quadraplegic*; the *ballad*, a two-story poem written in Medieval polka rhythm; and the *toilet*, which is no longer regarded as anything more than a formal exercise for beginning poets to cut their teeth on.

The verse form of Milton's *This Side of Paradise* and Wordsworth's "Splendor in the Grass," as well as of most of the verse of The Elizabethan Error, *blank verse* is unrhymed iambic pedometer with a predictable pause, or *Caesar*, in the middle of each line:

I come to bugger Caesar, not to praise him.

is an example of "Marlowe's Mighty Line" as written by Joseph Conrad Aiken. Wordsworth's peon "Michael," a humble Scots farmer of North Kensington and the father of six chickens, is famous for its blank last line, which is delivered with great laissex-faire and gravity:

And never lifted up a single skirt.

Simple scansion using stretch marks will show that only one syllable of this poetic line is emphasized:

And ne ver lif ted up a sin gle skirt.

Other prominent technical contributions to the blank verse movement include the so-called "variable foot" of William Tennessee Williams, the "club foot" of Lord Byron, and the "foot-in-mouth" of Charles "Bobo" Olson. Note the "dignity of hurry" Byron's club-foot imparts to the rhythms of his verse *epistle* to Wordsworth's concubine, Dorothy:

Nine months she grew in sun and shower,
But in my Lover's ear alone
Was ever sown a lovelier flower:
Strange fits of passion have I known.

An offspring of blank verse is *free verse*, which is often said to have contributed greatly to that watershed of modern and contemporary literary history, the twentieth century. From the French "amour libre," it eschews the rigors of formal verse, hence Frost's famous formula: "free verse is like playing tennis without a hairnet." Instead of rigor mortis, free verse makes use of musical katydids and speech-class rhythms derived from such diverse sources as the Bible and the dance hall on the one hand, and the psalms and the hygiene brochures on the other. Thus T.S. Eliot rewrites Rochester's stale, Neo-Calcified quatrain, "Written Under Nelly's Picture," into the much more footloose free verse poem, "Marianna":

Now the lily folds all manner of sweetness up
(O slip slip slip into the bowel of the lake).
Between the folding and slipping O my daughter
Quivers thy woodthrush. The palaver's over.

No wonder that free verse should become the whipping boy of just those Michelangelo-adoring courtesans Eliot castigates in *The Waste Land* for exposing their jugs to dirty ears.

Index